Divided Loyalties

Divided Loyalties

How the American Revolution
Came to New York

Richard M. Ketchum

A JOHN MACRAE / OWL BOOK
Henry Holt and Company · New York

Henry Holt and Company, LLC
Publishers since 1866
115 West 18th Street
New York, New York 10011

Henry Holt® is a registered trademark of
Henry Holt and Company, LLC.

On pages iv–v, B. Ratzer's map of New York City in 1767.
New-York Historical Society.

Library of Congress Cataloging-in-Publication Data
Ketchum, Richard M., date.
  Divided loyalties : how the American Revolution came to New York /
Richard M. Ketchum.—1st ed.
      p.   cm.
  "A John Macrae book."
  Includes bibliographical references and index.
  ISBN 0-8050-6120-7 (pbk.)
  1. New York (State)—History—Revolution, 1775–1783.   I. Title.
E263.N6 K48 2002
974.7'03—dc21   2002022814

Henry Holt books are available for special promotions and
premiums. For details contact: Director, Special Markets.

First published in hardcover in 2002 by
Henry Holt and Company

First Owl Books Edition 2003

A John Macrae / Owl Book

Designed by Kelly S. Too

Printed in the United States of America

1   3   5   7   9   10   8   6   4   2

For Bobs, Liza, and Tom

CONTENTS

_____

PREFACE

The American Revolution, the extraordinary act that gave birth to a nation and changed the history of the world, was not something that was plotted long in advance. No plans for revolt or independence from Great Britain occupied the minds of colonial Americans prior to 1760, and even then, only a handful of malcontents may have imagined a separation from what was thought of as the mother country.

The distant stirrings of what became a revolution dated back to the early 1700s, to the days when Robert Walpole was the first real prime minister in British history. Walpole's view of the American colonies was that they should be let alone, largely unhindered by restrictions from the home government, let alone to do what colonies were expected to do—which was to produce enough food to sustain themselves, to export raw materials needed in Great Britain, such as timber, tobacco, rice, and indigo, and to buy from England all the manufactured goods they required.

Walpole's policy, which became known as "salutary neglect," not only gave the colonies free rein, but unintentionally pushed them in the direction of self-government and an independent attitude. Over the years, without even realizing it, they became capable of managing their own affairs, and the habit was seductive, productive, and satisfying.

The struggle between England and France for possession of North America began in 1754 in what is now western Pennsylvania with an exchange of gunfire between some 150 Virginians led by the twenty-one-year-old George

Washington and a party of French and their Indian allies. Known in America as the French and Indian War (the fourth conflict of that name in the eighteenth century) and in Europe as the Seven Years' War, it became the first world war fought on three continents.

When the conflict at last ended in 1760 a sea change took place in America. That year the lucrative business of supplying the British army ceased, causing extreme financial pain for Americans in general and New York's merchants in particular. At the same time, old King George II died and was succeeded by his twenty-year-old, untried, inexperienced grandson, who was crowned George III. Stubbornly determined to reduce the huge national debt caused by the war, and equally resolved to make the colonists pay their share of it, George III and his ministers set in motion the chain of events that climaxed in the war of the Revolution.

New York was said to be the king's favorite of the thirteen colonies. It was centrally located between the fractious New Englanders and the middle and southern colonies. At a time when the easiest way to travel or to ship goods was by water, New York not only had one of the world's great ports, it had in the Hudson River unparalleled access to the vast interior of North America. That made it, for the British, a hugely important factor in the empire's economy.

During the early 1760s, when the colonists were increasingly frustrated and angered by Britain's efforts to impose taxes on them where none had existed before, officials in London had the impression that New York had a larger loyal contingent than other colonies. For as long as anyone knew, men and women had been subjects of a king and paid him homage. For a good many years after George III ascended the throne, most Americans instinctively revered him as a good king, a man to whom they owed loyalty and devotion. But in a few years' time things began to come apart, and that is the story of this book. It is, however, more than an account of the widening rift and the eventual rupture in the relationship between England and America. It is also about loyalties.

It took a long time—fifteen years or more—for people to realize that they had to take sides. Which is not to say that everyone did. As John Adams recalled it, about one-third of the colonists remained loyal to the king, another one-third did not, and the remaining one-third were uncommitted, or neutral.

It is with those first two-thirds that this book is principally concerned, for in the event of an upheaval as profound as a revolution, the people who take sides are those who care deeply enough to risk their lives, their families, and their fortunes in support of a cause in which they believe. More than two centuries later, if we think about this at all we are inclined to think that "our side" won the Revolution. After all, we are their inheritors, their beneficiaries, and what we have today we owe to those heroic men and women who struggled against all odds to obtain the freedom that meant more to them than anything else in life.

But because "our side" won, we forget that there was another side just as committed, just as dedicated, equally certain of the rectitude of their beliefs. Yet most of us have never given them a second thought because they were the losers. In the French Revolution the losers lost their heads, along with everything else. In America the treatment of Tories may have been less barbaric, but punishments were cruel, and it is worth asking whether a quick death may not have been preferable for some of those individuals who were forced to endure what amounted to a slow death in poverty and exile, deprived of what they regarded as their country, the land they loved, perhaps having lost a brother, a son, or a close friend who had chosen the other side.

We tend to think of the loyalists as rich, arrogant, unbending, concerned only for the privileges to which the wealthy are accustomed. And indeed many of them were arrogant upper-class snobs. But many were nothing of the kind—merely good people who chose to remain loyal to their king, as we today—most of us—are loyal to our government, despite its many faults, despite its flaws and blemishes, its frequent wrongheadedness and shortsightedness.

This is an account of how the Revolution came to one American town, New York, and the role people played as the forces of resistance and reform gradually gathered momentum and turned into something far more devastating and destructive—revolution. All this against a background described by Patricia Bonomi: "New York was almost continuously riven by one form or another of internal strife."

Insofar as possible I have tried to tell the colonists' story as they saw it and wrote it, drawing on their letters, journals, and diaries, as well as on contemporary newspapers. Often this has led to quoting a phrase that is unfamiliar to us, but that suggests their turn of speech. And of course the way certain individuals spelled a word can indicate how they pronounced it—a lively example is Marinus Willett's use of "Congersenal" for Congressional. In the mid-eighteenth century, "jail" was usually spelled "gaol" or "goal." "Lenity" was "lenience"; "jealousy" meant suspicion, not envy; where they said "least," as used in the phrase "least it might divide us," we say "lest"; writing to a friend in England, a New Yorker would say "on your side the water," not "on your side *of* the water"; describing where an open-air meeting was held, he might say it took place "without doors," rather than "out of doors."

More than two centuries have passed since these events took place, and it is important that we do not let different patterns of speech, the unfamiliar apparel, the wearing of wigs, lead us to conclude that these people would be strangers to us. Of course they were different from us in some respects, but in the same way that my children's generation differs from my father's. Beyond the surface differences, they were living, breathing human beings like us, with the same human needs, the same hopes and fears and dreams for themselves and their children. Like us, they did not see themselves as historical figures, but as normal people, living from day to day and not knowing what the morrow might bring.

Probably the most noticeable difference between New Yorkers of the eighteenth century and those of the twenty-first is the pace of life—a pace dictated by the speed at which a man traveled on foot or horseback or aboard ship. In the case of communications, for example, it meant that an event which was judged cataclysmic for their day occurred in Lexington, Massachusetts, and word of it did not reach New York for four days. News of the same event took twenty-one days to arrive in Charleston, South Carolina, and thirty-nine days to reach London. So uncertain were the transatlantic mails even under normal conditions that many officials or businessmen were accustomed to number their letters so the recipient would realize if he was missing one or more (probably lost at sea).

What is all but impossible for us to comprehend today was that our ancestors were subjects of a great power, three thousand miles and an ocean away, with their lives and destinies controlled by a distant monarch and his ministers. It took years for American colonists to realize that the imperial power was not being used for their benefit, but was often corrupt, arbitrary, humiliating, and beyond their capacity to change. Yet a break in the relations between colonies and mother country was years in coming, and some of the best-informed Americans—Benjamin Franklin, for one—believed as late as 1774 that the rift could be repaired.

Until the final hours before fighting erupted, revolution was never inevitable. Indeed, for most colonists it was unthinkable and need not have happened, had it not been for the intransigence of George III's government.

Divided Loyalties

PROLOGUE

It was nearing the end of March in 1776 and Alice DeLancey Izard was in Bath, England, presumably benefiting from the warm, healing waters at the spa, but in fact worrying incessantly about her mother, Elizabeth Colden DeLancey, who lived in New York City. On the other side of the Atlantic the fighting had been going on for almost a year now, making the mail even less reliable than it had been before the war began, but that troubled Alice less than her mother's safety.

"I suffer a great deal of uneasiness at hearing so seldom from you," she wrote. She had broached this subject several times, begging her parent to leave "so turbulent a scene as America presents, and take shelter with us here for a year, or two, till these calamities are past." It would be a simple matter for her mother to get away, she added, since her household was now relatively small, and if she came to England they could take a place in the country where they could live frugally. Alice said she would be enormously relieved to have her mother removed from danger.

"It is impossible for me to express how many anxious hours I spend in thinking of my friends, and my afflicted Country; how earnestly I pray for peace, which seems every day to fly farther from us, and how much I feel even for this Country, which seems to be seeing its own ruin and destruction. I am particularly distressed for you and my sister Nancy, as I know that the greatest part of your property lies in the Town of New York, and it is the general opinion that that beautiful—and by me, much loved place—will share

Ralph and Alice DeLancey Izard, by John Singleton Copley. *Museum of Fine Arts, Boston/Edgar Rugersoll Browne Fund.*

the fate of Norfolk in Virginia." Recently that unfortunate town had been bombarded on orders from Virginia's headstrong governor, Lord Dunmore, who had taken refuge aboard one of His Majesty's ships in the harbor to escape the skirmishing on shore, and for three days the place burned, until most of it was gone.

Before the Izards departed from New York, Alice had written her sister saying, "The hour of parting will soon arrive; I dread it but the hope of seeing you all in a few years will enable me to bear it." But almost five years had gone by now without visiting her family, and she could not help thinking that if it were not for this dreadful war she would be making preparations to return to America. How differently it had turned out.

She and her husband had sent their oldest son, Harry, to be with her mother, hoping he would be a comfort and an amusing companion. Her three little ones were well, she reported, and Mr. Izard, as she called her husband, joined in sending love and blessings to his mother-in-law and their dear boy. Alice had heard nothing about her Grand Papa, Cadwallader Colden, but hoped he was in good health and spirits. It was a relief to know that her younger sister Jenny and her husband, John Watts, Jr., were spending so much time with their mother. Since Alice was in the English countryside most of the time, she had seen little of the senior Watts, who had fled New York for England almost ten months ago, but Mr. Izard had seen him frequently and reported that he was well.

It is not easy to know just where Alice DeLancey Izard's loyalties lay. The letter to her mother contains a hint of her feelings, where she says how much she feels "even for this Country" (meaning England). But no matter. Her marriage to a patriot had already divided her own family, regardless of how she felt, and the tug of family against country must have been agonizing. Her husband, Ralph Izard, was a rice and indigo planter from Charleston, South Carolina, whose grandfather, Robert Johnson, had been the popular governor of that colony for two years and, for the last five years of his life, the first royal governor. Ralph, Alice, and their children went to England in 1771 but they moved to the Continent in 1776, probably because it was unpleasant living in what was by then enemy lands. Congress then appointed Izard commissioner to Tuscany. Recalled in 1779, he returned to America in 1780, but Alice did not follow him home until 1783. Izard was a strong Federalist, a supporter of the Constitution, and ultimately United States senator from South Carolina from 1789 to 1795. He died in 1804, but Alice lived on for another twenty-eight years.

Like so many of her fellow New Yorkers and her other countrymen, Alice Izard may have been loyal to two countries, to both Britain and America, may in fact have had a double allegiance, unable to decide which was her true home. No two people could have been more representative of their prominent position, or "rank" as they liked to call it, in New York society than her parents, Peter and Elizabeth Colden DeLancey. Theirs was a tightly knit group of staunch loyalists, active partisans of the crown, determined to resist the radical onslaught that threatened to split the colonies from the mother country, ending its membership in the British Empire.

Her father was the second son of Etienne DeLancey, a Huguenot refugee who made a fortune in the Canada trade and had become one of the most influential and popular men in the province of New York by the time of his death in 1743. Peter's brother James picked up where their father left off and as chief justice of the Supreme Court, lieutenant governor, and boss of the legislature, succeeded in dominating New York's political affairs for more than two decades. After James DeLancey's death, Grand Papa Colden became the perennial lieutenant governor, taking over the governor's office every time a royal appointee was recalled or died. Alice's sister Jenny was married to John Watts, Jr., whose father was a highly successful merchant, a member of the governor's Council, and a man who left New York rather than "turn Traytor to the Country that gave me being." So if Alice was predisposed to remain loyal to England even though her husband chose the opposite side, it is easy to understand that her attitude may have been based on her family's values.

But we do not know what was in her heart. We only know that she loved America—or New York, at least—and loved England as well. And perhaps she never had to confront the wrenching decision so many others had to face, which was to make the ultimate choice and gamble everything they owned— perhaps even their lives—on following the dictates of conscience.

The people of New York City, along with hundreds of thousands of other Americans, moved away from almost universal acceptance of their relationship with Great Britain and in less than a generation found themselves up against the profound and deeply disturbing question of where their loyalties belonged. Their story had its roots in the last of the French and Indian Wars that ravaged the frontiers of thirteen British colonies.

I

A Most Splendid Town

Long before they came in sight of land, European passengers bound for New York were greeted with the sweet scent of the continent's lush vegetation. Rounding Sandy Hook and heading for the harbor, they sailed through the Narrows between Staten Island and Brooklyn, up past the forested shores of New York Bay, and got their first, distant view of the settlement at the southern extremity of Manhattan Island. What they saw appeared to be no more than a village, surrounded by trees and open fields, but it was an experience few visitors forgot. It was "the most splendid Town in North America," according to one traveler, and few could argue with that. In surroundings of striking natural beauty, what had begun life as a tiny outpost of Holland's commercial empire was still, after 136 years, surprisingly small and compact—something like two thousand houses and a population of about twelve thousand.

The last of four great Pleistocene ice sheets that had blanketed Canada and the northeast deposited drifts of clay and sandy gravel up to one hundred feet deep across much of southern Manhattan. Where the ice stopped, as the glacier began to melt and withdraw, a terminal moraine, or accumulation of glacial debris, was left behind at either side of the Narrows, extending in a sinuous ridge from Staten Island across western Long Island.

Washed by two rivers and the ebb and flow of Atlantic tides, Manhattan had the magical, beckoning quality of all islands, but to most Dutch and its later occupants, the English, it was perceived less in spiritual than in physical terms. In addition to a central location among the colonies that were strung out along the Atlantic coastline, it possessed unparalleled access to the interior by way of the Hudson River. More important, Manhattan was blessed with a world-class deepwater port, protected by the Narrows and New York Bay, and was on the way to becoming the most important trading center in North America. Except for a handful of native hangers-on, most of the people regarded as savages were long gone, off on the frontier somewhere along with the bears, wolves, cougars, and other wild creatures that had once made their home on what the Indians called Manahata. The settlement had grown beyond the original Dutch wall erected to keep out the Indians and beyond the later palisaded barricade built across the island in 1745 by panicky residents as protection against possible invasion by the French, yet it was still a small provincial town, a community in which virtually everything was within easy walking distance, and where just about everybody was a neighbor.

The most tangible symbol of the British crown's presence was Fort George, perched on rocks at the southern tip of the island. Built by the Dutch about 1614, it had borne nine different names since that time and in the 1760s was in a state of advancing decrepitude. Despite its ruinous condition, it was the city's social and official center, since the royally appointed governor resided in a house inside the open rectangle, protected by ramparts of the Grand Battery. Behind this bulwark of a hundred ancient naval guns mounted on small wheels, the skyline bristled with church spires and the cupola and flag of City Hall. Houses clustered along and behind the waterfront, and beyond them were low-lying hills and woods.

The island was fourteen and a half miles long and ranged in width from half a mile to two and a half miles* or—as men tended to figure it in those days—two hours by cart from north to south, an hour's walk from east to west. But the city proper was only a mile long and no more than half that in width, which was a godsend to everyone involved in trade. In a day when nearly all business was conducted on foot or by horse-drawn vehicles, a visitor remarked that "the Cartage in Town from one part to another does not at a Medium exceed one-quarter of a mile. [This] prodigious advantage . . . facilitates and expedites the lading and unlading of Ships and Boats, saves Time and Labour, and is attended with Innumerable Conveniences to its inhabitants."

---

*It is much broader today as a result of fill that has been added to the shoreline over the years.

Manhattan's insularity was further intensified by problems of communication. Letters, news, and official documents traveled only as rapidly as a man on foot or horseback or in a ship could carry them. This was a world in which it took at least six weeks or more to get a letter from "home" in the British Isles, carried by a sailing vessel struggling against the westerly winds and subject to all the vagaries of weather, shipwreck, war, and piracy. Stockings, linens, shirts, kerchiefs, dresses, woolens, shoes—every item of clothing, it seemed, came from Britain, and New Yorkers were accustomed to delays of four or five months between the placing of an order and its arrival. A trip to Philadelphia, in good weather, with a good horse and solid footing on the roads, took at least forty-eight hours. A journey upriver to Albany—normally a three-day trip by schooner—might take twice that long if winds and tides were uncooperative.

Throughout the colonies, similar conditions existed, with the result that New Yorkers often knew more about goings-on in London than in the Carolinas or even Pennsylvania. Newspapers carried little but foreign news, largely because most colonials had almost no interest in what was happening in other colonies, and this self-imposed isolation was at the very root of the problems America faced during the seemingly incessant warfare along its vast frontier.

In theory, mail from England was put aboard a packet in Falmouth on the second Saturday of the month, but with the uncertainties of weather or possible damage to the ships one could only guess when it might be delivered. So the moment the packet boat was sighted sailing up the bay, word flew around town and people ran to the wharf to be on hand when the vessel docked, bringing official dispatches, letters, and the latest London papers.

When the Philadelphian Benjamin Franklin took over the slow, undependable colonial postal service in 1753, one of his innovations was to have newspapers print the names of persons who had mail waiting for them. Then he initiated the penny post, which provided that letters not called for on the day the post arrived were sent to the addressee the next day by the postman for an extra fee. (Letters which had been advertised in newspapers and remained unclaimed for three months were forwarded to the Dead Letter Office in Philadelphia.) But as welcome as these improvements were, long-distance mail, especially, remained uncertain at best. No wonder: as an instance of how mail was addressed and sent, Cadwallader Colden's father, in Scotland, directed a letter to his son thusly:

To Cadwallader Colden, Esq.
At New-York

How it was to be put on board ship left a good deal to the imagination:

To be Left at the Sun Coffee house
Behind the royal exchange   London

Yet somehow, it arrived.

The premise that the distance between two points divided by the rate of travel indicates the time it takes to get there governed relations between England and America, and it was significant in more ways than might come to mind. (One imponderable, of course, was the impossibility of predicting what the rate of travel across the ocean might be.) New York society, led by the mercantile aristocracy, was patterned on and imitative of that in London, which meant that court gossip about the foibles and follies and fashions of the highly placed were extremely important to provincials, who were prone to social insecurity. The faster they received word of what was de rigueur the more secure they felt.

Shopping seasons for English goods were a boom time and a boon for every kind of hostelry and eatery in the city. Crowds from near and far flocked to New York to see the large fleet of English ships sail into the harbor, as they did every April and October, and their arrival was followed by a shopping frenzy that might last for weeks. The ships made the round trip in about six months, taking half of that time for loading and unloading, and so it was that the very latest in garments—apparel from head to toe—along with books, pictures, furniture, and just about everything else was the main topic of conversation in those two months of the year.

From autumn into spring, New York's well-to-do attended assemblies run by the merchants William Walton and James McEvers, dancing classes, and concerts, which were almost always followed with balls. Gentlemen arrived dressed to the nines in silk or broadcloth suits trimmed with gold, boots with silver buckles, richly embroidered waistcoats trimmed with lace, and wigs freshly powdered and scented, lending support to Benjamin Franklin's comment that men "fear less . . . being in hell than out of fashion." On their arms, their companions were beautifully gowned in satin or silk hoopskirts, wearing shoes with impossibly high heels and tight bodices that covered stays cut high in the back and low in the front. And woe to the poor soul who had not yet heard from the staymakers who made regular trips from London and was unaware that waistlines had gone down this season.

At some balls the ladies were expected to stand in line according to their purported "rank," but this practice led to what Ann Watts described to her cousin Ann DeLancey as "a monstrous Fight," after which it was decided that "there shall be no Lady or Gentleman invited to dance that will not be willing to draw for a place, and that will be the only way to make things easy." The role of almost all women then was a restricted one, as Anne Moore complained to Ann DeLancey. "You will readily allow," she wrote, "that our sex can appear truly amiable in no light but the domestic," and only in that manner can she "find room to display every virtue."

The social whirl included regular evenings at the theater, musicales as well as more formal concerts, entertainments given by the governor at his house in the fort—often celebrating some event like a royal birthday—as well as parties given by British officers at the garrison. And moneyed New Yorkers had the same enthusiasm for sports as the English gentlemen they admired—everything from bowls to cockfighting, fowling, sailing, fishing, horse-racing, and foxhunting on Long Island, and they welcomed one governor who arrived at his post with "nine gouff clubs, one iron ditto, and seven dozen balls." The long winters were enlivened with shooting, skating, and sleighing parties just beyond town.

For a good many of these prosperous merchants' households the descriptive word was "luxury." They had their portraits painted by such fashionable artists as Benjamin West and Pierre du Simitière, and by itinerant limners. (During her lifetime, Alice DeLancey Izard and her husband had their portraits done many times, by the likes of John Singleton Copley, Gainsborough, Thomas Sully, and others.) They purchased fine clocks, silver, wall hangings, and figured wallpaper from England. They ate off Lowestoft, Wedgwood, and Canton china. They drank fine Madeira, claret, burgundy, and champagne. They were served by a butler and maids, and driven by a coachman—all of them Negro slaves.

These people were gregarious and convivial, meeting and gossiping in coffeehouses, inns, and private homes. One group of men called themselves the Hungarian Club and met regularly at Todd's Sign of the Black Horse in Smith Street. Astonishingly, they met *every night,* and a visitor noted that only good topers were accepted for membership. "To talk bawdy and have a knack at punning passes among them for good sterling wit," he observed sourly, but he concluded that "in this place you may have the best of company and conversation as well as at Philadelphia."

A newcomer from Philadelphia was similarly impressed: "This is a better place for company and amusements than Philadelphia," he said, "more gay and lively. I have already seen some pretty women." But his enthusiasm quickly palled. It was the novelty of the city that he had found enchanting at first, but before long he discovered that one day's exposure to the people, manners, living, and conversation conveyed as much as fifty days'. Making the rounds of many homes he found the same topics discussed—"land, Madeira wine, fishing parties or politics. . . ." What's more, in the coffeehouses they had "a vile practice . . . of playing backgammon (a noise I detest) from morning till night, frequently ten or a dozen tables at a time."

John Adams, accustomed to the ways of Boston, looked down his nose at New Yorkers. "With all the opulence and splendor of this city," he commented, "there is very little good breeding to be found. I have not met one gentleman. . . . There is no conversation. The people talk very loud and fast and all together and break in upon you in speaking."

Most of New York's streets were crooked, but many were wide, paved with cobblestones, with a gutter running through the middle, and lined with shade trees that made walking in summer on sidewalks laid with flat stones a pleasure. At night the lamplighter made his rounds and the streets were lit, as they had been since 1693, by "lanthorn & candle" hung from every seventh house, with the expense borne equally by the seven homeowners.* Over the years, the forest on the lower half of the island had been cut over for building, but in 1708 citizens were given permission to plant trees in front of their houses, and half a century later the leafy canopy caused visitors to comment that the place "seemed like a garden" because of the salubrious mix of beech, locust, elms, and lime trees, as the lindens were called. Many houses had balconies on the roof that enabled people to sit outside in summer and admire the lovely prospect of the town, with the sparkling rivers and bays beyond. In 1760 nearly every house lot of any size had a garden, as did the country estates north of town, many of which also had orchards growing all kinds of fruits, along with meadows and pastures for livestock. Saltwater fish were plentiful in the Hudson, as were oysters, from the huge beds on the New Jersey shore.

*Not until 1762 did lampposts with oil lamps begin to be used.

By 1760 the city's population was at least four times what it had been ninety years earlier and farms had sprung up over much of the island, but Manhattan retained most of the characteristics described by one Daniel Denton in 1670. He noted that the land grew corn and all sorts of grain, providing pasture in the summer—grass as high as a man's waist, he said—and fodder for winter. In the woods, "every mile or half-mile are furnished with fresh ponds, brooks or rivers, where all sorts of Cattel, during the heat of the day, do quench their thirst and cool themselves. . . ." Despite the number of streams that traversed the island, good, fresh drinking water was scarce, however. Numerous wells, public and private, existed in the city, but the output of most of them tasted so bad that people who could afford it purchased water by the cask or bottle from springs north of the settled areas. For those who wanted a daily supply of decent water for their tea or cooking, a horse-drawn cart made the rounds, hauling hogsheads of water from a spring where the Tea-water Pump was located, selling it for something less than a dollar a bucket.

The Hudson River was a constant reminder of Albany and the frontier that gave it such importance. For generations Albany had been *the* important end of the river, the collection point for all the furs sent from New York to Europe's hungry market, the source of so much wealth for the Dutch and their successors. It seemed that every well-dressed man or woman in Europe must have a beaver hat, and in the first year of Dutch settlement some fifteen hundred of the skins had been shipped to Holland. By the eighteenth century colonial hatters were exporting ten thousand beaver hats to Europe annually— infuriating English hatters, who petitioned Parliament to stop the importation of these finished goods from America.

But hats were far from the only end product: fur bands adorned costumes of velvet and silk; the so-called French hood was quilted and luxuriously lined with fur; gorgeous greatcoats for court wear, made of rich green velvet, were lined and bordered with ermine; men's habits were trimmed with spotted lynx; flowered taffeta was decorated with mink cuffs; muffs, too, were all the rage, especially those made from the long hair of fox and wolf. The beaver pelts—thick and soft with protruding coarse guard hairs—ranged in color from white to light brown (or rarely, black), and after the guard hairs were pulled out the pelts were ideal for felting by hatters.

As a consequence, Albany was the chief entrepôt in the British colonies for the immensely profitable animal pelts and hides so sought after by Europeans.

Yet as lucrative as the fur trade was for those who controlled it, the risks were considerable, for it depended entirely on Indians who trapped the animals and others who acted as middlemen.

No matter where you looked in New York City, the Dutch influence was pervasive and profound. It was almost a century since Peter Stuyvesant had surrendered New Amsterdam to the English—who promptly renamed the place in honor of the king's brother, James, Duke of York—but Hollanders who wished to do so had been generously permitted to remain in the colony, enjoying "all the privileges and immunities which they were possessed of before," with the result that the Dutch, though in a minority, remained an important presence in the town and the province. Many of them—especially the elderly—still spoke their mother tongue and clung to the old ways, but gradually this was changing, especially among the young, who were not only speaking English but attending the English church. (English was the language of commerce and officialdom, but Dutch was the common tongue in Albany and other upriver communities, and New York families often sent their children to New Rochelle to learn French.) Nonetheless, in many respects (commercially, in particular) New York still had overtones of a Dutch community. Dutch houses of brick, with their stepped gable ends facing the street, were prominent. Dutch was spoken at the fish market and Old Slip Market, and every other Sunday the sermon at the New Dutch Church was delivered in the language of the old country. According to a woman who lived in Saratoga, New York City was the place where those who lived upriver "sent their children occasionally to reside with their relatives, and to learn the more polished manners and language of the capital."

While the transformation from Dutch town to English city had continued for almost a hundred years, with the Dutch elite increasingly outnumbered by English and Huguenot and other arrivistes, as time passed it was clear that this island community was different from any other major population center in America.

It was a cosmopolitan, polyglot place, as most sailors' ports of call are, where newly arrived settlers and refugees from Europe's wars and pogroms mingled with longtime residents and filled the streets and taverns with the babble of eighteen different tongues. Indeed, the mix of races and religions meant that the community was for years destined to be divided by its interests and plagued with disputes between families and political enemies. One early resident complained, "Our chiefest unhappyness here is too great a mixture," yet it was the survival of that very mixture that saw the rough beginnings of a democratic society.

Between the Dutch patroon system, under which proprietary and manorial rights to huge tracts of land were granted to well-connected Dutchmen who brought fifty new settlers to the province, and the extravagant handouts of land by England's royal governors, enormous estates along the Hudson River had come into the possession of a relatively few colonial families—the Rensselaers, Schuylers, Livingstons, and others. Many leading families consolidated their huge landholdings and political influence by intermarriage, and it was hardly surprising to find that wealthy families such as the Livingstons, DeLanceys, Schuylers, Van Cortlandts, Beekmans, and others regarded as New York's elite had a disproportionate say in the membership of the Assembly and the Council and, more often than not, the ear of the royal governor.

Physically the city's size was determined mainly by the distance residents had to walk in order to go about their daily business. As a result the majority of New Yorkers lived within a mile of the southern tip of Manhattan, where Fort George's battery commanded the harbor ostensibly to prevent a French fleet from entering. Since the shoreline along the Hudson River was often iced in, only one important pier, King's Wharf, was located there, and consequently the East River wharves were the preferred destination in this magnificent harbor. (Michel Guillaume Jean de Crèvecoeur, who was in New York at this time, marveled at the skill of the inhabitants in constructing wharves, some of them in water forty feet deep.) Inbound vessels, sailing from the lower bay through the Narrows, passed Governors Island and were soon swallowed up in the mass of shipping lining the East River bank. Separating the city from Long Island and leading directly into Long Island Sound, the East River opened a sheltered passage to the lush farms of eastern Long Island and western Connecticut. Its docks could accommodate any size vessel, and this was home port for as many as five hundred sail of New York shipping, with ports of call in Europe, the Mediterranean, the West Indies, the Spanish Main, and the other American colonies.

The most desirable neighborhood for New York's powerful merchant traders lay between Wall Street and the waterfront, and at least seventy of them, in all, dwelt between Pearl Street and Crown. Running parallel to the river, Dock Street and Queen Street formed a continuous thoroughfare from the Battery to the Fly Market—the mercantile center of the city, where many wealthy merchants' houses adjoined their business quarters—on to the shipyards beyond Cherry Street. Crowded within its narrow twists and turns,

Dock Street held the very essence of eighteenth-century New York. Reeking with the pungent smells of cooking, salt air, the fish market, wood smoke, human slops, and horse manure, the cobbled way was one of the busiest places on Manhattan Island because of its proximity to open-air markets near Coenties Slip and Old Slip, the Exchange at the foot of Broad Street near Whitehall Slip, and the Custom House.

Here, alongside the impressive homes of such respected citizens as John Watts and Henry Van Vleck, were dozens of shops whose trade signs and storefronts proclaimed their wares to passersby. When the merchant Watts, who dealt primarily in wines and spirits, emerged from the handsome three-story town house that held his office as well as the family living quarters, he passed within a stone's throw of four purveyors of general merchandise and the stores of men whose names were reminders of how important the Dutch still were to the city's commerce—including Dirck Brinckerhoff's Golden Lock, where hardware and various metals were sold, Henry Cuyler's sugar emporium, and Anthony Van Dam's shop, where one could purchase imported wines and liquors.

As it had been from its founding in 1624 by the Dutch, the city was a maritime community whose lifeblood was commerce and whose consuming interest was money, derived from the endless variety of goods that longshoremen loaded and unloaded at the East River docks.

Surprisingly, what prosperity New York enjoyed depended more on the French and Spanish West Indies than on Britain, which produced ample food for itself and would not accept the grains raised in New York—wheat, Indian corn, oats, rye, and buckwheat. With so many British imports arriving at the East River docks the imbalance of trade was enormous, and it had to be made up insofar as possible through trade with the Caribbean islands.

British ships tied up at Cruger's Wharf and disgorged most of the dry goods which New Yorkers used in their homes or wore on their backs, along with earthenware and cutlery, saddles and bridles, silverware, tools, and luxuries of all kinds. Most of the latter came from London and included such niceties as perfume, mustard, tea, snuff, and gloves, along with handkerchiefs, ribbons, lace, sword knots, sticking plaster, and umbrellas. The hulls of American vessels bound for England were filled with the pelts of animals, potash and pearl ash, iron bars and pigs, and enormous white pine logs for masts for His Majesty's Navy. Traders crammed ships bound for the West Indies with pickled oysters, apples, Indian corn, peas, and rye, cheese and butter, salt pork, ham, and beef, lumber, planks, horses, and beeswax. On their return trip the ships brought sugar, cotton, and indigo, which were resold in England, plus rum and molasses for consumption at home. Sloops and other small craft that tied up at the foot of Broad Street brought fresh produce and poultry, cheeses, butter, and eggs from Dutch farmers on upper Manhattan and Long Island.

At the foot of Wall Street was the Merchants Coffee House, kept by Charles Arding, where John Watts and his colleagues met to discuss the day's news. A social club whose members included Watts and Judge Robert R. Livingston met at Fraunces Tavern (originally the DeLancey mansion) at the corner of Broad and Dock streets, and the King's Arms was a popular gathering spot for officers from the British garrison.

New York's streets were crowded with growing numbers of Irishmen, Germans, Scots, Sephardic Jews—some of them refugees from poverty, others from religious persecution—and Negroes, mostly slaves, who made up as much as one-fifth of the population. "It rather hurts an Europian eye to see so many negro slaves upon the streets," a visitor from Scotland remarked a few years later, but if any New Yorkers were troubled by the fact that one human being out of every five or six in their city was the chattel of another person, their voices were muted. An advertisement by the firm of N. B. Moore and Lynsen in the *New-York Mercury* suggests how slaves were regarded: "To be Sold To-morrow, at Twelve o'Clock, at the Merchants Coffee House, A Parcel of Sugars in Hogsheads. Also, Two Negroes, and a fine Horse."

The variety of religions was evident in the number of churches—seventeen of them within eleven hundred yards of the Fort. And the hodgepodge of nationalities and religions was echoed in the juxtaposition of fashionable residences, workshops, merchants' stores, law offices, and—especially on the waterfront—the dives, flophouses, and whorehouses patronized by seamen, all cheek by jowl as if they had been tossed into the air to settle higgledy-piggledy wherever they happened to land.

In every sense of the word, New York was a cosmopolitan place, with so many different points of view that it had a reputation for political instability. Its distinct difference from other towns in the colonies came from an extraordinary diversity that forced people to get along together, to accommodate and compromise in ways that shaped the city's politics and society. Crèvecoeur was struck by how hospitable New Yorkers were, saying the reception they accorded strangers was "enough to give them a high idea of American generosity, as well as of the simple and cordial friendliness which they are to expect in the other cities of this continent." Food was so cheap, he observed, that everyone lived comfortably—"the poorest not even excepted."

Complicating the religious, national, and cultural differences was the gap separating the rich, the middle-income, and the poor, and nowhere was it more visible than in their homes and neighborhoods. The most fashionable section was near the foot of Broadway, directly east of the Fort and the Governor's Mansion. Only a few blocks from Trinity and the First Presbyterian churches, it offered a superb view of the bay and the New Jersey shoreline. Facing the double row of trees lining the Bowling Green was a quartet of elegant homes. At No.1 Broadway, Captain Archibald Kennedy of the Royal Navy had just moved into the handsome dwelling he had built there. Next door was the residence of Justice Robert R. Livingston, abutting two houses belonging to the Van Cortlandt and Stevens families. A wealthy merchant, William Walton, owned a grand home on St. George's Square, fifty feet wide at the front and three stories high, built of yellow bricks from Holland. It had fluted, rectangular columns at the front door, over which the family's coat of arms greeted visitors, carved lions' heads in stone above the windows, a tiled roof surrounded by a double balustrade, paneled interior, and a stairway skirted with mahogany handrails and banisters. Typical of many successful merchants' homes was the three-story dwelling of Abraham de Peyster, furnished with fine mahogany and walnut pieces, brasses, leather-bottomed sofas, and the family's treasured silver plate—dishes, salvers, tankards, and bowls. One of the several upstairs bedrooms was called the "wainscot room," another the "tapestry room," and in addition to the usual living areas the house had an office, a storage room for apples, and a wine cellar. In the rear of the yard the stable contained a chaise and two sleighs—one for a single horse, one for a pair.

A sure measure of financial success was a country estate, and rich merchants, old moneyed families, and well-to-do government officials purchased land just beyond southern Manhattan with plenty of space for an imposing house, elaborate gardens, and cropland for livestock—a retreat for the summer where, if business called, the "commute" to town took less than an hour by carriage. Nor was that the end of it. Here as in all the colonies, the hunger for land was a disease—an obsession. Land was the goal of every man. For those who had little, a piece of land of their own could mean the difference between a good life and a life of servitude or squalor. For those who had money, land was the way to make more.

The New York merchant who had bought his home and his warehouse or store in lower Manhattan, and had a country place on the outskirts of town or on Long Island or in New Jersey, soon looked farther afield for a place to put his surplus money and sought speculative land development in newly planned townships or unsettled areas on the frontier—often on wild lands known to be Indian territory. Large landowners expected, and received, large profits. The merchant Charles Apthorp's real estate brought him more than £670 a year. Robert Livingston's income from his land was almost £850 annually, and James DeLancey's properties yielded £1,200—all this at a time when a truly well-to-do family could live comfortably on £500 a year.

Near the upper end of the island, rocky cliffs more than a hundred feet high extended almost all the way from the Hudson to the East River. In the middle was what became known as McGown's Pass—a gap about two hundred feet wide. Only two roads traversed the entire length of the island—the Bloomingdale Road, an extension of Broadway, which skirted the cliffs close to the Hudson shore, and the Post Road to Boston, which ran through McGown's Pass to King's Bridge (where Frederick Philipse, lord of a 92,000-acre manor in Westchester, had been given the exclusive right to operate the toll bridge across Spuyten Duyvil Creek).

From the southern end of the island, in the heart of the city, Greenwich Road ran up the west side of the island along the Hudson, or North River, passing a virtual catalog of privilege and wealth. First came Vauxhall, an estate leased by a British major, Thomas James. A few blocks to the east, between the road to Greenwich (known later as Greenwich Village) and the Fresh Water Pond, was the former estate of Anthony Rutgers, which had been transformed into a "pleasure garden" known as Ranelagh, where crowds gathered on Monday and Thursday evenings to watch the fireworks, listen to a concert, and amble through the gardens. Beyond Vauxhall was the residence of George Harrison, surveyor of customs. Then came estates owned by the merchant Leonard Lispenard, Abraham Mortier, paymaster of the British forces, Lady Warren, wife of the admiral, the importer John Jauncey, the merchant William Bayard, James DeLancey's brother Oliver, Colonel Thomas Clarke, and the attorney John Morin Scott.

The other main artery, in the shadow of Mount Pleasant, was Bowery Lane, which ran up the center of the island and intersected Broadway. On what were then the outskirts of town was a hugely impressive piece of

commercial real estate—James DeLancey's Bowery Farm—bounded by Bowery Lane on one side and on the other by the East River between Corlear's
Hook and the Salt Meadows. The DeLanceys, ever alert to opportunity, had
been quick to see that the only way for the city to expand was northward, and
they were ready for it to happen. A developer's dream, all laid out and ready
for the builders, consisted of seventy-two more or less rectangular lots, each
representing a city block and ranging in size from one and a half to two acres,
clustered around the eighteen-acre DeLancey Square. Beyond, extending to
lands of the Stuyvesant family, were open fields, several of them as large as
twenty to forty acres. Fronting on Grand Street—the principal thoroughfare
in the development—was a newly completed house owned by the attorney
Thomas Jones.

Jones was a successful lawyer following in the footsteps of his father, David,
the longtime member and later speaker of the New York Assembly and, from
1758 to 1773, a justice of the Supreme Court. Thomas was a governor of King's
College as well as its attorney, and was attorney as well for the Corporation
of the City of New York. In 1762 he married Anne, a daughter of James
DeLancey, and when DeLancey died* his son James Jr. gave his sister about
two acres of land on the highest part of the estate—indeed, the tallest eminence in that part of the city—where Thomas Jones built a large double house
and encircled it with gardens. The house had a spectacular view of all Manhattan and its surrounding waters—on the east beyond Hell Gate, which was just
south of Buchanan's and Montresor's islands;† on the west across the entire city
to the Hudson, the Jersey shore, and Staten Island; and south to the bay, Governors Island, and the heights of Long Island. Jones named the hill on which
his town house sat Mount Pitt, for the Great Commoner he admired.

For the middle class—artisans and mechanics, shopkeepers, grocers, carpenters, druggists, printers, and the like—housing was mainly in the central area
of the city, in the East, North, and Montgomerie wards. Their churches—
Baptist and Moravian meetinghouses and the Methodist, German Reformed,
and two Dutch churches—were close by in the North Ward.

---

*He died intestate and according to John Watts left "a large real Estate which all goes to Jemmy
[his oldest son] & a very small personal Estate which is unfortunate as to ye younger children."
The amounts were estimated to be £80,000 in real property and a personal estate of about
£12,000.
†Now Wards and Randalls islands.

At the bottom of the socioeconomic ladder, New York's poor occupied three different slum areas, all of them on the fringes of wealthy or middle-class society and the city's factories and industrial works. The worst slum was the waterfront along the East River, where the detritus that washed down from higher elevations in the city vied with the filth floating at the foot of the docks. Garbage and trash, broken timbers and barrels were everywhere; drinking water was foul; and food for the inhabitants of the wooden shacks and tenements, each of whose rooms might house three or four families, was as impure as it was inadequate. At any given moment as many as three or four thousand sailors and roustabouts, joined by criminal gangs and slaves who came here without the permission or knowledge of their masters, might be found "drinking, Tippling, Quarrelling, fighting, gaming, and misbehaving" in the waterfront taverns and brothels.

During the late French and Indian War this was fertile territory for the hated press-gangs from British naval ships, who swarmed ashore with firearms and clubs, with orders to seize anyone who had the look of a seafaring man about him, but who were just as likely to enter houses and grab whatever unlucky souls they found. In 1757, Lord Loudoun's expeditionary force was delayed by a shortage of hands aboard the ships, so he sent press-gangs into town and during the night they captured more than eight hundred men, or more than one-fourth of the city's adult male population. Fortunately, that was far more than Loudoun needed.

As might be expected in a community where the disparity between rich and poor was so pronounced, robberies after dark were frequent, as were outcries from the more privileged citizens over the inefficiency of watchmen. "Whipping at the cart's tail" was the punishment inflicted on many a culprit who was caught, which meant that he was tied to the back of a cart and followed it around town, to Furmans Corner, the meat market, Old Slip and Coenties markets, the Long Bridge, Livingstons Corner, and Dealls Corner, at each of which he was lashed five times on his bare back by the public whipper, to the delight of the crowd attracted to the scene. To finish off the sentence of thirty-nine stripes, he received four more at City Hall.

As cruel as life could be, New Yorkers were not entirely blind to the underprivileged in their midst. Subscriptions for the benefit of the poor were taken up because "Wood & all the Necessaries of Life, at this Time [were] at a much higher Price than was ever known in this City." And in September of 1760 a free school, supervised by Anglican clergy, opened near the New Dutch Church. The mission was to instruct some thirty Negro children five years old or more. Books were provided gratis and all that was asked of the children's owners was enough firewood to heat the building through the winter.

The waterfront area almost intersected a second slum lying along the city's northeast limits in what was called the Out Ward. It was just beyond a section given over to industry and activities that had been banished from better residential districts. Two tan yards were now located here because of the odors they generated. The public slaughterhouse (private slaughtering was against the law) was here for the same reason. And this was also the site of several ropewalks, pottery kilns, and five or more distilleries. Unfortunately for the occupants, it suffered from extremely poor drainage, which was unlikely to be remedied in the foreseeable future.

The Out Ward reflected an out-of-sight, out-of-mind mentality that had foisted many an unwanted enterprise on the neighborhood. Its southern border had been established along the line of palisades erected to guard against the French in 1745. Still standing, the rotting pales paralleled the old Dutch wall that gave Wall Street its name and ran from Warren Street on the Hudson to James Street on the East River. Beyond this barrier were the gallows and public executions that brought forth curious throngs of jeering, rowdy poor folk intent on viewing the spectacles, and a potter's field where black slaves, criminals, and paupers were buried. Cattle and pigs roamed the streets, the public slaughterhouse contributed its share of noise, filth, and smells, and the wooden hovels of desperately impoverished inhabitants were scattered willy-nilly throughout the district, where infectious diseases were often rampant.

In 1759 an epidemic of the dreaded smallpox broke out on Long Island; in March of 1760 it hit New York and Boston as well during the long, cold winter. Elizabeth Lloyd Fitch was living in Boston and wrote her father on Long Island to say that smallpox had spread to many places in town and might be contained were it not for "Some wicked people that have a mind to Spread it. I live in constant fear as none of the family has had it. . . ."

The third slum was a small pocket of poverty on the west side, near St. Paul's Church, which was under construction in 1765 in open fields at Broadway and Vesey Street, and King's College. By May of 1760 the "neat and commodious" college building, surmounted by an iron crown in honor of George II, was almost complete. Students were beginning to eat and lodge there, and the president, the Reverend Samuel Johnson, had moved in just forty years after he had done the same at the College in New Haven (later to become Yale). One of the city's largest assemblies of prostitutes flourished near the British soldiers' barracks behind the Fields, and although the nearby college was said to be "on one of the finest situations perhaps of any college in the world," one entered its grounds "thro' one of the streets where the most noted prostitutes live"—some five hundred "ladies of pleasure," a visitor reckoned. A certain number of the city's outcasts regarded as beyond the pale were provided for in 1760 when the Assembly voted funds for the purchase of Bedlow's Island,* where a pest house was erected, and for completion of a new jail.

In their occupations, manners, income, and general outlook on life the inhabitants of New York's slums were worlds apart from its more respectable, more fortunate citizens, but their physical proximity was a constant reminder of how difficult it might be to avoid trouble if the right combination of circumstances arose. The city's centers of poverty and misery were seedbeds of unrest, powder kegs ready for a fuse to be lit. As it happened, the events of the next decade began to break down the delicate equilibrium between the two groups, forcing men from all walks of life to decide where they stood.

New York's poor had ample reason to envy and resent the city's well-to-do, and there was a growing use among them of phrases like "big wig" and "silk stocking" to indicate their feelings about the affluent in society. Yet for many of those less fortunate the sight of a rich man's carriage or mansion was a symbol of what had brought them here in the first place. To many who had left behind family and friends and braved the Atlantic crossing, that symbol was concrete evidence that what another man had done you could do too.

For the upwardly mobile, Manhattan was where the new world began, and the numbers showed it. By 1762 New York's population would swell to almost 18,000, second to Philadelphia, which had more than 23,000, but outstripping Boston, which fell to third place with 15,600. The old world lay behind these people, and what lay ahead was something altogether different, with boundless prospects. The same Scottish visitor who was offended by seeing so many slaves on the city's streets concluded that this was "the best country in the world for people of small fortunes; or in other words, the best poor man's country. . . ." Writing to a friend back home, he elaborated on this. It takes time, he said, "to get established on an agreeable footing even in this country," and many obstacles lie in one's path—first, the long sea voyage, then a land where everything is strange and different. One has to begin life

---

*Later Bedloe's. Ceded to the United States government in 1800, it became the site of the Statue of Liberty.

anew, he added, acquire acquaintances, build friendships and a reputation, all requiring "courage and resolution in the adventurer," yet these difficulties are "easily overcome by young people or by those who have emigrated from hardships at home. . . ."

To men and women who had abandoned a land in which it was all but impossible to rise above class or station, New York promised opportunity for all except those in bondage. No matter what their nationality—British, French, Dutch, Spanish, German—or religion—Anglican, Presbyterian, Huguenot, Catholic, Jew—this was a country that offered hope for humankind, and New York was the portal favored by most who were seeking a new life.

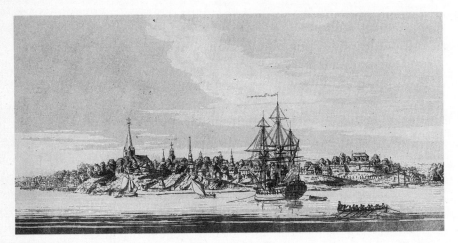

View of New York from the North West. *Stokes Collection.*

2

Salutary Neglect

Between 1721 and 1742, England's affairs were largely in the immensely capable hands of a stubby, coarse, 280-pound man named Robert Walpole, leader of the dominant Whig faction and the first real prime minister in the nation's history. Honest, plain, bluff in manner, and boundless in energy, Walpole reveled in the give-and-take of Parliamentary debate and had an unsettling habit of munching red Norfolk apples while he followed the arguments. This forceful man with large features and earthy speech that jibed with the rusticity he cultivated was a formidably efficient administrator and master of detail who understood the workings of government and used that knowledge to establish and maintain his political strength. Walpole rode to hounds, openly kept a mistress, and lived the high life in a small palace filled with paintings by such masters as Rembrandt, Van Dyck, and Rubens, but his prized possession was his own spoils system: for every office that became vacant, he had friends, relatives, or others who had proved their loyalty and could be relied upon to support him.

Recognizing that the House of Commons was the seat of power and the best place for a king's servant to be, he refused a peerage and assiduously cultivated allies among civil servants and political appointees, or placemen, as well as conservative country squires who could be counted on to provide votes when he needed them.

Few American colonists of that day realized it, but Walpole and his policy had a great deal to do with determining their present and future. He believed that England's ends and, by extension, those of her provinces were best served by avoiding war, encouraging trade, and keeping taxes as low as possible. Since colonies served a dual purpose—supplying the raw materials for British manufacturing and then providing a market for those manufactures—they were vital to the system, and it was clearly in the best interests of the mother country to follow a course Walpole so aptly described as "salutary neglect."

A number of factors that antedated Walpole's program were involved here. For one thing, the colonization of America was not at the outset regarded as a function of government, largely because seventeenth-century England lacked the resources—administrative as well as financial—to undertake such ventures. So where expansion occurred it was largely the result of private, not state, initiative. Merchants were granted charters, or patents, to form trading companies to carry on foreign commerce in various parts of the world. The prototype was the all-powerful East India Company, chartered in 1600 by Queen Elizabeth for trade with Asia, which conducted administrative, political, and military affairs as though it were a sovereign nation.

In America, no end of trading companies received charters that led to settlements (not all of which survived), while other charters were granted to individuals such as William Penn and Lord Baltimore, and all these became self-sustaining, independent corporations that governed themselves with minimal supervision or interference from London. In fact, one of the rare regulatory measures passed by Parliament during the early colonial period was the Navigation Act of 1651, which restricted the Americans' trade by stipulating that all goods brought into or out of the colonies had to be transported in English ships, and ruled further that the colonies were subject to regulations and laws of Parliament, though that body showed little inclination to become involved in pesky provincial affairs.

Until the eighteenth century was more than half past, the British Empire was an empire in name only. Occasionally, but only occasionally, Parliament stepped in and made a decision affecting the colonies, as did officials of the Admiralty, Treasury, or customs, but the lion's share of business with the provinces was left in the hands of the Board of Trade. For generations almost no English officials were truly conversant with colonial matters. Transatlantic communications customarily took anywhere from four to eight weeks. And when instructions were sent from authorities in London to the provinces, no means of enforcing them existed. In fact, until 1763 no British army worthy of the name was in North America on a permanent basis. At most, about 3,500 men were stationed in the colonies at any one time, and a majority of those troops were likely to be in a single location.

Yet another factor that kept the American colonies from receiving much attention was that they were hostage to the balance of power in Europe. In order to exclude the Roman Catholic Stuart line, the 1707 Union of England and Scotland provided that Sophia, princess of Hanover, and her Protestant heirs should succeed to the British crown. When Queen Anne of England died without an heir—not one of her seventeen children having survived infancy—Sophia's son George of Hanover was called to the throne. Stubborn, vindictive, and dull, George I spoke no English, never bothered to attend cabinet meetings, and satisfied his enormous libido with a succession of voluptuous German mistresses. His son, who came to the throne in 1727 as George II, spoke English but with a pronounced German accent. He inherited his father's receding chin, bulging eyes, short stature, and passion for large women and, according to the Earl of Chesterfield, had "all the weaknesses of a little mind, without any of the virtues or even the vices of a great one." Certainly he had none of the qualities expected of a ruler. Fortunately for England, however, his wife, Caroline, was an intelligent, no-nonsense woman, tolerant of his rages and his mistresses, who persuaded him to leave his adopted land's affairs in the hands of Walpole and the Whigs. Thanks to Parliament's aversion to a Catholic Stuart king, the Electorate of Hanover was for years an immense drain on Britain's finances, mostly in the form of huge subsidies for Frederick the Great's Prussia, its principal continental ally.

In Walpole's day the colonists, left to their own devices, got along as he knew they could. With a minimum of interference from London they had for years been exercising the mechanics of self-government, learning as they went, discovering through trial and error what worked and what did not, while growing ever so slowly into entities capable for the most part of running their own affairs.

In 1748 a native of Finland came to America on a mission for the Swedish Academy of Sciences. This was Pehr Kalm, a professor of botany, whose assignment was to conduct a search in the new world for useful seeds and plants—alternative sources of food for humans, fodder for livestock—hardy enough to survive on Swedish soil. Kalm was an indefatigable researcher, insatiably curious, and on his travels to Philadelphia, New York City, Kentucky, and the devastated frontier along New York's northern rim, he saw the effects of Walpole's hands-off policy and observed that "each English colony in North America is independent of the other, and that each has its own laws and coinage, and may be looked upon in several lights as a state by itself." Newspapers carried little but foreign news, largely because most colonials had almost no interest in what was happening in other colonies, and this self-imposed isolation was at the heart of the problems America faced during the seemingly incessant warfare along its vast frontier. Too often the views and policies of one province were diametrically opposed to those of another. Or it happened that the governor and the legislature in a colony were stalemated because they could not agree, thus preventing an action that might otherwise have been taken. Above all, no real unity among the separate colonies existed.

As Kalm saw it, "while the people are quarreling about the best and cheapest manner of carrying on the war, an enemy has it in his power to [seize] one place after another." That is, while one or several colonies suffered from attacks by French and Indians, other provinces simply sat on their hands and ignored the fighting, sometimes taking months to decide whether to provide assistance and, as like as not, concluding that they would not. Worse, instances existed where a supposedly neutral colony carried on extensive trade with the very enemy that was "attacking and laying waste some other provinces."

In terms of numbers, the French in Canada were insignificant compared to the English in America, yet they had been surprisingly successful in the ongoing wars of the late seventeenth and eighteenth centuries. With his talent for going to the heart of the matter, Pehr Kalm concluded that the French menace actually worked to England's advantage. The long, unprotected Atlantic coastline was particularly vulnerable to attack, as was the frontier with Canada, and threats from "dangerous neighbors in times of war [are] sufficient to prevent the connection of the colonies with their mother country from being quite broken off."

The proximity of the French, in other words, was a powerful incentive for the colonies to remain submissive to England, but conflicting factors were also at work. With the population of the provinces increasing so much that they began to "almost vie with Old England," the mother country insisted on prohibiting new manufactures that might compete with home industries and forbade Americans from trading with nations outside British dominion except in a few places. Nor were foreigners permitted to trade with the American colonies. The provincials, Kalm was astonished to hear, "are not allowed to dig for any gold or silver unless they send it to England immediately."

These restrictive measures were effective, he could see, but they seemed to be causing the colonists "to grow less tender for their mother country"—an aloofness with which Germans, Dutch, and French living in England's American colonies heartily sympathized. By the time Pehr Kalm had been in the provinces for only six weeks—from mid-September to early November of 1748—he had been assured by Englishmen, some born in America, some in the mother country, that in thirty or fifty years—as early as 1778, in other words—the English colonies in North America "would be able to form a state by themselves entirely independent of Old England."

It was clear in 1755 as it had been during Kalm's 1748 visit that the efforts of individual colonies were largely inadequate whenever the French and their Indian allies attempted to thwart the expansionist tendencies of English, Scottish, and Irish settlers who were continually reaching out for more land. As a few thoughtful Americans began to realize, the situation called for collective action, but too many jealousies intruded, too much turf was at stake, and in the meantime the situation in London changed dramatically.

A particularly nasty trait shared by George I and George II was that each despised his eldest son and heir. The second George described his son Frederick, Prince of Wales, as "a monster and the greatest villain that ever was born." And the young man's mother, Queen Caroline, was equally uncharitable: "If I was to see him in hell," she declared, "I should feel no more for him than I should for any other rogue that ever went there." Understandably, the public was sympathetic toward the young man, and that sentiment made it easier for the administration's opposition to attack Robert Walpole, who was a favorite of the king and, especially, of the queen. Walpole was aging physically, and after Caroline died in 1737, his power in Commons began to erode. War with France and Spain erupted, foiling the prime minister's frantic efforts to keep the peace; and in 1742 he resigned under pressure and accepted the title of Earl of Orford. In the meantime a cocky young supporter of the Prince of Wales had been elected to Parliament and it was evident almost at once that he spoke for a new generation.

And an eloquent spokesman he was. William Pitt was widely read, and while in school he had learned the art of speaking by practicing the orations of Thucydides and Demosthenes. Tall and thin, erect, with the eyes and beak of a hawk and the voice of an angel, he used his theatrical skills to run the gamut of emotions from ridicule and scorn to rapture and inspiration. Perhaps his greatest gift was a talent for giving his countrymen a vision of their nation's destiny—a future of eminence and glory. He was an exceptionally charismatic figure and a superb administrator, and despite his emotional instability and occasional fits of madness, the public loved him, largely because of what he said and stood for.

During the War of the Austrian Succession, George II, supported by his ministers, favored protecting his beloved Hanover and even fought at Dettingen—the last English monarch to appear on the field of battle. But he made the mistake of wearing the colors of Hanover, not Britain, lending special pungency to a speech Pitt delivered in Commons: "Neither justice nor policy," he told members scornfully, "required us to be engaged in the quarrels of the Continent. . . . The confidence of the people is abused by making unnecessary alliances. . . . It is now apparent that this great, this powerful, this formidable Kingdom is considered only as a province of a despicable electorate."

Pitt wanted to avoid large-scale military involvement in Europe and favored tactics that could be described as hit-and-run, or what would one day be called commando raids—quick strikes by small, mobile units along the Flemish and French coasts to keep the mighty French army continually off balance. Meanwhile he wanted above all to destroy France's navy and merchant marine and seize her overseas bases—Quebec, Mauritius, the sugar islands of the Caribbean. The program he advocated—"When Trade is at stake you must defend it or perish"—was the antithesis of Walpole's and that of his successors, Henry Pelham and the Duke of Newcastle. To them, war was anathema because they believed it would stifle commerce, produce confiscatory taxes, and plunge the nation hopelessly into debt. At most, they said, armed conflict should be limited to protecting the king's possessions on the Continent and defending British shipping in the Mediterranean and the Channel. But that was not Pitt's way.

In 1751, Frederick, Prince of Wales, suffered a chill after playing tennis and died unexpectedly, leaving behind his widow, Augusta, and their nine children, of whom the oldest was to become George III. (It was characteristic of George II to say, when he was told of the prince's death, "I have lost my eldest son, but I am glad of it.") After Pelham followed Frederick to the grave in 1754, George II was forced, reluctantly, to accept the inevitable, and three years later William Pitt became first minister and formed a new cabinet.* Now the golden opportunity on which he had set his sights lay before him.

Looking at a map published in 1755 by the engineer Lewis Evans, whose many interests and skills included cartography, one can see clearly the geography that dictated the strategic dilemma confronting Pitt in the American colonies.

From Massachusetts south to the Virginia capes, scores of English settlements crowd the Atlantic seaboard, clustered for the most part on the coast

---

*At the insistence of the king, the Duke of Newcastle was included in the cabinet, and although Pitt and the duke were frequently at odds, they managed—in the words of Lord Chesterfield—to "jog on like man and wife; that is, seldom agreeing, often quarreling; but, by mutual interest, upon the whole, not parting."

itself or inland along the rivers. But above Schenectady and Albany and Deer-
field the paper is almost blank except for geographical landmarks—lakes,
rivers, mountains—plus widely scattered forts at strategic locations.

From Albany, running northeast to southwest, are the "Endless Mountains," as Evans called them, seemingly impenetrable to judge from his anno-
tation: "A Vein of Mountains about 30 or 40 Miles right across, through
which there is not yet any occupied Path in these Parts." Beyond them to the
west are indications of Indian tribal lands, sites of buffalo licks, pipe clay,
rapids, salt springs, and warpaths, and the location of such oddities as Antique
Sculptures, Elephant Bones, Petroleum,* plus some isolated outposts bearing
the owner's names—Gist's, Stewart's, White Woman's, and French Margaret's—
along with places designated simply Cow Pasture or Meadows.

The mountains, it is plain to see, block the English settlements, hemming
them in, frustrating large-scale penetration of the vast expanse of virgin territory to the west, even though some provinces, like Virginia, claimed title to
everything "Bounded by the Great Atlantic to the East, by North Carolina to
the South, by Maryland and Pennsylvania to the North, and by the South Sea
to the West including California." In other words, a band as wide as Virginia
stretching from the Atlantic to the Pacific.

Geography, as Evans's map makes clear, greatly favored the French in North
America, since the mighty St. Lawrence River bypassed the Appalachian barrier to the north, enabling the intrepid *coureurs de bois* and Jesuit priests to
move by water from Quebec and Montreal into the heartland of the continent by way of the Great Lakes. With relatively short portages, they had
access to the Ohio River and clear sailing to the Gulf of Mexico, while intra-
continental travel by the English, on the other hand—until they hacked roads
through the wilderness—was limited to coastal rivers whose sources were
in the mountains, or the Hudson. By means of the latter, they could travel
by way of the Mohawk River (with portages) and reach Oswego on Lake
Ontario, or—again with portages—go from Albany to Lake George, Lake
Champlain, the Richelieu River, and on to the St. Lawrence. Either way, of
course, they would find themselves in an area claimed by the French.

Yet another barrier to the English was a broad territorial swath to the
north of their numerous towns. South of Lake Ontario and east of Lake Erie
as far as Albany, the labels on the map are the names of Indian tribes whose

*On this spot the Seneca and other Indians spread blankets on the oily surface of the creek water
and wrung out the slimy liquid into earthenware containers; they used it for medicine and lini-
ment and as a base for their war paint.

hunting grounds these were—reading from east to west, the Mohawk, Tus-
carora, Oneida, Onondaga, Cayuga, and Seneca—constituting a remarkable
alliance, the powerful Six Nations of the Iroquois Confederation. And to the
north and west, occupying the vastness beyond everything else, lay New
France, extending from the St. Lawrence to the Great Lakes, to the Ohio and
Mississippi rivers, and—well outside the confines of the map—to the
unknown immensity that geography effectively denied the English settlers.

To exacerbate the depredations of Indians and French on the frontier,
Europe's wars—fought over religious issues as well as the balance of power—
inevitably spilled over onto the American continent. If England engaged
France or Spain in Europe, sooner or later the conflict spread to America.
Between 1689 and 1697 the War of the League of Augsburg, known in Amer-
ica as King William's War, pitted the French and their Indian allies against the
English and the Iroquois. The War of the Spanish Succession, from 1702 to
1713, called Queen Anne's War by the colonists, produced more bitter fighting
between French and English in Massachusetts, Acadia, Port Royal, and else-
where. In 1739 the War of Jenkins's Ear broke out between England and
Spain, followed the next year by the War of the Austrian Succession, or King
George's War.

A significant triumph during King George's War was the remarkable expe-
dition in 1745 in which William Pepperell led an army of volunteers from
Massachusetts, Connecticut, and New Hampshire and, in cooperation with a
British fleet, captured the French fortress at Louisbourg on Cape Breton
Island. Glorious as that victory may have been for the New Englanders, it was
followed by two years of warfare along New York's frontier, when the French
and Indians from Canada attacked on a broad front, burning Saratoga and
Albany, among other communities. New York City had been in a state of alert
for years because of its vulnerability to attack by way of the Lake Champlain–
Hudson River corridor, and the severity of the renewed fighting increased
that awareness to the extent that municipal authorities in 1748 ordered construction of a new wall along the northern extremity of the town. The palisaded barrier of fourteen-foot cedar logs, standing upright in a trench, ran
from the Hudson to the East River* roughly parallel to the first wall, built by
the Dutch a century before. Militiamen stood guard in six blockhouses along
the route, and four gates provided access to the roads leading out of town. It
was a reminder, in case one was needed, that the destinies of the city and
province were firmly in the hands of powers across the sea.

---

*On a line from the present Chambers Street on the Hudson to Cherry Street on the East River.

More than most other colonials, settlers on New York's long northern perimeter knew what dangerous foes the French and their Indian allies were. They also knew that little aid had been forthcoming from other colonies, which meant a disproportionate drain on New York's manpower and other resources. Nor did the merchants of Albany and New York City have any enthusiasm for hostilities, since fighting inevitably interrupted the highly profitable trade with Canada.

So you had, on the one hand, two rival European empires that had already fought four wars in the past six decades, and each of those conflicts had produced, almost as a side issue, a struggle for control of the North American continent. On the other hand, you had numerous Indian nations or tribes which had lived on the land for centuries and whose existence was increasingly threatened by white newcomers who coveted their territory—many of them because they wanted to settle there, but many others because they believed possession of land would enable them to make a financial killing.

Even if Europe's monarchs and ministers of state actually believed that war and the slaughter or mutilation of thousands of their subjects would serve their ends, when the fighting at last came to a close and foreign ministers assembled in the town of Aix-la-Chapelle in 1748, they agreed to revert to the *status quo ante,* nullify all conquests, and—in a devastating blow to Americans—restore Louisbourg to France. Eight years of casualties and destruction of property on two continents, in other words, had yielded exactly nothing, except to make the colonials aware that they were so many pawns to be manipulated by a government across the sea.

Astonishingly, the governments of England and France were so determined to put an end to the interminable fighting that each appointed two "commissaries" who would spend the next five years in an effort to "examine and adjust" various issues between the two countries in America, as well as those relating to prizes and prisoners seized at sea. Alas, these prolonged conversations in Paris came to nought, ending in bickering and wrangling over who owned what and accusations of bad faith and treachery, until by 1754 the representatives of the two governments were thoroughly disheartened. By the time the commissaries admitted that they were at an impasse, events in America had taken charge.

All the while the diplomats were conversing in Paris, French and English activists on the other side of the Atlantic were moving in directions that made the commissaries' work pointless. The French had built a fort on the Niagara

River and another on Lake Champlain, and suddenly England's alliance with the Iroquois Confederation was threatened. At the same time, British traders were becoming more numerous and pushing deeper into the Great Lakes region and the Ohio Valley, challenging France's monopoly there.

The French were well aware that in 1749 a number of powerful Virginians—all land speculators (among them young George Washington and his half brother)—had formed the Ohio Company and received from King George II a grant of 200,000 acres, with the understanding that they would erect a fort to protect future settlers. But there was a problem here: the same land was considered by His Most Christian Majesty Louis XV of France to be his own.

The French acted quickly. The Marquis de la Galissonière, acting governor of Canada, sent the Chevalier Céloron de Blainville with two hundred men in thirty-three canoes into the Ohio Valley to reassert France's claim to the region, based on the premise that boundaries were determined by the watersheds of rivers. Covering some two thousand miles in Ohio territory, Céloron warned the Indians against the English and ordered English traders to leave the territory, saying that "should they make their appearance on the Beautiful River [as the Ohio was known] they would be treated without any delicacy." He then buried a number of square lead plates at strategic locations, warning potential trespassers that the lands on both sides of the Ohio River and all rivers flowing into it, "as far as the sources of the said rivers," belonged to France, as agreed in the treaties of Riswick, Utrecht, and Aix-la-Chapelle. To further thwart the Virginians' plans, the French began cutting a trail to the headwaters of the Ohio and constructed Forts Presque Isle, LeBoeuf, and Venango to cover the approaches to the Allegheny River. As Cadwallader Colden observed to New York's Governor Clinton, "it . . . appears that the French are resolved to destroy the British Trade Among all the Indian Nations where ever they can," and any pretensions of the governor of Canada to the contrary "are only very thin colourings to cover his designs." When news of this reached London a letter appeared in the *Gentleman's Magazine* warning, "If the French are not soon drove off and forts built by the English on the Mississippi they will have such strongholds that it will never be in our province to expel them."

The governor of Virginia, Lord Albemarle, was much too preoccupied to take action, since he was also George II's Groom of the Stole, colonel of the Coldstream Guards, and minister plenipotentiary to the French court, and had recently settled down in Paris with a reported sixteen cooks and a new mistress. So the responsibility for representing the crown fell to Robert

George Washington,
by Charles Willson Peale.
Washington and Lee University.

Dinwiddie, lieutenant governor, who was doubly outraged, since he happened to be a major investor in the Ohio Company. In 1753 he dispatched the twenty-one-year-old George Washington to Fort LeBoeuf on the upper Ohio River with a starchy message for the French commandant:

> Sir
> The lands upon the river Ohio, in the western parts of the colony of Virginia, are so notoriously known to be the property of the crown of Great Britain, that it is a matter of equal concern and surprise to me, to hear that a body of French forces are erecting Fortresses and making settlements upon that river, Within his Majesty's dominions.

The message went on at some length but predictably had no effect on the commandant, who informed Dinwiddie that he was barking up the wrong tree and should address his complaints to Ange de Menneville, Marquis de Duquesne, the new governor-general of Canada. After Washington returned to Virginia and reported that France planned to occupy the entire Ohio Valley and could be prevented from doing so only by force, Dinwiddie ordered a fort to be built at the Forks of the Ohio.* The effort was short-lived: no

---

*Where the Monongahela and Allegheny rivers come together to form the Ohio—at present-day Pittsburgh.

sooner was the fort under construction than a swarm of canoes carrying French and Indians appeared and sent the workmen scurrying back to Virginia.

By this time, officials in London were forced to admit that the skirmishes between colonials and French forces on the western frontier were getting out of hand and beyond the capacity of Americans to deal with unless they had the active support of British troops. There was a hitch here, of course, in that France and England were, for a wonder, not at war after 1748, which meant that putting a stop to French encroachment on His Majesty's territory must be deftly handled by a relatively small number of troops—not by any stretch of the imagination an army large enough to upset the fragile neutrality vis-à-vis France. Some of these soldiers would have to be British regulars who could be counted on to do things properly, the rest provincials, partly to add manpower but also to give the illusion that this was, after all, really a colonial matter, nothing for France to get alarmed about.

3

Year of Wonders

In August of 1754 at one of their interminable meetings, one of the French commissaries confronted the Englishmen with a report from the Marquis de Duquesne that forces led by an American officer named George Washington had killed a French officer named Jumonville in a "treacherous manner" near the Ohio River. A month later, the tables were reversed: the English received word of a French attack on Washington's troops at Fort Necessity and the defeat of that force.

When the Earl of Albemarle got word of the skirmish between George Washington's band of Virginians and the French scouting party he wrote to George II's prime minister, the Duke of Newcastle:

> Washington and such may have courage and resolution but they have no knowledge or experience in our profession [of arms]; consequently there can be no dependence on them. Officers, and good ones, must be sent to discipline the militia and to lead them on . . . we may then (and not before) drive the French back to their settlements and encroach upon them as they do at present upon us.

Newcastle agreed. "All North America will be lost if these practices are tolerated," he said, "and no war can be worse to this country, than . . . suffering such insults as these." But despite his bluster, Newcastle had no stomach for hostilities, especially since no major European ally was in sight just then, and he made no diplomatic protest. Whether or not George II's ministers willed it to be otherwise, the clock was running out, and in the months that followed both sides were preparing for the conflict that was all but inevitable in North America.

So it was that a minor skirmish fought in a place called the Great Meadows to settle a dispute about provincial boundaries began yet another French and Indian War in the new world and soon developed into the Seven Years' War in the old, embroiling the allied powers of England and Prussia against France and Austria, and eventually including Spain, the West Indies, and India. It was the first real world war and cost the lives of an estimated 850,000 soldiers and hundreds of thousands of civilians before it ended.

If you envisioned French Canada as an octopus, with its head in Quebec, you could almost see the long tentacles reaching up Lake Champlain and Lake St. Sacrément, up the St. Lawrence to Fort Frontenac and on to Niagara, south to Fort Duquesne and the Ohio country, southwest to the Mississippi and New Orleans, and northwest to Detroit and Michilimackinac, on the shores of Lake Huron. Nor was it difficult to imagine the stranglehold Louis XV's France would have on England's provinces so long as those remote outposts remained in French hands.

In fact, a good many of England's strategists, who had had enough of the patchwork solutions that achieved so little in the recent hostilities, agreed that the French in America were already on the road to war and should be stopped immediately, but Newcastle did nothing until September of 1754. Finally a plan was hatched to raise two regiments of provincials and send two regiments of regulars from England, led by "a general officer of rank and capacity." This was the genesis of an expedition that began to take shape on November 25 of that year, when eight long pages of detailed instructions from His Majesty George II were drawn up "for our Well Beloved friend Edward Braddock Esq., Major General of our Forces and whom we have appointed General and Commander of our troops and forces that are now in North America and that shall be sent or raised there, to vindicate our just rights and Possessions in those parts." On that same day in London, not entirely by coincidence, General Braddock signed his last will and testament.

A blunt, self-assured, profane man, Braddock was an experienced career officer who was known as a strict disciplinarian. He had a good record, was well regarded by his men, and was probably recommended for this job by

Lord Albemarle, his old colonel in the Coldstream Guards. On paper, the general's assignment may have seemed perfectly straightforward when he and his superiors discussed the operation over a map of Pennsylvania drawn in 1749 by Lewis Evans. But a map was one thing, reality another, and to anyone even remotely familiar with conditions on the American frontier the project was daunting, to say the least, since the army's route would take it overland, through heavily forested, uninhabited wilderness and over the endless mountains where nothing but a narrow track existed. This meant that every mile of the route must be widened to accommodate heavy wagons and monstrous siege guns. London figured by now that Fort Duquesne at the Forks of the Ohio was where the destiny of the empire might be decided. Ignoring the fact that England and France were not at war, the British ordered Braddock to drive the French from the fort and, leaving a garrison behind to hold it, press on and seize the French forts at Niagara, Frontenac on Lake Ontario (constructing a fleet if it proved necessary), St. Frédéric on Lake Champlain, and Beausejour on the isthmus of Nova Scotia. If he could not command these separate and wildly optimistic operations personally, he was authorized to name subordinate commanders and raise provincial troops wherever men were available. Whatever else he might decide, the Ohio expedition was to take precedence over the other campaigns.

In Alexandria, Virginia, Braddock—speaking now as commander in chief of all British forces in America—met the governors of Massachusetts, New York, Pennsylvania, Maryland, and Virginia, and after discussing strategy appointed William Shirley of Massachusetts to lead the attack on Niagara and William Johnson of New York to command the force against Fort St. Frédéric. Braddock himself would lead his troops across the Allegheny Mountains to take Fort Duquesne.

After a fairly easy march up the Potomac River, the army assembled at Wills Creek, the jumping-off place, where it was immediately apparent that they were badly in need of wagons. With more than 2,200 men, an artillery train of six- and twelve-pounder cannon, howitzers, and mortars, plus shot, shells, and powder, and all the other matériel required by an army on the march, the general had to reckon also with enough food for those soldiers for a month and a half, plus forage for the horses, since the dense forest afforded no natural feed. Fortunately for Braddock, Pennsylvania's assemblymen, reacting to harsh criticism from the general and his aide for their lack of preparations for his campaign, had sent Benjamin Franklin to smooth the waters. The two met for several days in Frederick, where the Pennsylvanian "had full opportunity of removing all [Braddock's] prejudices," and immediately arranged to furnish teamsters, horses, and 150 heavy wagons for the expedition.

Before they parted company, Braddock outlined his plans to Franklin. "After taking Fort Duquesne," he said confidently, "I am to proceed to Niagara; and, having taken that, to Frontenac, if the season will allow time; and I suppose it will, for Duquesne can hardly detain me above three or four days; and then I can see nothing that will obstruct my march to Niagara." Franklin may have smiled inwardly as he imagined the redcoats, uniformed in heavy wool, suffering in the stifling heat of summer as they struggled through the 110 miles of almost unbroken forest and mountains that lay ahead. He agreed with Braddock, however, about the ease of taking Fort Duquesne once he arrived there; after all, the place was only partially fortified and couldn't possibly withstand an artillery barrage.

Braddock may or may not have shared with Franklin his trump card—that he had in his possession a meticulously drawn scale map of the fort with a detailed list of its armaments, contrived by Major Robert Stobo while he was a captive of the French at the Forks, who risked his life to have it smuggled out by a friendly Indian. (The general also had a copy of Lewis Evans's 1755 map, "A General Map of the Middle British Colonies in America.")

But Franklin foresaw danger "from ambuscades of Indians, who by constant practice are dexterous in laying and executing them; and the slender line, near four miles long, which your army must make, may expose it to be attacked by surprise in its flanks, and to be cut like a thread in several pieces," which, since they would be widely separated, would be unable to come up in time to support each other.

Braddock told him not to worry. "These savages may, indeed, be a formidable enemy to your raw American militia, but upon the King's regulars and disciplined troops, sir, it is impossible they should make any impression."

The young Virginian George Washington, who had been invited to join the expedition as a member of Braddock's staff, also warned the general and his lieutenants to prepare for "the mode of attack" they could expect from the French and Indians, but the English officers were so obsessed with "regularity and discipline," he said, and held the Indians in such absolute contempt, that the admonition was suggested in vain.

On July 8, thirty-eight days after leaving Fort Cumberland at Wills Creek, with an enormously difficult and fatiguing march behind them, when men had sickened with dysentery and horses dropped dead of exhaustion and exertion, Braddock's men still had experienced not a shred of opposition and were within ten miles of the French fort at the Forks. With drums beating and fifes tootling the "Grenadiers' March," Lieutenant Colonel Thomas Gage led the advance guard into a clearing about a quarter of a mile beyond where they crossed the Monongahela River. Just then the scouts spotted a white man, dressed as an Indian but with an officer's silver gorget at his throat, darting from one tree to another. He waved his hat in the air, the unearthly shriek of Indian war whoops shattered the silence of the dense woods, someone shouted, "The Indians is upon us!" and Braddock's men were suddenly hit by a hail of musket balls. Within minutes the British force was surrounded on three sides, unable to advance, but the wagons and artillery kept moving forward into and among the frantic infantrymen, blocking their line of retreat, and almost no one could see an enemy to shoot at. For nearly three hours the redcoats were under continuous fire, fighting desperately, often hitting their own men in a futile effort to retaliate, until finally discipline collapsed and the survivors fled the field in wild panic. Every officer in the two grenadier companies was killed or wounded. Braddock was badly hurt; Gage was hit; Washington had two horses shot under him and four bullet holes in his coat. Of the fifteen hundred men who had gone into action, one thousand were casualties. Braddock died of his wounds an agonizing five days later, and to avoid having his body recovered and mutilated by Indians, Washington had him buried under the road so the boots of marching men, horses' hoofs, and wagon wheels would obliterate the site. A number of the unfortunate soldiers left alive on the battlefield who were not scalped were stripped, bound, taken to Fort Duquesne, and burned at the stake.

When news of the disaster reached New York, Lieutenant Governor James DeLancey moved quickly to suppress it. He told Alexander Colden, the local postmaster, to write immediately to his counterpart in New Haven and say that New York newspapers had been ordered not to publish anything about the defeat: ". . . It would be wrong [if] it should be printed any where on the Continent for some time lest the News reach our Indians and Army . . . which may be of bad Consequence."

Braddock's defeat was only the first in a series of calamities for British arms. Shortly after the debacle on the Monongahela, William Johnson led a colonial force northward from Albany with the objective of taking Fort St. Frédéric at the narrows of Lake Champlain. Along the way he learned that a party of French and Indians under Baron von Dieskau was on the prowl, and after much maneuvering by both sides the French ambushed about a thousand of

Johnson's men and killed the Mohawk Chief Hendrick but were driven off in a second battle. Reeling from the Braddock disaster, London was so elated to hear that Dieskau's French army—never mind how small—was repulsed that Johnson was made a baronet and given a purse of £5,000. But in fact the only positive result of the campaign was the construction of Fort Edward on the Hudson and Fort William Henry on the southern shore of Lake St. Sacrément, which extended the British frontier a little farther to the north and gave some protection to Albany and Schenectady. The French, however, were hardly idle: at the same time Johnson's men were building Fort William Henry they began construction of a bastion called Fort Carillon where Lake St. Sacrément (renamed Lake George by Johnson) empties into Lake Champlain.

Another expedition that had been planned by Braddock and the governors in Alexandria was expected to strengthen the vital post at Oswego on Lake Ontario, 160 miles from Albany, and Massachusetts governor William Shirley was put in charge of this operation. But the proposed campaign never got off the ground. In the spring of 1756, as Britain and France moved ever closer to formally declared war, Shirley was recalled to London and the French, who were now led by a dynamic career officer, the Marquis de Montcalm, handily seized the unfinished Fort Oswego. The two British regiments there, which had been raised in America, surrendered, but the Indians butchered the sick and wounded and a number of other men before the French could restore order. With the shocking loss of England's great trading post in the west, her foothold on Lake Ontario vanished and the frontier was suddenly pushed eastward to German Flats on the Mohawk River, halfway to Albany.

A plan to capture Louisbourg from the French in 1757 collapsed as a result of bad weather that delayed troop transports until early July, thick fogs that blanketed the place until fall, and a hurricane that scattered the British fleet in October. In that same year the French and Indians surrounded Fort William Henry and forced the surrender of its garrison. As at Oswego, helpless British soldiers, many of them wounded, plus women and children were killed and scalped or taken off as prisoners.

Nor was that the end of it. In Europe the Duke of Cumberland, second son of George II, commanding an army allied with Frederick of Prussia, was surrounded by the French at Hastenbeck in Germany, and after barely escaping capture he was forced to sign a treaty requiring him to deliver the king's Electorate of Hanover to the French and disband his Hessian and Hanoverian troops. Nothing could have been more humiliating, and after months of defeats on land and sea, William Pitt announced to the Duke of Devonshire, who presided in the cabinet, "My Lord, I am sure I can save this country, and nobody else can." And so it proved.

As secretary of state for war, Pitt began planning the campaigns of 1758. One of the young men he handpicked to execute his strategy was forty-one-year-old Colonel Jeffrey Amherst, who had organized a rearguard action that saved the Duke of Cumberland from capture by the French. Appointed as commander in chief of a task force that was to make another attempt to conquer the great stronghold of Louisbourg, Amherst set sail for North America in March of 1758.

Next on Pitt's list was Fort Carillon, guardian of the vital interior water route between Montreal and the Hudson River. Again Pitt wanted a young officer in charge, but the king insisted the command go to a senior man—General James Abercromby, an old-timer known to the colonial troops as "Mr. Namby-cromby." Abercromby was rated a good staff officer, but he was no leader and had never before taken troops into battle. Pitt did succeed in naming the young, enterprising Lord Howe as second in command (it was he who spent months planning the operation) and provided an army of some six thousand carefully selected regular troops plus nearly the same number of provincials.

Early in July, Abercromby's mighty force sailed down Lake George in nine hundred boats and landed at the outlet on the 6th of the month. As the advance party moved through the forest toward the fort it ran into a French detachment, shots rang out, and Lord Howe fell dead. The next day, Abercromby ordered an attack. Greatly outnumbered, Montcalm decided to make a stand on a low ridge about half a mile from the fort, and had his men throw up a six-foot-high wall of logs and sand bags. Inexplicably, Abercromby left most of his heavy artillery aboard the barges that brought them down the lake, and although a few light field pieces were brought up they were of no use against the log breastwork. Safe behind their barricade, Montcalm's troops slaughtered wave after wave of British attackers for more than six hours, and when the sun went down over the bloody field more than sixteen hundred of Abercromby's men were killed or wounded. More than half of the Black Watch regiment fell; that outfit alone lost 122 more men than the battle cost Montcalm's entire army. As night fell, Abercromby's shattered force reembarked and headed up Lake George, leaving behind provisions, baggage, and many of its boats.

As Pitt had warned, France loomed as the great, implacable enemy—the more so now because of its implicit alliance with the other Bourbon power,

William Pitt, Earl of Chatham, studio of R. Brompton. *National Portrait Gallery, London.*

Spain. Numbers told the story in stark terms. Against England's population of 7 million, France had 27 million and Spain 10 million. But William Pitt saw, as did Benjamin Franklin, that the population of the American colonies—already one-third as many as England's and increasing at a rapid pace—constituted a significant force in being and in the making. He recognized, too, that the vigor and success of those colonies greatly enhanced the reputation of England, positioning it as a power of the first rank.

During the years he spent in opposition, Pitt spoke frequently and fervently about the sanctity of the constitution, the independence of Englishmen, and, always, his vision of an empire of free men. Having resolved to extend British rule throughout North America, including Canada, to do so he must have new blood in the armed forces—young, imaginative, bold commanders, of which Amherst was the first to be selected.

Pitt's plans for North America included the taking of Quebec, which would deprive the French of Canada's furs and its timber. The ultimate objective, of course, was to eliminate France from North America and secure the British colonies against attack. He was determined to protect Britain's empire with a navy that was second to none, and every week that passed saw majestic ships of the line and sleek frigates slipping down the Thames—all with sealed orders, since Pitt did not trust his civilian colleagues to be discreet. He wanted his squadrons to appear where and when they were least expected, sailing in silently to destroy enemy vessels in harbors, burn the docks and warehouses, and depart as quickly and mysteriously as they had come, leaving the French to guess where they would strike next. As he suspected, the government at Versailles saw these lightning strikes as preludes to invasion, and France's armies were kept moving from one supposed trouble spot to another throughout the summer of 1758.

On August 17 of that year the brother of Major General Jeffrey Amherst arrived at William Pitt's home in London with the electrifying news that Admiral Edward Boscawen had defeated a French fleet and sealed off the harbor at Louisbourg, enabling Amherst and another of Pitt's young officers, the thirty-two-year-old Brigadier James Wolfe, to land troops at the rear of the city, ring it with cannon, and force the French to surrender. London went wild. A Louisbourg medal was struck, French flags taken at the surrender were paraded before the king and taken to St. Paul's cathedral, cannon at the Tower fired victory salutes, church bells tolled for hours on end, and bonfires were lit in streets near the palace.

The moment of triumph was just that, however. Two days later came word of Abercromby's disastrous defeat at Fort Carillon, with the further message that Mr. Nambycromby had decided to take no further action in America until spring. That, fortunately, was the last bad news Pitt was to receive for three years.

In August, Lieutenant Colonel John Bradstreet, an exceptional young officer, surprised the French at Oswego and Fort Frontenac, cutting New France's lifeline to the west. To the south, Brigadier General John Forbes and his second-in-command, the Swiss lieutenant colonel Henry Bouquet, were executing another of Pitt's plans. Charged with taking back Fort Duquesne at the Forks of the Ohio, Forbes decided not to use the road Braddock had built on his fateful expedition but to march west through Pennsylvania, traveling initially through settled country where food and forage were readily available and building a series of bases along the route. Each of these, stocked with supplies, was capable of reinforcing neighboring forts if help was needed. During the summer of 1758 the army hacked its way into virgin country, through what Forbes called "those hellish woods" and over the seemingly unbroken chain of the Allegheny Mountains, with the general himself so ill he had to be carried in a litter.

Passing the Susquehanna River and Shippensburg, Forbes's troops constructed forts at what became Chambersburg, Bedford, and Ligonier. With winter coming on, they were still forty miles from the Forks, and a council of war voted to proceed no farther until spring, but a prisoner they had taken recently revealed that most of the Indians and many of the French had left

Fort Duquesne and that the remaining garrison was too weak to defend it. At once, Forbes decided to move forward, and his force had reached a point near the site of Braddock's defeat when an explosion was heard in the distance that proved to be the end of the fort. The French, having learned of the fall of Frontenac, the source of their supplies, had blown up the fort at the Forks and departed, leaving behind only a long row of posts, each with the head of a Scot mounted on top with his kilt tied below. These were unfortunate Highlanders who had been captured by Indians in a skirmish near Ligonier, taken to Duquesne, and burned alive.

Writing to Pitt from "Pittsbourgh" about his successful campaign, Forbes explained, "I have used the freedom of giving your name to Fort Du Quesne as I hope it was in some measure . . . being actuated by your spirits that now makes us masters of the place."

With that triumph the tide at last turned in England's favor and New France was on the defensive. The mouth of the St. Lawrence was now vulnerable to attack, and except for Niagara the strong points in the west had been overrun. Pitt's strategy of taking the initiative was paying off, thanks in part to his choice of able young commanders and the men and supplies he gave them. In addition, the English had finally come to their senses and were beginning to adopt new tactics of fighting in the wilderness.

Not until September of 1759 did Pitt, who had been waiting impatiently for news from his fighting forces, learn from dispatches that Amherst had captured Carillon—which was renamed Fort Ticonderoga by the English— and had quickly moved to Fort St. Frédéric, abandoned by the French and renamed Crown Point. There, Amherst awaited news from the impetuous James Wolfe, who had been promoted to major general and assigned the challenging task of taking Quebec.* An Englishman named Samuel Denny, writing to his nephew at Combs, in Suffolk, did his best to describe the situation. "General Wolfe is, with his army, entrenched near the City and have beat it down to a heap of rubbish," he said. But since he was outnumbered two or three to one, Wolfe was "acting rather defensively." His scouts were out, "ravaging the country and . . . burning and destroying the inhabitants. . . ." Amherst, Denny added, was making his way north and had taken Ticonderoga and Crown Point, "but this is a strange country," he explained, and Amherst's men faced great obstacles—among them a French naval force in Lake Champlain, a strongly entrenched land force, and "a bog of 5 miles

*Wolfe's task was made easier because of another move by Pitt: he had sent James Cook to make a survey of the St. Lawrence River—information that was a key to victory.

across that cannot be skirted"—with the result that Amherst could not be expected to join Wolfe this year.

The first word Pitt received from Wolfe, written when he was approaching his destination, was that twenty sail of French ships blocked communication between him and Amherst and he was ill and in despair. Three days after Pitt read that letter came word of a near-unbelievable exploit by Wolfe. Risking everything, he had taken only a fraction of his entire force, landed upriver from the city, and scrambled up a narrow path from the St. Lawrence to the Plains of Abraham, where Quebec stood. Taking Montcalm by surprise, he destroyed his army, but Wolfe was fatally wounded and Montcalm was killed as he left the field of battle. The great citadel of Quebec, the rock of French power in North America, was now in English hands.

In a succession of triumphs, the newly knighted Sir William Johnson seized Niagara; the sugar islands of Martinique and Guadeloupe fell to British squadrons; and in India, Robert Clive won Bengal and defeated the French. Week after week in what Horace Walpole called this *annus mirabilis,* year of wonders, church bells in London and across the nation rang out incessantly, celebrating the victorious British arms. As the *Annual Register* said of Great Britain, "In no year since she was a nation has she been favored with so many successes, both by sea and land, and in every quarter of the globe." William Pitt, whose confidence that victory in war would produce enormous wealth and power, was the hero of England and America alike, for by the following year, with the fall of Montreal, France's power was destroyed in North America, the West Indies, Africa, and India, and the British navy ruled the high seas.

"Victories come so tumbling over one another from distant parts of the globe that it looks like the handiwork of a lady romance-writer," Horace Walpole wrote to a friend. "The park guns will never have time to cool. We ruin ourselves with gunpowder and sky-rockets." And in another letter he crowed that it took the Romans three hundred years to conquer the world, while the British had done it in three campaigns. "Our bells are worn threadbare," he exulted, "with the ringing for victories."

Those victories were attributable to more reasons than Pitt's able young men—above all else, the British navy's success in sweeping the French from the seas, effectively foreclosing France's ability to move troops and supplies from Europe to its North American colony. Of equal significance to the triumph at Quebec was the decisive battle of Quiberon Bay in 1759, when Sir Edward Hawke, in a daring, unconventional attack in a wild storm, virtually demolished France's only effective Atlantic fleet, along with two to three thousand sailors aboard the men-of-war. That triumph opened French merchant shipping to British attack and ensured that Louis XV's outposts in America could not be reinforced. Another factor in France's defeat was the defection of its Indian allies for a complex series of reasons, including a dwindling supply of trade goods and Montcalm's treatment of the native Americans as auxiliaries rather than allies.

In America, with the French defeat, the colonies were now free of any major threat along their borders, and beyond those unmarked boundaries lay untold thousands of empty acres, beckoning the adventurous and the bold to explore and settle. It began to dawn on many provincials that their destiny was now in their own hands if only they were left alone to manage their own affairs.

The latest clash of empires changed the balance of power in the world, ending France's claim to an immense slice of the North American landmass and feeding its determination for revenge against Great Britain. While France was decisively defeated, Britain, having triumphed at last, found herself with an increasingly fractious, unruly collection of disparate colonies whose most apparent bond was a common use of the English tongue. Americans believed that Britain was the freest society in the world and that they, as members of that society, were entitled to the same privileges as any Englishman. That they thought so was largely thanks to William Pitt.

Except for the years of peace under Walpole, England had been at war almost continuously for a century, and as William Pitt perceived, war had been a catalyst for Britain's economy. The thin, hawk-eyed, insightful man understood that trade, not empire, brought wealth, which is why his interest in America lay in its fisheries and forests, its furs and tobacco. He also knew that the expulsion of France from the new world would cost Louis XV timber that could be used to build his warships or vessels that provided a lively, prosperous trade with the sugar islands of the West Indies. Without France to threaten their borders, moreover, Britain's American colonies would be secure. Like Walpole, Pitt had no wish to control the provincials: he saw them as suppliers to England and a market for her goods and would argue in the future that they should be left alone. But the king and his friends were not listening.

In 1759, Robert Edge Pine painted a portrait of the little German king who had ruled England for more than thirty years, showing the blind, toothless monarch standing alone in his dark palace, a haunted expression on his face, his only companions the guards watching over him from a distance. On an October morning the following year the old man died in his water closet, to be buried at his wife's side, after a funeral, one observer said, that "was not well attended by the peers nor even the king's old servants."

Unmourned George II may have been, but the England he left behind was exploding with new projects and products, new jobs and opportunities, new wealth beyond all imagining. The Industrial Revolution was in full bloom, as anyone could see from the smokestacks spewing black smoke into the sky, docks piled high with raw materials and produce from across the sea—timber, tobacco, furs, sugar, molasses—to be made into finished goods for home consumption and export, and its fruits included a network of new roads and canals, and a growing number of beautifully proportioned, elegant mansions of the rich. England was truly on top of the world, brimming with newfound confidence, pride, and a sense of well-being.

This was the Age of the Georges—renowned for the beauty and proportions of its architecture, its landscape design, art, furniture, and fashions. It was also an era of unparalleled extravagance, but at the opposite end of the scale were appallingly crowded, filthy London slums, where smallpox, tuberculosis, and other diseases flourished, carrying off untold thousands of infants as well as adults. Angry mobs suddenly appeared on the streets, looting and burning, and had to be put down by force. Blood sports—cockfighting and bullbaiting—were the rage; gambling was an obsession of rich and poor alike; and among the city's most popular sights were the hangings at Tyburn, where young boys and girls were as likely to be seen dangling from the gallows as highwaymen and murderers.

Notwithstanding the dark side of life in his kingdom, seldom had a new monarch succeeded to the throne in such a climate of success, where everything pointed to further triumphs, to decades of growing prosperity and dominance of the world's affairs. But much would depend on the character of the young man who took the title of George III, for as yet no one could do more than guess what he might have in mind to do with the extraordinary good fortune that had fallen into his hands.

The first sign that change was in the offing came when William Pitt hastened, as was customary, to notify the Prince of Wales that George II was dead and he was now king. Before Pitt's coach and six, with his footmen in brilliant blue-and-silver livery, arrived at Kew, where the heir apparent resided, they met the new monarch's coach proceeding to London. He had already learned of his grandfather's death and in an affront to Pitt, waved him aside and headed for his destination. Pitt, of course, was *de facto* first minister; the Duke of Newcastle, who was in his cabinet at the insistence of George II, was nominally the ranking officer and it was to him, not Pitt, that George III granted his first private audience. At the end of their conversation, the king announced, "My Lord Bute is your good friend. He will tell you my thoughts."

Those words meant that Newcastle, an experienced man who had held high office for more than four decades and was a staunch friend of the colonies, and Pitt, who had been largely responsible for placing half the world's trade and a global empire in the hands of the new king, were to be cast aside, with consequences beyond all reckoning.

4

Join or Die

The summer of 1760 was oppressively hot and muggy, with violent rainstorms and flooding from the East Coast into the Ohio country and beyond. High winds brought rain for more than a month to Presque Isle on the shore of Lake Erie, and out on the lake after "a great squawl, Waves run Mountains high," according to George Croghan, Indian trader and agent. During the siege of Montreal by British regulars, American provincials, and Iroquois warriors, eight men drowned and eighteen boats were staved by raging currents and rapids on the St. Lawrence. At Fort Pitt at the Forks of the Ohio, torrential rains and high water in the rivers prevented Colonel Henry Bouquet from sending supplies by bateau to British outposts at Venango, LeBoeuf, and Niagara. Down in the Carolinas the Indians were unusually quiet. The corn they depended on for the winter was high but not yet ripe, and they were waiting anxiously, hoping it would survive the storms.

New Yorkers could consider themselves lucky. It had been uncomfortably warm on the island but the prevailing westerlies and breezes off the ocean kept the city livable, with no perceptible effect on its busy trade or social activities. On Tuesday, July 29, New York's acting governor, James DeLancey, went over to Staten Island and spent the day socializing with Governors Thomas Boone of New Jersey and Francis Bernard of Massachusetts, along with several local cronies. Despite the heat, by all accounts it was a lively affair, during which DeLancey was the butt of a good many jibes about his reputed skill at diverting public funds for his own use and his easy and

James DeLancey, by Henry Benbridge.
Private collection.

enduring popularity with New York constituents. Evidently DeLancey imbibed rather heavily and was "vexed and silent" by the time his boat headed homeward across the bay to Manhattan. There he stopped in to chat with his brother-in-law, the merchant John Watts, drank some wine, then mounted his horse and rode to his home, a mile from the heart of town.

The next morning one of his little children entered his study and found him gasping for breath, and before a physician could be fetched, he was dead of what was thought to be an asthma attack. DeLancey was only fifty-seven years old, but his career in the rough-and-tumble cockpit of New York politics had been remarkably long and successful. Richard Peters, an Anglican clergyman who was also Pennsylvania's provincial secretary, regarded his death as "a most sad stroke. Neither his Country nor his Friends can expect this loss will ever be replaced." And how to replace him was exactly what worried his friends, for DeLancey had been the most powerful man in the province of New York.

Nothing revealed the importance ascribed to him so much as the funeral held on the day after his death. At 6:45 in the evening a single gun was fired from HMS *Winchester,* lying in the Hudson River, signaling that the funeral procession was to depart the DeLancey home in Bowery Lane, and at the same moment cannon began firing from the Battery—fifty-seven shots, representing his age. These were followed by the big guns aboard the *Winchester* and those of the *General Wall* packet, slowly banging out fifty-seven times as the procession wound its stately way to Trinity Church.

James DeLancey was debonair and witty, and had been blessed with luck and money. His father, Etienne, was a Huguenot refugee who made a fortune as a merchant, became a convert to Anglicanism, and sent his son to be educated at Cambridge. The young man was canny enough to recognize that political success in America depended on an ability to accommodate the king's ministers in London while getting along with what he called the "touchy people" in America, and in England he made connections that were to prove immensely useful throughout his life. His former Cambridge tutor became archbishop of Canterbury. DeLancey married an heiress whose uncle was an influential politician in London, and whose cousin was a lieutenant of George II's longtime first minister, Robert Walpole. In fact, through his wife and his siblings, DeLancey was related to many of the eminent men in the province. One of his sisters had the good sense to wed Peter Warren, a wealthy British naval officer who was promoted to admiral after helping to capture the great French fortress at Louisbourg in 1745 and who, as a member of Parliament, pulled the strings that made DeLancey lieutenant governor. When Warren's secretary became New York's agent, he saw to it that DeLancey was regularly informed of which way the political winds blew in London. All in all, the connections could hardly have been better.

At the age of twenty-six, DeLancey was appointed to the governor's Council and two years later to the province's Supreme Court, with tenure for life. Four years after that he was named chief justice, and he so impressed Governor George Clinton that the latter named four of DeLancey's partisans to his Council. (A fellow councillor, Cadwallader Colden, was definitely *not* impressed and complained bitterly that "A Chief Justice known to be of an implacable temper is a terrible thing in this Country" and that DeLancey "makes use of the Power of his office to intimidate" his opponents.)

By 1753, when he became lieutenant governor, DeLancey effectively controlled all three branches of the colony's government—executive, legislative, and judicial—and held the province in his hands. Having put together the equivalent of a modern political machine, which was known as the court party for its strong ties to the royal government, he was unmistakably the boss of New York, but he owed his position of power to something more than luck, money, and connections, and the young lawyer William Smith, Jr., put his finger on it when he described how a demagogue who controlled the Assembly could also control the governor and his Council: "With Power to starve the Governor he had the whole Province at Command—This James DeLancey knew, & this Sway he held." Smith was a stern critic of DeLancey's cronyism and "his revels with low company," and undoubtedly resented his amazing popularity, but as much as he disliked him, Smith had to admit that the man's "accomplishments rendered him an ornament to the country which gave him birth."

The mechanism by which the province was governed was modeled upon that in Britain but was hardly conducive to harmony. Since New York City was the capital of the province, the governor and the lieutenant governor, both appointed by the crown, held office here, making the city the hub and hot seat of provincial politics. The governor's Council, consisting of seven to twelve members appointed by the governor, was patterned after the king's Privy Council and was often thought of as the upper chamber of the legislature, with the popularly elected Assembly of twenty-seven members as the lower house. Theoretically the governor held the power in the colony, but in fact, as William Smith, Jr., observed, the Assembly held the whip hand because it paid (or, on occasion, refused to pay) his salary. Since most governors came to America hoping to go home wealthy, a prudent executive was well advised to keep on good terms with the Assembly lest it refuse to compensate him. Powers the governor *did* have included the right to veto laws passed by the Assembly, convoke or dissolve that body, appoint a wide range of local municipal functionaries and militia officers, and—the juiciest patronage plums—grant titles to lands and award military supply contracts.

The Assembly also appropriated funds annually for running the province, specifying where and how they were to be spent, but the ministry in London had a check rein on this procedure, since all bills passed by the legislature were subject to review and possible rejection. The colony's only recourses in that event were to put pressure on British merchants, or send memorials to Parliament or the king, or instruct its London agent to lobby members of the House of Lords or Commons. These methods of appeal seldom produced effectual results, and the arbitrariness of the home government was a constant source of frustration.

The position of acting governor fell into James DeLancey's lap entirely by chance. In 1753, Sir Danvers Osborn, brother-in-law of the Earl of Halifax, had been appointed governor of New York to succeed Governor Clinton, who was recalled on grounds that New York's affairs were in such a mess that new blood was essential. Osborn arrived in New York on Sunday, October 7, and after taking the oath of office on Wednesday received an unwelcome admonition from the Corporation of the City of New York urging him not to

permit "any infringements of our inestimable liberties, civil and religious"—
an unmistakable reference to the unpopular policies of his predecessor. To
celebrate his arrival, "The city was illuminated, cannon were discharged, and
two bonfires lighted up on the common," but Sir Danvers took no part in the
festivities and retired to his lodgings "while the whole town seemed abandoned to every excess of riot."

Early next morning he strolled around town, visiting the markets, and
subsequently told DeLancey, to whom he had presented a commission as
lieutenant governor, that he felt poorly. Later, when he convened the governor's Council, he informed members of his intention to insist upon "the permanent indefinite support of government," but to his obvious dismay,
councillors said they did not believe the Assembly would agree to support the
administration in London on all matters. The New York Assembly, they told
him, was getting out of hand. Hearing this, he leaned against the window
frame, sighed, and exclaimed, "Then what am I come here for?" At dinner he
smiled at DeLancey and said mysteriously, "I believe I shall soon leave you the
government. I find myself unable to support the burden of it."

The following morning he was found dead, hanging by the neck from a
spike on top of the garden wall to which he had tied a silk handkerchief knot-
ted at both ends. On a table in his rooms someone found a paper on which he
had written, *"quem deus vult perdere prius dementat"* ("whom God wishes to
destroy he first makes mad"). Taking him at his word, a coroner's inquest
declared him a lunatic, and subsequently the poor fellow's secretary explained
his suicide by informing the authorities that Sir Danvers had been despondent ever since the death of his wife and had been given his post in New York
in hopes of distracting him from his depression.

The result of this unhappy episode was that James DeLancey was declared
acting governor. Shortly afterward he was handed a letter from the Board of
Trade, addressed to Sir Danvers Osborn, and opening it, realized that he, as
Osborn's successor, was obliged to summon representatives of the other
colonies to a meeting. The delegates were ordered to negotiate a treaty with
the Indians, improve the handling of Indian affairs, restore the friendship and
crucial alliance of the Six Nations, and henceforth see to it that if the natives
decided to sell any land it was to be purchased from them in the king's name
and with public funds—this, of course, to foil the speculators. That was the
genesis of what was known as the Albany Congress.

DeLancey was not keen on this idea of a conference, possibly because he
saw no way to control the representatives from other provinces, but he had

his orders and dutifully sent out invitations. By some stroke of luck, the men appointed by the various colonies were an exceptionally able lot, and as it turned out they had more on their minds than yet one more powwow with the Indians. A number of them, in fact, had come prepared to discuss some means of uniting the colonies, on the theory that this was the best way to achieve solutions to their common problems. Benjamin Franklin of Philadelphia had brought to the meeting what he called "Short Hints towards a Scheme for Uniting the Northern Colonies"—a revised version of a pamphlet he had written anonymously in 1750—and when the meetings with the Indians had concluded with the usual pious words and promises and wagonloads of gifts, the discussion turned at once to the question of unity.

Recently, in his *Pennsylvania Gazette* of May 9, 1754, Franklin had raised the issue of mutual defense through united action, coupling it with what was probably the first American cartoon—a woodcut of a snake cut in eight pieces, seven bearing the initials of a province (South Carolina, North Carolina, Virginia, Maryland, Pennsylvania, New Jersey, and New York), with the head labeled N.E. for New England. Below the snake was a dire warning in large block letters, "JOIN, OR DIE."

Franklin was asked to prepare a draft of a Plan of Union, and it was adopted and ordered transmitted to the seven colonies represented at the congress, plus New Jersey, Virginia, and the Carolinas, which had not sent delegates. It was essential, Franklin insisted, that the proposed government be established by act of Parliament, not by Americans. (Franklin was a realist and saw no hope of achieving union through some sort of voluntary association.) In accordance with his scheme, the government was to have an executive and a legislative branch. The executive, to be appointed and paid by the crown, and known as the president-general, was to have the power to make treaties with the Indians and declare war and peace, with the advice and consent of the legislative body. The legislature, known as the grand council, would consist of members chosen every three years by the assemblies of the colonies in numbers proportional to the taxes they paid into the union treasury. And placing power in the hands of provincial assemblies rather than the more aristocratic and conservative governor's councils was a decidedly democratic innovation.

All in all, it was a bold, novel proposal that would create a central government with the power to levy taxes and make laws concerning matters within its jurisdiction, even though these had to be submitted to the king in Council for approval. (If not disallowed within three years they would remain in force.) The new government would also deal with the many problems of defense— raising and supporting armies, building forts and ships, and regulating the

Indians. Significantly, the delegates resolved to limit the power of the colonies over western lands, stipulating that all land purchases from the Indians be made in the name of the crown and that the boundaries of some colonies be "reduced to more convenient dimensions."

The delegates' enthusiasm and support for the Plan of Union reveal a great deal about the mind-set of this representative group. Franklin and the others were American colonials, but they thought of themselves as Englishmen. That attitude was at the heart of the "Short Hints" Franklin took to Albany in 1754, which he and his colleagues refined until they had a highly original conception of the American colonies' place within the British Empire. They understood that the separate colonies must think of themselves not individually, but as a whole—a whole that was an integral part of the empire, and whose only separation from the mother country happened to be the ocean between them.

Although no one at the congress could have known of it, on the same day that James DeLancey delivered his welcoming speech to the Indians, fate took a hand in events some 350 miles to the southwest, when George Washington and about 150 Virginians were overwhelmingly defeated by a French and Indian force at Fort Necessity. That event prompted James Alexander, a New York councillor, to write Cadwallader Colden, saying he hoped the recommendations of the Albany Congress would "prevail on King & Parliament . . . to unite the force of the Colonies, and [do so] at the first meeting of parliament, for a Delay of it may be fatal, as there's nothing to hinder the french at this very time to make a Conquest of the Colonies, and put it then out of our power to hurt them by our intended union."

Despite the dramatic demonstration at Fort Necessity of the colonies' urgent need to unite, the warning was not heeded, and the Plan of Union was opposed or ignored by every provincial assembly that considered it, except New York's. In fact, the efforts of the commissioners—prominent as they were—were received with outright scorn by the very provincial governments that had deputized them. However surprising that seemed, it was extremely significant, for what it came down to was that as early as 1754 no colonial legislature was willing to yield any of its powers to a grand council and an executive appointed and paid by the crown.

Delegates to the congress had assumed that the provincial assemblies would comment on the Plan of Union, after which it would be sent to London. But DeLancey ignored their wishes and sent a copy of the proceedings to the Lords of Trade, who passed it on to George II without comment. When nothing favorable was heard from the colonies, no action was taken in England and the ambitious project died.

The Albany Plan of Union, which was Franklin's more than any other man's, may have been rejected, but it was far from forgotten. It became the basis of the form of governance that initially took effect with the First Continental Congress in 1774. The Articles of Confederation embodied a number of ideas included in the Plan of Union, notably federal control of western lands, which was established by the Northwest Territory Ordinance of 1787.

The ultimate recognition of Franklin's vision came in 1787 when the Constitutional Convention adopted the essence of the Plan of Union—substituting only a president for the president-general and adding a second house to the legislature. Congress was granted the same powers by the Constitution as those given the grand council, except the power to purchase Indian lands and make new colonies of them.

To no one had James DeLancey's success story been more galling than members of the Livingston family and Cadwallader Colden. Then, as later, politics in New York were turbulent and highly vocal, and two factions, or parties, dominated the scene—the DeLanceys and the Livingstons, representing, respectively, the urban merchant class and the landed Hudson River patroons. The bitter, long-seated enmity between them was economic, political, and social, further exacerbated by religious differences. As Peter R. Livingston wrote in 1769 to a friend, the two parties to the dispute were the Anglican Church (DeLanceys) and the Dissenters (Presbyterian Livingstons), which are "hott & pepper on both Sides." Speaking of the relationship, he said, "I have two uncles & two friends on our Side that Sitts up against a party that has from the beginning of this Province opposed our famaly."

Tax policy was one of the many issues on which they disagreed: the DeLanceys advocated raising revenues by taxing land; the Livingstons, as huge landowners, believed trade should be taxed. The Livingstons were fearful of their own safety and wanted military protection for their northern lands, to which the DeLanceys objected on grounds that trade with Canada might be adversely affected and an army would cost money that would strain the province's financial resources. And so it went, with no compromise in sight.

If the American colonies had had a peerage, the Livingstons would certainly have ranked near the top. With Livingston Manor, their huge estate in Albany County, and more property in Dutchess and Ulster counties, the family landholdings were truly ducal in scale. The first of the line in America was Robert (1634–1728), son of a Presbyterian minister who was exiled from Scotland after the Restoration and settled in Holland. Robert proved to be a precocious businessman in Rotterdam: by the age of sixteen he had built his own shipping business and decided to emigrate to America, where he made his way to Albany in 1674. There his acuity as a merchant was enhanced by his command of the Dutch language, and one of the most prominent and politically powerful Anglo-Dutch families was launched when the ambitious Scot married the widowed Alida Schuyler Van Rensselaer, daughter of Peter Schuyler.

According to Livingston family legend, when Alida's first husband, Nicholas Van Rensselaer, was dying he called for a clerk to record his will. A few minutes passed and Robert Livingston, pen in hand, entered the chamber and approached his then employer's deathbed. "No, no, send him away!" the old man cried. "He's going to marry my widow!" And with that he died. True story or not, the two were married less than eight months later, and since her former husband died intestate, Alida inherited everything.

Robert began purchasing wild acreage from the Indians; then friendship with Governor Dongan of New York, plus his connections in the valley, brought him an immense land grant that made him the lord of 160,000 acres—some 250 square miles—that became known as Livingston Manor. Following the first Robert's death, his son Philip (1686–1749) succeeded as proprietor of the major portion of the manor. The lower section, however, called Clermont, went to a second Robert, and his son Robert R. (1718–1775), known subsequently as the Judge, married Margaret Beekman, who came into his life with a dowry of 240,000 acres. One of their sons, yet another Robert R. (1746–1813), later became known as the Chancellor.

Through marriage and purchase (Robert of Clermont bought half a million acres in the Catskill Mountains), the acreage the Livingstons owned swelled to almost a million. Livingston daughters married into the best Hudson River families; the sons acquired yet more land, here and in the West Indies, and were active in the rum and sugar trade.

If land came first with this family, it sometimes seemed that opposition to the DeLanceys and Anglicans came next. Of the baker's dozen of denominations in New York, Anglicans were the most powerful, though not the most numerous—an eminence based almost entirely on the social prominence and wealth of the parishioners, plus the fact their denomination was the established Church of England. Pointing proudly to his own church's position in the province, the archconservative Thomas Jones observed haughtily that it was "of the most influence, and greatest opulence. To this Church, the Governor, the Lieutenant Governor, most of his Majesty's Council, many members of the General Assembly, all the officers of Government, with a numerous train of rich and affluent merchants and landowners belonged."

In second place, Jones ranked the Dutch Reformed; in third, the Presbyterians, whom Jones described condescendingly as "people of the middle rank" though admitting that some were "rich, wealthy, sensible men."

One of the chief sources of friction between Anglicans and Presbyterians was King's College.* Even before the institution opened its doors in 1754 it was a bone of contention. Since the president and most of the trustees were Church of England members, Trinity Church offered to donate a thirty-two-acre parcel of land granted to it in 1705 and now worth some £7,000 or £8,000. It was a superb site, and the college was eventually built on an eminence about 150 yards from the Hudson River, which it overlooked. From here one had a breathtaking, completely unobstructed view of the shore of New Jersey, Manhattan Island and the city of New York, Long Island, Staten Island, the bay with its islands, and the Narrows. As one of the college's presidents observed, it "has the benefit of as agreeable and healthy a situation as can possibly be achieved."

There was a catch to Trinity's gift, however. It was made on condition that all future presidents of the college be Anglican churchmen and that morning and evening prayer services be conducted according to the Book of Common Prayer. Lutheran, French, and Dutch Reformed churches went along with these conditions, but not the Presbyterians—in particular, three young lawyers castigated by the Reverend Samuel Johnson, then president of the college, as "the wicked triumvirate," William Livingston, John Morin Scott, and William Smith, Jr.

All three of these young men were born in New York and spent most of their early lives there. All attended Yale, had the same church affiliation, studied law with William Smith, Sr., one of the outstanding figures in the New York bar, and were related by marriage (Smith and Scott married Livingstons). All, it might be added, opposed James DeLancey and his faction and the man who succeeded him as lieutenant governor—Cadwallader Colden. Thomas Jones noted caustically that the young gentlemen were "educated at Yale College, at New Haven in Connecticut; then, and still, a nursery of sedition, of faction, and republicanism," and although he was himself a Yale alumnus, he added that the place was "a college remarkable for its persecuting spirit, its republican principles, its intolerance in religion and its utter aversion to Bishops and all Earthly Kings." Those comments were all of a piece with New York's distaste for what it perceived as the radicalism of New

*Later Columbia University.

England in general—an aversion that was reciprocated, since New York's lack of religious conformity was a red flag to New Englanders. The Yankees regarded their neighbors as backsliders and, in the years to come, foes of the common cause.

William Livingston was tall and ungainly, uncomfortable as a speaker in public, a rather homely man who enjoyed neither political meetings nor the social gatherings where he was often rebuffed by young women "who are tickled with an handsome appearance." He opened his law office in 1748 and was joined two years later by William Smith, Jr., son of the man with whom both had studied law. Smith was serious, a devout, some said puritanical, Presbyterian who abhorred drinking and cards. He was urbane, earnest, and charming, a quiet-spoken man who was a valued adviser to several governors. John Morin Scott, youngest of the partners, joined the firm two years after Smith and was quite different from the other two. He was a lively, outgoing fellow, an enjoyable conversationalist, easy and relaxed with people, and admired for his humor and frankness by friends and opponents alike. Scott was the partner who most relished political assemblies in the taverns and "out of doors."

Undaunted by the opposition of Jones or his fellow Anglicans, "the triumvirate" lashed out in the press and in a remarkable publication of their own, *The Independent Reflector,* questioning whether a school dominated by a religious minority was entitled to a charter that conformed to the terms of Trinity's gift and received public money. Surely, they argued, if such funds were to be used, they must go only to a nondenominational college. In the end, to the dismay of both parties, a compromise solution gave control of the college to the Anglicans, but only half the money (which was to be raised by a lottery)—the other half going to the building of a jail and a pesthouse.

The Independent Reflector was the brainchild of William Livingston, youngest of the six sons of Philip Livingston, lord of the Manor. He began thinking about a single-essay journal in 1749 and soon enlisted Smith and Scott in the project. While continuing to practice law, the collaborators planned and began work on what was to become the *Reflector,* and this, with other interests they held in common, engaged them for the next two decades. It was an extraordinary record of achievement. Newspapers were filled with their letters—some signed with their own names, more often with a pseudonym. They founded the city's first library, the New York Society Library; organized a reform group called the Moot where legal problems were discussed; wrote—at the request of the Assembly—protests against taxes levied by the government in London; initiated a Society for the Promotion of Useful Knowledge; and led the fight against the Church of England establishment.

While the *Reflector* was in the genre of Addison and Steele's *Tatler* and *Spectator,* it proved to be much more like a series of essays written by two other Englishmen, Thomas Gordon and John Trenchard, and published as *The Independent Whig* and *Cato's Letters.* Beginning in 1720, these publications attacked Tory politicians, standing armies, popery, high churchmen, and other perceived evils and came out for free speech, limited sovereignty, and the right of resistance. Shamelessly pirated by colonial newspaper editors, they fell on fertile ground and were wildly popular and highly influential. William Livingston was one of numerous dissenters who responded enthusiastically to the anticlericalism of *The Independent Whig.*

"Orthodoxy," Livingston wrote, "has caused the Effusion of more Blood than all the Roman Emperors put together." Dismayed by the "Popes and Persecutors of all Churches, whether . . . of Rome, England, Holland, or Geneva," and wary of every "little Flutterer in a Gown and Cassock," he rebelled against ecclesiastical "trumpery" and "tyranny" and switched from the Dutch Reformed to the Presbyterian church around 1752. That put him right in the middle of the fight against Anglican control of the college. New York's Anglican Trinity Church had a royal charter and received money from taxpayers, while the Presbyterian Church had neither—a situation Livingston and his friend William Smith, Jr., set out to change. They were equally outraged by the missionary work of the Society for the Propagation of the Gospel in Foreign Parts (SPG), an arm of the Anglican Church, and this opposition soon took the form of six issues of the *Reflector,* a crusade that turned the college issue into a far broader argument on politics and religion.

"The affair of the College," Livingston said, was "one of the most important matters that ever fell under the consideration of our Legislature" because it could determine "either the deprivation or the abridgment of our civil and religious liberties."

The first issue of *The Independent Reflector* came off the press in 1752 on William Livingston's twenty-ninth birthday, and after a slow start rapidly picked up subscribers and readers and gained an influence far beyond its relatively modest circulation. (Reading material was in short supply in colonial times and it is quite probable that each copy of a paper like the *Reflector* was read carefully by at least ten people.) When the triumvirate first began planning their publication they said it was "for correcting the taste and improving the Minds of our fellow Citizens" and their plan of action was to expose, attack, and reform. At the outset they planned to write an essay a month— not an easy task for busy lawyers—until they had a stockpile of 150 or more, after which time they would publish one or two a week. While religion was very much on their minds, they soon were writing about "the fashionable vices and foibles of the day" and other subjects of particular interest to New Yorkers—freedom of the press, taxation, firefighting, the evils of "Election Jobbers" and quack doctors, the regulation of beef and pork, and of course a whole series on the college.

During the magazine's brief lifespan of a single year, fifty-two issues saw the light of day and reached an audience far beyond New York. John Adams and Benjamin Franklin were among its readers, as were many Bostonians; college students quoted the journal in their recitations; and the *Reflector's* views on the rights of man became the common property of colonials everywhere. The people of America, Livingston argued, are subjects of the same king as the people of England and are "therefore entitled to equal Privileges with them." Governments are based on the "free consent of Mankind," and power is exercised in pursuit of the welfare of the community. If a king violates his oath to the people, "those who have cloathed him with Authority have a Right to strip him of it, whenever he abuses it."

These were views that appealed to many landholding aristocrats as well as men who became Sons of Liberty a decade later, but they were ideas that would eventually force colonists to choose between such principles and what amounted to treason. Unfortunately, *The Independent Reflector* was put to death by James DeLancey, to whom many of its ideas were abhorrent; he managed this quite simply, by putting pressure on the paper's printer and threatening to take the colony's printing work from him.

5

George—Be a King

A troubling ingredient in the bubbling cauldron of New York politics was the man who succeeded DeLancey as acting governor, Cadwallader Colden. Seventy-two years old in 1760, Colden had been a New York official for forty years and quite beyond that was an eminent figure in many fields, yet his personality was fatally flawed. In the scientific and other worlds he traversed, which included astronomy, chemistry, physics, mathematics, botany, medicine, natural history, and history, he was willing, even eager, to see and accept an opposing point of view and seemed to have an open mind for ideas of all sorts. In education, for instance, he advocated a real liberal arts program and higher education for women. As a physician, he was interested in epidemiology and the treatment of cancer. He was a surveyor and an authority on the fur trade as well as the Iroquois Confederation. He had, in fact, lived with the Mohawks and participated in conferences between Indians and whites before writing his *History of the Five Indian Nations Depending on the Province of New York in America*. And he had sought to alter the prevailing image of the Indian as murderous savage by explaining the social and political organization of the Iroquois, which he likened to an "Original Form of all Government."

In politics, however, Colden was utterly rigid and unbending, intolerant, tactless, a hopeless stickler for the letter of the law, forever on the lookout for a slight.

It is difficult to imagine any American more loyal to His Majesty George III than Cadwallader Colden, and his was a passionate fealty that had been given as well to the young monarch's grandfather and great-grandfather. His perception was that the king could do no wrong, therefore he did not. Minions of the crown might transgress—and did, all too frequently—yet Colden continued to believe that the man on the throne would set matters to rights and all would be well.

As surveyor general he had acquired a strong dislike for the great land-owners, Dutch and English alike, whose immense holdings hindered the orderly settlement of New York's frontier by smallholders (and whose failure to pay quitrents not so incidentally deprived Colden of a salary from that source). He quarreled with members of the Assembly and the governor's Council, conducted a vendetta with lawyers (especially William Smith, Jr., who despised him), warning that they and the landowners were "dangerous to good government" and a threat to the crown. To ensure the independence of royal officials he maintained that their salaries should be paid from quitrents (the rent paid by freemen in lieu of the services required by feudal custom). In so many of these and other matters he was right, of course, but it was his sanctimonious insistence that he *was* right that drove people crazy and made them dislike him intensely.

For several years he had served Governor Clinton as an indispensable aide, but finally he grew disgusted with politics and fled to his country manor, Coldengham—a house and farm several miles west of Newburgh—never ceasing to believe that he, not James DeLancey, should have been named to succeed Clinton as acting governor. And certainly he felt that justice was finally served when he, as senior councillor, was called to succeed DeLancey upon the death of that implacable enemy.

Although he knew it was only a question of time before a royal appointee came to New York as governor, he craved official recognition as lieutenant governor in fact—not as a temporary replacement. For all his tirades and complaints against political hacks who managed to get the plums he badly wanted for himself and his own family members, Colden was himself a place-man. Much as he might argue that he was the person best informed, most loyal, most determined to give the home government the truth about New York while managing the colony's affairs honestly and sensibly, Colden was a political appointee and thereby a placeman no less than those whose ethics and greed were so repugnant to him. As John Watts put it, "ministerial approbation is the balsam of his soul—next to pelf."

Colden knew he had a logical mind—a superior mind, at that—and above all, he knew he was right. But he had to put up with the "haughty & insolent Spirit of some men," the "slanderers," men with "an excessive vanity in their opinion of themselves," men who refused to admit the correctness of his views. Once in a position of authority, beginning in the early days of August 1760, Colden began to pursue a narrow-minded course of unquestioning loyalty and absolute obedience to the directives from London, never considering that leadership and persuasion—not coercion—might be the way to influence New Yorkers to accept the policies of George III's ministers.

It is quite possible that Colden, had he been of different temperament, might have influenced those ministers, too. He was certainly well enough informed about New York to have provided facts and the kind of inside information they needed. And indeed, he had tried—off and on for many years. The trouble was that the king's ministers had neither much interest in New York nor understanding of its very real problems, so whatever Colden told them—in numbing, repetitive detail—fell upon deaf ears. Colden had become his own worst enemy, for having heard from friends that British officialdom seldom if ever referred back to letters that had been received in the past, he made his points again and again and succeeded only in boring them to death.

All but ignored in London, scorned and disliked in New York, this was the man in charge of affairs at the time Britain determined to remake its suddenly expanded empire. Among the changes being discussed was a standing army to provide security for its American possessions and—as a means of recouping part, if not all, of the cost—taxing the colonists. If any one person may be said to have pushed New York toward rebellion against the government's new policies, it was surely His Majesty's loyal and faithful servant Cadwallader Colden.

Sixty-seven days after the death of King George II, the news reached New York, and Cadwallader Colden, acting as governor, found himself with an exasperating bureaucratic dilemma. On January 5, 1761, he wrote to John Pownall, secretary to the Board of Trade, who had notified him of the "melancholy event" while informing Colden that he would soon receive "the necessary forms for proclaiming his Present Majesty, together with Warrants for using the old Seals, Proclamation for continuing of officers & orders for the alteration of the Liturgy &c &c. . . ." Colden had communicated this immediately to the governor's Council, whose members determined that following Pownall's instructions "may put the publick affairs under difficulties."

The problem was this: upon George II's death the New York Assembly was automatically dissolved. A new Assembly could be summoned only by use of the Great Seal. But if Colden employed the seal for this purpose without waiting for arrival of the warrants that gave him permission to do so, the legality of the legislative meeting might be disputed. And that, Colden justifiably feared, "may be a great impediment to his Majesties necessary service."

In the meantime, Colden was not about to neglect his official obligations. Although "the Winter has sat violently in," he saw to it that the people and all the churches of New York were in proper mourning on Sunday, January 18. That was the day after the Council proclaimed (after the necessary warrants arrived) "with one full Voice and consent of Tongue and Heart . . . that the High and Mighty Prince George Prince of Wales is now by the Death of Our late Sovereign of happy and glorious Memory, become Our only Lawfull and Rightfull Liege Lord George the Third, by the Grace of God King of Great Britain, France and Ireland, Defender of the Faith, Supreme Lord of the said province of New York and Territory depending thereon, and all other His late Majesty's Territories and Dominions in America. . . ."

Behind his outward mask of certitude, what was gnawing at Colden was that ominous reference in Pownall's letter to the "continuing of officers." DeLancey's unexpected death had thrust him into the position of lieutenant governor, and he now had hopes of occupying the coveted post permanently, if only the new king's administration would do right by him. So a great deal depended on the young monarch and who his advisers would be.

The colonies' prevailing mood regarding their new monarch was one of hope, blended with caution, and was reflected in a bit of doggerel published in the *Boston Gazette* in January 1760:

> From all who dare to tyrannize
>   May Heaven still defend us,
> And should another James arise
>   Another WILLIAM send us—
> May Kings like GEORGE for ever reign
>   With highest Worth distinguish'd
> But Stuarts who our Annals stain
>   May they be quite extinguish'd.

But who was he, this new king? What manner of man? As eager as Colden and all other Americans were to have the answers, they were not easy to come by.

They knew he was just past twenty-two years of age and rejoiced that he was the first of the Hanoverian line to be born in Britain, but even in a day when childhood was short and maturity came early he was evidently not much more than a boy—and a mother's boy, at that—emotionally and intellectually. He was thirteen and devastated when his beloved father died, suddenly making him heir to the throne. Then began a struggle between his grandfather, George II, the king's ministers, Pelham and Newcastle, and the boy's mother, Augusta, each of whom wanted to control his education. The king overruled the others and ordered him sent to his palace at Hampton Court where he himself could supervise his upbringing. Separated from his mother until he was sixteen, George was withdrawn and desperately lonely. His tutors—second-raters, all of them—complained that he was a difficult child, unable to concentrate on his lessons, unable to read until he was eleven.

Physically he was tall—five feet ten and a half inches—with prominent, almost bulging blue eyes, a long nose, small chin, and full lips. Painfully uncomfortable in the company of relative strangers, he had an awkward, nervous, self-conscious habit of speaking very rapidly, repeating "What? What? What?" to astonished listeners. Raised inside a royal cocoon, he had no conception of what the world at large was like, yet he had very definite ideas concerning kingship, which he once expressed in a boyhood essay, writing that a prince should be "feared and respected abroad, adored at home, by mixing private economy with public magnificence." This may have explained his insistent refusal to relax court etiquette and his inability to unbend in front of others, of whom he was often extremely inconsiderate. On more than one occasion he kept Pitt—who suffered terribly from gout—standing for long periods of time.

Unhappy, all but friendless at the time he returned to his mother's household, within two years he had become infatuated with her friend and adviser John Stuart, third Earl of Bute, whom she had appointed as George's tutor. A Scottish peer (and therefore regarded as socially and politically inferior by titled Englishmen), Bute was forty-seven years old, girlishly handsome, an amiable but pompous man known for his skill as a dancer and amateur actor and his good legs—which counted for much in a day when men wore breeches and tight stockings to the knee—though he had few accomplishments beyond sociability. He had been neglected and ignored by the court of George II, and young George saw him as a fellow sufferer, an outsider on the fringes of society, and equated the indifference to Bute with his own lonely situation. He made him his Groom of the Stole, and therefore part of his innermost circle, and began addressing him as "My Dearest Friend."

The Earl of Shelburne called Bute cowardly and insolent; Lord Chesterfield said he was "too cunning to have great abilities"; George's father once described him as "a fine showy man who would make an excellent ambassador

George III.
Colonial Williamsburg.

in a court where there was no business"; and after Frederick's death, gossips whispered that he was the lover of George's mother. Savage cartoons appeared in the press showing him displaying his long legs to a rapturous Princess Dowager; jeering crowds held up petticoats and a boot to represent Augusta and Bute. But whatever the world may have thought of him, the Scot was assured by the man who was about to become king that "I will exactly follow your advice, without which I shall inevitabl[y] sink." And again, in another letter: "I will defend my Friend and . . . show the world the great friendship I have for him, and all the malice that can be invented against him shall only bind me the stronger to him."

"George—*be a king!*" Augusta told her son repeatedly, and many who saw him in the early days of his reign were persuaded that he was heeding her command. Horace Walpole described him as "tall and full of dignity . . . good-natured . . . graceful and obliging." The secretary at war spoke highly of his "great civility" and said it was a pleasure to do business with him. Soon other, less winning, traits became apparent. Observers noted that he was headstrong and obstinate, determined to end the long ascendancy of the Whigs and restore the prestige of the monarchy. It was clear that he intended not only to reign but to rule the empire. Before long, his self-doubts seemed to have vanished and he was issuing streams of orders and pronouncements, all written in his own hand, all influenced by Bute. Again and again, attacking the hated Whig politicians who had dominated his grandfather's reign, he railed against "party" and "faction" and those who aimed to dominate him. In a letter to Bute he referred to the old king as a "shuffling devil" of whom he was ashamed. The Duke of Newcastle was a "knave," and although Pitt had been his father's friend, he too was tarred with the same brush: he was "a true snake in the grass" and "the blackest of hearts, the most ungrateful and in my mind the most dishonourable of men. I can never bear to see him in any future ministry."

In the first year of George's reign the foremost business was the matter of his marriage. After all, a queen and an heir were essential. Because of his mother's opposition, George had been denied marriage with a lovely young German princess chosen for him by his grandfather. His mother and Bute then overruled his own choice of the beautiful Lady Sarah Lennox; instead, he was informed that he would marry a fifteen-year-old princess named Charlotte Sophia from the obscure Duchy of Mecklenberg-Strelitz, who was said to be "accomplished in music and of amiable temperament." As was evident when she arrived in England in September of 1761 aboard a royal yacht, she was also extremely homely—short, thin, with a turned-up nose and a large mouth. Before George could raise any objections the couple was whisked to the altar, and two weeks later the young man and Charlotte were crowned king and queen of England. The question of an heir was solved many times over: she bore the king fifteen children before she was forty.*

As early as 1757, before he became king, George had begun worrying about the nation's finances, insisting to Bute that they must plan to free England from her present load of debts. As the war dragged on and the costs mounted alarmingly—especially those for subsidizing the war in Germany—the then Prince of Wales and his tutor turned increasingly against Pitt, the man they held responsible for the conflict and its potential damage to the British economy. George was priggish and penurious by nature—a cheeseparer in his own household and in public affairs—and in his first speech to Parliament as king he pointedly stated, "The greatest uneasiness I feel at this time is in considering the uncommon burdens necessarily brought upon my faithful subjects." (This was a grudging compromise by the king: at Pitt's insistence the word "necessarily" was added at the last minute.)

---

*On September 8, 1762, the heir presumptive—a new Prince of Wales—was christened George Augustus Frederick.

Although the Seven Years' War had engulfed much of Europe, the general impression in England—fostered by many a British minister—was that it had been fought "for the long injured, long-neglected, long-forgotten people of America," in William Pitt's words. So it was hardly surprising that a heated discussion began at war's end as to what Britain should demand at the peace table.

With the fall of Quebec in 1759 a fierce pamphlet war had erupted in England, the goal of which was to influence both public opinion and government policy. Although Britain had won the real war by then, it was widely believed that France would insist on a price for making peace, and the price, interestingly, came down to a choice between Guadeloupe or Canada. Guadeloupe for its sugar, or Canada for its furs—that was the question. If England did not retain Canada, one argument went, "you lay the Foundation of another War," so the French should be excluded from North America "*absolutely* and *entirely*." Moreover, an America with all of Canada added to the colonies would be an increasingly significant market for British manufactures, the source of masts for the Royal Navy, along with rice, tobacco, and fish for Britain and Europe, and an essential contributor to a booming commerce with the West Indies and the mother country.

The opposition position was that possession of Canada had never been an objective of the war, but Guadeloupe—ah, there lay the prize. It produced more sugar than all the British islands put together, and commercially was infinitely more desirable than Canada. Furthermore, if the people in the colonies were not threatened from Canada, the likelihood was that they would move inexorably west into those vast open spaces, losing their ties with England and becoming a dangerous competitor commercially, and then where would the mother country be? One opponent wrote, "The Possession of Canada . . . may in its Consequence be even dangerous. A Neighbour that keeps us in some Awe, is not always the worst of Neighbours."

The provincials, a pamphleteer said, are "numerous, hardy, independent People, possessed of a strong Country," and could hardly be expected to remain in thrall to England much longer. It was clear, therefore, if Canada became British, the independence of the colonies would be inevitable. And that state of affairs was precisely what Pehr Kalm had foreseen in 1748.

As might be expected, Benjamin Franklin had decided views on this subject. He had gone to London in 1757 as agent for Pennsylvania (and subsequently served other colonies in that capacity) and three years later wrote and published a pamphlet entitled "The Interest of Great Britain Considered with Regard to the Colonies and the Acquisition of Canada and Guadeloupe." In it he reiterated his thesis that America would surpass England in population in another century, while reassuring English readers with a reminder that the mounting number of new subjects would constitute an ever-expanding market for British-made goods. To soothe those who worried lest America's population growth and territorial expansion would lead to greater strength and ultimately to independence, he reminded them that the colonies were so suspicious of each other that they had never even succeeded in forming a united front against the French and Indians—as witness his own experience with the ill-fated Albany Plan of Union. To an Englishman who was convinced that independence was the goal of Franklin's countrymen, he insisted that "no such idea was ever entertained by Americans, nor will any such ever enter their heads, unless you grossly abuse them." After all, he added, there was no danger "of their uniting against their own nation."

His message seems to have sunk in. As a writer was to comment in the *London Magazine* in 1766, "The American is apparelled from head to foot in our manufactures . . . he scarcely drinks, sits, moves, labours, or recreates himself without contributing to the emolument of the mother country."

There is no reason to suppose that Franklin was dissimulating, because he was every inch the loyal subject of his king, and his pamphlet evidently persuaded many Britons that they had little to fear from colonial ambitions for a century or more, since Americans entertained no thoughts of independence.

Years later, however, John Adams was to write that "immediately upon the conquest of Canada from the French in the year 1759, Great Britain seemed to be seized with a jealousy [a word that then connoted suspicion] against the Colonies, and then concerted the plan of changing their forms of government, of restraining their trade . . . and raising a revenue within them by authority of parliament, for the avowed or pretended purpose of protecting, securing, and defending them." Certainly it was true, as Adams suggested, that the departure of the French from Canada and the diminution of the threat to America's northern frontier caused many British leaders to suspect the colonials' intentions and be on the alert for any sign of what was called "independancy."

Thomas Hutchinson, lieutenant governor of Massachusetts, argued later that an insidious conspiracy was at work during this period. Americans were well aware of the Guadeloupe–Canada debate, he wrote; they were all too familiar with the argument that the cession of Canada would cause the colonies to split from the mother country; and "enterprising men"—by which he meant Boston's radical Samuel Adams and his ilk—capitalized on this knowledge of British fears to consider "how far such a separation was expedient and practicable."

While the question of Canada or Guadeloupe was settled officially in 1761, with Britain's treaty negotiators instructed to hold out for Canada and let the French keep the island, the debate continued for years, with many British believing it had been a terrible mistake to demand that the French give up Canada. Samuel Johnson, for one, was heartily of that opinion in 1775. "Let us restore to the French what we have taken from them," he wrote. "We shall see our Colonists at our feet, when they have an enemy so near them."

A letter in a London newspaper reminded readers how the Americans "are constantly boasting of the prodigious services which they rendered *us,* in the course of the last war, when it is notoriously known, that the last war was entered into for their *own* immediate protection," and whatever efforts they made "were entirely from motives of *private interest. . . .*" The moment Canada was ceded to Britain, the writer continued, "The dutiful colonies began to change their tone; America was no longer *ours,* but *theirs.*"

In support of John Adams's views, it was evident by the time George III ascended the throne that the attitude of those Englishmen whose opinions mattered was beginning to harden against the colonials. For centuries the landed gentry had dominated village and county life in England, providing militia officers, church wardens, justices of the peace, looking after the impoverished, sending their own to Parliament. This conservative, property-owning class was the voice of tradition and privilege, and when Benjamin Franklin declared that every Englishman "seems to consider himself as a piece of a sovereign over America [and], with the King . . . talks of *our subjects in the colonies,*" he was speaking of those solid country squires, churchmen, and aristocrats who represented the heart of Britain. As long as Walpole's laissez-faire policy and the ensuing French threat from Canada prevailed, there was little reason to alter the relationship between America and the mother country, but after 1760 signs of change began to appear as the months wore on.

The landed gentry had supported William Pitt's war as long as he gave them victories; but now the fighting was over and they wanted an end to his costly ministry. Asking what Britain had gained for the vast expenditures of life and treasure over the war years, they concluded that the beneficiaries were the colonials, and now it was time they faced up to it and started to pay their own way. Increasingly annoyed and angry with the Americans, the country gentlemen stood foursquare behind King George. And Parliament, they insisted, must maintain its absolute sovereignty as laid down in 1689 after the Glorious Revolution ended the Stuart dynasty. The provincials were getting out of hand and must be held on a short leash. Furthermore, they must be required to contribute revenue to the government—money for their own defense and money for administering their own affairs.

For justification, the conservatives needed only to point to the financial facts of life. It goes without saying that a government runs on money, and for a government at war, peacetime revenues are vastly inadequate. For instance, the British government that operated comfortably on £2.5 million in 1754 required £19 million in 1761, and conventional means of raising these funds had to be greatly supplemented by long-term borrowing.

In peacetime the land tax in England was usually kept at two shillings in the pound—a 10 percent tax on assessed value—which brought in £1 million to the Treasury. In wartime the land tax was doubled—to four shillings in the pound, producing £2 million a year. Other sources of revenue, such as the malt tax and the sinking fund, brought the total up to a maximum of £4.65 million per annum, but more—much more—was needed, as indicated by government borrowings of £8 million in 1760 and £12 million in 1761 and 1762. Furthermore, each of those loans required an additional tax, which was set at the rate needed to pay the interest on the loan.

Remarkably, during the Duke of Newcastle's tenure at the Treasury, interest rates were kept low, ranging from 3.4 percent to a high of 4.8 percent, and inflation never became a serious factor. The duke held strong views on taxation, notably that the land tax was unfair, since it fell most heavily on a small percentage of the population (the landed gentry, obviously), with the result that it was held at what he considered its outer limit—a figure that no politician ever challenged. But since customs duties were extremely uncertain during wartime, the tax burden was shifted onto such consumer taxes as malt, newspapers, beer, soap, and coal, putting a heavy burden on those least able to bear it.

Newcastle was keenly aware of the people's concerns: as he observed in 1759, "The real cause of the misfortune is, that we are engaged in expences infinitely above our strength; and the people do not see the end of it." Then, in words aimed squarely at Pitt, he went on, "Expedition after expedition; campaign after campaign. No approach *now* from any quarter towards peace, and an aversion to . . . those . . . who may either think of it, or talk of the necessity of it."

In the year of George III's coronation, the word in London was that an army would be established for the protection of the colonies and the Americans must pay "at least the greatest share of charge for it. This will occasion a tax." The national debt had soared to £140 million, on which the interest was

£5 million a year—more than 60 percent of the annual budget—and Pitt seemed incapable of facing up to the consequences of that, let alone what was necessary for the colonies' continuing defense.

Even so, with the king heckling his first minister to get on with a peace treaty and put an end to the military expenditures, Parliament in 1760 was not yet ready to take the step of forcing Americans to support the troops and administrative functionaries needed in the colonies. It would be left to one of Pitt's successors to bite the bullet, for Pitt, as far as George III was concerned, was on the way out. The king had already made it known that he would "put an end, at all events, to the uncertainty about Mr. Pitt," and Bute and Newcastle were sufficiently in the know to be conferring on the makeup of a new cabinet.

While the peace proposals floated back and forth between London and Paris during the summer of 1761, cabinet meetings turned into ugly trials of strength between Pitt and his fellow ministers. Pitt had learned from his spies that Charles II of Spain was about to form an alliance with France and would declare war on Britain the following year, and his immediate thought was to take preemptive action—at once. He alerted the Royal Navy to prepare for hostilities against Spain, and on October 2 pleaded with an antagonistic cabinet to support him. Now, he argued, was the moment for humbling the House of Bourbon, and if they let the opportunity slip by it might never be recovered. If his views did not prevail, he warned, this was the last time he should sit in that council. . . . He would no longer remain in a situation which made him responsible for measures he was no longer allowed to guide. When Lord Bute announced that under no circumstances would the king agree to any such action, the cabinet voted against the motion and William Pitt immediately turned in the seals of his office and resigned from the government he had led for five triumphant years. As the *Annual Register* reminded readers, "he revived the military genius of our people; he supported our allies; he extended our trade; he raised our reputation; he augmented our dominions." It was no small achievement.

During nearly half a century of Whig dominance, public life in Great Britain had been stable, largely unruffled, but after 1760 it gave way to turmoil and change, and suddenly the king pushed his way to the center of the political arena. George realized that the Whigs' control of patronage had enabled them to monopolize political power, and he determined to seize it from them. To rid the government of the "factions" he detested, he tore a page from Walpole's book and established a political circle of his own—the "king's friends"—which proved to be a virtually unbeatable party with the monarch at its head, dispenser of patronage and power.

The patronage system was a controlling factor in Parliament. Of 588 men elected in 1761 to serve in the House of Commons for seven years, at least 271—nearly half—were on the government payroll in one way or another. Nor did Commons faintly resemble a representative assembly: since the right to vote was based on property ownership, only 215,000 of the eight million adult males in England, Scotland, and Wales were eligible. Furthermore, voting districts were designed in such a way that wealthy landowners controlled who could stand as candidates. Members of the House of Lords—many of them hugely rich—determined which of their constituents could stand for election to the Commons, and those fortunate few were known as placemen, because they were expected to do no more than sit in their places and vote as ordered. The election results of 1761 revealed the system at work: for example, the Duke of Newcastle controlled forty-nine votes in Commons; Lord Bute a bloc of seventy-six, mostly Scots; the Duke of Bedford ten; the Earl of Hardwicke eleven. And so it went.

With Pitt's departure the transition was anything but smooth: a sorry parade of first ministers came onstage and their ministries rose and fell, taking with them remnants of a Whig bureaucracy that had been in place for longer than most men could remember. The king sought a compatible leader who suited him and would do his bidding, but he found only inexperienced, narrow-minded men who possessed his own failings—a lack of foresight and generosity, a quickness to anger—men who were driven by frustration over the American situation to miscalculations and actions that were as unfortunate as they were unforeseen. For ten turbulent, unhappy years those ministers managed to foster increasingly ugly confrontations with George III's dominions on the western shores of the Atlantic.

William Pitt was succeeded by the Duke of Newcastle, who had served in every government since Walpole's time and was the last emblem of the Whig power so despised by the king. George wanted to be rid of him too, and seven months later he was gone, Bute took over, and the Whigs' decades-long domination of Britain's government finally ended.

And still the war continued, but by September of 1762 it was clear to the French that their alliance with Spain was more hindrance than help, and in December diplomats at last agreed on terms that ratified British victories in North America. France lost all of Canada and its vast territory east of the

Mississippi River, except the island of New Orleans (which she later ceded to Spain), while Spain yielded East and West Florida. As expected, France retained Guadeloupe and several other islands, plus fishing rights off Newfoundland.

When the treaty came before Parliament the vote in favor was an overwhelming 319 to 65, but 174 members (most of them Whigs) had abstained, and retribution was swift. The king informed Bute that those who had opposed the government "must be made an example of," and the purge of men who owed their patronage or positions to Pitt and Newcastle was ruthless, shattering forever what remained of Whig power. As Horace Walpole put it, "A more severe political persecution never raged." Anyone who voted against the treaty was instantly dismissed, with the friends and dependents of the Duke of Newcastle singled out for particular retribution. This cruelty, Walpole added, went so far that old placemen, "who had retired and been preferred to very small places, were rigorously hunted out and deprived of their livelihood." It was a dramatic preview of what would happen to those who opposed ministerial measures approved by His Majesty King George III.

Even before the peace treaty was in hand, the king had begun work on a scheme to reduce the size of the armed forces. Huge numbers had been involved in the Seven Years' War—nearly 200,000 Britons in all, including 120,000 in the army alone, plus 60,000 Germans hired by the crown to augment forces on the Continent. But more than the national debt and the king's desire for economies had to be considered as Lord Bute, executing the king's wishes, prepared a peacetime budget.

Scores of thousands of demobilized soldiers and sailors, a majority of them poor, many of them mutilated, would be coming home, seeking employment. At the same time it was necessary to consider England's lonely eminence in the world. With France and Spain humiliated, quite likely seeking revenge, and with Britain's ally Prussia alienated, who could say how strong the British military must be? Radical changes had taken place since 1755, forcing England to come to terms with its unprecedented power in the world and the responsibilities that accompanied a global empire. These considerations raised questions as to how traditional British liberties could be preserved while maintaining what Edmund Burke called "the strong presiding power that is so useful towards the conservation of a vast, disconnected, infinitely diversified empire."

This was a question that demanded answers, for as anyone could see, the immense postwar empire required a greatly expanded administrative network and a military force adequate to protect all those far-flung possessions. The problem was particularly acute in the American colonies, to which an enormous territory had been added (along with some seventy thousand Roman Catholic inhabitants of Canada), and where—even with the French menace gone—the frontiers continued to be threatened by hostile Indians.

An army substantially larger than the small forces that had operated during the French and Indian Wars was deemed essential, and its support would require a heavy flow of capital. So it was apparent to every thinking member of Parliament that the Americans must contribute to the increased cost of their defense and the administration of their affairs.

By this time, however, the colonials had been on their own too long to accept unquestioningly a sudden infusion of demands and controls from London. The threat from Canada was removed, and despite Benjamin Franklin's assurances to the contrary, the colonials felt more secure, less dependent on the mother country.

6

Gentle Shepherd

William Pitt had known it all along, but ever so slowly it began to dawn on ordinary people that in winning a war Britain had also won an empire, and on both sides of the Atlantic there was a growing perception that nothing would be quite the same again. No one was aware of it at the time, of course, but the Peace Treaty of 1763 proved to be the great watershed in relationships between Great Britain and its American colonies.

The question of whether Canada or Guadeloupe would be awarded to Britain had long been settled in a decision that was supremely interesting to Charles Gravier, Comte de Vergennes, the shrewd Anglophobe who was to become minister of foreign affairs under Louis XVI of France. "England will ere long repent of having removed the only check that could keep her colonies in awe," he remarked. "They stand no longer in need of her protection; she will call on them to contribute toward supporting the burdens they have helped to bring on her; and they will answer by striking off all dependence." Paradoxically, fear of France had until recently created what little sense of union the colonies achieved, but England now provided the real provocations that drove them to act collectively.

Indeed, the decade that began so triumphantly with George III's accession soon became a time of confusion and growing mistrust, as untried ministries grappled with problems beyond their ability to solve, and men took sides on a constitutional question once undreamed of: was Parliament to be sovereign or was it not?

Curiously, no one had ever scrutinized the relationship between mother country and offspring in order to define the rights of Americans within the structure of empire. Quite simply, such an examination had never been thought necessary. But once Englishmen began questioning to what extent Americans had contributed in blood and treasure to the fighting of the French and Indian Wars, the next questions to be asked were: How long must our support for them go on? And why should they not pay for their own defense?

Those questions led inevitably to a discussion of what rights and how much authority the colonials were to have. And as Edmund Burke observed, when people begin to define their rights, it is "a sure symptom of an ill-conducted state."

Readers who picked up copies of Weyman's *New-York Gazette* on January 24, 1763, were greeted with the words of King George's November 26 speech, in which he informed Parliament that preliminary articles of peace had been signed with France and Spain, ensuring that "an immense Territory" would soon be added to the British Empire, laying a solid foundation "for the Increase of Trade and Commerce." The king went on to praise the "unwearied perseverance and unparallelled bravery of my officers and private men, by sea and land," who had shown that "no climate, no hardships, no dangers can check the ardor or resist the valour of the British arms." But it was not lost on American readers that the speech included no mention whatever of any contributions the colonials may have made during the long, bloody conflict.

In the weeks that followed, snippets of information concerning the treaty—mostly rumors—dribbled into New York. On April 21, John Watts told a friend that a peace treaty had finally been signed in Paris, though no official confirmation of the agreement had been received. He hoped the peace would be a lasting one, so "that we may throw off the Load of Warr, which tho' very glorious, has been very expensive too." And further financial drain lay ahead, he observed ruefully. Fifteen or sixteen regiments were said to be heading for America, to be quartered at the colonies' expense, and he hoped those provinces that had borne little or no cost of defending the frontier in the past could be forced to contribute now. As matters stood, New York was required to send every fifth man between the ages of sixteen and sixty to the military and was also expected to pay £40,000 annually until 1767 to support that force. It was a heavy burden.

The treaty was signed on February 10, after which Lord Bute resigned and a new ministry led by George Grenville took office in April. Bute's departure was not unexpected: his unpopularity had been brought home to him with a vengeance when his carriage was attacked and stoned by an angry mob, inflamed by his role in Pitt's resignation, and now that he had presided over the peace treaty he begged leave to retire. The king, one suspects, was not sorry to see him go, having learned that Bute was not a man he could depend on to assist in what the monarch considered the awesome task of governing.

George III did not like Grenville, who no sooner took office than he began nagging the king on how he must defer to the new cabinet. The king had previously declared that "Grenville is very far out if he thinks himself capable for a post where either decision or activity are necessary; for I have never met a man more doubtful or dillitory." Grenville had reason to be doubtful, thanks to a political insecurity that stemmed from having a patchwork ministry and little support in Parliament or outside it. He was Pitt's brother-in-law, but had broken with him and, because of that, with other Whigs. But few doubts troubled his sleep. And dilatory he certainly was not. In fact, his conscientious attention to business and its most minute details was the reason the king held him in contempt and condemned him as having the mind of a countinghouse clerk.

The king chose him because he had no other choice. And so it happened that a pompous, domineering, bad-tempered man who nevertheless had good intentions, a strong will, and an orderly set of ideas for solving the problems of America came to power and succeeded in enraging the colonials with every new program he devised.

For his own sake and his empire's, the king could hardly have made a worse choice. George was determined to rule; Grenville seemed equally determined to keep him from doing so. As the thoroughly annoyed monarch observed on one occasion, "he had the insolence to say that if people presum'd to speak to me on business without his previous consent, he would not serve an hour." It was a pity for all concerned that the man on the throne did not give Grenville the excuse to leave, but he did not, and for three stormy years the king was alternately badgered and bored, forced to make do with an abrasive minister he hated for his tiresome lectures and his long-windedness. As the king complained, he "would talk for an hour and look at his watch and then go on for another half-hour."

On the big issues, however, the two agreed: both wanted economy in government, a reduction of the national debt, and revenue from the colonies to defer the expenses of their upkeep. Both subscribed to Grenville's concept of empire as an entity with a "supreme centre and subordinate parts." In financial matters, Grenville's enthusiasm for cost-cutting exceeded even that of the king: he went so far as to turn down a request from the royal household for money to enlarge the grounds around Buckingham House (later to become Buckingham Palace), which the king had purchased. A row of houses had gone up on empty land opposite the gardens, giving residents a choice view of the royal family whenever they went outside, but the king's privacy meant less to Grenville than the £20,000 the king had requested to buy the houses. One of the first minister's tightest economy measures inflicted woeful damage on the Royal Navy, causing ships to be laid up at dockside with no money for maintenance and not enough to pay off the crews, thereby reducing the fleet to the same pitiful condition that had prevailed before the Seven Years' War.

Soon the Grenville austerity program began to be felt in America. The first minister was quick to see that customs officials were part of the whole rotten patronage system. The most lucrative jobs were sinecures, handed out to royal favorites who continued to live in London while hiring agents in the provinces to do their jobs for them. Poorly paid, those agents discovered that enterprising local merchants were willing to reimburse them handsomely to look the other way, and as an American newspaper put it, they found it "easier, and more profitable, not only to wink but to sleep in their Beds, the Merchants' Pay being more generous than the King's." James Otis, the Boston attorney, observed that an insignificant position in the customs service in America could make a man a fortune sooner than an important government job: people were profiting handsomely from the estimated £700,000 of merchandise that was smuggled into the colonies annually. So much of the New Yorkers' trade with Indians was in exchange for goods smuggled from Holland that the governor warned that "the greatest part of the Commerce of the American Colonies will be withdrawn from the Mother Country, and be carreyed to Holland."

To the average English politician—indifferent though he might be toward America—the role of colonials was to ship raw materials to the mother country and buy manufactured items in return, all of this trade, naturally, being carried in British ships. Only it did not work that way in practice. Smuggling was a fact of life in colonial America, and it was rampant, engaged in by merchants in every colony. Not even a war interrupted the illegal trade: during the French and Indian War, Manhattan merchants doing business with the French West Indies off-loaded cargoes out of sight beyond Sandy Hook and sailed into port ready for customs inspectors while their illicit goods came into the city by wagon. The vast extent and irregularity of the coastline and the collusion of customs collectors with the smugglers made it all but impossible to check illegal entry.

In an effort to remedy the situation, "An Act for the further Improvement of His Majesty's Revenue of Customs" was passed in 1762, granting a customs official half the value of a ship and its cargo if the vessel was seized for violating the trade laws. The following year, Grenville sent a circular letter to governors, condemning the "iniquitous practice" of smuggling, which resulted in diminishing the public revenue at a time when the nation was struggling under a heavy debt "incurred [during] the last War for the protection of America." The letter demanded compliance with the laws and made it clear that no more jobbery by colonial customs officials living in Britain would be tolerated: customs officers were ordered to be at their appointed stations by the end of August and comply with their responsibilities or face dismissal.

Walpole, characteristically, had chosen to ignore colonial infractions of the rules where commerce was involved, his argument being that the more America's trade flourished, so would Britain's. If the colonies profit by £500,000, he had said, "I am convinced that, in two years afterwards, full £250,000 of their gains will be in his majesty's exchequer." Thanks to his conviction that the more money the Americans made, the "more of our produce will be wanted," in those halcyon years few quarrels marred the serene relationship between mother country and her children.

Now the situation had changed, and in more ways than one. For years Americans had conducted their affairs through the Board of Trade, a small group of men, many of them known personally by colonials. But with Parliament's awakening to the meaning of the peace settlement came a day of reckoning—a sudden awareness of how enormous America was, far beyond the confines of the coastal colonies—and a new sense of Parliament's own responsibilities and the power that accompanied them, and it was soon apparent that they wanted revenues from two sources—trade and taxes.

In terms of trade alone, North America was the biggest and fastest-growing part of Britain's economy, and the prosperity of England's chief cities was a direct result of that commerce. Think, then, of what might happen if the vast lands to the west became populated as Benjamin Franklin had foretold, opening huge new prospects for business. Clearly, the problems and prospects were beyond the capacity of the Lords of Trade to handle—too important by far. So for the first time, Parliament began to assume control over colonial issues.

Unfortunately for the Americans, Parliament was largely unreceptive—even hostile—to colonial suggestions or appeals and, having taken the bit in its teeth, was determined to exercise its power. That determination was reflected in one bill after another passed between 1763 and 1765, each more troubling to the colonials, each leading inexorably to such a radically different policy that the Americans finally realized they must resist before they were undone. The first indication of what was afoot came with the new emphasis on collecting customs duties, but more—much more—was in store.

Word reached New York of a debate in Commons, when the ministry introduced a proposal to levy an excise tax on cider made in England. America's hero, William Pitt, immediately attacked the measure, protesting the means of enforcement on grounds that they violated the rights of the individual. George Grenville responded with a sharp criticism of Pitt for his mishandling of finances while in office, adding that it was time now to consider new sources of revenue. If the Opposition found the cider duty objectionable, he invited it to suggest where new taxes should be laid.

"I say, Sir, let them tell me *where*!" he whined in his high-pitched voice, and then repeated the question.

At that William Pitt began humming, loud enough for members to hear, the tune of a popular song, "Gentle Shepherd, Tell Me Where." The ludicrous picture of the somber Grenville in the role of Gentle Shepherd, with a voice like a shepherd's pipe, brought down the house, and the nickname stuck. But it was clear in the weeks ahead that the Gentle Shepherd had harsh measures in mind.

"The Indians are proving dangerous Neighbours, now the French are removd [and] their plan seems extensive & determind . . ." wrote John Watts in July of 1763. That was an apt description of what provoked the latest outbreak of savage warfare on the frontier—an uprising led by Pontiac, chief of the Ottawas. The peace treaty ending French power on the North American continent had deprived the western Indians of their long-standing allies, leaving them alone to resist the continuous encroachment of Americans onto their territory, and the whites' renewed westward drive had actually begun in 1761, two years before the treaty was signed, as Richard Peters of Pennsylvania warned Sir William Johnson, the colonial superintendent of Indian affairs. "The Connecticut People are making their grand push both in England for a new Grant from the King, and in this province for a forcible entry and detainer of the Indian Land, on no other Pretence than that their Charter extends to the South Seas [i.e., the Pacific]," Peters wrote, ". . . and so like mad men they will cross New York and New Jersey, and come and kindle an Indian war in the Bowels of this poor Province. . . . I wish you or General

Amherst could fall on some means to have it laid aside, for it will breed a civil war among our Back Inhabitants, who are sucking in . . . the Connecticut Poison and Spirit & will actually, in my Opinion, go into open Rebellion in the opening of the Spring."

By June of that year, Johnson knew in his bones that trouble was coming, and he wrote Sir Jeffrey Amherst, governor-general of British America, that he was very apprehensive that something dangerous was brewing among the Indians. "I do not only mean the six Nations," he said. "I fear it is too general whatever it be." But Amherst was unimpressed. If an Indian plot was afoot, he wrote, it "never gave me a moment's concern, as I know their incapacity of attempting anything serious," and if the tribes gave him any trouble, he would "punish the delinquents with entire destruction . . . extirpate them root and branch."

Pontiac was the incarnation of the settlers' age-old fear, harking back to King Philip's War—a leader capable of uniting the Indian nations against whites. Angered by the intruders' cheating and land-grabbing, Pontiac formed an alliance of western tribes, which was attacking white settlements from New York to Virginia in the spring of 1763 and had already seized a number of forts formerly held by the French.

Early in June, John Watts wrote a friend, "Some Indians, supposed[ly] the Delawares, have been troublesome about Pittsburg, scalpd some people & as the report goes have cut off an advanced Post, either St. Josephs or San-duski. . . ." A month later he could see that the situation was more serious: "We don't know what is the fate of Detroit, Machilimachinack & St. Josephs, but Presq' Isle, Sanduski, Le Beuf & Venango are cut off & the poor Soldiers butcher'd all except a very few." Captain Dalzell, Amherst's aide-de-camp, led a party of three hundred men west from Oswego on July 3, heading for Detroit, by which time, Watts reported, "We have now not one Post or Fort left from Pittsburg outwards on the one [line of] communication, or from Niagara on the other, except Detroit." And in September, confirming Watts's fears that Captain Dalzell would lose "the Skin off his head, among the mys-terious & savage Race of Vermin," that officer died in an abortive attempt to surprise a group of Indians several miles from Fort Detroit. Ambushed by a superior force that had word of his coming, his command lost forty wounded and twelve or fifteen killed.

The New York Assembly appealed to Cadwallader Colden to ask General Amherst to demand that "Governments to the Eastward" send their quotas of troops for the common defense. "On the success of this War," the address to the lieutenant governor read, "their, as well as our, very Existence depends." The assemblymen reminded Colden that New York had enjoyed friendly relations with the Six Nations for nearly a century, but now "Those inestimable Blessings have been ravished from us by a Savage Enemy" at the very moment that peace at last seemed at hand. It was all very well for Amherst to request troops from New York and New Jersey, but what about Massachusetts and Connecticut, Rhode Island, and New Hampshire? In the meantime, New Jersey turned down his demand for six hundred men and sent only two hundred, while Philadelphia did nothing about the thousand Pennsylvania troops the general wanted, and the squabbling among the colonies and between colonies and Amherst went on. New York's treasury had been exhausted by the demands of the recent war, when all its specie had been sent to Great Britain, and it was clearly impossible now to pay a large number of men.

It was plain to see that Amherst had grossly underestimated the severity and seriousness of the Indian uprising. His contempt for the native Americans, his refusal to heed William Johnson's warnings, and his reliance on small, undermanned, and widely separated garrisons in the west had revealed the stupidity of his policy, and he was recalled by London and replaced in November of 1763 by Thomas Gage, now a major general. But the border warfare dragged on.

The following spring, Watts told of the investment of Detroit by two thousand Indians under Pontiac; in September of the "scalping & butchering [of] poor innocent defenceless people"; and in November of the burning of the Moravian mills in Bethlehem, Pennsylvania. More than once he lamented, "I cannot for my Life see yet a probable end of this infernal War, either by Force or Treaty, the one is so difficult & the other so uncertain & tame."

A treaty of peace may have been signed in Paris, but life had become no easier in His Majesty's provinces, and not until December of 1764 was Governor Penn of Pennsylvania able to proclaim that the "Enemy Indians" had sued for peace "in the most humble and submissive manner" to Colonel Henry Bouquet.

Grenville's reaction to Pontiac's rebellion was the Proclamation of 1763, which reserved lands west of the Appalachians to "the several Nations or Tribes of Indians . . . who live under Our Protection," forbidding white settlement there, denying the purchase of western lands by any "private Person," and restricting commerce with the Indians to traders licensed by the government in Britain. Nor was that the end of it: the Privy Council notified governors that the granting of Indian lands to whites must cease, and fur traders were required to deal with the natives inside designated posts and in the presence of crown officials.

The reaction in America was outrage. For the first time in colonial history, territorial expansion was to be under the thumb of British officials. From the day of the original white settlements, land speculation had been a right taken for granted. The lure of profits from buying land cheap and selling dear was in men's blood, and no proclamation was going to deny it to them. George Washington was one of many determined to bypass the new rules. He regarded them as no more than "a temporary expedient to quiet the Minds of the Indians" and secretly arranged with a surveyor friend "to secure some of the most valuable Lands in the King's part [of the west] . . . notwithstanding the Proclamation. . . ." As Washington and other speculators knew, the edict could not be enforced: therefore it could be ignored. Nor did the fur traders behave as London wished: instead of dealing with the Indians inside the walls of a British fort, they conducted their business outside, where they were able to provide the native Americans with liquor to make them as pliable as possible.

Belief that the proclamation was unenforceable was not shared by London, however, and the cabinet decided that ten thousand troops, stationed along the frontier, could handle the task. Immediately the question of money arose—very considerable amounts of it, possibly £250,000 a year—and this the colonials would be obliged to help pay, since it was for their own defense.

As logical as it might be for Americans to regard the Proclamation of 1763 as a means of pacifying the Indians, the underlying thinking behind it was quite different. The Board of Trade insisted that all western settlement must be carried out according to the rules of trade and commerce of the kingdom and under its authority, in order to keep "the colonists in due subordination to, and dependence upon, the mother country." As one British official put the case, mincing no words, it was essential to prohibit settlement beyond the Alleghenies to keep the colonists "as near as possible to the Ocean." They must remain "subservient to the Commerce of their Mother Country" and not engage in manufacturing, for they were "merely Factors for the Purposes of Trade." The interior, therefore, should be as open and wild as possible. And to accomplish all that, a standing army was essential.

Seeking new sources of revenue for the Gentle Shepherd, while doing its utmost not to alarm the testy colonials, the Treasury Department hit upon what it considered an ideal solution. This was to resuscitate the moribund Molasses Act. Passed in 1733 and repeatedly renewed, it had levied a duty of sixpence a gallon on molasses imported by the Americans. Since that amount was regarded as ruinous by New England rum manufacturers, they proceeded to ignore or circumvent it, and customs officials went along with them, charging rates (unless they accepted bribes to do nothing) ranging from one-tenth to one-quarter of the statutory duty and more often than not pocketing the proceeds as a perquisite of office. The practice was abhorred by many a merchant, one of whom urged repeal of the old act, since it only encouraged fraud and worked a hardship on the honest trader.

Molasses was a vital component in the colonial scheme of commerce. A sweet, brownish liquid that remained after sugarcane was pressed and heated to produce sugar, molasses came primarily from the French West Indies—in particular, the islands of Guadeloupe, Martinique, and St. Domingo, where France forbade the distilling of molasses into rum in order to protect its domestic brandy makers. The consequence was that hogsheads of molasses were imported in vast quantities by Americans. Massachusetts, for instance, brought in 1.5 million gallons annually, two-thirds of which was consumed locally as a sweetener or in distilled form, with the balance exported as rum. Rhode Island's economy was based almost entirely on the product, which was then transformed by more than thirty distilleries into rum, to be exchanged on the west coast of Africa for gold dust, elephant tusks, and, principally, slaves, who were taken to be sold in the British West Indies, the Carolinas, and Virginia.

The African slave trade began in the Americas when a Spanish missionary, Bartolomé de Las Casas, suggested early in the sixteenth century that Negroes be imported to replace the West Indian natives who had perished from disease and depression, having fought unavailingly against their appallingly brutal treatment in servitude. Las Casas later repented his folly and spent the rest of his life working against the inhuman practice, but he was too late by far.

Before the sixteenth century, sugar—an addictive and unnecessary substance—was all but unknown in Europe, where honey was the common sweetener. For some time after sugar was introduced it was an expensive novelty, affordable only by the wealthy. But when coffee, tea, and chocolate became all but essential to the middle classes, they created a huge demand for sugar, which Dr. Johnson called "the indispensable companion of tea." Initially the Portuguese and Spanish established sugar estates in the islands of the eastern Atlantic and West Indies. It was a reliable cash crop in an ever-expanding market, but it was extremely labor-intensive, and the planting, cultivation, and harvest in the hot sun was too much for whites (or so they thought), and West Africa's Negroes, moreover, proved to be immune from the severe form of malaria because of the incidence of sickle-cell anemia.

After the canes were cut they were crushed in mills and boiled in open vats, with the heavier, blacker portions drained off first, leaving crude brown or yellow sugar, which had to be dissolved again and crystallized into white, except in the small mills that produced only molasses and one grade of sugar. The heat in the sugar houses was unbearable, with temperatures up to 140 degrees Fahrenheit and the humidity extreme. The reason the sugar islands imported timber from America was that their own forests had been cut down to fuel the vats.

During the years of the slave trade as many as twelve million Negroes were exported from Africa, and it is estimated that three-fourths of them may have been involved in raising sugar. No one can possibly say how many others perished in the tribal wars and ambushes when they were first captured and marched to the coast, before being chained together in the stinking hold of a ship where they lay prone for as long as three months. The Middle Passage, from West Africa to the West Indies, took as few as twenty-three days and as many as ninety-five, passing through the Doldrums on the equator before the ship sailed from island to island where its human cargo was sold. That done, the vessel was transformed from slaver to sugar carrier, loaded with rum, molasses, and crudely refined sugar for the voyage to America or England. There it took on a cargo of trinkets, alcohol, salt, fabrics of various kinds, firearms, and gunpowder for delivery to African slave traders, and the cycle began anew.

To justify the trade a biblical argument was made: the heathen blacks of Africa were children of Ham, the son of Noah, who had cursed Ham and declared that he should be "a servant of servants." But justification or no, the trade was hugely important for Britain's merchant fleet, and only slightly less so for those of the Dutch and the Americans. A 1770 ruling by the Earl of Mansfield, a British judge, put an end to trafficking in slaves from British ports, but even so, in that year 192 ships sailed from those ports bound for the coast of Africa to carry off slaves to British America and elsewhere in the world. Until that year the British were the largest slave traders anywhere. In 1768, for example, when some 97,000 Negroes were carried to America from Africa by Europeans, more than 60 percent came in British vessels, and almost depopulated the African coast, forcing traders to move farther and farther inland. The risks were high—extremely so, considering the vagaries of weather, pirates and privateers, and leaky or cranky vessels that might stagnate in the Doldrums or founder in the North Atlantic—but for those whose human cargoes survived, the profits could be immense. In the early days, a Negro bought for £3 might sell for £25 or more (later the slave traders charged £20 and the selling price in the Americas was more like £30, but even at that it was a 50 percent profit for the ship owner). It was little wonder that many Britons considered the sugar islands more important than Canada in 1763, despite Dr. Johnson's condemnation of Jamaica, a typical island, as "a place of great wealth, a den of tyrants, and a dungeon of slaves."

By the time of the American Revolution virtually every spoonful of sugar consumed in England was grown and harvested by slaves, and it was estimated that for each two tons of sugar produced, one black man died.

When Parliament began reviewing the matter in 1762, members were dismayed to learn that revenues from the Molasses Act totaled no more than £1,000 or £2,000 annually, while the cost of collecting the duties amounted to £7,000 or £8,000 for the same period. In fact, studies revealed that colonial exports had produced duties of a mere £35,000 over thirty years, with import duties a pitiful £22,000 during that time. More often than not, American ships cleared for Great Britain but instead sailed to other, duty-free ports. Faced with this ridiculous situation, Grenville decided it was time to get tough.

In April of 1763 the navy (which regarded the task as well beneath its dignity) was enlisted to enforce the acts of trade. Eight men-of-war and twelve armed sloops were assigned to North American waters and captains were ordered to seize and condemn any vessels found to be breaking the laws.

At first it was assumed by colonial merchants that the molasses trade would be winked at and carried on as before, but in November customs officials were warned to do their duty or face immediate dismissal, prompting Governor Francis Bernard of Massachusetts to comment that this caused greater alarm in the northern colonies than the French capture of Fort William Henry in 1757. A carrot was added to the stick: customs officers were now to be paid on the basis of the revenue they collected.

In April of 1764 the Sugar Act was passed, amending the Molasses Act. It was to take effect in September of that year and continue for an unlimited period—placing a duty of threepence per gallon on all imported molasses, including the previously untaxed output of the British West Indies. Importation of foreign rum was prohibited.

The idea behind the scheme was this: since the colonials refused to pay sixpence a gallon, why not reduce the duty to something they *would* pay?

After considering a number of proposals, the ministry decided to reduce the tariff by half and enforce it rigidly. The act incorporating this decision provided a further sop to Americans by declaring that the funds collected would go not to the general Treasury but would be used specifically for "defending, protecting, and securing" the North American colonies, to help pay for the regulars soon to be patrolling the frontiers.

The catch here was that the duty of threepence was regarded by American merchants as equally inequitable and impractical—less than sixpence, to be sure, but still far more than the traffic would support. As Rhode Island's Governor Hopkins declared, the molasses duty is "much higher than that article can possibly bear and therefore must operate as an absolute prohibition." Jared Ingersoll of New Haven, who represented Connecticut distillers, wrote Thomas Whately, a secretary of the Treasury, to say that "Parliament have overshot their mark" and predicted that not a single captain trading with the French or Dutch West Indies had the slightest intention of paying the duties. British attempts to stop smuggling, he added, were like "burning a barn to roast an egg."

In England some of the most conspicuous nouveaux riches were absentee owners of sugar plantations. The tale was told of the king, out for a drive in the country with the first minister at his side, encountering a showy carriage with numerous outriders in fancy livery. When George III was told that this ostentatious equipage belonged to a Jamaican he turned to his companion and said, "Sugar, sugar, hey? All that sugar! How are the duties, hey Pitt, how are the duties?"

For New York, the Sugar Act came as terrible news. The colony's imbalance of trade—the value of imports over exports—was already nearing £470,000, but the deficit was largely made up by means of the lucrative molasses trade with the West Indies. Grenville's decision to peg the duty at threepence per gallon (if enforced, as it appeared that it would be) made it impossible to turn a profit. At the same time, shipments of timber were required to go to England instead of the more remunerative West Indies or European markets; a new duty on wine from Madeira drastically reduced that trade; and new restrictions on textiles from non-British suppliers and new tariffs on indigo, coffee, and other commodities reduced or shut off still other sources of profit at the same time the molasses business was in ruins.

On the heels of these unpopular measures came another blow—the prohibition of paper money. The so-called Currency Act, which was to take effect on September 1, 1764, forbade the colonies from issuing paper currency or paper notes, which were backed by mortgages on land purchases. The colonies depended for hard currency on what they received for their exports of lumber, furs, tobacco, horses, rum, and other goods, but cash was always in short supply, and to make matters worse, a provision of the Sugar Act required that customs duties be paid in sterling. As New Yorkers saw it, the shortage of specie would virtually reduce them to bartering, and they then learned that the Mutiny Act was to be extended, forcing them to provide barracks and certain supplies for General Gage's troops.

The New Yorkers most affected by these measures were the merchants, who happened to be the wealthiest and most influential men in the city. They performed a broad array of vital functions as wholesalers and retailers, importers and exporters, shipowners and insurers, and they were in continuous touch with each other and their counterparts abroad. Respected though they were, some of them were not above ignoring the law on occasion, and a number of them had secret chambers in their houses to conceal smuggled goods. Of far greater significance was their open resistance to the government's recent policies—a resistance that became institutionalized in the provincial Assembly and resulted in a growing contest between that body and the governor, who represented the king's government.

Many of the city's merchants were solid, esteemed citizens like John Watts, who served as an assemblyman and later as a member of the New York Council. Keenly interested in New York City's cultural and social progress, he was a founder and trustee of the New York Society Library and a governor of King's College and the Society of New York Hospital. His financial success was publicly visible in a three-story mansion on Great Dock (now Pearl) Street with stables in the rear on Bridge Street, as well as a "country seat"— Rose Hill, 131 acres of woods and meadowland with frontage and a landing on the East River between what is now East 24th Street and Kips Bay—plus numerous properties in Westchester and Dutchess counties and elsewhere.

Watts had a look of authority about him—a prominent hooked nose, heavy eyebrows, sharp eyes with a penetrating, questioning quality. All his business letters contain flashes of his lively sense of humor about human failings. (Commenting on the famous *Commentaries* by Sir William Blackstone, the distinguished British jurist, he observed that they brought the "mysterious Business [of the law] to some System besides the System of confusing other People & picking their Pockets, which most of the Profession understand pretty well. . . .") His candor and inquiring nature are evident in his correspondence with such English political figures as the former governor-general Robert Monckton. After the general departed for London, Watts looked after his affairs and saw to it that he received half of the salary owed him, the rent from property he owned, and wines of the finest quality that Watts had set aside for him.

Watts was married to James DeLancey's sister Ann, by whom he had seven surviving children close enough in age that he fancied they "will cut me out work enough till they are all provided for," and he took a warm, fatherly interest in their education, marriages, and future careers. Essentially conservative and a stalwart of the court party, he had an innate sense of fair play and usually managed to see both sides of an issue. He was frequently bemused by the frosty Cadwallader Colden, whom he referred to as "the old gentleman" or "the old Man," but he took strong exception to such actions of the lieutenant governor as his move to strengthen Fort George "as if he had been at Bergen-op-Zoom when the French besieged it." Despite his skepticism over Grenville's policies and his belief that they might even result in independence for the colonies, he believed strongly that America's future lay within the empire and he remained determinedly loyal to the king.

Watts was no admirer of the Sugar Act. He had wished the old one amended or scrapped entirely, and he regarded the new duty of threepence as excessive—"injurious," he called it. What was more, the act "certainly cramps Navigation & Shipping, which helps to keep a Community alive, Stops up . . . many of the Outlets to the Brittish Manufactorys, & not a little disables the Colonys from paying for those they import." In the long run, he predicted, England would be the loser from this folly.

New York's Assembly concurred. In an address to Cadwallader Colden, that body expressed hope that peace with the Indians would free New Yorkers from further military expenses, allow them to retire war debts, and "enable us to pay those Taxes which the present and increasing Scarcity of Cash renders extremely burthensome." Then, turning to the issue at hand, they urged the lieutenant governor to join them in securing "that great Badge of English Liberty, of being taxed only with our own Consent." And on October 18, 1764, the assemblymen adopted a memorial to the House of Commons stating that exemption from the burden of involuntary taxes must be the guiding principle of every free country. That exemption was not a privilege—it was a *right*, whose deprivation would "dispirit the People, abate their Industry, discourage Trade," and introduce poverty and slavery, eventually turning the colonies into "a dreary Wilderness" while impoverishing Great Britain. On the same day, the legislature appointed a committee to correspond with the assemblies of other colonies about the Sugar Act and appointed Robert R. Livingston to lead it.

Increasingly, speakers and pamphleteers began to question the right of the ministry and Parliament to perpetrate these outrages. Were they not an infringement on the rights of Englishmen? As James Otis of Boston saw the situation, the Sugar Act set people to thinking, in six months, more than they had done in their whole lives before.

It had been an extremely trying year for George Grenville and his sovereign. Four days after the king closed the spring session of Parliament in 1763 with a speech praising the Peace of Paris, an article appeared in Issue No. 45 of a relatively new weekly publication called *The North Briton,* accusing the ministry of putting lies into the mouth of George III, condemning the peace treaty, and characterizing Grenville and his colleagues as "wretched tools of Bute, who, to their indelible infamy, have supported the most odious of his measures, the late ignominious peace."

The attack, which shocked London, was written by John Wilkes, founder of *The North Briton.* An ugly, brilliant, witty lecher, with squint eyes and the nose of a boxer, Wilkes was also a member of Parliament who was widely known as an impecunious, dissolute champion of liberal causes. The son of a nouveau riche distiller, at thirty-eight years of age he had the reputation and look of the devil* and was continually in debt and eager for fame and fortune. Surely nothing could have brought notoriety quicker than his daring insults to the ministry and the king himself, of whose crown he said, "I lament to see it sunk even to prostitution." Yet Edward Gibbon, the historian, impressed with his "inexhaustible spirits, infinite wit and humour," said he had "scarcely ever met with a better companion."

For months every facet of the Wilkes affair was trumpeted by the press. The king and his ministers decided Wilkes must be punished and had him arrested on a general warrant in which he was not named, along with forty-eight others charged as being implicated in the attack. Almost at once Wilkes became the darling of the discontented, while at the same time he was applauded by many middle-class Englishmen who resented the domination of politics by the landed gentry. He was bundled off to the Tower of London

---

*A savage caricature by Hogarth shows him holding a liberty cap atop a staff, his hair curled to resemble the devil's horns, his expression a sinister leer.

John Wilkes, by William Hogarth.
Laurie Platt Winfrey, Inc.

while his home was ransacked and his papers searched, but he continued to defy the authorities, sued for his release, won on grounds that he was privileged as a member of Parliament, and then was awarded £1,000 on grounds that an illegal warrant had been issued for his arrest.

Wilkes's moment in the sun was brief, but it produced a series of victories with an abiding effect. Establishing the illegality of general warrants was a triumph for individual rights. His attacks on Parliament revealed how unrepresentative of the people it was, how corrupt, and how subservient to the crown. And not least, by his actions and shameless self-promotion he exposed the folly of the government's rash acts to an increasingly informed public that began to seek a role in politics.

A blanket indictment of *The North Briton* by Frederick, Lord North, denouncing it as "a false, scandalous, and seditious libel," was approved by a large majority in Parliament. The Earl of Sandwich—a former drinking companion of Wilkes's—unearthed an obscene parody of Pope's "Essay on Man" called "An Essay on Woman," and Wilkes was accused of writing it. Wilkes was expelled from Parliament, copies of *The North Briton* were burned by the public hangman, Wilkes was badly wounded in a duel by a thug who was probably paid to attack him, another attempt was made on his life, and finally he slipped away to France, where he spent the next four years living on contributions from his supporters. Behind him he left a changed political landscape in which thoughtful citizens were forced to come to grips with such fundamental issues as Parliamentary privilege of a member, Parliament's right to hold debates in secret, the right of the press to report on Parliamentary debates, and the right of a constituency to be represented by a delegate of its own choice.

Whether or not Wilkes recognized the significance of his role, he proved to be a harbinger of a growing hostility toward Parliament that was to polarize relations between Britain and her American colonies. And thanks to Wilkes, ordinary people in London and provincial English towns were made aware that their constitution was threatened by a Parliament that was corrupt and unrepresentative of the people's wishes. Nor was the lesson lost on Americans. To a great number of them the man George III called "that devil Wilkes" became the very personification of liberty.

On the reverse side of the coin, the combination of the Wilkes affair and the growing tide of protest in the colonies provoked a new, more strident conservatism in London. There, as in America, the political scene was increasingly fluid, with the opposing forces moving ever closer toward a collision.

7

A Stamp Tax

In March 1764, Parliament passed a resolution offered by George Grenville, affirming its right to tax the colonies and stating, in what seemed almost an afterthought, that "it may be proper to charge certain stamp duties in the said colonies and plantations. . . ." Curiously, Grenville decided not to take action on a stamp tax until the next session, saying that he wished to sound out the colonies on the matter, while suggesting that the Americans could take advantage of the hiatus to offer objections to the tax or suggest an equivalent method of raising the necessary revenue—even to the extent of taxing themselves. In fact he had no such idea in mind, but the delay was a major mistake. A little knowledge may have been as dangerous as full disclosure, and the resulting apprehension among the provincials turned quickly to resentment and anger, while the postponement gave colonial legislatures time to ponder the implications of a stamp tax. It did not take long for them to act.

A group of legislators in Connecticut, including Governor Thomas Fitch, came forth with the notion that the trans-Allegheny lands belonged to the crown, not the colonies; therefore the latter should not be charged for their defense. But very quickly the protests became widespread and focused on something entirely different—the rights of colonials, as British subjects, to be represented in Parliament if they were to be taxed by that body.

A great many Americans had read, or heard about, James Otis's 1764 treatise "The Rights of the British Colonies Asserted and Proved," in which he argued that every colonial subject of the king was "entitled to all the natural, inherent, and inseparable rights of our fellow subjects in England," and that any taxes imposed on Americans without their consent violated their rights as British subjects.

The debate over America's representation in Parliament soon intensified on both sides of the Atlantic, and an example of the colonial view came from a New Yorker who urged that representatives from each colony be given seats in the House of Commons. No law limited the number of members to 550, he said, so surely there was no reason why "two Gentlemen should not represent a whole colony, as well as a little Cornish borough of ten barns and an ale house."

The attitude of Englishmen who supported the ministry was expressed by a Londoner who signed himself Pacificus. The New Yorker's idea was preposterous, he stated unpacifically. "The Mother Country has a supreme Power over her Colonies; . . . they were settled for her Benefit; and are to be made subservient to her interests." What's more, the loyalty of Americans was suspect: they had ungovernable tempers and were inclined to "disorderly practices." Virginians, he observed, were libertines, New Englanders a crabbed race, not unlike "their half-brothers, the Indians, for unsocial principles and an unrelenting cruelty." What sensible Briton would permit American representatives to serve in the House of Commons? "Would our morals be safe under Virginian legislators, or would our church be in no danger from pumpkin senators?" Surely Britain would never yield up her birth rights to satisfy the whims of Virginians, who are "far fitter for an engagement with our Covent-garden ladies" than with British regulars, or to the "pumpkin gentry" of New England, who are "the joke of America."

In any event, the peevish Londoner concluded, the idea that Americans might rebel over such an unimportant dispute as the stamp tax is "merely chimerical . . . a silly Utopian fancy which can never be midwifed into existence."

The first real outburst against Grenville's announcement that a stamp tax was in the offing came from Samuel Adams, the lisping, palsied, impecunious Boston politician who was, somewhat ironically, collector of taxes for that town. (As his constituents were amused to report, he was not opposed to *all* taxes—only those imposed by the British.)

Adams may not have been an accomplished tax collector but he was a master propagandist, and when charged with providing instructions to members of Boston's Assembly on how to deal with the threatened stamp tax, he wrote: "If Taxes are laid upon us in any shape without our having a legal

George Grenville.
Laurie Platt Winfrey, Inc.

Representation where they are laid, are we not reduced from the Character of free Subjects to the miserable State of tributary Slaves?" If our trade is to be taxed, our lands will be next, he predicted, then the produce of our lands and everything else we own—all of which strikes at our "Brittish Privileges." And where would it end?

During 1764 six colonies—Massachusetts, Rhode Island, Connecticut, New York, New Jersey, and Virginia—took a stand against the Grenville tax program. The General Assembly of New York attacked the plan submitted to Parliament "to impose Taxes upon the Subjects *here,* by Laws to be passed *there,*" which would "reduce the Colonies to absolute ruin." Without immunity or protection from ungranted, involuntary taxes, the complaint continued, there can be no liberty, no happiness, no security. Writing to a friend, William Smith, Jr., reported that New Yorkers "have fearful Apprehensions of being soon burdened by internal Taxes," a concern common to all the colonies.

Writing to his father in June of 1764, Robert R. Livingston passed along news from England indicating that "the ministry appear to have run mad." The stamp duty was reportedly deferred until it was clear whether the colonies would "take the yoke upon themselves," but already New Yorkers were talking about what they would do if the tax was levied. "They will wear nothing but homespun; another will drink no wine because it must pay a duty;

another proposes to dress in sheepskin with the wool on." The resentment was so general, he added, that if a French army of only three thousand men were to land in the colonies, "I doubt whether they would meet with any opposition from the inhabitants."

A month later Livingston was writing Henry Beekman, the merchant, to say that the only news from England was "bad prospects." A reliable source—a member of Parliament and an officer in the Treasury—had written to say the stamp duty would definitely be levied, and beyond that the ministry "think of no other yet but a duty on negroes, a poll tax, which I think will make negroes of us all, what the consequences of these things will be God knows. . . . I much fear that we are in the greatest danger of ruin."

Thanks to Grenville's casual prediction of a stamp tax and rumors like those Livingston had heard, the groundwork for what amounted to a legal brief denying Parliament's right to tax the colonies was being put together in America (notably by lawyers, who were likely to be major victims of such a levy). Remarkably, although the opposition was largely unplanned and unco-ordinated, it was beginning to resemble a united front, whose common theme was quite simple: Taxes require consent by the colonies. Consent requires that the colonies be represented in Parliament. But since the distance between colonies and motherland is too great to permit real representation, the power to tax must reside in the colonial legislatures, where the colonists *are* represented.

Grenville, of course, had no intention whatever of deferring to the colonies or giving them a voice in the matter and had already assigned to Thomas Whately, one of two undersecretaries at the Treasury, the task of preparing the tax legislation. Writing to Richard Temple, surveyor general of the customs in North America, Whately inquired what the Americans might think of a stamp duty. "To Us," he explained, "it appears the most eligible of any [tax], as being equal, extensive, not burthensome, likely to yield a consid-erable Revenue, and collected without a great number of officials." The last point was important: in England, where a stamp tax had existed since 1694, it was said to be "self-collecting."

So in August the Earl of Halifax sent a letter to Cadwallader Colden in New York and other governors, requesting a list "of all Instruments made use of in publick Transactions, Law Proceedings, Grants, Conveyances, Securities of Land or money . . ." on which "certain Stamp Duties" might be charged. (Colden, pleading inability to prepare such a formidable list accurately, turned the job over to New York's attorney general, who complied.)

. . .

Again, distance and the difficulty of communications conspired to drive America and Britain farther apart. Beyond any legal justification for objecting to a stamp tax, many Americans had pressing financial reasons for resisting any increase in the cost of living. The late war against the French had effectively ended after 1759, at which time the action shifted to the Caribbean. With that, military contracts ended and immediately New York, which was a supplier of arms and matériel, felt the pinch. Oliver DeLancey, his partner Beverly Robinson, and the mayor John Cruger, who had all benefited handsomely from supplying the armed forces, saw profits fall off dramatically. John Watts, who dealt in spirits, once rejoiced that the military was "exceedingly publick Spirited in the Consumption of strong Liquors," but with the pullout of British troops local tavern-keepers were left with nothing but a memory of those happier days. Watts said he now had his hands full with his sons, with not enough business to employ them, "which is the worst Situation a Youth can be in." The province's income from a duty on incoming cargoes dropped by one-half. During the war some 128 privateers had been fitted out in New York, and in the first years of the conflict they brought in £200,000 in prizes, which profited such owners as Alexander McDougall by an estimated £7,000 and Isaac Sears by £2,000 or more, with many levels of the citizenry sharing directly or indirectly in the booty. Now, with France and Spain defeated, no prey remained for the privateers, and all New York was the poorer for it. As the effects of the Sugar Act were felt, the number of debtors rose, rents increased, and the cost of firewood soared, as did the price of food. These were bad times.

Quite apart from objections to a stamp tax on legal grounds, many Americans could plead personal hardship. Nature itself seemed to be against them. In 1761 and 1762, drought hit the northeast, affecting the production of hay for livestock as well as corn and grains, which were major food crops. The next two years saw a series of killing frosts in May and early June, and in 1760, 1761, and 1764, early-September frosts also hit the crops. All too frequently, spring plantings of corn, killed after the plants first leafed out, had to be reseeded at great cost in time, seed, and precious specie, while early-fall frosts cut the season short and meant an immature or badly damaged crop. With poor harvests, farm families—and their customers—often had to do without.

On the farms, surpluses were essential. Without sufficient hay to fill his barn, a farmer could not hold on to the calves he planned to sell in the spring and had to let them go before they could bring good money. Too often the shortage of feed meant less meat for the family, as well, and the ripple effect was that the cost of food rose on what the merchants exported and on what the growing urban population ate.

The notion of using a stamp tax to raise money in the colonies had been around for a long time—in fact, a royal governor had proposed it for New York as early as 1734. One of its enthusiastic advocates, Henry McCulloh, who had spent a number of years in North Carolina, thought it was such a good idea that when he returned to England in 1747 he declared himself an adviser to the government on colonial affairs and began lobbying for a stamp tax.

McCulloh was of Scottish descent and for decades had engaged with single-minded passion in land speculation. Typical of his operations was a patent he obtained for 54,000 acres, rights to which he sold to friends in Ireland while promising to pay the quitrents. Not surprisingly, he never made those payments, and when McCulloh became commissioner of quitrents in the colony he saw to it that those who had purchased land from him were exempted from doing so. McCulloh was a man with an eye to the future and an ear to the ground, a trait he cultivated by holding a position in the colonial customs service and having a young protégé of his made governor of the province.

His land deals were facilitated no end by the fact that no one knew exactly where North Carolina's boundary with South Carolina was, enabling him to offer huge, vaguely defined parcels to a variety of speculators. In the 1740s and 1750s he disposed of some 525,000 acres; under an agreement with Lord Granville, the earl received 175,000 acres while McCulloh retained 300,000; and in 1765 McCulloh gave up 339,325 acres to the crown, keeping 129,335 for himself and his children.

As a self-styled expert on colonial affairs, he did make some constructive suggestions to the government. One was that Britain should issue a uniform, interest-bearing paper currency for all the colonies. Another was that duties on molasses from the West Indies be lowered to an affordable level to discourage smuggling. And as early as 1751 he wrote to the Earl of Halifax urging that "all Writings, Deeds, Instruments or other matters relating to the law in the said Provinces should be on Stamp Paper or Parchment," purchased from the crown, with the proceeds to be devoted "Only to the Security and Advantage of the Colonies."

By 1763 McCulloh was old and jobless, but still seeking profit or place—or both—in the colonies, and in July he sent an unsolicited proposal to the Treasury, outlining his thoughts on how to curb the colonial trade in contraband goods, as well as his plan for a stamp tax. It could hardly have appeared at a more opportune moment, for Charles Jenkinson, an undersecretary at the Treasury, was just then conducting exhaustive studies for Grenville on the best methods of increasing revenue from America. Jenkinson was keenly aware of the first minister's determination to eliminate smuggling and knew he would be interested in McCulloh's belief that a stamp tax would raise £60,000 or more annually. And he figured Grenville should heed McCulloh's warning that the Americans "have always given great opposition to any [duties] passed here, and . . . conceived very wrong notions of their privileges." Shortly after his proposal reached the prime minister, McCulloh learned that the plan was approved in principle and he was employed as a consultant, assigned to redraft his suggestions and create a plan for a general stamp law throughout America and the West Indies. As it turned out, Jenkinson had also engaged another man with similar ideas, one Thomas Cruwys, who was working separately on the same project.

By the autumn of 1764, both men had completed their task, each having arrived at a different projection of how much revenue would be raised by a stamp tax. McCulloh's estimates had skyrocketed to the astonishing figure of £500,000 a year, but his calculations were predicated on collecting the monies not only for defense but to defray the costs of a civil list to administer the colonies. Grenville vetoed that scheme and, to McCulloh's great disappointment, accepted Cruwys's plan and had him draft the final bill for submittal to the Lords of Trade in January of 1765.

While this was going on, Grenville held a number of meetings with agents for the colonies. These well-placed individuals were authorized to look after the interests of their clients in America and constituted the real channel of communications between each colony and officials in England. As quasi-ambassadors, they could commit colonial governments to certain agreements, but they were also paid lobbyists who forwarded news, documents, and petitions, obtained acceptance of legislation passed by colonial assemblies, resolved land disputes, handled finances in London for the colonies, and did their best to prevent hostile bills from passing in Parliament. It goes without saying that they had to know the right people.

For example, the agent for the New York Assembly, Robert Charles, had important connections with such luminaries as the dukes of Argyle and Newcastle and Admiral Sir Peter Warren, whose recommendation to James DeLancey launched Charles on a twenty-two-year relationship with the colony of New York. Charles was a haughty, insolent man, by all accounts, known to Whitehall's bureaucrats as a "conspicuous busybody." Frequently caught in the middle of New York's perennially vicious factionalism, on several occasions he encountered difficulties in London because of Cadwallader Colden's animosity toward him and interference with his activities. Charles was never financially secure, and his continuing worries about losing his job finally led to his suicide in 1775.

Of all the colonial agents in London, Benjamin Franklin was the most accomplished. He began representing Pennsylvania in 1757 and served in London until 1775, during which time he recognized the need for unity among his fellow lobbyists and became the dean of what was, by 1765, an eighteen-man group.

In the wake of Grenville's vague announcement in March 1764 that a stamp tax would be forthcoming, eight colonies sent formal protests to Parliament, after which Grenville, hoping to mollify the Americans while quietly and determinedly pushing ahead with his plans, arranged to meet a representative group of agents—Charles Garth and Richard Jackson, who were both members of Parliament, and Jared Ingersoll of New Haven and Franklin of Philadelphia, who were most *au courant* about the colonies. Almost certainly, these men realized by now that Grenville had decided a year ago to impose a stamp tax, and they warned him that "'twill forever be dangerous to America that [the colonies] should be taxed by the authority of a British Parliament." The reason, they went on, was the great distance between Britain and America, which prevented a genuine familiarity or even acquaintance of one for the other, resulting in mutual jealousy and ill will.

Serenely confident that what he was doing was right, Grenville was reassuring to the agents—the soul of reasonableness. Why, self-interest alone would keep England from overburdening the colonies and damaging the relationship, he said. In the House of Commons, he argued that "the colonies were all virtually represented in Parliament, in the same manner as the subjects in Great Britain, who did not vote for representatives." By now he may have recognized that a docile acceptance of a stamp tax was not in the cards, but he had made a commitment to Parliament that he would levy such a tax and he firmly intended to go forward with it.

At the same time, he was telling members of Parliament, most of whom knew little or nothing about America, how prosperous the colonies were, and spoke of their "opulence." (A letter from a Londoner to a friend in New York echoed Grenville's opinion, saying, "The Report of your Gaiety and Luxury has reached your Mother Country; and they infer from thence your Opulency, which is further confirmed by the extravagant Expences of your Youth sent here for Education, and therefore you are well able to bear Part of the expences your Defence has cost the Nation. . . .")

Behind all the fuss about stamps, Grenville told his colleagues in Commons, you have to realize that the Americans are no different from anyone else—they don't like paying taxes. But members should not forget how much Britain had suffered in behalf of the colonies, and he was only doing his duty in insisting that the provincials pay their fair share. Indeed, if Parliament failed to tax them now it would set a precedent for the years ahead. The colonies must "remain dependent," he added firmly, and "they must be subject" to Parliament. "If [they] are not subject to this burden of tax, they are not entitled to the privilege of Englishmen."

Continuing, he assured doubters that a stamp tax would not affect the poor—only the rich, and America was full of wealthy men. Then he closed by stating piously that the stamp tax "is founded on that great maxim that protection is due from the governor, and support and obedience on the part of the governed."

During the debate the former secretary at war, Charles Townshend, referred to the colonials as "these . . . children planted by our care, nourished by our Indulgence . . . and protected by our Arms," and then asked, "will they grudge to contribute their mite to relieve us from the heavy weight of that burden which we lie under?" At this, Colonel Isaac Barré rose, "and with Eyes darting Fire and an out-stretched Arm," according to the newspaper account received in New York, replied in words that quickly made his name a household word in the colonies.* A veteran of the French and Indian Wars who had been wounded at Quebec, Barré was an eloquent spokesman for the Americans and responded heatedly to Townshend. "Children planted by your care? No! your oppression planted them in America; they fled from your tyranny into a then uncultivated land, where they were exposed to almost all the hardships to which human nature is liable. . . . They nourished up by your indulgence? They grew by your neglect of them. . . . They protected by your arms? They have nobly taken up arms in your defence. . . ."

*Barré and Wilkes became eponyms of Wilkes-Barre, Pennsylvania.

But eloquence was not what produced votes, as the first reading of the bill on February 6, 1765, revealed: the vote was 245 in favor to 50 opposed. Afterward, when petitions from the colonies were introduced, the House of Commons refused even to consider them. The one from New York, in fact, was regarded as so inflammatory that agent Robert Charles could find no member of the House willing even to present it.

On March 22, 1765, the long, complicated, sixty-three-section Stamp Act became a statute of the realm. George III was ill at the time, suffering from a worrisome pain in the chest, coughing, fever, a fast pulse, and fatigue,* and was urged by his physicians to stay quiet, so a special commission gave the bill the royal approval. Finally, to allow time for the necessary paper to be produced, stamped, and shipped across the Atlantic while giving Americans time to digest the terms of the tax, the new levy was not to take effect until November 1, 1765.

For a number of reasons, the ministry viewed a stamp tax as an ideal vehicle for raising revenue in the colonies. In England the crown had a monopoly on the sale of paper and in order to preserve the monopoly had ruled that papers used for certain purposes had to be stamped in order to be legal. Accepted without question by the British public, the so-called stamps were in fact impressions embossed on sheets of paper by means of a die in a screw-type press. The stamps designed for use in America were from one to one and a half inches high and looked like a modern notary public's seal. Since the clear impression of the seal was difficult to see on parchment, small blue or beige squares of paper, slightly larger than the die, were embossed, glued to the parchment, and reinforced with a staplelike device in case the glue dried out.

Various decorative embossing patterns were used—the Tudor Rose, the Cross of St. George, the arms of George III on a shield, for instance—and usually bore the words "AMERICA" and the motto "Honi Soit Qui Mal Y Pense," the crown, and the denomination of the stamp in pounds, shillings, or pence.

According to the act, a user had to buy the necessary stamped paper or parchment from a stamp distributor, who not only dispensed the paper but collected the tax. There seemed no end to the items on which the stamp tax was levied—playing cards and dice, pamphlets, licenses to sell liquors,

---

*His ailment was diagnosed nearly two centuries later as the onset of a rare disease, porphyria, which worsens with the passage of time and attacks the brain.

diplomas for college graduates, licenses to practice law. Courts of law would be awash in stamped paper—wills, deeds, land transfers, judgments, subpoenas, depositions, affidavits; almost every legal document required a stamp. To complicate matters further, different classes of documents demanded different rates, so that a deed for less than 100 acres took a one-shilling-sixpence stamp; 100 to 200 acres required a two-shilling stamp; 200 to 320 acres a two-shilling-sixpence stamp, and so on.

All American ships leaving port for a foreign destination were required to have their bills of lading and clearance papers on stamped paper before they could sail. If they failed to comply and arrived without the proper documents the captain was subject to severe punishment.

Perhaps the heaviest burden fell on editors and publishers, since every sheet of paper in a newspaper, pamphlet, or almanac had to be stamped, and every advertisement in a publication was separately taxed. This meant, of course, that consumers would have to pay substantially higher prices for their reading matter. Nor was the process as simple as taking unstamped paper to the distributor to be stamped: on the contrary, only paper that had been stamped in England could be used, which spelled ruin for several score colonial paper mills. Worst of all, stamped paper had to be paid for in hard currency—pounds sterling—which was chronically in short supply in the colonies. And to compound the problems, violations were to be tried in admiralty courts, where a royally appointed judge—not a jury—rendered the verdict.

As may be imagined, all this put immense demands on stamp commissioners in Britain, who had to estimate the amount of paper and parchment needed by each of the colonies, on the English paper mills, which had to supply sheets of paper in numerous sizes and stamped denominations, and on ships that carried the huge tonnage of paper from England to North America and the British islands. Four vessels laden with paper for New York alone sailed between the end of July and September 20, 1765.

To handle the sale of stamped paper in the colonies, stamp distributors were to be appointed, and on the somewhat dubious premise that Americans known to local people would be more acceptable than Englishmen, Grenville let it be known that he preferred colonials for the job (the more "discreet and reputable" the better, Benjamin Franklin reported). Not only would the appointees have a say in the choice of subdistributors, thereby heightening the prospects of patronage and power, but the pay was rumored to be large and the responsibility great. Not surprisingly, the job was considered a plum and a number of Americans began pulling strings to be named.

The colonial agents, lulled by Grenville's assurances of how rational this project was, helped with the selection of stamp distributors. Franklin, for instance, saw to it that his Philadelphia friend John Hughes was appointed and persuaded Jared Ingersoll to take the job in Connecticut. Andrew Oliver, the secretary of Massachusetts Bay and brother-in-law to Thomas Hutchinson, was to be the distributor in Boston. In Virginia, Richard Henry Lee applied for the post but was passed over in favor of Colonel George Mercer, a planter and member of the General Assembly.

Grenville began deciding on these appointments on April 3, 1765, but the names were not immediately released. Indeed, in at least one instance, a man did not know he was the appointee until a ship carrying a consignment of stamped paper addressed to him arrived in port. And not until the names were made public did anyone conceive what fury would be released with their disclosure.

By mid-April the king felt well enough to deal with affairs of state, but he recognized that his illness had been quite serious and found it unnerving to contemplate what could have happened had he not survived. So his first order of business was to have a bill enacted providing for a regency in case he was again incapacitated for any length of time. The second item on his agenda was to get rid of Grenville. The king had had enough of him.

Once George became aware that patronage meant power, he bitterly resented his first minister's invasion of what was clearly the crown's prerogative. "No office fell vacant in my department," he complained, but what Grenville declared he could serve no longer unless the man he recommended was appointed. And all the while Grenville pecked away at the king's expenditures, lecturing him on economies at every opportunity.

The royal patience finally snapped when Grenville introduced the bill to establish a regency council, naming the king's wife, his uncle, and his younger brothers as members. But George's mother, Augusta, Dowager Princess of Wales, was conspicuously missing from the list, and the king was furious. What appeared to be a gratuitous slight was more likely an inexcusable lack of tact by Grenville, Halifax, and Sandwich, who had drafted the bill, but no matter. The king decided to invite Pitt to form a ministry. But Pitt was ill, he would accept only under conditions the king would not grant, and the monarch suffered the humiliation of recalling Grenville. In June, however, Grenville left London for the country, giving the king the opportunity to say he had resigned. Now he turned to the young, inexperienced Marquis of Rockingham and the dukes of Newcastle and Grafton, convinced that they had "principles and therefore cannot approve of seeing the Crown dictated to by low men."

Before Grenville stepped down, he had a final stormy audience with the king on July 10, during which he bluntly warned him, "as he valued his own safety," not to permit anyone "to separate or draw the line between his British and American dominions." The latter, he said, were "the richest jewel of his crown" and anyone who attempted to undermine the Grenville ministry's regulations affecting America should be dealt with as "a criminal and the betrayer of his country." And with that, George Grenville joined the opposition at the very moment that colonial reaction to his policies came to a head and the American problem became a flashpoint of British politics, driving a wedge between friends and political allies.

Even out of office, Grenville worked tirelessly to persuade the House not to yield an inch to American entreaties, not even to receive, let alone consider, such moderate efforts at compromise as a petition from Massachusetts Bay for relief from the Stamp Act. Grenville understood, as few others did, that Britain was going to find it increasingly difficult to govern and control her colonies, and this realization lay behind the reform program he had devised to exact increased revenues from the Americans while simultaneously ensuring the government's domination of them. The likelihood that this might succeed was what produced disaster.

Ignoring the numerous signs of dissatisfaction and malaise, he had plunged ahead with his plans, all the while seeking to calm Americans with honeyed, reassuring words, telling them it was not his purpose to abridge their rights. But the colonials, sure that he was deceiving them, never believed him. As James Otis put it, "'Tis possible he may have erred in his kind intentions . . . and taken away our fish, and given us a stone."

Unluckily for Grenville and his successors, the introduction of his program happened to coincide with widening poverty in America's cities. Not only were the prosperous times of the war years over, now there was a heightened sense that the rich were getting richer and the poor poorer, that the class divide that had existed from the earliest times was worsening. Less fortunate Americans began to suspect that the stamp duties would only widen the gap between the top levels of society and everyone else.

Logically enough, the colonials most likely to capitalize on this malaise were those most adversely affected by the stamp duties—editors, publishers, and lawyers. It seems to have escaped the notice of the Grenville ministry that these were the people in the best position to voice complaints about the tax, the people best equipped to propagandize against it.

It was the loveliest time of year in Virginia as the month of May and the session of the House of Burgesses were winding down, with members beginning to leave for their homes and plantations before the fearsome heat and humidity descended on Williamsburg. Most of the older legislators, in fact, had already departed, leaving only thirty-nine of the 116 seats occupied. As the voices droned on, detailing mundane issues like road-building and the amount of bounty to be paid on wolves, several spectators stood in the lobby, watching and listening, one of them an unknown visitor from France who recorded in his journal what he saw and heard on that 30th day of the month.

Arriving in Williamsburg at noon, the Frenchman had passed by the lifeless bodies of three Negroes hanging from the town gallows—their reward for having relieved a Mr. Waltho of his purse. Proceeding to the handsome pink brick building where the legislature was sitting, he arrived in time to hear a lively debate on the stamp duties and see a man whose "name is henery" rise and say "he had read that in former times tarquin and Julius had their Brutus, Charles had his Cromwell, and he Did not Doubt but some good american would stand up in favour of his Country. . . ."

This is the only known contemporary eyewitness account of the fiery speech delivered by the twenty-nine-year-old first-term delegate from Hanover County—Patrick Henry. A former farmer and storekeeper who was known as a pretty fair fiddler and a first-rate storyteller, Henry had read law for a year and acquired a reputation as a skillful courtroom lawyer. He had a gift for oratory—an extremely useful talent in a day when the spoken word was more often than not the means of disseminating information—and he had already gained a popular following for arguing in court that the crown, in overturning a law passed by Virginia's Assembly, had broken the compact between ruler and the governed.

Over the years, the words he supposedly spoke on May 30 took on the halo of Scripture as "Caesar had his Brutus; Charles the first his Cromwell; and George the Third . . . (cries of 'Treason!' from the Speaker of the House) . . . *may profit from their example.* If *this* be treason, make the most of it!"

According to the Frenchman, the speaker of the House did say that Henry "spoke traison," but contrary to legend, Henry then asked forgiveness for his outburst spoken in the heat of passion, adding that he would remain loyal to

His Majesty George III "to the last Drop of his blood," and attributing what he said "to the Interest of his Countrys Dying liberty which he had at heart."

In the wake of Patrick Henry's emotional speech, the burgesses passed five resolutions—one of which won by a single vote. Two others were either adopted and then expunged or rejected when offered—the record is not clear. What is indisputable is that the resolutions that passed avowed the Virginians' rights as Englishmen "to all the Liberties [and] Privileges . . . as if they had been Abiding and Born within the Realms of England." One such right was to be taxed "by Themselves or by Persons Chosen by Themselves to Represent them." In short, the Virginians were not having any of George Grenville's *virtual* representation.

Conservative members managed to reject or rescind two resolutions. The first had stated that Virginians were "not bound to yield obedience to any law or ordinance designed to impose any taxation upon them other than the laws or ordinances of the General Assembly" of Virginia. The second added that any man who held a contrary opinion "shall be Deemed an enemy to this his Majesty's Colony."

In overruling the radicals' most incendiary resolutions the conservatives may have thought they had put an end to the matter, but they failed to reckon that word of such momentous news would leak almost immediately. Three weeks later the *Newport Mercury* printed a version of them, followed soon afterward by the *Maryland Gazette* and *New-York Gazette,* and before long the so-called Virginia Resolves—which served, one man said, as an "alarum bell"—had inspired similar resolutions from other colonies defining their rights and denying Parliament's power to tax them. Patrick Henry's resolutions had passed by the slimmest of margins, but that was hardly noticed at the time: for all anyone outside Virginia knew, they represented the sentiments of the entire colony.

Less than a month after George Grenville left office the Virginia Resolves were received in London, upon which the ousted first minister labeled them "dangerous and desperate doctrines" which not only accused members of Parliament as "enemies of their country" but asserted that "the sole right of imposing taxes is in themselves." The Resolves were the work of demagogues and hotheads, Grenville charged, and would be recognized as such by responsible people in America, who would soon be convinced that the necessity of having stamped paper made the outcries against it extraneous. But it did not work out that way.

One colonial official who had the same view of agitators in America was Governor Francis Bernard of Massachusetts. On June 8, 1765, the lower house of the Massachusetts Assembly sent a circular letter to the other colonial assemblies, inviting them to attend a congress at New York in October "to consider what dutiful, loyal and humble Address" might be made "to our gracious Sovereign and his Parliament . . . to implore Relief." Despite those honeyed phrases, Bernard saw a sinister motive. At first glance it might seem "only an Occasional measure for a particular purpose," he wrote the Lords of Trade, "yet I have reason to believe that the purposes it is to serve are deeper than they now appear." In his view, the call for an intercolonial meeting was designed "to lay a foundation for connecting the demagogues of the several Governments in America to join together in opposition to all orders from Great Britain which don't square with their notions of the rights of the people. Perhaps I may be too suspicious; a little time will show whether I am or not."

As time would indeed show, Governor Bernard was not far off the mark. Change had been in the wind since 1763—since 1760, in fact. Ever since the war ended, the government's increasingly coercive tax plans had the colonists dumfounded and angry. After all, they had contributed blood and money to that war and now were apparently being told they must pay for it again. As they saw it, George III and his ministers were bent on keeping them subordinate, second-class citizens of a restrictive society such as those which characterized much of Europe.

8

Slavery Fenced Us In

It was October of 1764 and the commander in chief of His Majesty's armed forces in North America was house-hunting in Manhattan. General Thomas Gage, second son of Viscount Gage of Firle, had just arrived in town after enduring three boring years as governor of Montreal, and initially he and his wife—who was pregnant with what would be their third child—were as unlucky in finding a suitable home in New York as Gage had been in building a military reputation in the colonies.

After purchasing a lieutenant's commission in 1741, Gage had seen action in Flanders, had fought in the bloody battle of Fontenoy, and participated in the campaigns that ended the dreams of the Young Pretender, culminating at Culloden. Bringing his regiment to America in 1755, Gage was with Braddock in that ghastly affair on the Monongahela, where he and his advance guard were the first to be fired on by the Indians and French. He did what he could to rally the troops, was wounded, and with George Washington organized a rear guard to cover the retreat. Three years later he took over as second in command of Abercromby's force after Lord Howe was killed near Fort Carillon and once again was an eyewitness to a slaughter of British troops. At the end of that campaign he left the demoralized army and hurried south to marry Margaret Kemble, a tall, slender belle of Brunswick, New Jersey, whose ancestry was equal parts English, Greek, Dutch, and French.

His American record was undistinguished, and one of his admirers observed that although he had been unlucky, he was too nonchalant for his own good. Whatever the case, he did not receive the promotions he thought he

General Thomas Gage, by
Jeremiah Meyer.
National Portrait Gallery, London.

deserved, nor the relief he wanted from the "cursed climate" and lack of culture in what he and his wife regarded as the tiresome backwater of Montreal. New York was far more to their liking.

Gage was a handsome man—thin, of moderate height, with a rather long nose and large eyes, popular with both sexes, dignified, courteous, genial, but viewed by fellow officers as something of a sobersides, since he had no fondness for gambling or drinking. At the time Amherst was recalled, when Pontiac's rebellion was at its peak, Gage had been given temporary command of the British forces, and when Amherst finally declared in September 1764 that he had no desire to return to America, Gage was formally commissioned commander in chief. By then he and his wife had found a proper home—a large double house, surrounded by gardens, on Broad Street. Attractive as it was, it was not in a particularly fashionable setting, since it was across the street from a wigmaker-hairdresser and an embroiderer. But here, for the next nine years, Thomas and Margaret Gage were as happy as at any time in their married life.

Margaret Gage was described by contemporaries as a very pretty woman, but her portrait suggests that she may have been one of those women whose charm and sensitivity spell beauty in the eye of the beholder. More, as an American married to Britain's top military man in the colonies, she was a great asset to her husband, and they were immediately caught up in a swirl of social events, attending the theater, dances, and numerous tea parties, while meeting most of the important visitors to town, and entertaining frequently despite Margaret Gage's many confinements. (All of their children were sent "home" to school at an early age, to be cared for by Gage's parents. Henry, their first child, later became the third Viscount Gage and was reputedly the first British viscount to be born in North America.)

Gage was the most powerful British official in the land, and his family home and his office at Fort George were headquarters for all of the government's military activities on the continent. For months now the general's correspondence with Lord Halifax, secretary of state for the Southern Department, to whom he reported, was almost exclusively devoted to affairs on the frontier. As a result of the Proclamation of 1763 the interdiction of settlement was in the hands of the military, which meant controlling western expansion of the land-hungry colonists. At the same time the military had its hands more than full policing the activities of French settlers, English merchants, Indians, and Indian traders, settling boundary lines, and supervising Indian congresses. Gage was also communicating with subordinates all over the country—Major Gladwin in Detroit, Major Hamilton in Halifax, Colonel Bouquet at Fort Pitt, Colonel Robertson in Florida, and Colonel Bradstreet on Lake Erie, not to mention the two Indian superintendents, Sir William Johnson and John Stuart, who had their own sets of problems.

This was all new ground for Gage, and just when he began to see what an overwhelming task it was, he was faced with an entirely new and even more important challenge, caused by the revenue acts levied by the ministry in London.

Traditionally, provincial opposition to London's policies had been directed against the royal governors and took place mainly in the colonial assemblies. But after 1763, when Parliamentary legislation became a tool used to control the colonies, the situation called for a more organized and united opposition. The legislatures, which were subject to being summoned or dissolved by the governors, were too vulnerable, with the result that opposition came to be centered in extralegal bodies—Sons of Liberty, committees of correspondence, and provincial congresses.

The significance of this phenomenon was that these organizations strengthened the unruly, most vocal elements at the same time they tended to undermine the efforts of moderates, who preferred to channel resistance through accepted governmental entities. Conservatives were handicapped by their attachment to traditional authority and gradually lost their ability to dominate or control any protest movement.

Despite the many changes that had occurred in New York, much remained the same as it had been for several decades. The squabbles and feuds between Anglicans and Presbyterians continued undiminished; other denominations resented the Church of England, supported by taxpayers' money; the Assembly bickered incessantly with the lieutenant governor and the Council, with members of the legislature holding back money from the executive whenever it suited their pleasure. The old political arguments continued as before, bitter and nasty as ever. It often seemed that the one belief virtually all New Yorkers held in common was affection for their king and loyal devotion to him.

In the waning days of 1764 a new, positive idea captured the imagination of a number of New Yorkers. The direct result of worsening economic times was a notice that appeared in the *New-York Gazette* announcing that "a Number of Gentlemen" had decided to form the Society for the Promotion of Arts, Agriculture and Economy. Membership was open to "every real Friend and Lover of his Country, of whatever Rank or Condition" (although sponsorship by the unnamed "Number of Gentlemen" strongly suggested that not *all* ranks would be welcomed). Soon meetings were held on the first Monday of every month, committees were formed, and it was evident that the economy was to be the focus of the organization's agenda. The manufacture of flax, for instance, was especially to be encouraged, since it would enhance the value of land, employ the poor, and save the public considerable expense at a time "when Trade is at a Stand and our english debts increased to an intolerable Burden."

Evidencing the society's determination to support farming, fishing, and mining, an array of prizes was announced, to be awarded for the greatest quantity and quality of potash, linen cloth, tow cloth, and "wove thread" stockings, for tanning the finest belt sole leather, for the best-quality one hundred pairs of women's shoes, the best-dressed deerskins for breeches, the finest beaver-skin gloves, the greatest quantity of roofing tiles, and so on. Before long a gold medal was offered by the society—this to be awarded for the first three flax mills erected in the province—and a committee was appointed to organize the making of flax spinning wheels and looms and present certificates to those farmers producing the greatest quantities of plants such as flax and hemp that were used in making fibers, along with hops, barley, and cheeses. It did not take much imagination to see that the society had it in mind to foster home industries and agriculture at the expense of the British.

As interesting as the range of activities to be encouraged by the society was the membership of the organization—a cross section of the important families, professions, and political opinions that made New York what it was: the New York Establishment. Anglicans and Presbyterians, DeLanceys and Livingstons, merchants and men of the cloth, great Hudson River landowners—luminaries from every important group were represented. Philip Livingston and Leonard Lispenard were on the Committee for Arts. Colonel Philipse and Captain DeLancey were two of the five-member Committee for Agriculture; another Livingston—the lawyer William—with James Jauncey and Isaac Low, served on the Economy Committee; and two other attorneys, William Smith, Jr., and John Morin Scott, were on the Committee for Correspondence.

In New York and elsewhere in the colonies, when the economy turned sour it appeared all but inevitable that the bad times would worsen when the accursed stamp tax became operative. Better to forget our differences, society members seemed to be saying, and for once all the city's factions seemed willing to pull together to set matters straight.

The year began with wicked cold. On January 29 the Hudson was frozen from shore to shore, with ice so solid that horse-drawn carriages flew back and forth across the river. After a year of rumors about the promised stamp tax, the long-awaited January and February mails from England arrived with official word of its passage and its provisions. Four columns in the *New-York Gazette or, the Weekly Post-Boy* listed in numbing detail, paragraph after paragraph (each concluding with an exclamation point emphasizing the sense of shock felt by the editor, John Holt, who observed that they would "make the ears of every American . . . tingle and fill him with astonishment"), the taxes that would affect just about everyone in some way. From a half-penny tax on every pamphlet or newspaper printed on half a sheet of paper or less, to one shilling on a pack of playing cards and ten shillings on every pair of dice, to taxes in varying amounts on every conceivable land transaction, affidavit, judgment, bill of lading, license to practice law or notarize documents, license to sell spiritous liquors or wines, bonds, the appointment of officials, advertisements, almanacs, calendars, and fees paid by apprentices. Nor did foreign-language journals escape. "Every Skin or Piece of Vellum or Parchment, or Sheet or Piece of Paper on which [anything is] ingrossed, written or printed in any other than the English language" was to be charged at double the regular amount.

In the debate in the House of Commons, it was reported, every single member who spoke had declared that America should be taxed, and the initial reaction throughout the colonies was a stunned silence and, as Robert R. Livingston said, "a general disgust." One resident, thinking back on the occasion, said it seemed like a "frightful dream" with every avenue of escape "barred up with a tenfold Guard" so that "Slavery . . . fenced us in on every Side." The Boston cleric Jonathan Mayhew, who regarded resistance as a religious obligation, noted that some colonists were despondent, and that "even the wise and good men, tho' equally against the measure, could not agree . . . what was to be done." The times, John Watts observed, "are as sore as a bile," and he despaired of the ministry's "severity & contempt."

William Smith was quick to see what the consequences would be, saying, ". . . when the Americans reflect upon the Parliament's refusal to hear their Representations . . . and find themselves tantalized and contemned . . . what can be expected but discontent for a while, and in the end open opposition . . . This single stroke has lost Great Britain the affection of all her Colonies."

In June, publisher Weyman announced that his *New-York Gazette* would cease publication until new (and presumably higher-priced) subscriptions took effect. It was the third New York paper to close because of the Stamp Act's punitive terms. And summer's weather remained as oppressive and foreboding as the news. Captain John Montresor's diary entry for July 13 was "a prodigious hot and sultry day" and that night he was "scarce able to exist— very close and cloudy and scarce a breath of air." A week later came "the Hottest day I ever felt." Late in August a violent thunderstorm brought lightning that split the mast of an Albany schooner and killed a man, while September saw foul winds and gales so strong ships could not sail up the Hudson.

Although more than a year had elapsed since Grenville first announced that a stamp tax would be forthcoming, the colonials were remarkably unprepared when reality finally hit home. Early that summer in Boston a group of tradesmen and artisans formed a social club called the Loyal Nine, having concluded that they could not rely on their representative assembly to alter Parliament's decision to tax them. These men were not radicals—far from it—nor were they particularly distinguished. One man, John Avery, Jr., was a Harvard graduate and therefore deemed respectable; another was Benjamin Edes, who with his partner John Gill published the *Boston Gazette;* two were braziers, others a jeweler, a painter, a distiller, a merchant, and a master of a ship. Not only were they not rabble-rousers or troublemakers, it seems likely that they deliberately distanced themselves publicly from Samuel Adams and James Otis, those radical leaders of the Assembly (although they were probably surreptitiously in touch with both of them, as well as John Adams).

By mid-August the Loyal Nine prepared to act. The *Gazette* had published a stream of articles condemning the Stamp Act—on August 12 attacking the stamp distributors as "mean mercenary hirelings . . . who for a little filthy lucre would at any time betray every right, liberty, and privilege of their fellow subjects." By then the Nine had enlisted the services of Ebenezer McIntosh, a shoemaker from the South End, who customarily took his neighbors into violent action against the rival North End gang on Pope's Day, also known as Guy Fawkes Day, November 5. They talked McIntosh into putting his bully boys to better use against the Stamp Act, and on August 14 the action began when the effigy of Andrew Oliver, who was rumored to be the stamp distributor for Massachusetts, was seen hanging from a tree on Newbury Street. Alongside the dummy was a large boot—representing the hated Earl of Bute (who had nothing to do with the Stamp Act)—with the figure of the devil crawling out of it.

Governor Francis Bernard and Lieutenant Governor Thomas Hutchinson were justifiably alarmed. They ordered the sheriff to cut down the effigy, but that gentleman returned shortly to report that his men could do so only at the risk of their lives. McIntosh's men, whose numbers had swelled, headed for a building in which Oliver had his office, destroyed it, and moved quickly to Oliver's home, where they beheaded an effigy of him. Finding the entrance to the house blocked, they tore down the fence, broke in windows and doors, and began destroying the furniture. Fortunately the Oliver family had been warned in time to flee, but the pillaging of the house continued until midnight, when the mob tired of its work and went home. The rioters had wreaked the worst violence in Boston's history.

The following day, several men called on Oliver and suggested that he resign the office of stamp distributor. Since he had not received his commission he really had nothing to resign, but promised to do nothing to carry out the stamp duties and said he would write the authorities in London and request permission to give up his appointment.*

Massachusetts had discovered a way to beat the Stamp Act, and within two weeks the Newport, Rhode Island, stamp man resigned, followed by the distributor in New Jersey. The latter quickly realized the danger he was in when he tried to rent a house and was turned down unless he would insure it against loss or damage.

In New York a local merchant named James McEvers had been named to the post and initially found that people seemed pleased that he, and not a stranger, got the position. But in the wake of the Boston riots, friends warned him that a storm was rising and he would soon feel the brunt of it. In August he wrote Cadwallader Colden, begging him to take possession of the stamped paper when it arrived and stow it safely in Fort George while he appointed another person to distribute it. The cruel fate of Mr. Oliver, said McEvers, had forced him to decline the office, which would be "Attended with very

---

*Oliver eventually got notice of his appointment but as late as November 1, 1765, had not received his official commission as stamp distributor. Nor had Governor Bernard ever received an official copy of the Stamp Act he was required to enforce.

dangerous Consequences," which he went on to enumerate: "My House would have been Pillag'd, my Person Abused and his Majestys Revenue Impair'd." Not daring to leave his fate solely in the lieutenant governor's hands, he wrote a friend in England, explaining that his appointment was so "odious to his fellow citizens" that he had resigned publicly and now beseeched his friend to have someone else appointed stamp distributor. He had worked long and hard in his store, he explained, and at any given moment it contained about £20,000 worth of goods "with which the Populace would make sad Havock." But if he should lose his property, he went on, he hoped he might be reimbursed at least by the amount of income his stamp distributorship would provide if the act was reinforced. (McEvers, to his enormous relief, had acted quickly enough to save his property before the mob destroyed it.)

In Maryland, Zacharias Hood was determined not to resign, even after his house was destroyed, forcing him to flee with nothing but the clothes he wore. Arriving in New York, he found lodging at the King's Arms, but only momentarily. He was discovered there and the landlady, fearing for her own safety, told him he would have to leave. Poor Hood, in bed with a fever, wrote a note to Cadwallader Colden, pleading for sanctuary inside Fort George, and the lieutenant governor took him in. Although it was clearly impossible for him to distribute stamps in Maryland from that vantage point, there he remained, fearing for his life, unable to move, and on November 26 a New York mob forced his resignation.

Jared Ingersoll, the man Benjamin Franklin had persuaded to take the stamp man's job in Connecticut, was forced to resign in September by a mob that seized him and was prepared to lynch him if he did not give up the post. Even after Ingersoll resigned he was kept under strict surveillance by radicals, who opened his outgoing letters, saw that none reached English friends, and kept tabs on the correspondence of Ingersoll's friends. In New York his effigy was paraded through the streets and finally "executed" as people shouted, "There hangs a traitor. There's an Enemy to his Country!" And so it went, in colony after colony. By November, Robert R. Livingston informed a friend, all the stamp distributors "have resigned their offices or have been obliged to desist from all attempts to carry the Act into execution."

In Massachusetts, twelve days after the riot that had destroyed Andrew Oliver's property, mob action took a new, more sinister turn. This time the homes of two royal officials connected with customs and the admiralty court were partially destroyed and ransacked. Then Ebenezer McIntosh, as skilled as any general at manipulating his troops, led a shouting, drunken, rampaging mob to the home of Lieutenant Governor Thomas Hutchinson and wrecked it, tearing out windows and doors, smashing furniture and paintings, stealing cash and silverware, clothes and anything else that was portable, cutting down the trees in the yard, and scattering to the winds the precious documents Hutchinson had collected for his history of the Massachusetts Bay Colony.

This went far beyond any protest of the Stamp Act: it was fed by an intense dislike of Hutchinson, a cold, haughty man of considerable wealth, and, some whispered, by a desire to destroy certain records that implicated local merchants in smuggling, or papers revealing that a certain grant of land had not been made to those who claimed it. But something far more alarming was involved here, for Hutchinson was the local representative of royal authority. Lieutenant governor, chief justice of the colony, and judge of the Suffolk County Probate Court, he was an appointee of the king himself, favored with the salary and patronage and other perquisites of office, and to strike at him was to strike at the institution he represented—the crown of Great Britain. It was small wonder, taking all these factors into consideration, that the well-to-do and well-placed in every other colony experienced a shiver of fear they had never felt before—a terror just as real as that felt by men and women in the lonely cabins on the edge of the wilderness.

Within weeks, personal letters from Massachusetts residents to friends and business associates in the other colonies, sailors aboard coastal vessels, plus copies of newspapers exchanged by one printer with others, had spread the word of these violent acts to every part of the continent.

The circular letter from the Massachusetts Assembly sent in June to speakers of the houses of representatives or burgesses of all "the several Colonies on this Continent" had invited them to "consult together on the present Circumstances of the Colonies." Delegates were to meet in New York City on the first Tuesday in October—the first of the month and one month before the Stamp Act took effect—and on September 16 the brigantine *Caroline* sailed into New York Harbor, bringing three Charleston passengers to the meeting. These delegates from South Carolina, who had the greatest distance to travel, arrived two weeks before the conference began, and a distinguished lot they were. Christopher Gadsden, the oldest of the three at forty-one, was a wealthy Charleston merchant, owner of a large plantation, his own wharf, and stores. Thomas Lynch, three years his junior, was also a member of the landed gentry and owned several estates near Charleston. John Rutledge, who had studied law in England, was, at twenty-six, the youngest man attending the meeting. He had been appointed attorney general of his colony the year before, probably because "He fronts a fact more quickly than anyone I ever knew," as one of his law clients remarked. Like his two colleagues, he was a prominent advocate of resistance to Parliamentary intrusion on the rights of the colonists.

Whether the rest of the delegates to the Stamp Act Congress, as it came to be called, would be as determined in their views as the South Carolinians was anyone's guess, but New York's lieutenant governor was both uneasy and angry about the coming invasion of his territory. Writing to Henry Seymour Conway, now secretary of state for the Southern Department, a week after the South Carolinians arrived, Colden said he "discountenanced" the assembly as "an illegal convention . . . inconsistent with the Constitution of the Colonies" and worried that "Whatever possible pretences may be used for this meeting their real intentions may be dangerous."

Increasingly unpopular with his constituents, disliked by both the Livingston and DeLancey camps (who for once agreed on something), Colden was now virtually alone, facing a hostile populace. "The triumvirate"— William Livingston, John Morin Scott, and William Smith, Jr.—had attacked him repeatedly in the courts and newspapers, most recently in connection with a lawsuit in which a creditor stabbed a debtor in a quarrel over an unpaid debt. In the case of *Forsey* v. *Cunningham,* Colden, crabby and arrogant as ever, insinuated himself into the dispute by asserting that an appeal from the jury's verdict could be heard—not by a higher court, but only by himself and the Council, as representatives of the crown, and that he could reexamine the facts in the case, not just look for legal errors.

As ever, Colden was zealously guarding what he took to be the prerogatives of the king. The triumvirate—and, in this instance, the justices of New York's Supreme Court—opposed him vigorously on a matter that threatened the citizen's right to trial by jury amid increased suspicions that the lieutenant governor was attempting to expand his own power. Lampooned in the press, feeling insulted, Colden took the unfortunate step of publishing a pamphlet vindicating his views on the proper avenue for appeals, the tenure of judges (he had urged the replacement of Justice Robert R. Livingston on grounds of conflict of interest, and the dismissal of the attorney general for incompetence), and—the hottest potato of all—enforcement of the Stamp Act.

John Watts's view was that the "old gentleman's" legal opinion was "so unconstitutional that not one lawyer . . . would draw the writ of appeal," and that Colden's position would "entirely destroy the use of juries & Court too." As a result, he added, "the old body was dislik'd enough, but now [the people] would prefer Beelzebub himself, to him."

Colden also read a long and unwelcome dissertation on the law to members of the Council and a hundred or more other people in attendance at the Council meeting, claiming that his understanding of the points of law at issue was a notable accomplishment and boasting how even a man of eighty could, after a few weeks of reading, be more adept in such matters than the entire legal community.

The result of what William Smith, Jr., called the lieutenant governor's obstruction of justice was that Colden "has inflamed the whole country," making people believe that "the Crown is aiming to deprive the subject of his most valuable rights," and he predicted that the Assembly would vote against every measure recommended by Colden, who was now regarded with the most unreserved disgust.

The worst of this unfortunate matter, as John Watts saw it, was that Colden had created such an uproar "in these sore times" during the Stamp Act troubles, "but like Satan he would damn himself & his posterity to seem great, which he thinks such controversies make him, having an unbounded opinion of his own parts & being on the side of prerogative for which he would sink all America right or wrong."

With the entire legal fraternity and much of the public outraged by his position, Colden faced the city's growing anger over the stamp duties. Talk of the New England riots was on everyone's lips, and tension grew as the town spoke of little but the unpopular act. The approaching Stamp Act conference had been arranged without his consent, Colden complained, he had disapproved of it from the beginning, and although he could do nothing about it, he was sure he would be criticized in Whitehall for permitting the extralegal meeting to take place. The injustice of it was all the more painful inasmuch as he was serving as acting governor until Robert Monckton—who had gone to England in poor health in June of 1763—either returned or was replaced.

For Colden, moreover, the resignation of McEvers as distributor meant that he could not enforce the Stamp Act, since it would not be possible to obtain stamped paper. To make matters worse, an organization calling itself the Sons of Liberty was threatening violence against anyone buying or selling the stamped English paper. And to add to the lieutenant governor's misery, the delegates from eight other colonies were arriving almost daily.

They came singly, by twos and threes, traveling on horseback, by stage, on packet boats and ferry, and New York had never seen anything to equal it. As one of the delegates remarked, they were "an Assembly of the greatest Ability I ever Yet saw," and Manhattan residents agreed. Surely, they could boast, this was the most notable group of American colonists ever to gather in one place. Not even the Albany Congress eleven years earlier had seen so many men of such distinction. Indeed, more men of note would have been present had not the governors of Georgia, North Carolina, and New Hampshire either refused to call their legislatures into session to name delegates, or recessed the assembly, or—in the case of Virginia—dissolved the House of Burgesses so no action could be taken.

New Yorkers could be forgiven for feeling that their city was suddenly the center of the world—a small world, to be sure, but the focus of attention of all Americans. The authors of the Massachusetts circular letter, inviting delegates to the convention, had chosen this city as the site because it was accessible by land or water and was much closer to the southern and middle colonies than New England. Besides, as soon as delegates finished their business—which was expected to be done quickly—petitions for relief from the stamp duties could be sent at once to England.

A few of the delegates knew each other, having met on one occasion or other; many were virtually unknown; but all, it turned out, had served in the legislative bodies of their colonies, and all, it hardly needed saying, were deeply loyal to His Majesty George III, whom they revered. These twenty-seven men, averaging about forty-one years of age (the youngest was twenty-six, the oldest more than sixty-five), were a good cross section of reasonably well-to-do Americans. All but three were American-born. Ten were merchants, ten lawyers, the other seven were men of the land—planters and farm owners.

Eleven years after the first real effort at colonial unity—when the Albany Congress met and drew up its ambitious plan—the second attempt began in the old City Hall on the northeast corner of Wall and Broad streets in New York. None of the delegates knew it, but as background accompaniment to their deliberations, New York City was about to erupt.

9

Petitions and a Dagger

When the twenty-seven delegates to the Stamp Act Congress held their first session on Monday, October 7, 1765, the first order of business was to elect a chairman. Since Massachusetts had called for this meeting, it seemed appropriate for one of that colony's three representatives to be the presiding officer, and Timothy Ruggles was elected, beating James Otis by a single vote—the conservative over the man with the radical reputation. John Watts had only just met Otis but felt he should have been chairman. "Otis aimed at it and would have succeeded," he said, "but they thought as he had figured much in the popular way, it might give their meeting an ill grace, but it is observed Otis is now quite a different man, and so he seemed to me . . . not riotous at all." Caesar Rodney of Delaware also favored Otis, who, he wrote later, "displayed that light and knowledge of the interest of America, which shining like a sun, lit up those stars which shone on this subject afterwards." In fact, Otis's behavior during the congress was not at all "in the popular way" but as dignified and subdued as could be; the insanity that doomed his later years seems not to have afflicted him at this time. But Ruggles it was, and John Cotton, a thirty-seven-year-old Harvard graduate and deputy secretary of the Massachusetts House of Representatives, was chosen to be secretary.*

*Delegates were: Massachusetts—James Otis, Oliver Partridge, Timothy Ruggles; Rhode Island—Metcalf Bowler, Henry Ward; Connecticut—Eliphalet Dyer, David Rowland, William Samuel Johnson; New York—Robert R. Livingston, John Cruger, Philip Livingston, William Bayard, Leonard Lispenard; New Jersey—Robert Ogden, Hendrick Fisher, Joseph Borden; Pennsylvania—John Dickinson, John Morton, George Bryan; Delaware—Thomas McKean, Caesar Rodney; Maryland—William Murdock, Edward Tilghman, Thomas Ringgold; South Carolina—Thomas Lynch, Christopher Gadsden, John Rutledge.

After each day's session the delegates gathered for dinner about four in the afternoon and continued their discussions well into the evening. By all accounts these informal conversations were often spirited, even acrimonious, for these were men of strong convictions, along with regional and other biases. They took care that they were not overheard in their meetings in taverns or private homes, and secrecy was a hallmark of their formal sessions, too, since no member of the public was admitted, nor did information about their sessions reach curious ears outside the meeting rooms. Nothing about the debates or opinions voiced by any of the delegates was recorded, nor did any representative write his own minutes of the proceedings. (William Samuel Johnson kept a diary but confined the entries to where he ate or spent the evening or a notation of the hours the congress opened and adjourned.)

Since everything was off the record, opinions were undoubtedly more candid than would otherwise have been possible, but a frustrating result of the strict confidentiality was that John Cotton's official journal notes the election of Ruggles, the appointment of several committees, the objectives of the congress, and then, in maddening repetition for ten days, states only, "The Congress met according to Adjournment &c as yesterday And then adjourned to 10 Oclock tomorrow Morning."

Judge Robert R. Livingston, in a letter to his father written after entertaining the other delegates at dinner, revealed that the congress, while discussing many minor issues, dealt with "three great points—trials by Juries; a right to tax ourselves; [and] reducing admiralty courts within their proper limits." Although the congress had no legal standing in the British view of affairs, the delegates—who were mostly conservatives—insisted that their deliberations be conducted with scrupulous attention to parliamentary procedure, and the judge was proud of the group's achievement. "Every man amongst us that can contribute anything to this grand work stands on tiptoes & calls himself a Patriot," he observed.

Other New York delegates, as well as merchants like Watts and other "gentlemen of the town," as John Dickinson describes them, were hosts to their fellow congressmen, entertaining them at their homes or, more often, at George Burns's City Arms Tavern. General Gage invited the three Massachusetts representatives to dinner, presumably to question them and give advice, and almost certainly made his opinions known to William Bayard, a delegate from New York and a cousin to Mrs. Gage. The general took a dim view of the proceedings and after seeing who the delegates were described them to Henry Conway, secretary of state for the Southern Department: "They are of various Characters and opinions, but it's to be feared in general that the Spirit of Democracy is strong amongst them. The Question is not of the inexpediency of the Stamp Act, or of the inability of the Colonys to pay the Tax, but that it is unconstitutional and contrary to their Rights. . . ." By "Democracy" Gage did not mean governance by the people; it was his way of saying the colonists were getting out of hand. To be sure, Gage continued, some moderate men were present—enough to give hope to "well Meaning People" that the meeting would draw up a "Modest, decent, and proper Address" to the king and Parliament. But he had little good to say of those noisy elements in the city who would urge delegates "to the most violent, insolent, and haughty Remonstrance." He thought it impossible to predict how much opposition to the Act would be raised in other colonies, but feared "if it is began in some . . . it will soon spread over the rest."

When word of the pending congress first reached London, the Lords of Trade were so disturbed that they wrote at once to the king, stating that "this appears to us to be the first Instance of any General Congress appointed by the Assemblies of the Colonies without the Authority of the Crown, a Measure which we Conceive of dangerous Tendency in itself. . . ." But the wheels of bureaucracy grind slow, and it was two days before a committee of the Lords of Trade reported to the king that "this is a Matter of the Utmost Importance to the Kingdom and Legislature of Great Britain . . . and Proper only for the Consideration of Parliament." Once again, distance was a factor: by the time Parliament was properly informed, the Stamp Act Congress was already in session.

In July, Cadwallader Colden had retired to Spring Hill, his country place in Flushing, Long Island, "for the preservation of my health during the heats of summer." (John Watts's acerbic comment on the lieutenant governor's absence was that "he never sees any of us but in Council & then reluctantly enough, 'tis strange doing business when all confidence, harmony & real respect is banish'd.") When word of the violence in Boston reached the old man, he hurried back to town and urged Gage to beef up the garrison at Fort George (which then consisted of three or four invalids) to protect it "from a Mob or from the Negroes." What threat Negroes may have posed is a mystery, but the fear of a slave uprising was never far beneath the surface. (In 1740, after a series of unexplained fires broke out in the city, panicked citizens believed that Negroes were the culprits and that an insurrection was planned in which inhabitants would be massacred. The consequence of the infamous "Negro plot" was that thirteen blacks were burned at the stake, twenty were hanged, and some seventy deported.)

Recognizing the fort's vulnerability (its guns were "Honey comb'd & the Carriages rotten, and . . . there was no powder in the Fort"), Major Thomas James of the Royal Artillery brought in fieldpieces, howitzers, ammunition, and two companies of artillerymen in early September, but Colden remained ill at ease, knowing he would have to take the heat until the new governor, Sir Henry Moore, arrived. It was clearly his duty to enforce the Stamp Act, and although the presence of British troops was reassuring on the one hand, it made him nervous on the other. With tempers worn thin and the populace thoroughly aroused over the act's likely consequences, the slightest provocation between redcoats and town rowdies might lead to a clash.

After the lieutenant governor asked for a battalion of troops to put down "seditious attempts," General Gage ordered an engineer, Captain John Montresor, to report on what needed to be done to strengthen the fort's defenses. Colden had seen a copy of that report and was not reassured, yet the last thing Gage wanted was to alarm the townspeople, and wisely he told Montresor that whatever precautions were taken should have no "very conspicuous appearance" of rendering the fort stronger. Indeed, he reminded Colden that the military "can do nothing by themselves; but must act wholly and solely in obedience to the Civil Power." When troops were granted, he continued, "they are no longer under my Command." And that, he added, was the way it ought to be "in every Country of Liberty."

The engineer's report left no doubt that the place was in no condition to hold off a determined assault. The works were entirely exposed to rising ground to the north—a deficiency that could only be ameliorated by having three or four frigates in such positions that they could rake those attacking the works. Sorties needed to be blockaded and repaired; firewood must be removed from outside lest it be piled up and used to scale the walls; five thousand crow's feet* should be scattered on the ground to cover salients, sally ports, and other vulnerable spots. The recommendations went on in great technical detail, but it was clear to Colden that much needed to be done.

In the meantime, Gage was offering to send troops to other colonies—wherever they were most needed—an offer that would have been more com-

---

*Four-pointed iron devices similar to a child's jacks (though much larger) used primarily against cavalry.

forting to the several governors who had called for assistance had the small number of regulars not been stationed at remote outposts in the west, Canada, and the Floridas. Nevertheless, Gage—trying to fulfill his responsibilities for maintaining Britain's authority in America, and figuring that New York was of great strategic importance—decided to order some two hundred of his force to Albany and another one hundred to Lancaster, where they would be relatively close to Manhattan. (Even so, no troops reached their destinations until mid-December.)

Hoping to avert the problem of the stamps as long as possible, Colden wrote to Captain Archibald Kennedy aboard HMS *Coventry* urging him to order all ships under his command to ascertain as quickly as possible which vessel arriving off Sandy Hook was bringing the stamped paper to New York. That ship, he said, should anchor offshore until the best means for protecting the stamps was determined.

By mid-September, replying to a request from Jared Ingersoll that Colden "take care of" Connecticut's stamps when they arrived in New York Harbor, the lieutenant governor loftily informed the Connecticut distributor that he should look after his own problems, since Fort George was "crowded with Men & military Stores."

September 23 found Colden writing to Secretary of State Henry Conway, informing him that a "secret Correspondence has been carried on throughout all the Colonies . . . concerted to deter by violence the Distributors of Stamps from Executing their office, and to destroy the stamped Paper when it arrives." But once the stamps were distributed in New York, which he promised to supervise, "I believe the present Bustle will be done." On that same day he wrote his successor, Sir Henry Moore, to assure him that the difficulties he had successfully surmounted would make life easier for Moore. But, he added, "Nothing could give me more pleasure than that you were in this Place at this time, as I am confident that your presence would contribute to bring the People to their senses, who seem now to be running Mad in opposition to the Stamp Act . . . no man can more earnestly desire your speedy arrival than I do."

Little could either man have imagined what would greet Sir Henry upon his arrival, but the violence in Boston preyed on Colden's mind, making him ever more apprehensive of what lay ahead for New York on November 1, when the act took effect. With no one willing to sell the stamped paper, no ships could sail from port, the courts would come to a dead halt, newspapers could not be published, and the Lord only knew what other calamities might be in store.

. . .

Those New Yorkers who were "running Mad in opposition to the Stamp Act" had been aroused by a year-long barrage of handbills, ballads, and letters published in the city's papers, memorials to the houses of Parliament and petitions from the Assembly to the king, and Colden was convinced that the town's prominent lawyers and certain members of the judiciary were behind this incessant propaganda.

As early as May 24, 1764, the New York Assembly had warned that "if the Colonist is taxed without his consent, he will, perhaps, ask a change"—an extraordinary statement for that day. On October 18 of that year—the same day the legislators sent a memorial to the House of Commons complaining of the burden of "involuntary Taxes"—the Assembly appointed a committee to correspond with the legislatures of other colonies on the subject of the Sugar Act, trade, and "the impending Dangers which threaten the Colonies of being taxed by Laws to be passed in Great Britain"—an obvious reference to the proposed stamp tax.

During the late spring and summer of 1765 a small group of merchants who were threatened by what they now knew of the stamp tax decided that it must be resisted. These were not the older, well-established, wealthy merchants like John Watts, but ambitious younger men, on the way up, who had less of a financial cushion to fall back on in hard times. Philosophically they were closely related to the lawyers of the triumvirate, especially John Morin Scott.

It was an article of faith with them that free men had a right to resist the actions of a government that failed to honor its implied contract with the citizens. For them, the seminal event in England's history was the Glorious Revolution of 1688–1689 and the constitution that was its result. That compact demanded that rulers as well as the ruled be subject to laws, and if they failed to do so, resistance was not only legitimate but obligatory. Even so, nothing like revolution had entered the minds of New Yorkers, most of whom believed that resistance must be kept within bounds lest it become anarchy.

At the outset of 1765, many thoughtful Americans had figured that the Stamp Act, as undesirable as it was, would probably be submitted to, albeit with much grumbling. But as the weeks passed, propaganda against the act increased in intensity, resistance grew, and by September the fatalistic attitude of springtime had vanished. The question was no longer if they should resist, but how they would go about it. The violence in Boston and Newport had shown what could be done, the stamp men in other colonies had resigned or fled, and with New York's McEvers out of the way with his resignation, the villain of the despised Stamp Act became Cadwallader Colden.

The most vocal opponents of the act were the young merchants and members of the middle class. Men of like mind, they met in the city's taverns and coffeehouses, scheming for hours on end about what they could do and how best to go about it. Without thinking of their group in a structured, organizational sense, they began calling themselves sons of liberty—a term that had been around for a long enough time to have become generic. To them, the phrase signified that they were inheritors of a freedom won by their parents and grandparents who had come to North America from Europe in search of a new life. Recently the term had been given an extra cachet when used by Colonel Isaac Barré in a speech to the House of Commons that had been much admired in America. Sons of Liberty, Liberty Boys, Sons of Freedom— all had the same meaning, and by the autumn of 1765 they were synonymous with those who intended to resist the Stamp Act.

With the Livingston party in control of the Assembly and the triumvirate writing in the press or speaking out against the Stamp Act, with workingmen generally anxious and angry because of low wages, and with more radical leaders beginning to appear on the scene, the city was ripe for trouble.

On June 6, 1765, the *New-York Gazette* published an essay which was attributed to John Morin Scott, and a remarkable document it was. If the interests of mother country and colonies could not be made to coincide (which the writer believed they could), and if the constitution could not function the same way in both (which it certainly ought to do), and if the welfare of Britain demanded the sacrifice of the colonies' rights, then "the Connection between them ought to cease—And sooner or later it must inevitably cease, and perhaps end in the total ruin of one or both of them. . . ." The government, he went on, could not insist that the colonies be governed by "principles diametrically opposite to its own without losing itself in the Slavery it would impose upon the Colonies. . . ."

The author pooh-poohed the notion that the colonies were "virtually" represented, as Grenville would have it. Genuine representation demanded that a representative have complete knowledge of his constituent's circumstances and concerns so that his interest was identical to that of his constituent.

John Watts was quick to see the dangers of this kind of talk: in a letter to Robert Monckton he called the essay "a bold stroke at John Bull," and went on to say that no one he knew would even hazard a guess as to the writer's identity, but by the author's sourness and perseverance "(for it seems he is not yet done) I should guess him a Presbyterian, & a rash One too, who does not know what he is about, I mean what risque he runs." It was all very well to bait one of the king's ministers, Watts added, but this fellow had better keep his "hands off of edg'd Tools."

Yet the lieutenant governor was silent, not daring to punish the publisher, John Holt, "for fear of adding more fuel to a very dangerous fire," as Judge Livingston put it. Indeed, Colden said the attorney general feared for his own safety if he prosecuted any of the publishers.

Writing to Secretary Conway, Colden complained that "virulent papers were published in the Weekly Newspapers, fill'd with every falsehood that malice could invent to serve their purpose of exciting the People to disobedience of the Laws and to sedition." First they denied Parliament's authority to levy internal taxes; now they denied its authority to legislate in the colonies.

A week later, the author of the first essay published a second, more temperate installment, vehemently denying that American colonists sought independence. On the contrary, he said, they simply wanted the same rights and freedom that were their due under the British constitution.

Still, the talks at City Hall droned on, day after day, until the time finally came to draft a "Declaration of the Rights & Grievances of the Colonists" which would serve as the basis for petitions to king and Parliament. This was touchy business: delegates knew they must not appear to infringe on Parliamentary power or the royal prerogative, while at the same time they had to make clear—very respectfully—their position regarding the colonies' rights and privileges. As John Dickinson put it, they had to assume the posture of dutiful children who had received harsh treatment from their beloved parents, and voice their complaints in "the language of affection and veneration." They were Englishmen, after all, with the same rights as all other Englishmen, and firm in their conviction that the colonies would remain tied to Great Britain with Parliament maintaining jurisdiction over them.

Robert R. Livingston wrote that what gave delegates the most trouble and kept them arguing for almost two weeks was whether to acknowledge the authority of Parliament to regulate trade even though they fully accepted its right to do so. The Sugar Act had made them wary, for its purpose was not only to regulate trade but to raise revenue as well, and if they admitted that Parliament had the authority to regulate trade it could be construed as an admission that a tax to raise revenue was acceptable. While this may seem like dancing on the head of a pin, the argument was deadly serious, and many

Americans could argue interminably over the difference between "external" and "internal" taxes and their unwillingness to accept the latter because they were not represented in Parliament. On the other hand, as Livingston well knew, if Britain could not regulate America's trade, her colonies would be useless to her.

One of the more interesting aspects of this Stamp Act convocation was the size of the gap between the two extreme points of view. Timothy Ruggles was probably the most conservative member of the group, and the suspicion was that he had been handpicked by Massachusetts governor Francis Bernard and dispatched to the meeting with an agenda representing Bernard's views. As indeed he had. Bernard opposed the very idea of the congress but figured he had more to gain by seeming to play along, perhaps persuading the delegates to recommend submission to the Stamp Act until Parliament could be induced to repeal it. So he managed to have two "prudent and discreet men"— Ruggles and Oliver Partridge—named, along with the unpredictable James Otis, as the colony's representatives.

Ruggles was fifty-four years old, a judge of the Worcester County Court and former speaker of the House of Representatives who had accumulated a tidy fortune from his law practice. He had served under Sir William Johnson as a colonel of militia and with Jeffrey Amherst as a brigadier general, and he was pro-English to the core.

At the other end of the spectrum was Christopher Gadsden of South Carolina, a prickly character who felt passionately about his beliefs and carried that passion into the daily dialogues. While Ruggles wanted no real change in the existing relationship with the mother country, Gadsden was probably as close to being an independence man as there was in those days—not quite there, but very, very close—and a man who intended to take no more nonsense from the legislators in London or the ministries of George III.

Somewhere in the middle was Pennsylvania's John Dickinson—a first-rate thinker, like Ruggles and Gadsden a man of conviction, but one who saw both sides of the enormously controversial and potentially divisive issues that underlay this conference. Dickinson, who had been a leading spokesman for and writer of the Pennsylvania Resolves, was probably one of the chief draftsmen of the documents that emerged from the congress's sessions.

Christopher Gadsden was dead against admitting the colonies' subordination to Parliament: because colonial charters differed, he maintained that the congress should not base its arguments on charters but on Americans' natural and inherent rights as descendants of Englishmen. "There ought to be no New England men, no New Yorker, &c. known on the Continent, but all of us Americans," he said, since the colonies' rights were based on something broader than those granted in the charters. Just what that something was appeared in the Massachusetts Resolves on the same day the congress adjourned. These resolutions, drafted by Samuel Adams, stated that Americans' rights "are founded in the law of God and nature, and are the common rights of mankind." Similarly, the Pennsylvania Resolves, published on September 21, had declared that the colonists' constitutional rights were "founded on the natural Rights of Mankind, and the noble Principles of English Liberty. . . ."

After much debate the congress came up with language maintaining that while Parliament could make laws and levy taxes for George III's subjects in Great Britain, it could only make laws in the colonies, since the colonials had no representation in Parliament and therefore could not be taxed. It is "inseperably essential to the Freedom of a People, and the undoubted Right of Englishmen," the declaration's third resolution read, "that no Taxes be imposed on them, but with their own Consent, given personally or by their Representatives."

On a number of points conservatives and radicals agreed. To a man, they wished to declare their allegiance to the king, as affectionate and dutiful subjects. As for Parliament, they could not be represented there, nor did they *want* to be represented; therefore they could be taxed only by those who *did* represent them. Ever mindful of the practical problems they faced, they expressed great regret over the scarcity of specie, which made taxes levied by Parliament even more impracticable, and made it impossible for them to purchase British manufactures.

When the time finally came to write the petitions, the South Carolinians again opposed the general view, saying that only a petition to the king was needed. It was to the king—not to Parliament—that they owed allegiance, so to petition the House of Lords or the Commons was absurd. The majority prevailed, however, on grounds that it would be insulting to members of Parliament to be ignored, especially since they were the ones who enacted the stamp tax in the first place. After addresses to the king, the House of Lords, and the House of Commons were read, amended, and approved, the decision was made that those present would sign the documents and deliver them to their respective assemblies for submission, which would then forward them to England. And at that point the Stamp Act Congress suddenly threatened to come apart at the seams.

The five New York delegates, who had been instructed only to attend the congress, felt that they were not entitled to sign without the New York

Assembly's approval. Similarly, the Connecticut and South Carolina representatives said they were obligated to submit the documents to their assemblies
for signature. Then arguments broke out. Ruggles and Robert Ogden of New
Jersey refused to sign, even though they were authorized to do so, and Ruggles
went so far as to move that *no* delegates should sign, that all members should
take the petitions home to their assemblies for adoption.

Ruggles's attitude was inexplicable to the others. Why had he presided
over the congress for the entire two and a half weeks, seeming to approve of
the proceedings, only to refuse now to sign the documents they had labored
over? If he had not agreed, why hadn't he resigned and gone home?

As these and other questions were being asked, Thomas McKean of
Delaware lost his temper and demanded that Ruggles give the reasons for his
refusal to sign. Ruggles was two decades older than McKean, he was a big,
dour-looking six-footer, he resented being questioned by the younger man,
and he said he had no intention of explaining himself. At that, McKean
snapped back at him, saying they had gathered here with common purpose,
hoping to persuade Parliament to repeal certain oppressive acts, and it was
curious, to say the least, that a man who had seemed to agree with all the
proceedings should refuse to sign his name to the work they had done. Did
Ruggles consider their actions treasonable or offensive? If so, surely he owed it
to his colleagues to say so.

When Ruggles replied shortly that it was against his conscience to sign the
petitions, McKean lit into him in front of all the delegates, at which Ruggles
challenged him to a duel. "Young man, you shall hear from me tomorrow," he
said abruptly. And McKean, who related the story in an autobiographical
sketch years later, retorted that he would give Ruggles satisfaction the next
morning and, what's more, would wait in New York for ten days if necessary.
But the next morning Ruggles was gone, having left before daylight, bound
for Boston.

The Massachusetts Assembly was in no mood to let his behavior pass
unnoticed, and he was reprimanded publicly by the speaker for not signing
the petitions and for leaving New York before the congress adjourned.
Ruggles prepared a written defense of his actions and read it to the House,
but members would not permit his remarks to be published in their journal.

Ogden, for his pains, was burned in effigy in towns in New Jersey and castigated by the Assembly, as a result of which he resigned the office of speaker
and gave up his seat in the legislature.

Undaunted by Ruggles's actions, Otis and Partridge sent copies of the
petitions to Richard Jackson, agent for Massachusetts in London. Since two

vessels were to leave New York Harbor almost immediately, they sent one copy aboard each ship in case one was lost at sea. By coincidence, one of the vessels was the *Edward,* which had arrived in New York with the stamped paper just five days earlier.

When the Rockingham ministry learned that the colonial agents had received these petitions for the king and the two Houses of Parliament, they had as much difficulty deciding how to deal with them as the congress's delegates had experienced in drafting them.

Dutifully, the agents for the colonies delivered the appeals to men they considered friendly—George Cooke, a member of Parliament, Secretary Conway, and Lord Dartmouth, head of the Board of Trade. And there the trouble began. The recipients all knew that members of both houses were debating the Stamp Act behind closed doors, and that Rockingham was eager to have the act repealed. But they also knew that the worst possible outcome would be for anyone to think that Parliament had bowed to pressure from the colonies or the petitions of the upstart Stamp Act Congress. It was a question of face.

Dartmouth rejected the memorial to the Lords on a technicality, saying it was an inappropriate document, diplomatically incorrect. The House had all sorts of reasons not to consider the petition: it had been submitted by an unconstitutional assembly; it denied Parliament's right to levy taxes; it smacked of "Independency"; to accept it would be to admit that Parliament had erred; and so on. James Otis knew full well what was afoot. In a letter to a friend he said: "'Tis much feared the Parliament will charge the Colonies with presenting petitions in one hand and a dagger in the other." But long before Parliament decided how to handle the hot potatoes handed them by the colonies, events in New York had taken charge.

An unpleasant surprise awaited Captain William Davis of the *Edward* when he sailed up New York Bay on the night of October 23. The ship's arrival was announced by the firing of cannon aboard a man-of-war. Then one of the naval vessels came alongside and an officer handed him a letter from Lieutenant Governor Cadwallader Colden explaining that "repeated public Declarations" had been made here and throughout the colonies threatening that the stamped paper would be destroyed on arrival. Since these warnings had been accompanied in some areas with "violent and riotous proceedings,"

Cadwallader Colden, after Matthew Pratt. *New-York Historical Society.*

Colden was taking every precaution to prevent the destruction of the stamps and had instructed Captain Kennedy to provide all necessary protection to the *Edward* and its valuable cargo. As the ship was convoyed toward the harbor, some two thousand New Yorkers gathered at the Battery, "most furiously inraged," watching to see if the stamps were unloaded.

As a result, the *Edward* now rode at anchor in the North River, off lower Manhattan, covered by the guns of Fort George and those on the *Coventry* and other naval craft, backed up by a sloop at Sandy Hook and a frigate midway between Sandy Hook and the fort. That accomplished, Colden could breathe a sigh of relief, and he summoned members of the governor's Council for their advice. To his mounting irritation, repeated messages brought forth only three of the ten members, each of whom protested that he could give no advice without a quorum present. What worried them was that the *Edward* was carrying a full cargo of merchandise along with the stamped paper, and they told Colden that if the unloading of the cargo was delayed they, the three councilmen, were likely to be sued by merchants waiting for their goods. (What no one realized was that Captain Davis had no idea where the packages of stamps were stowed in his hold: to avoid the possibility that colonial agents might discover what ship they were in, they had been handled with such secrecy in England that the bundles had been carried aboard at different times, with other cargo piled on top of them.)

Recognizing that the lieutenant governor was in a real bind, Captain Davis suggested that an Albany sloop be hired to come alongside the *Edward* and unload the cargo so they could get at the stamps. After prolonged argument, the Council members finally advised Colden to do just that, but another stumbling block appeared. No sloop was for hire at any price. Owners were having nothing to do with this business, and Colden began to suspect that "they"—the enemies he saw all around him—were hoping he would commandeer a vessel, in which case he would have a riot on his hands. Abandoning this idea, he decided to have sailors from one of the frigates remove the stamp packages. This went smoothly enough until only three bundles remained, but those were buried so deep in the hold that they could not be removed without putting the *Edward* at risk of capsizing in a brisk wind.

Writing to Secretary Conway on October 26, Colden reiterated his determination to have the stamps distributed, but complained that he had had not so much as a word of instruction from the Stamp Commissioner's Office, not even a bill of lading—only boxes and two bales of stamped paper marked "No. 1, J. McE NEW YORK," and one box and one bale labeled "No. 1, J. I. CONNECTICUT" (the initials, of course, stood for James McEvers and Jared Ingersoll). He was unable to discover the contents of the packages without opening them, and that he was unwilling to do. It would have to await the arrival of the new governor, Sir Henry Moore, who was expected daily, since he had already been more than eight weeks at sea. Meanwhile, he informed Conway, the night after the *Edward* dropped anchor, placards were tacked up all over the city, in taverns and on street corners, warning that the homes and personal belongings of anyone buying or selling a stamp would be destroyed. Signed "Vox Populi," these and similar broadsides "Threatened vengeance in terms the most terrifying imaginable, till the first of November approached." That date, Robert R. Livingston explained, was bruited about as "the last day of Liberty."

Despite the mounting danger, Colden's son David—who, like his father, was no man to pass up an opportunity—was writing to the stamp commissioners in London, telling them of McEvers's refusal to perform his designated duties and asking them "to favor me with an appointment as Distributor of Stamps in the Province." In the same breath he warned that if the new governor did not arrive before November 1, "this momentous affair will lay entirely upon my Father, and I under him must be exposed to the fury of the Populace, whom designing, licentious Men have excited & blown up to a dangerous highth." He would need the commissioners' protection, he added, and if he ran the risk, he believed he deserved an appointment.

By noon on the 26th the stamp packages were landed from the frigate and carried into the fort uneventfully without a guard, and there they remained until Thursday, October 31. That was the day Colden, along with every other governor in America, was required to renew his oath of office. And in doing so he pledged to enforce all laws, which meant promising to see that the provisions of the Stamp Act would "be punctually and bona fide observed . . . So help me God." Friday was the fateful day, yet the man responsible for putting the legislation into effect in the face of a hostile populace had never seen an "authentick Copy" of the act he had sworn to uphold.

On the morning of the 31st a number of people took to the streets dressed in mourning, grieving, they said, for "the Interment of their liberty." At the Merchants Coffee House even the backgammon boxes and the dice were wrapped in crape. In the harbor, merchant ships rode at anchor with flags at half mast, indicating "Mourning, Lamentation, and Woe."

That evening, more than two hundred local merchants met at Burns's Coffee House, and after passing a resolution to enforce opposition to the Stamp Act they took the extraordinary step of voting to order no more goods from England and to sell nothing consigned to them until the act was repealed. Before adjourning, they approved the appointment of a committee to correspond with the other colonies in hopes of broadening their support and creating a unified front against the government's new tax, and a number of prominent merchants were nominated. When it became apparent that those named preferred to keep a low profile on this sensitive issue, several of the more ardent Sons of Liberty stepped forward and offered their services. The volunteers were Isaac Sears, who had been a privateer in the Seven Years' War and was now a successful merchant dealing in the West Indies trade; John Lamb, an accomplished linguist who was a dealer in wines; and Gershom Mott, William Wiley, and Thomas Robinson.

When the meeting broke up, the merchants filed out of the Coffee House and started to walk home, only to find that a crowd—largely made up of sailors and young men from the docks—had gathered, having heard a rumor that a foolish ceremony of "burying Liberty" was afoot. Disappointed to learn that the meeting had been a serious, peaceable one, they began roaming the streets, whistling and shouting while systematically smashing streetlamps, shattering windows, and threatening certain citizens that they would pull down their houses the next night. It began to look as though God's help was exactly what Cadwallader Colden would need.

The City in Perfect Anarchy

On Friday the first indication that more serious trouble was brewing arrived at Fort George in the person of one John Bridge, who had heard from John Ketcham, a shoemaker in town, "that there was a design to bury Major James alive this Day or Tomorrow." From other sources Colden learned that "a Riot or Tumultuous Proceedings were intended," and he implored Mayor Cruger and the city magistrates to do everything in their power to preserve order. Then he sent an urgent request to Captain Archibald Kennedy for marines to reinforce the garrison troops. The naval officer replied at once: Lieutenant Owen and twenty-four marines were on their way to the fort. But he added a cautionary note revealing the woeful state of the fleet under his command: ". . . by doing this I leave the Ships without Marine Sentrys, & as most of our men are imprest there is a great risque of their deserting."

These continuing efforts to strengthen defenses at the fort gave rise to a rumor that the lieutenant governor planned to enforce the Stamp Act by force if necessary, and Major Thomas James of the Royal Artillery, who had reinforced the works in September, was said to have made an arrogant boast that further inflamed the people. He was quoted as threatening to "cram the stamps down their throats with the point of my sword," and he said that if they dared to resist, he "would drive them all out of town, for a pack of rascals, with four-and-twenty men."

That was all that was needed to bring out an angry crowd, and not long before sundown people began to gather in the vicinity of the Fields, the triangular commons that bordered Broadway, across from the upper British barracks. Peaceable at first, the throng was growing in size, with many of them carrying clubs. Along with sailors and young men were numerous mechanics, blacks, and people who had come in from villages and farms in the countryside. An enthusiastic bystander named Carther, newly arrived in town, called it "A Wonderfull Large Mob," women as well as men, and seemingly led by a large number of boys bearing torches and carrying a scaffold. One sailor could be seen balancing a chair on his head, on which sat an effigy representing the gray-haired lieutenant governor with a piece of stamped paper in one hand, in the other a boot, representing the villainous Lord Bute; on his back was a drum, a reference to the popular belief that he had been a drummer in the Pretender's army in Scotland in 1715. Next to that effigy a man carried an image of the devil, who appeared to be whispering in Colden's ear. Hooting and laughing, yelling curses and insults, occasionally firing a pistol at the governor's effigy, the mob passed in front of James McEvers's house, where they gave him three loud huzzas for resigning as stamp master.

When the rioters arrived at City Hall they were met by a worried Mayor John Cruger, aldermen, and a glum group of constables. The officials had been hoping they could put a stop to this demonstration before it got out of hand, and the constables managed to pull down the effigy, but the leaders of the mob demanded that it be returned, assuring the mayor and the others that none of them would be harmed as long as they made no attempt to interfere.

From City Hall the mob moved on, bigger now but still orderly. Judge Livingston stood at a window of his house, silently watching, and wisely concluded that he should stay indoors, since the aim of those behind this shocking affair was "to expose a man universally odious"—Colden, of course—and no one could possibly have deterred the rioters from their work. Finally the surging horde headed for the fort, hoping to confront Colden with his effigy.

To General Gage what was happening had all the earmarks of an insurrection, made up of great numbers of sailors, plus captains of privateers and other vessels, inhabitants of the town, and hundreds of others, who had come in from outlying communities and even other colonies. Among them were carpenters, masons, blacksmiths, keepers of taverns and shops, barbers, jacks of all trades, and some of the merchants. It was impossible to tell how many there were, but he put the number in the thousands. The worst of it, he later told his boss Henry Seymour Conway, secretary of state for the Southern Department, was that "many people of substance are amongst them," but whoever they were, "from the highest to the lowest," all opposed the Stamp

Robert Livingston. *Culver Pictures.*

Act. Despite his outward appearance of calm, the general's state of mind was very near panic: he was certain the worst would happen.

It was a dark night without a breath of wind, and as Carther ran toward the fort to have a closer look he was struck by the "Butifull Appearance" of the approaching mob, their faces illuminated by what he thought must be five or six hundred candles and scores of torches, and he saw Major James standing on the wall of the fort, shouting, "Here they come, by God!" Cannon were loaded with musket balls, which would be devastatingly effective against a mass of people, and the ramparts were lined with British soldiers and marines, ready to fire on the crowd if ordered, but the defenders numbered no more than 130 and fortunately no order was given.

Nearing the fort, the rioters gave three cheers, ran beneath the looming cannon, and yelled to a soldier to tell Major James or "the drummer," as they called Colden, to open fire. Leaning the makeshift gallows against the gate, they beat on it with clubs and grabbed at the top of the walls, yelling to the troops to fire if they dared, and heaved bricks and stones at the men on the ramparts. But the disciplined redcoats, though provoked almost beyond endurance, obeyed orders not to break ranks, and not a man moved or said a word in reply to the taunts. Even so, it was a close-run thing: some three hundred of the city's carpenters were prepared to hack down the gate and storm the fort if a shot was fired, and the slaughter could have been appalling.

While the boys hoisted the effigies within eight or ten feet of the gate, others broke open Colden's coach house outside the fort's walls, hauled away his beloved chariot—a proud symbol of his office—and after perching the effigies on top of it, ran off on a wild circuit of the town, flames from the torches bobbing up and down through the narrow, cobbled streets, casting crazy shadows on the sides of buildings. Hoarse from shouting, the rioters finally spread out on the green about a hundred yards from the gate of the fort, erected the gibbet, and hung the effigies from it.

For a while the crude figures swung in the air before someone cut them down and threw them onto the carriage. Then Colden's buggy and two sleighs were brought up and the whole pile set on fire to wild cheers from the crowd. While the flames leaped higher into the darkness, Colden noted bitterly, "a great number of Gentlemen of the Town, if they can be called so, stood round to observe this outrage on their King's Governor."

Then the rioters began reviling Major James, calling out that his house was next and "If he was A Man he should Go and defend it." With the terrifying, deep-throated snarl of an angry mob out of control, they ran off through the night toward Vauxhall, the estate James rented and had just finished remodeling for his own use, filling it with his collection of books, paintings, and objets d'art. Driving the few guards out the back door, the rioters broke every window in the house, cut down the shutters, and smashed all the partitions, and in less than ten minutes, Carther wrote, they had destroyed windows, doors, mirrors, mahogany tables, silk curtains, some three hundred books, all the china and furniture, and all the family's clothing, plus uniforms belonging to two of James's officers. Mattresses and bolsters were slit open with knives, the feathers scattered in the street and set afire. More than nine casks of wine were consumed. All the silver was stolen, along with the family's larder, and everything left behind was smeared with butter. The beautifully planted gardens that ran down to the Hudson were trampled to ruins. Last to go were the red silk colors of the Royal Regiment, carried off in triumph.*

Sometime after nine-thirty the rioters—suddenly turned peaceful—obtained permission from all the ministers in town except the Anglicans to toll the church bells. "Thus, with an attack on some bawdy houses, the mischief ended for this night," wrote Judge Livingston. And that, he and other moderate citizens hoped, would be the end of it, as the mob, exhausted and

---

*Several days later Major James reckoned his losses conservatively at £2,000 sterling.

sated after their savage work, broke up into smaller groups and vanished into the darkness around four in the morning.

For more than ten horrifying hours, New Yorkers had witnessed their sane, comfortable, infinitely promising world being ripped apart by what seemed a pack of savages, sending a shiver down the spine of perplexed, sensible citizens, who could only wonder at what was happening to their city and what was yet to come. Men like John Watts and Judge Livingston and their families, folk with comfortable fortunes and confidence that life in this outpost of empire would go on in an orderly manner, had to ask themselves what on earth the government at home had done and why it had allowed matters to come to this.

In the days and weeks that followed the night of terror, it was impossible to escape the feeling that an undercurrent of violence remained, just beneath the surface, coiled like a serpent to strike again. But strangely, it never quite erupted. It was as though someone behind the scenes was manipulating the strings, seeing to it that the threat was always present, but making certain that the situation never got out of control.

It is possible, even likely, that James DeLancey, Jr., understood why and how this had come about, for in a curious move that seemed completely out of character this wealthy patrician, son and heir of the former political leader, suddenly declared himself one of the Sons of Liberty.

On Saturday morning, November 2, five members of the governor's Council met at Fort George, where Cadwallader Colden began angrily by reporting how his own and several other carriages had been smashed and burned by the mob in "the Great Riot and tumult." Just before violence erupted, he informed the others, a man had brought a letter to the gate of the fort and told the sentry to deliver it to the lieutenant governor. It contained the same chilling message that had been posted at the Coffee House, which he now read to them. By taking the oath to enforce the Stamp Act, the letter stated, Colden had made himself "the Chief Murderer" of the people's rights and privileges, "an enemy to your King and Country, to Liberty & Mankind," and unless he swore not to execute the act, the anonymous writer assured him, his fate was in the people's hands. If he dared to open fire on them from the fort, as a rumor had it, "you'll bring your grey Hairs with Sorrow to the Grave, you'll die a Martyr to your own Villainy & be Hang'd . . . upon a Sign Post as a Memento to all wicked Governors, and . . . every Man that assists you Shall be surely put to Death."

So there it was, and what was to be done? he asked them. Should he "order the Fort to be put into the best posture of Defence possible"? Threats had been made that unless the stamped paper was put aboard naval vessels in the harbor, the people would set fire to the works, and how was that to be prevented?

To his questions the councillors replied unhelpfully that while they were no judges of military matters, they believed the fort perfectly safe, but of course "if anything further was necessary, everything proper and absolutely necessary ought to be done."

At about this time the mayor and aldermen were meeting at City Hall to decide what they could do to keep the uneasy peace, and they were floundering, paralyzed into inaction, when Judge Livingston came in to see how he might help. "I found the whole body extremely dejected," he said. They had come up with no solution to the dilemma and were waiting to hear if the lieutenant governor was willing to make any concessions "to quiet the minds of the people." Some of the aldermen were for calling out the militia, others for forming an association of moderate men to serve as peacemakers, but no conclusions were reached. Finally a message came from the fort: the lieutenant governor said he would distribute no stamps but would put them aboard a man-of-war if Captain Kennedy would accept them. That was all Colden would say in order to "quiet the Ferment" he had been instrumental in creating.

Meanwhile, Colden's attempt to have Kennedy take him off the hook went nowhere. The naval officer refused to receive the stamped paper on board one of the king's ships. For one thing, the onset of winter would soon oblige the vessel to tie up at the wharves, where the stamps would be at greater risk than they were at the fort. For another, it was too risky to move them, so they should remain safely intact, behind the walls of Fort George. (Left unsaid was Kennedy's fear that his accepting them would mean the almost certain destruction of his elegant house on the Broad Way.)

That afternoon eight Council members attended another emergency meeting, and again they took the easy way out. Responding to Colden's question of what he should do with the bundles of stamped paper that were now in the fort, they said since his honor the lieutenant governor had no instructions, he should do nothing with the stamps. And since Sir Henry Moore "is hourly expected," Colden should leave it to the new governor to decide. But that, it developed, was easier said than done.

Judge Livingston and the civil authorities, assessing the impasse, decided to take matters into their own hands, since Colden so stubbornly refused to reassure the people by saying he would not carry out the terms of the Stamp

Act. James Duane, a well-known lawyer, had joined Livingston as a peace-maker and volunteered the suggestion that since any further disturbances would probably begin with the sailors, they should talk with captains who commanded privateers. The group at once began making the rounds of the dock area, and one of the privateer captains* accompanied them all over town, where they spoke to a number of people and "found the highest resent-ment against the Lieutenant Governor everywhere prevailing. . . ." Heading toward Major James's ruined house, they ran into seven or eight men carrying candles and holding a barber's block on a pole, wrapped in rags—the makings of another effigy, obviously.

The peacemakers persuaded about half the men to go home, but the dis-cussions attracted attention and before long a crowd of more than two hun-dred surrounded them. When Livingston realized that these fellows planned to attack Fort George, he was aghast. "It was a mad project," he said later, quite beyond belief. "Never before this could I think that this was really intended." While they stood there, arguing heatedly, someone brought word that Colden had finally declared that "he would not meddle with the Stamps"—an admission that persuaded even the most outspoken activists to give up their plan to assault the garrison.

On Sunday morning, November 3, a sentry discovered a large oyster shell that had been left by the gate, containing another message, signed "Benevolus," addressed to "Honourable Cadwallader Colden Esq., Lieutenant Govr. of New York," informing him that his life depended on swearing that he would never enforce the Stamp Act and that he should do everything in his power to have the hated legislation repealed in England. That same day, customs offi-cials received a threat: unless they cleared all ships intending to leave port and returned any duty they had collected, the Custom House would be destroyed. And a notice appeared at the Coffee House, signed "Sons of Neptune," alert-ing people to ignore the "peaceable orators" who had talked them out of assaulting the fort. Be resolute! they were told—soon they would be com-manded by men who had proved their courage in the last war, and an attack was scheduled for Tuesday, November 5.

These warnings came on the heels of a report completed on Saturday by John Montresor and two other engineers listing in great detail what should be

---

*Although the man's identity is not known, there is reason to suspect that he may have been Alexander McDougall.

done to strengthen the fort's defenses, after which the lieutenant governor ordered the troops to spike all the cannon outside the fort's walls—making them unusable for action. It was a sensible idea from the standpoint of safety, but it infuriated the public. The seventy-seven-year-old Colden, advised erroneously by informants that arms were being distributed to people, was preparing for battle, predicting that it would be "attended with much bloodshed," since some former privateers and disbanded soldiers were determined to "plunder the Town." Wild rumors were being spread, but often enough they were followed with equally ominous confirmation. On Monday, Montresor brought word that "stragglers" from Connecticut were drifting into New York and milling around, evidently bent on looting. "It was high time now for those inclined to keep the peace of the City to rouse their sleeping courage," Judge Livingston decided, and to that end officials summoned townspeople to a meeting at the Coffee House at ten o'clock on Monday. It was clear that most of those who attended came to present a united front against violence, but few were willing to declare their views openly, so fearful were they of "the secret unknown party"—the mysterious "Vox Populi"—whose threats had so intimidated the government that work on the fort's defenses intensified with every passing day.

Livingston spoke to the anxious, deeply troubled crowd. They simply must keep the peace, he told them, and he conjured up in vivid detail the terrors of government by mob that would ensue if they did nothing. Fortunately, his appeal had the desired effect, and that evening peacekeepers were out in force, determined to head off any new disturbances. Making the rounds, they were greatly relieved to hear that a group of ship captains had met at a tavern and sent word to the mayor and the Corporation of their determination to support law and order. But the lieutenant governor, the mariners insisted, must carry out his promise to put the stamps aboard a man-of-war.

November 5—Guy Fawkes Day, the anniversary of the 1605 conspiracy to blow up Parliament—dawned, and found Colden and his family aboard HMS *Coventry*, where they had fled for protection. It was "The day which all feared," Judge Livingston wrote, not knowing whether it would bring an attack on the fort or open rebellion, not knowing how formidable "Vox Populi" was, or who was behind it. How much the Sons of Liberty were responsible for this mystery was anyone's guess. When they were not out on the streets, the Liberty Boys operated in great secrecy. Few people knew anything about their organization, their activities and plans, or the size and makeup of the membership, but as it turned out they were extending their reach well beyond the island of Manhattan. Later that month one of the leaders, Joseph Allicocke, wrote to John Lamb expressing concern over "the disunion of the People of Philadelphia," who, "at this critical conjuncture," had failed to force their local stamp master to resign. The New York Liberty Boys, he declared, were "more than ordinary enraged with their wonted Patriotic Fire" to learn that someone in Philadelphia planned to make use of the stamped paper. If it was true, a respectable number of New York Sons were prepared to set things straight in the Pennsylvania town, and he expected they would be joined by "a noble possy of Jersey Folks," supplemented by "Eastern Lads kept ready at a moment's warning who upon occasion will swarm like the Industrious Bees . . . to scourge the base Enemies of our Country and our greatest Darling L I B E R T Y. . . ." Clearly, the Sons were organized and ready for action.

On November 5, Colden informed the Council that city authorities were urging him to turn over the stamped paper to them to avoid "any Effusion of blood." Members of the Corporation promised to store the stamps inside City Hall under constant watch and make good financially any losses. In other words, the city would pay for the loss of revenue that would have been produced by the stamped paper, should the stamped paper vanish or be destroyed.

Colden viewed this solution as no solution. He had taken an oath to carry out the will of Parliament and failed to see why the stamps were any safer in City Hall than they were inside the fort. In fact, the offer simply confirmed what he had suspected all along: if the Corporation was sufficiently powerful to safeguard the stamps in City Hall, that same power could be employed to protect them where they were—in the fort. Those who ran the city were behind this whole evil affair, and if he and the councillors acceded to this demand, more would certainly follow and would only "draw the Government into still greater Contempt," while his own compliance with the Corporation would be seen as a breach of his oath.

After careful deliberation, the councilmen declared themselves "thoroughly sensible of the Weight of his Honour's Reasons, but . . . the City appeared to them to be in perfect anarchy." Not only that: the government—both military and civil—was patently unequal to the task of protecting citizens from the fury of the mob. General Gage had recommended that the stamps be put on board one of the king's ships; Captain Kennedy had refused to take them; and large areas of the city would surely be destroyed if it proved necessary to defend the fort against attack. The lieutenant governor had done all he could to carry out his responsibilities, but under the circumstances they unanimously advised him to turn the stamped paper over to the Corporation.

It was a sobering judgment. Those men expressed their fears clearly when they called the situation "perfect anarchy," for so it seemed to everyone who had witnessed events on the night of November 1. And when Colden sent the minutes of the Council meeting to General Thomas Gage, that officer defined the circumstances in even starker terms. If the fort was attacked, he warned, gunfire "might disperse the Mob [but] it would not quell them, and . . . the consequence would . . . be an Insurrection, not only of the Inhabitants, Sailors &c in this City, but of the Country People who are flocking in, and those from the Neighboring Provinces who would likewise assist." He reminded Colden that the army's military stores, artillery, and ammunition (left over from the last war and housed outside the fort in stone buildings alongside the East River) would quickly fall into the hands of the mob, and what followed would be "the Commencement of a Civil War," at a time when no preparations had been made to oppose one.

With the magistrates and other leaders of the town pleading with him to save their families and the city from destruction, Gage wanted to impress on Colden what lay at the heart of his advice: "The fort tho' it can defend itself, can only protect the Spot it stands on." Undoubtedly a factor in Gage's argument for conciliation was the fact that he lived outside Fort George and was unwilling to face the humiliation of seeking sanctuary inside its walls.

Colden later admitted to Judge Livingston that he had been willing to accept the Corporation's proposal at four o'clock that afternoon, when an enormous crowd gathered at City Hall. But—ornery, contrary, and arrogant as ever—he refused to signify his assent until later in the evening, when Gage gave full approval to turning over the stamped paper to the city fathers.

"O how we pant for the new Governor's arrival," John Watts said, "even tho' he should be as hot as pepperpot itself, 'tis better than the venomous stream we at present drink from." Later he summarized the problem in a letter to Monckton: ". . . the extreme aversion to the old man's person and character rooted at the very heart, was a noble stock to engraft the stamp act upon, and it flourished accordingly."

For the moment at least, the crisis was over. As Livingston assayed the roles played by Gage and Colden, "tranquillity is restored by the humanity of one gentleman, which was so unnecessarily disturbed by the perverseness of another." But as he confided to his cousin Robert at Clermont the morning after the rioting, "every man is wild with Politics & you hear nothing but the

Stamp act talked of. Last night . . . we had mobbing" such as "never was seen before in the City."

The moral of the story and the lesson for Britain, Livingston informed General Monckton in a letter, was that enforcing the Stamp Act "will be attended with the destruction of all Law, Order & government in the Colonies, and ruin all men of property. . . ." In fact, such was the state of the colonists' minds—from one end of the continent to another—that he saw no way, short of repealing the act, to prevent its most outspoken opponents from carrying a tide of people along with them, with consequences beyond all imagining.

Nor was that all. Britain would surely suffer more from resistance to the stamp tax in one year than she would ever receive from this tax or any other. The merchants of New York, he observed, had made a collective decision to order no more British manufactures, and those men—and, although Livingston failed to say so, the women who supported them—carried enough weight that "Shopkeepers will buy none, Gentlemen will wear none." Indeed, home manufactures were being encouraged in New York, "all pride in dress seems to be laid aside, and he that does not appear in Homespun, or at least a turned coat, is looked on with an evil eye. The Lawyers will not issue a writ. Merchants will not clear out a vessel." This was not hearsay or exaggeration, he assured the former governor: it was the plain truth and it was vital that it be known in England.

The judge's worst fear was that the government would decide to enforce the Stamp Act at all costs, and if that happened, "there is the utmost danger . . . of a civil war." Those frightening final two words had been used by the commanding officer of the king's armed forces in North America and a justice of New York's Supreme Court. They were also spoken by William Smith, Jr., a respected attorney, who feared "that a general Civil War will light up and rage all along the Continent" because the stamp duties had cost Britain "the affection of all the Colonists." These were men who were keenly aware of the deadly direction this dispute had taken.

II

Madness and Folly

On November 13 the long-awaited Sir Henry Moore arrived in New York aboard the *Minerva*, which also carried nine more boxes of stamped paper for the colony. Born in Jamaica, Moore was a sophisticated product of Eton and the University of Leyden, and his appointment as royal governor was evidently a reward for his brutally efficient suppression of a slave revolt in Jamaica. John Watts, for one, had misgivings about the new man: he may be very good, the merchant said, but "the northern colonies have always considered the planters of the southern their enemies from self interest. . . ." Moore's heart, he suggested, lay "where his treasure is," and he was unlikely to be unprejudiced or disinterested when making decisions affecting New York businessmen. Whether Moore had been well briefed at Whitehall or knew instinctively to present New Yorkers with a persona entirely different from that of old Colden, his first move was to ask the Council's advice: what was to be done about the stamps and the fort? When the councillors urged him not to distribute the stamps and to restore the fort to its previous state—that is, to that of a stronghold that posed no threat to anyone, least of all to the citizens of New York—he quickly agreed.

Moore was a pragmatist. Realizing that he lacked the force with which to support the law, he decided to placate New Yorkers and let them suffer the consequences of their actions. Already they were beginning to feel the pinch of having brought trade to a standstill, and as General Gage observed confidently, once they felt the loss of all business, "many will soon wish to take the

Stamps, tho' all [are] afraid to be the first." The nine boxes of stamps that accompanied Moore on the *Minerva* were packed off to City Hall for safe-keeping with the others. Then the new royal governor ordered the fort to be dismantled on grounds that it bore "too hostile an appearance in a friend's country." He recalled the assembly, which Colden had prorogued months earlier. And, best of all for his relations with the people, he delivered an ingra-tiating address to the citizens while wearing a homespun jacket. A congenial climax came in the Fields on November 21 when hundreds of people gathered to welcome Moore and put on what someone called "the greatest bonfire ever exhibited in the city."

One New Yorker who did not warm to Moore was Cadwallader Colden, who was thoroughly annoyed by the new governor's using "every method to ingratiate himself with the People" and departed for his country place shortly after Sir Henry's arrival despite a warning from "Benevolus" that "You are not safe at Flushing." Moore obviously intended to have nothing to do with Colden, and the old man was willing to risk danger rather than suffer humiliation.

For all Moore's efforts to encourage harmony among the people, however, too much discord had been stirred up on the night of November 1 to subside quickly. British military men were uneasy, and with good reason. The day after Captain Harrington led the 2nd Battalion of Artillery from Detroit and Niagara into what had been described to him as "the Rebellious town of New York," he was summoned by the new governor and ordered to dismantle the fort's defenses at once. When Harrington acquainted Gage with these orders, the general "desired I wou'd put them in execution." But the captain spoke for a good many of his cohorts when he said, "Various are the opinions with regard to dismantling the Fort but no one chooses to speak publickly. It is cer-tain that at present the people have every thing in their own hands—our Mil-itary Force is small; and the grand Arsenal of America is liable to be insulted by any villain that may chuse to set fire to the Stone Houses." Harrington, along with Montresor and other British officers, resented the collapse of civil-ian authority that had led to mob action and the widespread sense that the sit-uation was still out of control. The soldiers' attitude was an early sign of trouble in a decade of rising ill will and ugly incidents between American Whigs and anti-British agitators (especially New York's laboring class and waterfront workers) on the one hand and British military men on the other.

The term "Whig" was heard more and more these days in New York. It was Scottish in origin, and had been used in the seventeenth century as a label applied to Presbyterians who opposed the royalist Cavaliers and supported the English Puritans. Later these same folk were against the Catholic Duke of York's claim to the throne and threw their support to the Protestants William and Mary. In America, the word came into use in the 1760s to characterize those who opposed the policies of the Grenville ministry, and in 1765, after passage of the Stamp Act, "Whigs" became almost synonymous with "Sons of Liberty" and meant opposition to the hated ordinance. Two of the most vociferous foes of the act were Isaac Sears and John Lamb.

Sears came from a family with a New England background dating back more than a century; his paternal ancestor was living in Plymouth as early as 1633. Born in 1730, the sixth of nine children, Isaac was a child when his parents left Cape Cod and moved to Norwalk, Connecticut, where the boy worked peddling shellfish throughout the area. At the age of sixteen he was apprenticed to the skipper of a coastal vessel. He had a bent for the sea and by his early twenties commanded small sloops sailing between Halifax and New York, with winter cruises to the West Indies.

During the French and Indian War he became a captain of several privateers, commissioned to prey on enemy shipping. The profits could be high,

Old Methodist Church in New York. *Stokes Collection, Iconography of Manhattan, New-York Historical Society.*

but the risks could be enormous, and the line between privateering and piracy was razor-thin, since the privateer's letters of marque were not always recognized. Sears was bold, he had a string of adventures, including shipwreck, that enhanced his reputation on the docks of New York (he married the daughter of Jasper Drake, who operated a tavern popular with seamen near Beekman's slip), and by the end of the war he was successful enough to become a merchant, investing in ships trading along the North American coast and the West Indies. Like so many others, he was a victim of the postwar depression, the Currency Act, tightened customs regulations, and the scarcity of specie, and he became an ardent supporter and spokesman for the nonimportation agreements. As Henry Moore, the new governor, informed the Earl of Hillsborough, "many of the poorer inhabitants have been ruin'd and all Ranks greatly impoverish'd." When the Stamp Act was about to take effect, "Sears now became a great man, he headed the mob in New York, was upon every committee, in every riot, and obtained the name of 'King Sears.'" So wrote the loyalist Thomas Jones, who had no use for Sears or his cause. As Jones put it, "His tune is for mobbing; committees and popular meetings are his delight, his greatest pleasure, his hobby-horse." Although the tone of voice was nasty, the description was apt.

John Lamb was another of whom Thomas Jones had nothing good to say. The son of a skilled optician and maker of mathematical instruments, he was five years younger than Sears and began his career apprenticed to his father. Not for long, though—by the age of twenty-five he had become a wine merchant, was married to a Huguenot woman, had three children, and was fluent in Dutch and German and spoke passable French. He was a good speaker and his talent for writing was put to use in many handbills and letters to the newspapers, when Lamb's business, like Sears's, suffered increasingly under the strictures imposed by London. It was fitting that he—with Isaac Sears—should be among the merchants who assembled at the Coffee House on October 31, 1765, the day before the Stamp Act was scheduled to take effect, and resolved to enforce opposition to the distribution of the stamps and to form associations to curtail the importation of British goods until the act was rescinded. These were men who had made their own way in the world without benefit of family money or influence, men who could be trusted by seamen, artisans, and dock workers, men who had the common touch.

Disagreements over how the Stamp Act was to be resisted caused an open break between radical members of the Sons of Liberty, led by Sears and

Lamb, who were challenged by the more moderate wing of the organization that included another former privateer, Alexander McDougall, and by patricians of the Livingston faction, notably the triumvirate of lawyers—Livingston, Scott, and Smith. The Liberty Boys insisted that the stamps be ignored in all transactions and other activities for which the act required them. The Livingstons argued that whatever resistance was to be offered must be kept within legal limits, while the lawyers were nervous about preparing unstamped documents for fear of prosecution and possible confiscation of their own and their clients' property. Adding to the friction, the patricians and wealthy lawyers could afford to bide their time; the Sons could not, for economic conditions were worsening, more men were out of work, and with winter coming on the poor were going to be up against it.

One astonishing outcome of this internecine dispute was the marriage of convenience between Sears and James DeLancey. Both men were motivated by a desire for power and the prospect of making life miserable for the hated Livingstons. DeLancey, of course, was eager to recapture some of the political prestige and popularity his father had enjoyed, and since a good many prominent merchants with strong ties to the DeLanceys were appalled by what had occurred on the night of November 1, it took little to convince James that he should use his budding relationship with the Sons as a means of counseling caution, seeming to support the Liberty Boys while doing his best to prevent renewed violence or destruction of property.

Even though Judge Livingston and his followers were equally anxious that violence be avoided, the alliance between DeLancey and Sears signaled the beginning of a decline in the Livingston faction's influence. Whichever side one favored, of course, the universal interest was in opening the port so that commerce could go on as before. In the December 19 issue of the *Gazette* a writer signing himself "Freeman" bemoaned the state of affairs: "Our Business of all Kinds is stopped, our Vessels, ready for Sea, blocked up in our Harbours as if besieged by an Enemy."

General Gage had a bird's-eye view of what was going on and was quick to see the division between conservative and radical elements. "The Wiser and better Sort of People," he told Secretary of State Conway, "have certainly disapproved of the outrages that have been committed, tho' they have Approved of Clamor and Noise." In other words, the aristocrats endorsed public outcries against the act to put pressure on the government, but only as long as "the Inferior Sort" were kept under control. He added that everyone was unified in opposing the Stamp Act, differing only over the method to be pursued. One side wanted the act undone "by open Force and Violence," while the better sort preferred to "Quibble that no Stamps were to be had, and every other Pretence that could give Some appearance . . . of the legality of their Proceedings. . . ."

The plan of the propertied class, he went on, was to encourage the hoi polloi to prevent the Stamp Act from taking effect. They even encouraged the rioting, but not to the point where the mob got out of hand, becoming treasonable and rebellious and threatening to destroy property and endanger lives. These aristocrats wrote their friends in England and laid the blame on "the unruly Populace," hoping to terrify the government into repealing the act at the same time New York's merchants canceled their orders for British goods until the act was repealed, knowing the merchants in London and trading towns would assist them.

New York's lawyers, Gage informed Secretary Conway, were the worst offenders—the source of most of the trouble—for in New York, "Nothing Publick is transacted without them," and even judges on the bench were culpable. Indeed, had it not been for the instigation of the legal profession, merchants, assemblymen, and magistrates, Gage declared, "the inferior People" would have been quiet, for they were not easily stirred to action. Sailors, he explained, were the only ones who deserved to be called a mob, and the seamen were acting at the bidding of those who employed them—the merchants.

Never in all his time in America, the general admitted, had he been at such a loss over how to perform his duty for king and country while preventing any outbreak that might tarnish the military's power and influence. Had he given the rioters the least opening, they would have taken advantage of it. "I have kept within my Sphere," he continued, "Not to interfere further than by Advice," unless the civilian authorities asked for assistance. But the general had resolved never to be caught so unprepared again, and that resolve was behind his order bringing two hundred Royal Americans from Canada to Albany and one hundred Highlanders from Fort Pitt to Lancaster, Pennsylvania.

The state of affairs was confusing, to say the least. On the one hand a substantial number of merchants were more troubled by the prospect of harming commerce with Britain than they were by damage to private property, and these men tended to side with the radicals, many of them as members of the Sons of Liberty. On the other side were conservatives more concerned about the sanctity of property, who also resented the insolence and impertinence of the lower class and had little sympathy for their plight.

Most of Sears's followers were sailors and mechanics—"leather shirts"—whose livelihoods were at stake if the port remained idle, and they naturally

demanded that trade be resumed without stamps—a practice customs officials in Philadelphia had recently smiled upon. In fact, the Sons persuaded
New York's collector of customs, Andrew Elliot, to permit vessels to leave
without properly stamped documents, but Captain Archibald Kennedy balked
at that and denied them laissez-passer unless they had the governor's permission to sail or had papers that were in order—which is to say, stamped.

It looked to be a long, comfortless winter—no trade, growing unemployment, money in ever shorter supply, dispositions rankled, even friends at
odds, exacerbated by the frustrations caused by an absolutely unknowable
future dependent on the Stamp Act's repeal. Everything seemed to have
turned sour at once. Strict enforcement of the Sugar Act, coupled with the
growing shortage of paper currency and an almost total lack of specie caused
the prices of sugar, molasses, and rum to soar and closed the doors of at least
two major sugar houses in town. Poor harvests sent the price of grain out of
sight, and "trade in this part of the world is come to so wretched a pass that
you would imagine the plague had been here, the grass growing in most trading streets," as one New Yorker described conditions. Merchants no longer
looked for clerks to hire, he added—they were too busy seeking employment
for themselves.

No one dared use the stamps, and between that and the fear of *not* using
them business was at a standstill. It was as John Watts had predicted:
"If [the stamps] are not issu'd," he had written to General Monckton, "Confusion will ensue, I am sure. If they are not, 'twill be as bad if not worse."
While New Yorkers had been virtually unanimous in opposing the Stamp
Act, what to do about it was another matter. The Sons of Liberty, by virtue
of their role in inciting the mob, had become a real force to be reckoned
with, but most merchants wanted no more rampaging, lawless crowds and
relied increasingly on the DeLancey–Sears partnership to keep matters under
control.

Even so, the threat of violence was palpable. Captain Montresor said control was so lacking that "Children nightly trampouze the Streets with lan-
thorns upon Poles & hallowing. . . . The Magistracy either approve of it, or
do not dare to suppress it. . . ." The British officer had no doubt whatever of
what should be done. He was outraged by what occurred on January 7, 1766,
when the brig *Polly* arrived at Cruger's dock with packages of stamped paper
for New York and Connecticut and was boarded by Liberty Boys, who

searched the vessel from stem to stern, removed the parcels, and took them upriver, where they poured tar over them and lit a bonfire. When the job was done, the *New-York Gazette* reported, the Sons dispersed quietly, without alarming the sleeping city.

Governor Moore, Montresor reported, gave the mayor and magistrates a stern lecture, telling them that if they couldn't keep the peace he would, that he would not hesitate to ask General Gage for troops if the civil authorities failed to act. But in Montresor's opinion, more than lectures was needed: "troops and fleets to enforce his Majesty's orders" would soon put an end to the lawlessness.

In the meantime, Governor Moore was behaving "sensibly and coolly," according to John Watts; "he lets the stamps sleep till he can hear from home." But whether the stamps slept or not, unsettling incidents continued.

On November 19, Peter DeLancey, Jr., Colden's grandson, arrived from London aboard the *Hope,* expecting to assume his position as a stamp inspector, only to discover the enormous antipathy toward the act. He hardly knew what to say or do, John Watts observed, "so odious is the Person of every Officer in America" who has anything to do with the stamp tax. Just "fix the Term to any Mans Name & he becomes a Scare Crow," said Watts. "Here it would certainly be more than his Life is worth, to attempt to execute the Office," besides which every other DeLancey would have "his Name in the Dust. . . ." On November 27 the young man resigned.

When Colden departed in high dudgeon to Flushing, he was followed by Zacharias Hood, the stamp master to whom the lieutenant governor had given sanctuary in Fort George after he fled from Maryland. His continuing presence in the fort was an embarrassment to Governor Moore, so Hood departed in haste, only to be spotted in Queens, where he was tracked down by several hundred New York Liberty Boys, and caught. Told that he could either resign his office or be turned over to "an exasperated Multitude," Hood took the safe way out, since Colden could no longer help him and Moore would not. Loudly cheered by his captors for this unremarkable decision, Hood was invited to "an Entertainment" but prudently declined the honor, saying he was "in such a Frame of Body and Mind that he would be unhappy in Company"—especially in that company.

The unfortunate fellow went back to Annapolis, hoping to rebuild his life there, but no one would do business with him, and in 1771, broken in health and spirit, he sailed for England, hoping to be compensated for his losses. He never returned to America.

"Strange Scenes we have had, Madness & folly triumphant," John Watts wrote to Monckton, informing him that the fort was dismantled and all the cannon removed or spiked. To a colleague, Moses Franks, he opened his heart, commenting sarcastically that the behavior of the "wise ones" in London reminded him of the old woman who was dissatisfied with only one egg a day from her hen so she killed the poor bird figuring she could have them all at once. His warmest wish, he added, was that Parliament might be dissolved, though whether even that would help America he could not foresee. The gulf between mother country and daughter was so wide and "the Tempers of People . . . so alterd by the frightfull Stamp Act, 'tis beyond Conception. . . ." In his judgment the government would never recover its stature in the colonies until better people—better than those "fit for nothing at Home"— were sent out to fill the important offices.

He concluded with a prophetic warning to Franks. Do not think the tie between England and America is indissoluble, he wrote: "Providence in mercy has reserv'd the power of dissolving it as Alexander did the Gordian Knot, by cutting the thread."

Sir Henry Moore was content to stick with his hands-off policy and his feigned indifference to what was happening, for he was certain that the economic distress caused by New York's refusal to accept the act would do more than he could to end resistance. But the Sons persisted and the turmoil continued. Effigies were burned, fighting broke out between Liberty Boys and the soldiers, a mob was narrowly dissuaded from destroying Captain Kennedy's house, the Sons boarded a ship and ransacked the hold, searching in vain for stamps supposedly destined for Connecticut.

As the year wound down, thoughtful men everywhere had ample reason to reflect on what had happened and what the future might bring. In Braintree, Massachusetts, the young lawyer John Adams wrote in his diary that 1765 had been "the most remarkable Year of my Life." He had seen the Stamp Act—"that enormous Engine, fabricated by the british Parliament, for battering down all the Rights and Liberties of America"—result in a spirit of resistance that had spread throughout the continent. Above all, he noted, "The People, even to the lowest Ranks, have become more attentive to their Liberties, more inquisitive about them, and more determined to defend them, than they were ever before known or had occasion to be."

Adams rejoiced in the remarkable unanimity of resistance to the stamp tax and those who supported it, which had brought about a vibrant spirit of liberty everywhere—such a union as had never been achieved here before, certainly not during the French and Indian Wars.

This was a time of profound change, and on the final day of 1765, Adams recorded his thoughts about the new year to come. "This Year," he wrote, "brings Ruin or Salvation to the British Colonies." America's eyes were on Parliament, waiting to see if the Rockingham ministry would repeal the despised Stamp Act. "Britain and America are staring at each other," he observed, "And they will probably stare more and more for some time."

John Watts was deeply disturbed by the course of events, but where Adams perceived salvation in the spirit of liberty and the new engagement of "The People, even to the lowest Ranks," Watts was determined that the empire must be preserved, and he had no illusions that the common folk were likely to be helpful in that cause. Surely, he thought, "some New Constitution will be form'd in time between the Mother Country & the Colonys." What he had in mind did not exist anywhere, so far as he knew, but he believed that "a supreme power lodged somewhere" was a requisite.

Then the first signs of doubt crept in: since the population of the colonies would exceed that of Britain in a few years' time, it simply would not work to treat Americans as second-class citizens—"unrepresented & of course unheard." Barring an unlikely change in the nature of man, Watts mused, that sort of government could only become an oppressor.

To the intense chagrin of Cadwallader Colden and Captain Archibald Kennedy, they got much of the blame for what had happened in November. Secretary Henry Seymour Conway informed Colden that the king was thoroughly annoyed to hear that "the unjustifiable Demands of the People met with so much Compliance" by the lieutenant governor, who had incomprehensibly decided "to suspend the Power of Government 'till the Arrival of the governor," Sir Henry Moore. Mincing no words, Conway told him "you had no Right" to refuse to act. Adding salt to Colden's wounds, the Assembly voted to give Major James £1,745 to cover his losses but ignored Colden's request for £195 to compensate him for the destruction of his chariot, buggy, and two sleighs.

Meanwhile, Kennedy was out of a job. He informed Colden that "he was superceded in his Command of His Majesty's Ship Coventry on a Complaint of having refused to take the Stamp'd Papers on Board" at Colden's request. Now Kennedy, in disgrace, was on his way to England, and Colden tried to wriggle out of his embarrassing dilemma by laying the blame on the city magistrates and the Council, saying they had advised him to ask Kennedy to take the stamps, and that Kennedy had said "he thought it unnecessary."

Major James, safely arrived in England, was questioned in Commons along with other victims of the riot "who had sufferd unheard of Cruelties by the unprovok'd Americans." These unfortunates were reassured by members that they were now safe and need no longer fear "being murder'd or having their Effects destroy'd."

Cartoon presumably by Benjamin Franklin. *Laurie Platt Winfrey, Inc.*

12

An Act to Repeal an Act

On December 18 a northeaster dumped six inches of snow on the city, and when John Watts wrote to General Robert Monckton on the last day of the year it was still bitter cold, with a full moon on the wane. Describing the mood of the city, Watts told the former governor how lucky he was to be out of the colony—out of America, for that matter—where "the ill boding of things, cramping of trade, suppression of paper money, duties, courts of admiralty, appeals, internal taxes, &c, have rendered people so poor, cross, and desperate, that they don't seem to care who are their masters, or indeed for any masters. I expect to see this City go one day or other," he added gloomily, reminding Monckton that it had already come close to coming apart when the people demanded the stamps be removed from the fort.

Watts may not have realized it, but popular uprisings were nothing new in the colonies, or in England for that matter. America had seen frequent disturbances over such issues as impressment, smallpox inoculation, food shortages, and the White Pine Acts, which reserved *all* white pines to the crown—not only those to be used for the navy's masts. Governor Hutchinson of Massachusetts once quoted members of the House of Lords as saying that "if the people really don't like something, then they wreck our carriages and tear off our wigs and throw stones through the windows of our town-houses. And this is an essential thing to have if you are going to have a free country." Similarly, the noted seventeenth-century lawyer John Selden, when asked what law book contained the statutes for resisting tyranny, replied that he did not know, "but I'll tell [you] what is most certain, that it has always been the custom of England—and the custom of England is the *Law* of the *Land*."

What was deeply troubling to John Watts and others in the ranks of the elite, who were highly visible because of wealth or property or official position, was the underlying threat that what had happened on the night of November 1 could happen again—anywhere, and at any moment. Governor Moore seemed unconcerned, though, so certain was he that his decision to forbid any business transactions that would require the use of stamped paper would quickly bring the people to their senses. "All their commerce must inevitably be ruined if they persist in their obstinacy," he declared. But he was dealing unwittingly with a new group of people, an unknown quantity, who were giving voice to the voiceless for the first time—the city's working class.

The first signs of change had come when the Sons put up placards all over the city, headed LIBERTY, PROPERTY AND NO STAMPS, inviting all residents to meet on October 31 at Burns's Coffee House—the meeting at which resolves were passed against the stamps and for nonimportation. From that day until spring of 1766 the Sons played an increasingly active role in the agitation that plagued the city, with its members endlessly busy—organizing, poised for action at the slightest indication that the stamps were being used, urging other colonies to join them and do the same—and all of their business being carried on as subtly as possible. In the process of organizing, they were acquiring skills that were to prove useful in the days to come: propaganda, especially, and a knowledge of how to enlist the interest of the diffident or unengaged members of New York's middle and lower classes. General Gage, never imagining that "the lower sort" could possibly achieve what the Sons had done, was convinced that whatever they were up to must be because they were being manipulated by either the DeLanceys or Livingstons or both, but he was wrong. The Liberty Boys had their own agenda.

From New York a continuous stream of letters went out to the brethren in Long Island, Westchester, Connecticut, Massachusetts, and beyond, invariably including an acknowledgment of George III as "our rightful and lawful King," while stressing the need to augment "our strength and Union," which was essential for the "preservation of Liberty and perfecting an Union of the Colonies." That word "union" began to appear regularly in the incoming mail as well as what emanated from the Sons' headquarters in New York.

From Huntington, Long Island, came a long list of resolves, along with a discourse on how their forefathers had come to the "uncultivated howling Desert" in America, where they eventually "enjoyed an incontestible Right of taxing themselves by Representatives of their own chusing untill an unjust

Ministry, endeavouring to subvert the Constitution and destroy the Liberties of their Country, invented new Ways of taxing other than by the Consent of the People. . . ." The Sons in "Oisterbay" chimed in, pledging solidarity, as did those in New Brunswick, White Plains, Albany, Philadelphia, Newport, and Norwich, Connecticut, who "rejoiced at the prospect of a General Union without which we must fall an easy prey to our most Inveterate Enemies."

Word went out to Annapolis, to Norfolk. In North Carolina a similar association was taking shape, while South Carolinians and Georgians adopted some of the techniques developed by the New Yorkers. While not all groups called themselves Sons of Liberty, the pattern was nonetheless the same. And so it went, with the web of connections expanding as the need for union was increasingly recognized. But possibly the most important result of this growing correspondence was that like-minded individuals became acquainted with others across the country and found that they were not alone, that a host of other Americans shared the same views.

While both parties were hoping desperately to prevent further outbursts like that of November 1, it turned out that Robert R. Livingston's efforts to mediate the crisis had backfired, while James DeLancey's overture to the Sons of Liberty would eventually produce a sea change in New York politics. At a meeting on Tuesday evening, January 6, 1766, the Sons adopted a number of resolutions that put them on record as pledging to "go to the last Extremity, and venture our Lives and fortunes . . . to prevent the said *Stamp-Act* from ever taking place in this City and Province." As significant as the resolutions was the participation at the meeting of half a dozen DeLanceyites, including James. As William Smith, Jr., described the origins of this bizarre alliance, at the time the Stamp Act "threw the whole Continent into Confusion," the ardor of the mob "outstripped the Zeal of the Assembly [which was controlled by the Livingstons] & the Livingstons lost Ground by the Moderation which their Responsible Characters & the Novelty of the Dispute inspired." He went on to accuse the DeLanceys of planting agents with "the Rabble" and doing their utmost to gain the people's confidence so that when the next Assembly was prorogued they might win a majority in both houses and rule the colony. And so it proved.

The DeLanceys were playing a dicey game by allying themselves with Sears and his fellow radicals. They knew what would happen if the government decided to take a hard line and send troops to enforce the Stamp Act.

Indeed, Oliver DeLancey was at this time gathering up the family papers and putting them in a secure place lest "the ravages of the population" destroy them. He told his sister Susan that violence in enforcing the act would mean civil war, in which case "all Distinction will then be lost and our family will hardly be unobserved in such a Scene of Confusion and Distress."

The support of the DeLancey elite was hugely gratifying to the Liberty Boys, but rather than slowing down their activities, the opposite was true. After boarding the *Polly* and destroying the stamps aboard her, forcing Peter DeLancey, Jr., to resign, and capturing Zacharias Hood, the Maryland stamp collector who was in hiding, the Sons forced poor McEvers, the New York stamp man, to resign yet again—publicly, this time. In a February meeting they promised to "fight up to their knees in blood" to prevent the stamp tax from being imposed in New York or elsewhere, and one of their most far-reaching decisions led to establishment of a committee of correspondence, intended to establish communications with Sons of Liberty throughout the land. (Isaac Sears, John Lamb, and three others volunteered to serve on the committee, which promised to be hazardous work if Britain got tough.) The result was a network of provincial correspondents—radicals, all of them—connecting the resistance movement from Massachusetts to South Carolina.

Already a certain amount of organizing had been done behind the scenes. In January of 1766, Governor Francis Bernard of Massachusetts reported to Secretary Conway a conversation he had had with a man from Connecticut, who told him that two men from New York had arrived at a tavern in New London, summoned six or more inhabitants who were known to oppose the Stamp Act, and told them that British troops would be arriving from England to enforce the act. New York would undoubtedly be attacked first, they said, and they had come to find out how many Connecticut men could be counted on to assist the people of New York. The New York messengers said further that they were going on to Norwich and Windham, and that other Sons were heading for Boston on a similar mission.

After learning that two merchants named Pintard and Thompson had obtained stamped passes to the Mediterranean from Charles Williams, a customs official, Isaac Sears, Joseph Allicocke, and John Lamb rallied several thousand of the faithful, marched on the Custom House, and forced the hapless Williams to hand over any similar passes he had, and then made Pintard burn them. That evening the mob came close to getting out of hand: they broke down the door to Williams's house and began destroying furniture before someone remembered that the house was rented by the customs man from James DeLancey, to whom it belonged, and persuaded the mob that they could deal with Williams and Pintard the next day. (Thompson escaped punishment by claiming not to have known that the passes were stamped.)

That Saturday morning, according to Captain Montresor, the unfortunate Williams and Pintard "were carried to the Common with an intent of being pilloried but through the intercession of the clergy of this place who attended them and harangued the mob, they were allowed only to make their confessions first there, and after being conducted to their Houses to repeat it." Montresor went on to say that the "General Officers" in charge of this action were a pair of ship carpenters named Tony and Daly, who seemed able to raise or suppress a mob instantly. It was this air of mystery surrounding the Liberty Boys as well as their capacity for violence that made them seem so sinister and threatening.

On February 17 the packet from Falmouth brought word of a speech by the king, in which he had declared that there was to be no appeal in England from the verdict of a jury—a direct rebuke to Cadwallader Colden. That was not the only indignity suffered by the recently displaced lieutenant governor. When Monckton still occupied the governor's office, Colden had made an agreement with him under which half the governor's salary and the perks of office went to the lieutenant governor when Monckton was out of the country. Members of the Assembly, who did everything possible to deny Colden any money, were balking at doing so now and were ignoring the old man as if he were in another world—"where they heartily wish him," John Watts wrote, "for he and the Stamp Act at present are exactly alike, without a single friend."

In the same mail that arrived by the Falmouth packet was a newspaper report of George Grenville's statement that the recent behavior of the colonists could only be construed as rebellion. A week later came evidence that all but corroborated that remark: a Connecticut militia colonel named Israel Putnam sent word to the New York Sons of Liberty that he and his men "would assist them . . . to the utmost lives and fortunes to prevent the stamp act being enforced in this Province or any other." And on February 26 the Liberty Boys were quoted as saying that if orders were received to enforce the Stamp Act they would seize all crown officials, put them aboard ships sailing for England, and then do their best to convert British troops to their own point of view.

March arrived on gale winds, bringing snow and rain, at a time when the capacity of the Liberty Boys to keep the pot bubbling seemed to have no bounds. One day they were quoted as saying they favored "shaking off the Yoke of Dependency [on] their Mother Country." A few days later, when the cannon Colden had ordered spiked (by driving a sharp piece of metal into the vent) were finally unspiked after two months of work, the Sons announced plans for a parade, to be held on the first fair day, and on March 6 the weather cleared long enough for a cannon to be hauled through the streets by a large crowd, with an effigy of the lieutenant governor seated on it, drilling the vent.

On their circuit of the city's streets the marchers stopped in front of General Gage's headquarters and gave him three cheers, but when the salute was not acknowledged they warned the commander in chief and his aides that "they would have their Hats off yet before they were done with them."

The ice in the Hudson had melted sufficiently for the first Albany sloop to sail, but the next day the weather turned foul again, a hard wind from the northeast brought a foot of snow, and not until March 25 was the river free of ice and navigable from New York to Albany. When the *Halifax* packet from Falmouth arrived at last, after running aground eight times coming up from Sandy Hook and springing a leak, an estimated twenty tons of ice had to be removed from her masts and rigging. The captain reported that it had been the stormiest voyage he had experienced in twenty-two crossings. One of his passengers was Captain Conner, sent to take command of the *Coventry* in place of Archibald Kennedy, who had been ousted for refusing to accept the stamps in November.

On March 12, the same day the *Garland* man-of-war docked, Montresor's journal noted almost casually, "Lieut Governor Colden's life daily threatened by the Sons of Liberty," and several days later one of the *Garland*'s officers was embroiled in the city's troubles. A ship's lieutenant named Hallam, speaking to a justice of the peace, had unwisely likened the Liberty Boys to the rebels in Scotland in 1745, adding that John Holt, printer of the *New-York Gazette*, deserved to be hanged and that he, Hallam, "would not be against putting a halter about his neck." Warned by the justice that he should mind his words lest the Sons put a halter around *his* neck, Hallam retorted "that they may be damn'd and might kiss his arse." Sears and Allicocke promptly paid a call on the vessel, but Lieutenant Hallam refused to talk with them and ordered them off the ship. At that the situation turned ugly. A crowd gathered on the wharf, shouting, "Bring the lieutenant ashore with a halter about his neck!" and demanding that he apologize or deny what he had said.

Next day a larger crowd of people made their way onto the wharf, yelling that they would attack the ship if the lieutenant was not turned over to them, prompting General Gage to intervene. He sent word to the captain of the *Garland* that he would give him all the assistance necessary, and reinforced his intent with a supply of powder and cartridges from the ordnance stores. Twenty-four hours later the Liberty Boys were down at the docks again, but when they discovered that the several men-of-war in the harbor were prepared for them and that they ran the risk of losing their lives, they made the rounds of houses in the area to assess how much support they had. In the days ahead the tension never let up and the city remained in torment, plagued by uncertainties, by increasing friction between individuals and groups, by the threat or the actuality of violence. Leaders of the Sons said they intended to ask Gage why he had sent support to the *Coventry* and the *Garland* and why he had ordered additional troops to New York—an insolence Captain Montresor attributed to Sir Henry Moore's failure to intervene in "all the tumults and disturbances" which the mob regarded as an invitation "to daily pursue their disloyal Irregularities. . . ." Until Gage acted, he went on, not a shadow of opposition to "the Rabble" had been evidenced.

On March 23 the Liberty Boys threatened to tear down the house of the brigade major who had carried Gage's message to the ship captains, and on the 24th word reached New York that Colonel Putnam in Connecticut had acquired arms and ammunition and had ten thousand men ready to oppose the stamp tax. Putnam, Montresor noted disdainfully, had "received his Majesty's money, having been employ'd during the War as a Provincial Colonel." And the show of force was all to no purpose, the captain added huffily, for not a stamp had entered Connecticut: they were all safe inside Fort George.

(Montresor was probably unaware of it, but Israel Putnam had seen more than his share of action in the French and Indian War, having been one of Robert Rogers's Rangers and, after being captured, having been rescued just as Indians were about to burn him at the stake. He went with Amherst to Montreal, was shipwrecked during an ill-fated expedition to Havana, and commanded Connecticut troops in Bradstreet's march to Detroit in Pontiac's War. Now he was a prominent member of the Sons of Liberty in Connecticut.)

On the night of March 24 a ship from Philadelphia, which had originally sailed from England, brought the worst possible news: the Stamp Act would not be repealed. At once a crowd assembled at the Merchants Coffee House while the town crier and newsmongers roamed the streets all night, shouting "Bloody news for America!"

At four o'clock the next afternoon an express rider from Philadelphia clattered into town, having made the trip in only twenty-two hours, with a completely different account: a vessel from Ireland had entered the Choptank River in Maryland after a remarkably fast passage, and a passenger claimed to have seen a letter from a member of Parliament to a friend in Ireland stating that the Stamp Act had in fact been repealed on January 24. Immediately several hundred boys took to the streets to spread the news, but people seemed to realize that what amounted to a third- or fourth-hand story was hardly enough to pin their hopes on, and the Sons, in particular, were not about to relax their vigilance or their pressure on the authorities until solid evidence of repeal arrived. As if to dampen spirits further, a foot of new snow fell, accompanied by strong west winds and intense cold.

Out of the blue, General Gage decided to put a thousand barrels of powder and twelve thousand stands of arms aboard the men-of-war for safekeeping, and he requested wooden boats to ferry them to the ships, since no owners of merchant vessels could be persuaded to assist in the transfer. Gage had applied to the governor for a press warrant to procure a vessel, but when the request was refused on grounds that "'twas time of Peace," the commander in chief "waited on the governor for an Explanation regarding some late affairs," according to Montresor. It was an exchange that must have produced some lively comment from the general.

On the final blustery day of the month, Gage met with governor and councillors to see what was behind their "denying his Majesty a vessel for his Ordnance Stores." Put like that, it was hard for them to refuse permission, and granted it was. At dusk that day, five "Ruffians or Sons of Liberty," as Montresor described them, attacked a British officer, "beat him unmercifully and broke his sword. . . ." Next day the transfer of ordnance to the men-of-war was blessed with warmer weather, but the crew worked under the eyes of "the Sons or Spawns of Liberty and Inquisition," as Captain Montresor called them, who cursed the workers, their officers, and the crown, while threatening to attack the lieutenant governor's home if the Stamp Act was not repealed. The engineer was troubled by the fact that these "Heroes of Liberty" maintained an office and kept a record of everything that happened, which they sent on to "their licentious fraternity throughout the different Provinces."

On the first warm spring day, when droves of New Yorkers went outside to cultivate their garden plots, another report, coming by way of South Carolina to Philadelphia, indicated that the detested act was repealed on February 10—not January 24 as rumored earlier. The days passed with no further word, but the Sons had sufficient confidence to announce that in the event of repeal they would insist that all restrictions on trade be removed, and that the Post Office and admiralty courts be prevented from infringing further on personal liberty.

Another report of repeal came in from Maryland on April 8, giving February 8 as the date of Parliamentary action, and still the wind and rains continued, as did the loading of weapons and ammunition, additional rumors of repeal, and worrisome questions of what the Liberty Boys might or might not do next. But despite the Liberty Boys' threats, by mid-April all the arms and powder were safely aboard a hired transport and sloop, guarded by a dozen artillerymen, and watched over by the *Coventry* and *Garland.*

Behind all the tantalizing rumors about repeal of the Stamp Act were the realities of political maneuvering in London. The new and largely inexperienced Rockingham ministry, which succeeded Grenville's, had been intimidated by the violence in the colonies and was seeking a solution that would accommodate the colonial agents in London and Britain's merchants while not compromising Parliamentary authority and not capitulating to American extremists. It was no easy row to hoe.

In early December 1765 a group of London merchants held two days of meetings, after which they sent a letter composed by Barlow Trecothick* to commercial towns throughout England, urging support for the repeal of the Stamp Act. While this was being circulated, Rockingham held two dinner parties at which leading merchants discussed American affairs with administration officials. Quite simply, the questions confronting them were how to alleviate the distress of British merchants while repairing the wounded honor of Parliament and at the same time ensuring that body's authority over the contentious colonies. A vital consideration was the one Lord Dartmouth cited in Parliamentary debate, that "not less than fifty thousand men in this kingdom are at this time ripe for rebellion for want of work from the uneasy situation in the colonies." The group agreed that the colonies should have "every possible Relief in Trade & Commerce"; they were undecided on how to deal with the Stamp Act—whether to amend, suspend, or repeal it; but they agreed that a declaration of Parliament's right to legislate for the provinces was imperative.

---

*Trecothick was himself a prominent merchant who had lived in Boston for a time and was now the London agent for New Hampshire.

By this time the Stamp Act was universally opposed in America and even in England the sentiment for repeal was compelling, thanks largely to the efforts of British merchants, who had rallied public opinion behind such a move on grounds that the tax would punish Britain economically. Surprisingly, the king himself—never mind how reluctantly—now believed "Repealing infinitely more eligible than Enforcing, which could only tend to widen the breach between this Country and America." Only Grenville held out, demanding that the army enforce the tax.

By mid-January, Trecothick's skillful lobbying produced a petition to Parliament from the London mercantile community along with petitions from manufacturing and trading towns in the countryside. These gave added incentive to Rockingham, who knew he had to repeal the Stamp Act because he lacked the political strength to uphold it and declared he would "wish no Man so great a Curse as to . . . be obliged to enforce the Act." He decided to push through one bill aimed at repealing the act because of its adverse effects in England, plus a separate bill declaring Parliament's legislative authority over the colonies.

When the colonial agent Richard Jackson wrote to Governor Thomas Fitch of Connecticut on January 11, he said he could see no indication that the act would be repealed, but after Parliament opened on January 14, William Pitt rose to deliver one of his most powerful speeches. He began by complimenting the Rockingham ministry on its address to Parliament, while chiding it for its delay in calling the House together for such an important matter. Then he referred contemptuously to Grenville's late ministry, whose every measure "has been entirely wrong," after which he praised the Americans, saying, "I rejoice that America has resisted," and went on to urge "that the Stamp Act be repealed absolutely, totally, and immediately." At the same time, however, he insisted that the sovereign authority of Britain over the colonies must be asserted in unmistakable terms and made to "extend to every point of legislation whatsoever." England could "bind their trade, confine their manufactures, and exercise every power whatsoever, except that of taking money out of their pockets without their consent."

Beginning on February 3, the House sat as a committee of the whole, working as long as ten hours a day, while a numbing array of witnesses—merchants, agents, and American visitors—predicted disastrous consequences if the act was not repealed. Trecothick alone spoke for four hours, but the star turn was by Benjamin Franklin, who gave the performance of a lifetime on February 13. No one knew as much about America and its people as Franklin did; no other colonial was so well informed about the country's affairs or was better equipped to describe the facts about them and the people's attitudes; and his replies to his questioners were clear, unhurried, reasonable, and persuasive. Even those who disagreed with his arguments had to admire the depth and breadth of his knowledge. One Briton told friends in America, "I believe he has left nothing undone that he imagined would serve his Country."

His comments, recorded by a secretary, were published in London, New York, Philadelphia, Boston, and Williamsburg during the year and eventually in France. In them he made a convincing case that Americans objected to internal, not external, taxes, adding, "I never heard any objection to the right of laying duties to regulate commerce; but a right to lay internal taxes was never supposed to be in Parliament, as we are not represented here."

He argued that the recent war had been waged for British interests, not American, that it had been fought over national boundaries, territories to which the crown laid claim, and the right of Britain to trade in Indian country. Not until the ill-fated Braddock expedition was launched, he reminded them, were the colonies attacked by the French.

That led to his comments on the enormous expenditures approved by colonial assemblies in support of the war (his own colony of Pennsylvania, he observed ruefully, had spent £500,000 and had been repaid only £60,000 by the crown). Furthermore, "the colonies raised, paid, and clothed near 25,000 men during the last war, a number equal to those sent from Britain, and far beyond their proportion. . . ." One result was that the colonies now had barely enough specie to pay the stamp taxes for a single year. And in a rebuke to Grenville's demand that troops be employed to enforce the Stamp Act, he warned that such a move might provoke a rebellion.

One of his most cogent arguments was his answer to the question "What was the temper of America towards Great Britain before the year 1763?"

A. The best in the world. They submitted willingly to the government of the Crown, and paid, in all their courts, obedience to acts of Parliament. Numerous as the people are in the several provinces, they cost you nothing in forts, citadels, garrisons, or armies to keep them in subjection. They were governed by this country at the expense only of a little pen, ink, and paper. They were led by a thread. They had not only a respect but an affection for Great Britain; for its laws, its customs and manners, and even a fondness for its fashions, that greatly increased the commerce. Natives of Britain were always treated with particular regard; to be an Old England man was, of itself, a character of some respect and gave a kind of rank among them.

Q. And what is their temper now?

A. Oh, very much altered. . . .

Then, to the question of whether Americans still have the same respect for Parliament they once had, he replied, "No, it is greatly lessened."

The man who was the most famous American in the world concluded his testimony with responses to two questions. To the first, "What used to be the pride of the Americans?" he replied, "To indulge in the fashions and manufactures of Great Britain." And to the second, "What is now their pride?" his answer was simply, "To wear their old clothes over again till they can make new ones." It was a statement carefully calculated to make the case for Britain's merchants.

Nine days after Benjamin Franklin's appearance in the House, a bill for repeal was brought before that body. The debates went on night after night, and when they ended at last a weary merchant who had attended the sessions wrote an American friend saying, "I am glad this ugly affair is over, for we are heartily tired, and have slaved like horses, sometimes not coming home till two or three o'clock in the morning, and then perhaps fasting." The bill for repeal passed on March 4 and was approved in the Lords on March 17, but in both houses the margin of victory was narrow, with many members bitterly opposed, and it was clear that the measure would have failed had it not been for a Declaratory Act, passed at the same time, asserting the right of Parliament to make laws binding the colonies in all cases whatsoever.

In spite of the strong opposition in Parliament, the British populace in general had favored repeal overwhelmingly, largely because of the economic depression for which they blamed the Stamp Act.

The *London Gazette,* quoted in New York's papers, portrayed the moment when the royal carriage made its way through the streets carrying George III to the House of Lords on March 18 to give his assent to the repeal, saying that "there was such a vast Concourse of People, huzzaing, clapping Hands, &c. that it was several Hours before His Majesty reached the House." Seated at last on the throne in his royal robes, the king dispatched the Gentleman Usher of the Black Rod to the House of Commons, commanding the members to attend him, and when they were assembled, "his Majesty was pleased to give his Royal Assent to An Act to Repeal an Act made the last Session of Parliament, entitled, An Act for granting and applying certain Stamp Duties. . . ."

Immediately after the ceremony on March 18, someone acting for the British merchants rushed word to Captain Wray of the *Dispatch,* riding at anchor in the Thames, and he set sail at once to deliver the news to the first port he could reach on the North American continent, while at the same time ships in the river broke out their flags in a riotous display of colors, and illuminations and bonfires all over town made "the Rejoicings . . . as great as was ever known on any Occasion." Through the streets of London the next morning an extraordinary procession made its way from the King's Arms Tavern in Cornhill to the House of Lords—more than fifty coaches carrying a host of merchants eager to express their gratitude to George III for signing the repeal bill. And that night the merchants dispatched an express to Falmouth with fifteen copies of the bill to be forwarded to New York, while several merchant ships put to sea with the news and messengers galloped off to spread the word in Birmingham, Manchester, Sheffield, and other manufacturing towns.

On Tuesday, May 20—nine full weeks after George III gave the royal assent—the "authenticated, glorious news" that the Stamp Act had been repealed finally reached New York, and the reaction was all that could have been expected. The city went wild.

"Long Live the KING!" trumpeted the *New-York Gazette,* praising "his sacred Majesty [who] so graciously assented to the wise Measures of his Ministry" (adding gratuitously that had it not been repealed the "most direful Consequences" would have been visited on the city). A huge celebration immediately began, honoring the king, friends of liberty at home and abroad, and the guardian of America—William Pitt. The Sons of Liberty began their day at the Old Church, where the rector was preaching a "congratulatory Discourse," and after a royal salute of twenty-one cannon they repaired to their favorite tavern to enjoy an elegant entertainment, a band concert, and twenty-eight toasts which they "chearfully drank," raising their tumblers to the king, the Prince of Wales and the royal family, and Pitt, concluding with drams for the committee of merchants in London and the true Sons of Liberty in America.

Captain John Montresor, ever one to find a sour note in the actions of New York's unruly underclass, noted that there was a "Grand Illumination" throughout the city except where he and other military officers resided, and that the night ended in "Drunkeness, throwing of Squibbs, Crackers, firing of muskets and pistols, breaking some windows and forcing off the Knockers off the Doors." To cap it all, a large crowd of Liberty Boys went to the fort to congratulate the governor, and to Montresor's disgust, three of them, "drunk as they were, had admittance."

The next day, as the revelry continued, a "Flag Staff" was erected in the Fields. A large board was attached to the pole, bearing the words "George 3rd, Pitt—and Liberty," and sometime in the days that followed, it came to be known as the Liberty Pole. Since it stood directly in front of the upper bar-racks occupied by British troops, it was a particularly galling sight to the red-coats and a symbol of pride and defiance to townsfolk. No more than a tall pine log, it was to become for four years the focus of all the rancor and bitter-ness between Thomas Gage's soldiers and the increasingly combative populace.

Repeal of the Stamp Act led many Americans to believe that they had tri-umphed, and in New York they not only did away with the hated stamps but also had the satisfaction of humiliating the hated Cadwallader Colden. Yet the grounds for the Stamp Act remained: Britain still demanded revenue from its colonies, and it still had in place several means to collect it—the Sugar Act, the Currency Act, certain new commercial regulations, and, above all, the Declaratory Act, which bluntly asserted Parliament's "full power and authority to make laws and statutes of sufficient force and validity to bind the colonies and people of America subjects of the Crown of Great Britain, in all cases whatsoever." Furthermore, the men who grasped the reins in Parliament in the mid-1760s were hard-liners, inflexible and determined to curb America's growing autonomy.

Their mistake, it turned out, was caving in to colonial demands that the stamp tax be repealed, for in doing so they all but negated the Declaratory Act, making it likely that the radical element in America would challenge future Parliamentary measures. They had done it once, they could do it again—or so they reasoned. And now, of course, the American radicals had experience under their belts. They had created the Sons of Liberty, organized, cultivated brethren in other colonies, and achieved a certain solidarity. If nec-essary, they figured they could do that again, too.

For his role in the affair, Benjamin Franklin became a hero. He had done more than hold his own against the harshest critics in Parliament while upholding the cause of all America, and in his home city of Philadelphia, cof-feehouses presented gifts to the sailors on the ship that brought the news of repeal and gave free beer and punch to anyone wanting to drink the health of the king. On the king's birthday in June, several hundred Philadelphians gave their homespun clothing to the poor and wore suits of British manufacture, while cannon aboard a barge named the *Franklin* fired salutes to the monarch.

Amid the almost universal jubilation, a few voices of caution were heard. Benjamin Franklin, for one, was uneasy. Repeal of the Stamp Act, he knew, was a bandage, not a cure, which only imperial union could bring about. But

Benjamin Franklin, by Joseph Sifrede
Duplessis. *New York Public Library.*

he was sure that Parliament would not consider admitting representatives
from the colonies until it was too late, and by the time they did so, those in
the colonies would think too highly of themselves to accept it.

A Londoner wrote to a friend in the colonies asking, "And will you Americans look upon this as a Victory gained over your Mother Country?" and
warned: "If you do, you are ruined: You will lose the greatest part of your
Friends by such a Conduct, and effectually disable the few who remain from
serving you."

The same powerful British merchants who had circulated the letter
throughout England urging repeal of the act (which Edmund Burke, Rockingham's private secretary, called "the principal instrument in the happy
repeal of the Stamp Act") reminded Americans of the odds against which
they had prevailed while warning the provincials not to carry their protests
too far. No government is perfect, they said. Misinformation, misunderstand-
ings, and mistakes are bound to occur, but government works for the good of
the whole. Then, as the lecture began, you could almost see the index fingers
wagging: "flagrant Breaches of public Order" must stop. Remember, they
continued, you are indebted for repeal to "the Clemency and paternal Regard
of His Majesty for the Happiness of his Subjects" and the "Abilities and Firmness of the present Administration," along with "the Humanity, Prudence,
and Patriotism . . . of those who compose the Legislature, and the most considerable Persons of every Rank in this Kingdom." Which was to say, the
entire power structure of Great Britain.

This and similar warnings prompted assemblies in various colonies to send addresses of thanks to king and Parliament, expressing their filial duty and gratitude. Celebrations were held up and down the Atlantic coast, with houses brightly lit by night and countless toasts drunk publicly to William Pitt and other champions, but few excesses were reported and people were generally well-behaved. Since most of the revelry was staged by the Sons of Liberty, it was somewhat surprising that it did not get out of hand, but it was evident then and later that the Liberty Boys were not about to forget what they thought they had achieved. Although they dissolved their association as they had promised to do once the Stamp Act was repealed, they nevertheless pledged "to keep up that glorious spirit of liberty which was so rapidly and so generally kindled throughout this extensive continent," and from 1766 until 1775 they commemorated the glorious 18th of March in such a way that it was not forgotten.

In New York a group of petitioners that included James DeLancey and Isaac Low appealed to their representatives in the New York Assembly to provide for "an elegant statue" of the great patriot William Pitt, who had for the second time been the preserver of the country. (Not until later did someone stop to think that it might be insulting to the king if he was not given a statue, so that was also ordered.) And New Yorkers breathed a sigh of relief, hoping that peace and quiet would return to their city now that the Stamp Act was dead at last.

13

An Unsupportable Burden

If an American had been privy to the correspondence between General Thomas Gage and Secretary of State Conway in London, he would have realized at once that major changes were afoot in the governance of the colonies and in the imperial relationship between the provinces and the mother country. The signs may have been subtle, but they were unmistakable.

After 1760, once the French were defeated and the threat of invasion removed, the colonists largely lost interest in military affairs, but the king and his ministers were keenly aware of the need for a standing army in America. It was expensive and largely unprecedented, but essential. Once the enormous territory in what had been French Canada and the American west had been set aside as a reservation for the Indians, it had to be policed. The Indians had to be guarded against, as Pontiac's uprising made abundantly clear, but at the same time they had to be protected from the covetous maneuvering of land speculators. Whites who traded with the Indians had to be safeguarded; so did French settlers in Canada. More important, civil disorders in the colonies had to be dealt with, and unless the army was substantially enlarged, that had to be handled with more emphasis on diplomacy than force, as Gage's recent experience in New York suggested.

As yet no colony-wide civil mechanism existed for the administration of Britain's new holdings on the continent, and it was all but inevitable that the military should move into the vacuum by default. The commander in chief and his subordinates were given the power to act in a host of unprecedented situations, since the colonies lacked any administrative unity and the difficulties of communication meant that action had to be taken more often than not without instructions from home. As a result, the man in charge of the army became the single most powerful imperial authority in America.

For instance, the superintendents of Indian affairs were instructed to obey Gage's orders on all occasions. His location in New York, at the center of the colonies, meant that he would be corresponding regularly with all the governors and would also be the "Medium of material Intelligence either to or from England or the Colonies." Salaries of officials dealing with Indian affairs, the expenditures of congresses with the Indians, and the drawing of boundary lines—all were paid out of the general's office. Army officers supervised trade with the natives and oversaw the operations of merchants dealing with them. And Indian affairs were only one of the myriad responsibilities of Thomas Gage.

He was in touch with provincial governors and customs officials, with the leading American merchants and public figures. The secretaries of state and war in London sought his advice on everything from colonial commerce and industry to the reasons for colonial discontent and how to deal with it. They wanted his opinion on taxation and trade laws, relations with France and Spain, smuggling, what to do with Frenchmen stranded in Detroit and other remote outposts, how to pare expenses, western expansion, the desirability of establishing new colonies beyond the Appalachians. It was a tall order.

Gage's letters from the ministry in London reveal the growing trend to make him and his army the chief agents of imperial administration, and the general himself the man on whom government relied for information and counsel on virtually every significant question concerning America. Not only that: the ministry repeatedly refrained from giving him specific orders, telling him that he would know best what to do. Until recently the army had been envisaged as the defender of the colonies' frontiers; now Britons were beginning to think it should defend the king's authority within those frontiers.

In the wake of the Stamp Act rioting, Henry Seymour Conway wrote to Gage bewailing "the disordered State of the Province where you reside & the very riotous & outrageous Behaviour of too many of the Inhabitants." His Majesty, Conway added, was aware of the delicacy of Gage's position and the many difficulties faced by the general, which were made more acute by his lack of adequate forces, but the king was also disturbed by the mob's insulting treatment of Lieutenant Governor Colden and thoroughly annoyed by Captain Kennedy's refusal to take charge of the stamps. Gage had given Conway the impression that tempers would soon cool in the province, and the secretary urged the general to take every possible opportunity to improve the situation, while supporting "the Honour of Government" and suppressing "any riotous or rebellious Resistance offered to The Laws, or those Magistrates who have the Execution of them."

All well and good, but the general was in a major bind. When Cadwallader Colden asked for military assistance at the time of the Stamp Act riot, he managed to turn the army into an enemy of the people, an instrument for oppression, and an object of hatred. At the same time, influenced by the imperious attitude of such officers as Major James and Captain Montresor, the soldiers in the ranks came to detest what they regarded as the rabble of New York. Ironically, the redcoats were drawn from the same underprivileged class that produced the unemployed dock workers, seamen, and mechanics of New York. Many of the troops were castoffs and convicts and were unwilling soldiers—few of them were volunteers. Punishment in the army was horrifying—anywhere from a hundred to a thousand lashes for offenses that were often no more than petty crime. A man's rations, which consisted of beef or pork, flour, peas, rice, and butter, were deducted from his pay, as were clothing, medical treatment, and even his pension. The poor fellows were no better off than slaves, and were itching for a fight.

Soon a series of ugly incidents drove these two antagonistic parties farther and farther apart, to a point where even a chance encounter might spark an explosion. Even after the Stamp Act's repeal, when the Sons of Liberty disbanded, Gage noted the continuing activities of "violent and unruly Spirits," and observed that "the spirit of Riot is contagious, it spread lately into the Country." Add to this inflammatory situation the fact that the troops were quartered in the city and the public was being ordered to pay for the dubious privilege of having them there and you had the makings of serious trouble. The former Sons aimed to drive the troops out of the city and made the rounds of taverns, inns, and stores, trying to persuade the proprietors not to serve the hated lobsterbacks, not to sell to them.

These difficulties were nothing new: a year earlier Gage had heard from the provincials that the Mutiny Act did not extend to America, and he complained to London that "Soldiers are seduced from the King's Service, Deserters protected and Secreted, Arms, Cloaths &c purchased, Quarters and Carriages [i.e., wagons] refused, without incurring any Penalty." Outrageously, officers had been prosecuted and fined for seizing deserters, and had been "seduced from their Regiments and indented as private Servants; sent to Jail for being in the Quarters which had been allotted for them. . . ."

Gage and other senior officers who had fought in the French and Indian War had already experienced the difficulty of prying money out of colonial assemblies to pay for quartering and provisioning their troops on the march and now asked Parliament to do something about it. The result was an extension of the Mutiny Act to include the American colonies and the Quartering Act of 1765, which went well beyond what the generals requested and gave the colonials—especially in New York—yet another bone of contention. The act demanded that assemblies pay for housing and feeding soldiers in settled areas—an expense that had previously been borne by the crown. And since most of Gage's men were likely to be in New York, that province would be obliged to pay a disproportionate share of the total costs. Troops were to be garrisoned in colonial barracks if available (and of course in New York City and Albany that was the case). They were also to be supplied with cider, small beer, and rum diluted with water, plus such essentials as firewood, bedding, candles, vinegar, and salt—most of which the colonies had provided in wartime with little grumbling, but now the issue was hotly disputed.

The Quartering Act immediately raised serious questions. Why was it necessary to station the king's troops in colonial towns and cities in peacetime? Was this not another instance of taxation without representation, since the colonials had neither requested the soldiers nor had a say in bringing them here? Was this not, in fact, the first step toward a standing army that could tyrannize the people of America?

Gage's dilemma came down to this: he was determined to concentrate his forces in and around Manhattan, but in the event of civil disturbances he could not act in a military capacity unless invited to do so by the civil authorities, and those authorities were not likely to extend such an invitation. Not only that: if the authorities *should* call on him for assistance, the military "must act wholly and solely in obedience to the Civil Power," in which event the troops would no longer be under his command but under civilian control.

There were several anomalies in all this. Isaac Sears and John Lamb wanted to get rid of the army, while the last thing moneyed New Yorkers desired was for Gage's troops to leave the city. The confusion and disorderliness that had erupted the previous year were bad for business and a worse threat to property, and the only safeguard against anarchy was the army. On the other hand, elected city officials did not want to offend the followers of Sears and Lamb, for those were the voters who could elect them or throw them out.

In any case, while Gage's motive was to provide order and political stability, his move had the opposite effect. He had badly misjudged New Yorkers' reaction by failing to see their resentment and fear of a standing army, whose presence in the city was a daily reminder that it might be used against them.

Since the general's immediate problem was that the New York magistrates lacked money to pay for billeting his troops, he was obliged to take his case to Governor Moore, but that gentleman was forbidden to request military aid without the consent of his Council. So when that body, in its turn, passed the request on to the Assembly, it was as good as dead on arrival. Dominated by the Livingstons, the Assembly had mastered the art of frustrating crown officials; as Gage put it, "They have not directly rejected the Act, but Set the Demand aside by Evasion." In response, Gage spoke with some of the leaders in the Assembly, had the act explained to them to show that Parliament had taken steps to quarter troops "in the Manner the least Burthensome to the Inhabitants," and told the assemblymen if they could come up with a better method of doing so he would see to it that Parliament considered an amendment to the act.

Privately, Governor Moore gave his approval to billeting the soldiers at the province's expense, but with repeal of the Stamp Act and the widespread rejoicing that followed, the sense of crisis passed. Gage, however, who strongly favored the idea of taxing the colonists to support the army, was not happy to lose the opportunity to strengthen his force. At the end of April 1766 he wrote to the governor of Georgia, James Wright, expressing chagrin that no civil authority had requested military help to meet the Stamp Act crisis, though he hoped that attitude would change, enabling him to bring in more troops, while wishing that "other measures will soon be taken to defend the powers of government."

The governor of New York was as frustrated as Gage was. He had published a proclamation offering £100 reward for information leading to the discovery of the culprits who burned the stamped paper from the *Polly* but had had no response whatever. Writing to Conway in January of 1766, Moore said that "the disorders have become so general that the magistracy are afraid of exerting the powers they have [been] vested with, and dread nothing so much as being called upon in these troublesome times for their assistance." Civil authority, it seemed, was as impotent as the military.

Along with everything else, the Gages and the Moores were feuding. Gage claimed that he was superior to all governors in America on all occasions, which ran counter to the governor's instructions. Rumors were abroad that Lady Moore and Mrs. Gage were bickering over who took precedence at public events, and when the governor dispatched two councillors to invite the general to join him in celebrating the king's birthday, Gage refused because Moore had not personally invited him. Gage tried to shove the dispute under the rug, calling it "ridiculous," but it was not. As Moore described it, the general's claim of precedence was a "step toward the total abolition of the Civil

Power in order to introduce a Military Government." While the quarrel sim-mered down, the problem did not go away, but recurred during the later administrations of governors Dunmore and Tryon.

The situation was not without its humorous moments. Montresor wrote in his journal that the Liberty Boys had assembled in the Fields for a grand supper but arguments broke out ("which is generally the case") and the crowd dispersed in anger and went home just as food was brought to the table.

The truth was that no one knew what might be coming next, and chances were it would not be amusing. Early in May, for instance, when billboards announced the opening of a play featuring strolling players and comedians, much grumbling was heard from people "who thought it highly improper that such Entertainments should be exhibited at this Time of public Distress, when great numbers of poor people can scarce find Means of subsistence." This was before news of the Stamp Act's repeal arrived, when nerves were on edge and tempers short, but no one anticipated what happened on the evening of May 5.

A rumor had spread that if the play was staged it would be greeted with "some Disturbance from the Multitude," and that warning was enough to keep many people from attending. But others disregarded the threat, arrived at the theater, and took their seats, and when the curtain went up for the sec-ond act they were horrified to see a mob storm inside, shouting and shoving, stealing watches, picking pockets, throwing bricks, bottles, and glasses, and crying "Liberty! Liberty!" while terrified theatergoers who could not push their way to the doors jumped out the windows. The lights were extinguished and people began screaming with fear, while the howling mob gleefully tore down the building and took the pieces to the Fields, where they were con-sumed in an enormous bonfire. At some stage of the melee a young boy's skull was fractured, and a number of other people were injured.

Although Montresor laid the blame on the former Sons of Liberty, their participation was by no means certain. An equally likely possibility was that rioting—inspired, to be sure, by the Liberty Boys' example—was becoming endemic in New York, and this night's violence was the work of another gang. Street brawls were increasingly common, and nowhere were they more appar-ent than in the relationship between civilians and soldiers.

The first ugly episode between soldiers and civilians had occurred as early as January of 1764, when a large crowd of citizens turned out on a Sunday night to the ringing of alarm bells. To everyone's surprise, it was not a fire but a call for help to prevent a group of soldiers from freeing an officer from jail, where he was being held for nonpayment of a debt. The jailer had struggled with the soldiers when they demanded his keys; they beat him and broke the locks on all the cell doors, though not before several other people were wounded and a sergeant was killed.

Frequent instances of impressment and harassment of colonial vessels by the British navy kept the pot bubbling, as did the bayoneting of a Son of Liberty by a Royal Artillery member several weeks after the Stamp Act rioting. Hostility had peaked in those early days of November 1765, with the threats to Fort George and the looting of Major James's house, but while the frequency of ugly incidents lessened for a time, their intensity heightened—with the focus of anger on the Liberty Pole erected on May 21, 1766, when the town was celebrating repeal of the Stamp Act.

As part of General Gage's plan to concentrate about fifteen hundred soldiers in and around New York City, troop reinforcements began arriving in the city during the summer—ninety-nine Highlanders, a detachment of artillery, and the 46th Regiment in June, followed by the 28th Regiment in July.

To exacerbate what was already a tense situation, the Assembly refused to provide quarters for these troops despite Gage's repeated demands to know if the legislature intended to refuse compliance with Parliament's act requiring billeting. All this while the Highlanders and the men of the 46th, who had arrived aboard ships from Detroit and Albany respectively, had to remain on board, suffering from thunderstorms, pelting rain, and a sudden cold snap. They were raging mad.

The Liberty Pole belonged in the Fields, or commons, New Yorkers maintained, but they were well aware that it would be a daily insult to every British soldier living in the barracks in front of which it stood, and it was not long before the redcoats had had enough and chopped it down. Daylight on August 10 revealed the flagstaff lying on the ground, the *New-York Gazette* announced—an affront to the town which "gave great Uneasiness." The following day was uncommonly hot, but the weather did not deter a surly, threatening crowd estimated at two to three thousand from assembling on the common. Led by Isaac Sears, the mechanics began by demanding an explanation of why the Liberty Pole had been cut down and then, according to Captain Montresor, used "the most scurrilous and abusive language" against the officers and soldiers, who were suddenly pelted with brickbats. Naturally enough, the troops defended themselves with bayonets until word arrived from Gage, carried by his aide-de-camp, a captain, and by Major Brown, commanding officer of the 28th Regiment, who were "grossly Insulted in the streets and publickly called Rascals to their Face" by a former colonial officer named Dawson who swung a stick at the aide and tried to knock him off his horse. The captain drew his sword and some in the crowd pulled out pistols, but before it turned into a pitched battle (as it was, Sears and one of his crew were injured) the officers succeeded in quieting the crowd by declaring that if the soldiers proved to be guilty they would be punished. Though not entirely mollified, the crowd withdrew, and soon afterward the controversial pole was erected again. Commenting on the affair, Montresor—who had no use for Moore's apathetic reaction to these hostile confrontations—observed contemptuously, "The Governor Sir H Moore never Interfered."

Conditions worsened and the hatred mounted on both sides. The radicals vowed to break up military formations in the streets, the vulnerable British drummers were obliged to march under double guard, and after another pole was set in place with the sign "George, Pitt and Liberty" affixed, the 28th Regiment was reviewed by the commander in chief on a devilishly hot day and suffered the humiliation of having to do so protected by artillerymen with fixed bayonets, who formed a square around the regiment to keep the mob from pushing through its lines. Soldiers were insulted daily. The former Liberty Boys pressured innkeepers and market vendors to have no dealings with the lobsterbacks and even had the temerity to request that Gage bar soldiers from carrying sidearms while off duty.

On September 23 the Liberty Pole was a casualty once again but was restored without incident. A month later, in the dead of night, a band of soldiers roamed the Fields area with bayonets, terrorizing the residents. This had nothing to do with the Liberty Pole, it was said, but was retribution for ill treatment the redcoats had received from the city's ladies of pleasure, "at some of those infamous Houses which to the great scandal of our wholsome Laws, are suffered to exist as so many Receptacles for loose and disorderly People."

The hatred of the army so rife in New York was not confined to that city. The next year Gage was in Boston briefly, where troops newly arrived from Halifax were being denied quarters by "Every Art and Evasion" in order to drive them out. This was a town, the general decided, "where every Man studys Law, and interprets the Laws as suits his Purposes. And where the Measures of Government are opposed by every Evasion and Chicane that can be devised." By the time he left Boston, where "the Writers for the Gazettes will always endeavor to raise a Clamour and invent News that has not the least Foundations of truth," the general was almost glad to see New York again.

John Watts had a clear sense of what was wrong. The colonies, he told a friend, are "extremely incensed at the treatment they have had from the Mother Country"—so much so that they wished Canada were French again. When it had been, "it made 'em feel of some consequence," but they had lost that feeling after Canada was conquered. In fact, he speculated, if the French and Indian War had to be fought again, the colonies "certainly would not grant a man for that or any other use. . . ."

Yet the people's pocketbooks were as much involved as their pride. What drove numerous workmen and some of the elite to take the actions they had was their certainty that Britain had to be challenged to prevent something worse from happening. A great many former Sons of Liberty were men on the make—men like Alexander McDougall and Isaac Sears and John Lamb—who realized that government was getting in their way, passing unfair legislation that made it more difficult—perhaps impossible—for them to conduct their businesses profitably, threatening their livelihood and their future.

Repeal of the Stamp Act had brought joy and the steady clink of silver coins into the countinghouses of merchants. As business boomed, one man described the welcome affluence, saying "money began to flow in all sorts of channels, and riches, long hoarded, came into prominent view." New warehouses, new churches, new mansions in open land beyond the city—all soon attracted the envious eyes of Britain's landed gentry, who resented the showy opulence in what was said to be the king's favorite colony.

Just as suddenly as it had come, the financial boom went flat and times were tough in the city again. "Never was a Country so embarrassed as this," John Maunsell wrote to a friend, "our paper Curr[ency] Almost exhausted: all the Gold and Silver sent home & trade quite dead, the difficulty to live here is inconceivable, the marketts as high as ever, Labour as expensive. . . ."

Meanwhile, the crown had no intention of letting the New York Assembly get away with refusing to quarter the king's troops, and on August 9 the Earl of Shelburne—who had recently replaced the Duke of Richmond, who had replaced Henry Conway, as secretary of state for the Southern Department—wrote Governor Moore, "acquainting him" that His Majesty "expects &

requires a due and chearfull Obedience on the part of the provinces to the Acts of the Legislature of Great Britain"—among them, most emphatically, the order for quartering His Majesty's troops "in its full Extent and meaning."

Several things had happened in New York in the interim. Governor Moore had tried his hand at getting the Assembly to pay for billeting the troops and to his surprise was told that some money had been left over from French and Indian War funds for use by the commander in chief, and Gage, when he heard this, said he would use the money. But more was going to be needed, and that presented the Livingston-dominated legislature with a real dilemma. If it flatly refused to provide the money, it would be defying George III and Parliament and would certainly antagonize Gage, whose support was now especially important in light of growing unrest among tenant farmers.

Another factor in the legislature's decision was the continuing economic downturn and its effect on the province's declining revenues from duties on trade and licensing fees. What's more, the Assembly had recently been ordered by Parliament to compensate victims of the Stamp Act riot for their losses—notably Major James and Cadwallader Colden—to the tune of some £2,000.

In a letter to one of the newspapers someone suggested that if improved land were to be taxed at a penny per acre and unimproved acreage at a farthing, or a mere one-quarter of a penny, the annual income to the province would be as much as £35,000 a year. But the land barons were dead set against that. To a man like Robert R. Livingston, who owned vast acreage, it meant financial ruin.

When, in November, Governor Moore prodded the legislative body again, this time less gently, reminding members of the king's demand for "due and chearfull Obedience," he waited for nearly a month for a reply, and what he heard was simply astounding. Apologetically, but firmly, the Assembly refused, saying it was too much to expect them to shoulder a "ruinous and insupportable" burden if additional troops were brought into the province. They would be "guilty of a breach of [the] most sacred trust" of the citizens they represented if they agreed to vote additional funds for the troops.

And now from another quarter came further resistance to Parliament. A number of New York merchants, alarmed by the effects of the Revenue Act of 1766 on the vital West Indies trade, sent a petition to Parliament protesting the new duties on sugar and Madeira wine and the jurisdiction of vice admiralty courts, on top of other complaints. Unfortunately, the catalog of their woes was accompanied by a veritable lecture on policy, on the nature of commerce within the empire, and on the "reforms" painstakingly worked out by members of Parliament and British merchants—all in a condescending tone that infuriated the recipients.

Benjamin Franklin did his best to smooth the ruffled waters. "Petitioning is not rebellion," he noted in a letter to the press. "The very nature of a petition acknowledges the power it petitions to, and the subjection of the petitioner." Writing to his friend Monckton, John Watts said that, after all, "'tis really beneath the dignity of a great government to be so much alarmed by [the petition], be it ever so absurd or ill drawn, when it is considered as coming from only Some Merchants of one Single Trading Town of America. . . ." Absurd though it was, he went on, it contained "much truth."

The merchants' petition and the Assembly's defiance of Parliament could not have reached London at a worse time. The Rockingham ministry had recently fallen, and only William Pitt seemed capable of mustering the necessary support to form a government in a Parliament deeply divided on the question of America. Pitt was determined to settle colonial affairs. No one was more aware than he was of the size and importance of the problem or the urgent need to resolve it, but he overestimated his strength, political as well as physical. In the process of forming his ministry the man known as the Great Commoner left the House of Commons to become Earl of Chatham—shocking his thousands of loyal adherents on both sides of the Atlantic, many of whom considered that he had betrayed them by trading his principles for a title— and cobbled together a makeshift cabinet that was an unpromising assortment of personalities and proved to be as weak as it first appeared. Edmund Burke characterized it as "a diversified piece of mosaic . . . a tesselated pavement without cement . . . treacherous friends and open enemies . . . it was, indeed, a very curious show. . . ."

This was the sixth ministry in seven years, and from the start it proved unstable—largely because Chatham was now in extremely poor health, cranky, alone with his pain, and incapable of giving his time or attention to the business at hand. Knowing his condition would not permit him to attend Parliamentary sessions regularly, he took for himself the minor office of lord privy seal and gave the most important job, first lord of the Treasury, to Augustus Henry Fitzroy, Duke of Grafton. The duke, who was far more interested in social pleasures and a mistress he took everywhere—even to the opera when his wife and the royal family were present—was an odd choice. But he worshiped Pitt and would "take up the spade and mattock" or do anything else for him. However, the only cabinet post Grafton was permitted to fill was chancellor of the Exchequer, and against Chatham's wishes Grafton picked Charles Townshend. Once more the relationship between Great Britain and her American colonies was to be jeopardized by a man singularly ill suited to handle it.

Although Townshend had suffered for years from epilepsy and other physical ailments, he was said to be a man of considerable ability. But according to Horace Walpole, he was immensely vain and apt to be "restless in any situation, fond of mischief." He was also contemptuous of Americans, distrustful of them, and determined that they be brought to heel. (It was he who had spoken in favor of Grenville's Stamp Tax, asking, "And now will these Americans, children planted by our care . . . grudge to contribute their mite to relieve us from the heavy weight of that burden which we lie under?" Which brought forth Barré's famous retort: "They planted by your care? No! Your oppressions planted them in America.")

Townshend was ambitious and was being pushed by George III to reopen the matter of taxes, so although he knew Chatham would not approve, he thrust himself into the project with a vengeance, at a time when Chatham was so ill and in such pain he was unable even to comprehend what was happening. For many years Townshend had felt the colonials were getting away with actions that threatened or undermined "the ancient and established prerogatives wisely preserved in the Crown," and now—thanks to the disarray in the cabinet—he had the opportunity to get back at them. Soon after the opening of the 1766–1767 session of Parliament, he set to work on a revenue plan.

Without consulting the other ministers, he announced that he would extract more revenue from the colonies, and in this he certainly had the support of the House of Commons. As Burke was to remark, Townshend "conformed exactly to the temper of the House; and he seemed to guide it, because he was always sure to follow it." When Benjamin Franklin learned what Townshend had in mind, he wrote his friend Joseph Galloway in Philadelphia saying, "People in Government here will never be satisfied without some revenue from America, nor America ever satisfy'd with their opposing it; so that disputes will . . . be perpetually arising. . . ." There was, he observed, a "general Rage against America," and he went on to note that "the Idea of an American Tax is very pleasing to the landed Men."

A man who heard Townshend propose his tax program to Parliament reported him as saying that ambitious men in several colonial assemblies were determined to end the colonies' dependence on Great Britain. To Townshend this meant that steps must be taken to show the Americans "that this country would not tamely suffer her sovereignty to be wrested out of her hands." He fully intended to "strike an awe into the factious and turbulent" with his program, and in June of 1767 he introduced a bill calling for colonial import duties on glass, lead for paint, paint colors, paper, and tea. To prevent the Americans from condemning them as "internal taxes," they were couched as import duties, and they were to take effect on November 20. The revenue from them was to be used for paying governors and judges, thus making those officials solely dependent on the crown for their salaries. The Townshend Act of 1767 also provided for a board of customs commissioners in North America, to be located in Boston. And—the real bombshell—as of October 1, 1767, the New York Assembly was suspended from doing any legislative business until such time as it supplied the king's soldiers with billets and all the items listed in the Quartering Act.

In September of 1767, Charles Townshend died suddenly at the age of forty-two, to be remembered as the man who eventually cost Great Britain her American colonies. His departure forced new changes in the ministry. The Duke of Grafton was recognized as *de facto* substitute for Chatham; Frederick North took Townshend's place at the Exchequer; and the office of a third secretary of state was established to deal with American affairs. Grafton was indolent and moody and preferred the racecourse to matters of state; North, thirty-six years old, was amiable, good-humored, and obligingly pliable; and Wills Hill, a young Irish nobleman with the title Earl of Hillsborough, who took over the third secretaryship, was a man of questionable judgment who knew enough to take orders. Shelburne, who *did* have strong views on American affairs but was too friendly with the colonials, remained as southern secretary of state but no longer had jurisdiction over the colonies. The very weakness of the ministry ensured that George III would be thrust into a more active role.

To New York the summer of 1767 brought intolerable heat and an epidemic of the "bloody flux"—the dreaded cholera morbus—which killed fourteen or fifteen residents every day. It also brought a chilling realization of what lay ahead when the Townshend Revenue Act and the punitive New York Restraining Act took effect. "What a dismal Prospect is before us!" one tradesman predicted; "a long Winter, and no Work; many unprovided with Firewood, or Money to buy it; House-rent and Taxes high; our Neighbors daily breaking, their Furniture at Vendue at every Corner."

Charles Townshend, after Sir Joshua Reynolds. *New York Public Library.*

Vociferous opposition to the Townshend Act and the Restraining Act was immediate and widespread, for the Restraining Act was an implied threat to *all* colonies, while the revenue bill was regarded as yet another tax without representation, especially since the monies raised were to pay the salaries of royal officials, making them independent of the assemblies. The ultimate insult under the Townshend Act was the sanctioning of writs of assistance, which authorized customs officials to enter and, if necessary, break into warehouses and homes to search for smuggled goods without any evidence of the owner's malfeasance.

The program devised by the late Charles Townshend was about to unleash a whirlwind.

14

A Tax on Tea

The flammable mixture of rival families, politics, and religion in New York was seldom more venomous than in the elections of 1768 and 1769. The warring families, as ever, were the Livingstons and DeLanceys, who had been feuding for three decades and more. Following the death of the elder James DeLancey in 1760, his family and their supporters slid into political decline, to be succeeded by the Livingstons and their allies. Robert R. Livingston, who was named to the Supreme Court in 1763, also served as a representative to the assembly from Dutchess County; his cousin William, the lawyer, represented the manor even though he resided in New York City; another cousin, Henry, was also elected in Dutchess County; while cousin Philip, from Brooklyn, was a delegate from New York City and County. Those four kinsmen, plus their numerous friends, translated into a potent political bloc—enough to control the legislature. In the wake of the Stamp Act upheaval, which sparked a great divide in New York politics, the Livingston faction held on to its dominance in the Assembly and for the next four years enjoyed the patronage of Governor Moore, thanks to amicable relations with him.

Judge Livingston was one of the most popular men in the city—admired for his intellect and sense of humor, his many achievements, his even disposition, and his sense of fairness and what was right. The social world in which he had grown to manhood was a relatively small one, and he had married his second cousin once removed, eighteen-year-old Margaret Beekman, whose inheritance of vast lands was added to his own Clermont holdings. Important though her dowry may have been in their union, theirs was a genuine love match that lasted for thirty-three years of married life.

They were often separated, since Margaret and the children spent most summers at Clermont to escape the city's heat and frequent epidemics of contagious diseases, while the Judge was preoccupied in town with family business and his civic duties. But Clermont, the brick mansion built by his father on a bluff that afforded a spectacular view across the three-quarter-mile breadth of the Hudson to the Catskills beyond, was seldom far from his thoughts. Even though he and his wife were apart, he was in constant touch by letter, asking her advice on business matters, teasing her when she failed to write, saying that her letters "bring me back to such a train of thinking as is most comfortable to a Christian." He wrote love letters, telling her his imagination "paints you with all your lovliness," reminding her that "without you I am nothing."

When Edward Livingston was born in 1764, shortly after his mother's fortieth birthday, he was her tenth child. The oldest was Robert R., Jr., who was twenty-one years old. It was a closely knit family, emotionally attached, living in what Margaret Livingston called a house of peace and love. All the children were interested in learning, and Robert R., Jr., who studied Greek, Latin, and "natural and moral philosophy" at King's College, delivered his graduation oration on a subject close to his father's heart—"in Praise of Liberty." Very quickly, the younger Robert took up the profession of law and was regarded as one of the promising newcomers in the field.

As the leading peacekeeper after the Stamp Act rioting, Judge Livingston had received a number of angry threats, and his deep concern at the time was that enforcement of the act would lead to "destruction of all Law, Order & Government in the colonies, and ruin all men of property. . . ." The ultimate danger, he feared, was the possibility of civil war. Now, in 1768, he was keenly aware of potential changes in the legislature's coloration, as the DeLanceys, led by the younger James and his uncle Oliver, brought fresh vigor to their party through alliance with Isaac Sears and the former Sons of Liberty.

That relationship had come about when the Sons took the Judge's efforts to calm and contain the rioters and prevent further outbreaks as interference with their tactics, and abandoned the Livingstons. The most tangible evidence of their disfavor was Isaac Sears's support of James DeLancey as a candidate for election to the Assembly in 1768.

Not all of Sears's followers approved his decision, but no matter, he prevailed, and when the election campaign opened in January 1768 the Liberty Boys launched an attack on John Morin Scott of "the triumvirate," the

Livingston-backed candidate for one of the four New York City seats in the Assembly. The DeLanceyites, known also as the popular party, evidently decided to concede one of the seats to Philip Livingston, an incumbent who was enormously popular (even with Isaac Sears). Although he was a cousin of Robert Livingston, Jr., third lord of Livingston Manor, he was, more important, a prominent merchant, and had been a delegate to the Stamp Act Congress. That left three seats, and two other wealthy merchants—James Jauncey and Jacob Walton—were chosen to join James DeLancey on the ticket.

The "leather-aprons" resented John Scott's criticism of their violent tactics in opposition to the Stamp Act, and as a prominent lawyer he was viewed with dark suspicion by them and many of the city's merchants—among them Isaac Sears. A broadside circulated during the campaign went straight to the point: The good people of the City, it declared, are supported by trade and the merchants. Lawyers are supported by the people.

The popular party kept printing presses clattering busily for weeks producing pamphlets, broadsides, and newspaper articles denouncing Scott and lawyers in general, who "fatten and grow rich upon the ruin of the people," while linking Scott to the landowners and their actions against their tenants. The moderates did their best to counter these attacks, and it was not long before religion became a burning issue.

In the 1760s in America, religion was as deeply entwined in many people's lives as it had been in the Middle Ages, and the strife that erupted in New York was the latest in a schism that went back to the 1640s in England, when Protestantism was splitting into a numbing array of splinters—Anglicans, High Church and Low, Puritans, Baptists, Separatists, and others. More recently, the dispute reflected a bitter argument in 1693 during the reign of William and Mary, when New York's Governor Fletcher had pushed through a reluctant New York Assembly an act calling for an Anglican church to be established in each of the five counties surrounding New York City. Fighting back, the Assembly voted that the minister in each parish must be selected by a majority vote of Freeholders, thus assuring that a Dissenter would be responsible for the souls in each church.

Under orders from the crown, however, successive governors blithely ignored or misinterpreted the law, ousting Dissenting ministers and replacing them with tax-supported Church of England men. The result was a permanent state of enmity between Anglicans and Dissenters. Too many of the latter had come to America seeking religious freedom or escape from an autocratic church to submit to teachings that the English king ruled by divine right, that obedience to that monarch and his administration was a duty of Christians, or that the Church of England was the one true church.

At the root of the Dissenters' anger was the well-founded suspicion that an ecclesiastical plot was woven into the policies of the king's ministers, animated by fear that the Society for the Propagation of the Gospel in Foreign Parts (the SPG) and Thomas Secker, the archbishop of Canterbury, were out to "episcopize" the colonies by weakening Dissenting religions, proselytizing, and sending bishops to American communities. Some years later, Samuel Seabury, an Anglican clergyman in Westchester, derided the charge that the clergy and the SPG had a plan "for enslaving America," saying it was preposterous, and that the people who spread such a lie do not "believe one Syllable of it But only intend it as an Engine to turn the popular fury upon the Church; which . . . will probably Fall a Sacrifice to the persecuting Spirit of Independency." Dissenters, however, thought otherwise.

They were well aware of the Anglican prelate's scheming and his opinion of them. Archbishop Secker was, in fact, the son of a Dissenter and had been raised and educated as one, but he joined the Church of England and through hard work, ability, and useful connections was eventually consecrated bishop of Bristol, then bishop of Oxford, from which pulpit he preached a sermon deploring the irreligion of American colonists, referring to non-Anglicans as "wicked, and dissolute, and brutal in every Respect."

In July of 1760 the then president of King's College, Samuel Johnson, had written to Archbishop Secker offering a plan for restructuring the governments of the colonies to rid them of "republican mobbish principles and practices." He proposed that Rhode Island, Connecticut, and Massachusetts be consolidated into a single province that would be governed by a viceroy appointed by the crown, and that as many as three bishops be appointed to ordain and govern the clergy and instruct and confirm the laity. Since Johnson had discussed his notion with a number of friends, news of his scheme spread like a raging fire through New England and the middle colonies, as did a rumor that a group of Anglicans in Newport were urging a colonial "Nobility appointed by the King for life." At about the same time a rich young clergyman named East Apthorp arrived in Boston and had a mansion built for him near Harvard Yard. The elegant home was promptly labeled "the Bishop's Palace" when word spread that it was to house the first American bishop.

All this was too much for Dissenters and nonchurchmen alike, whose animosity toward Anglicans had been in full sway since the archbishop of Canterbury opened a campaign for an American episcopate after the Peace of

Paris in 1763. The reaction to that was so quick and so heated that Archbishop Secker decided to drop the plan for the time being and await a more favorable climate. But the pressure continued unabated in New York, abetted by such figures as Charles Inglis, Samuel Auchmuty, Myles Cooper, who became president of King's College in 1763, and Samuel Seabury in Westchester.

The line that separated religion and politics grew ever dimmer until it was virtually indistinguishable. On the one hand, Anglicans were convinced that members of the Dissenting clergy were responsible for "promoting and spiriting up the People to that Pitch of Madness, Tumult, and Disaffection which so generally prevailed" during the Stamp Act troubles.

For their part, Dissenting ministers believed that the Anglicans were threatening liberty itself—both religious and civil. Their fear of an American episcopate was that it would apply political pressure to deny religious freedom to nonconformists, who had fought so hard for it during the past century and a half in America. In 1769, Presbyterians and Baptists founded the Society of Dissenters to oppose an episcopacy. Much of their grudge had to do with the fact that they were forced to pay taxes to support a church to which they did not belong, and although they constituted a majority of the population they could do nothing to induce the Anglican-dominated Council to relieve them of this financial burden. In the same year, Lewis Morris moved in the Assembly to "exempt protestants of all denominations . . . from the payment of taxes raised for the support of a religious persuasion to which they do not belong"—this on grounds that such taxes were "palpably partial and unjust." His bill passed on May 15 but was rejected by the Council four days later. William Smith, Jr., a Presbyterian, cast the only vote in favor of it.

John Adams of Braintree, Massachusetts, described how "our pulpits have thundered," arousing "the unconquerable rage of the people." It delighted him to see how those in all levels of society had become more attentive to their liberties and more determined to fight for them. What outraged the young lawyer was the effort to introduce canon, or ecclesiastical, law, convincing him that "there seems to be a direct and formal design on foot to enslave America."

The attitude of nonconformists hardened when they learned that eleven of the thirteen Anglican bishops in the House of Lords opposed repeal of the Stamp Act. Henry Cruger, Jr., son of a Council member, wrote his father from England on February 14, 1766, saying that all the "King's Friends," including nine bishops, were "for carrying Fire and Sword to America, with this Argument, that since you snarle and begin to shew your Teeth, they ought to be knocked out before you are able to bite."

The Reverend William Gordon quoted the English evangelist George Whitefield as saying, "My heart bleeds for America. O poor New England! There is a deep laid plot against both your civil and religious liberties, and they will both be lost. Your golden days are at an end. You have nothing but trouble ahead of you." And Gordon himself believed that "once Episcopacy has got a footing, there's no knowing where it will stop."

One great advantage the Dissenters possessed was an unparalleled communications link, which had been developed over the years among colonial clerics and with their fellow ministers across the Atlantic. One Sunday morning in June of 1766, the Reverend Jonathan Mayhew, who was an early champion of religious freedom in New England and "one of the great polemical writers this or any other country has ever seen," according to the *Boston Gazette,* got to thinking about the committees of correspondence developed by clergymen and sent a note to James Otis, suggesting that the Massachusetts Assembly send circulars to all the other assemblies on various matters of common interest. Mayhew had been impressed by the common bonds that developed during and after the Stamp Act Congress, which had "contributed not a little towards our obtaining lately a redress of grievances," and believed that "Pursuing this course, or never losing sight of it, may be of the greatest importance to the colonies, perhaps the only means of perpetuating their liberties." Mayhew warned, "It is not safe for the colonies to sleep; for it is probable they will always have some wakeful enemies in Great Britain."

As the ugly dispute between Anglicans and Dissenters continued, the former argued that the independent religions "produce Republicans in the State and from their Principles . . . the greatest evils may justly be apprehended." Since the Church of England was the national as well as the true Christian church, it followed that Dissenters had no rights. They would be countenanced—but only just—until such time as they should conform to the established church. The Reverend Samuel Auchmuty, rector of Trinity Church, wrote to Sir William Johnson in 1767, speaking of the Dissidents, "These restless People enjoy Privileges enough already by the Act of Toleration; should they be vested with more, they will indanger the established Church, to say nothing of the State."

The fighting between sects could be vicious, as Ambrose Serle, civilian secretary to Admiral Richard Howe, discovered. In November of 1776, a year and a half after the War of the Revolution began, he wrote to Lord Dartmouth to say that of all the causes of the war, religion and "the preachers here of all denominations" represented the major obstacle to peace and reconciliation. In New York, he said, "the ministers were all Politicians to a Man," and he could not have believed that so many teachers of "public Inflammation" could be found, or that they could have universally forgotten that the "first Principles of their Profession are Peace, Love, and Goodwill towards all Men."

Anglicans and Dissenters alike were to blame for the fact that "Under the Notion of Godliness, so much evident Hypocrisy and Wickedness are not to be found in all the World as in our Colonies of North America."

Then, proceeding to list all the men of the Anglican Church, followed by those of the Dissenters, he told Dartmouth that he named them with some pain. Most, he said, disseminate principles "which only make Men bad Subjects and bad Neighbours," rather than to "inculcate that Purity of Doctrine which tends to promote Happiness in a Man's own Heart, and Peace and Forbearance with all the world."

This war, he concluded, is "very much a religious war."

In 1769, Cadwallader Colden—a staunch Anglican—wrote to the Society for the Propagation of the Gospel and tried to describe the attitude of the Dissenters living near his country place, Coldengham. They were members of several different denominations, he said, and were extremely disputatious among themselves. "One thing however they seem to agree in & the only one in which they do, viz., a blind, bigoted prejudice & opposition to the church of Engld. . . ."

In 1767 the Presbyterians petitioned the king for the fifth time to grant them the premises of their church on Wall Street and a charter, only to be turned down on advice of the Lords of Trade as a result of lobbying by the New York Council, which was dominated by Anglicans. In the election campaign, the Livingstons hoped to capitalize on the Presbyterians' resentment by inducing other dissenting faiths to turn against the DeLancey candidates in the election. Further antagonism toward Church of England partisans arose in reaction to a campaign by the Anglican cleric Thomas Bradbury Chandler for an American episcopate, when the old fears of ecclesiastical courts and an American bishopric surfaced again. As an added fillip, moderates spread the word that James DeLancey, who was visiting in England, was doing his best there to have an Anglican bishop appointed for the colonies.

Describing the 1768 electioneering, one New Yorker said the "Contagion of Politiks" was such that we "know Nothing Else nor Discourse upon Anything Else," and the "Contagion" meant no holds barred, including bribery, buying votes, and outright threats against backsliders who might be tempted to vote for the other faction's candidates.

Unfortunately for the Livingstons, their efforts to attract Dissenters failed for several reasons. People voted their stomachs, not their souls, in these days of economic distress, and many simply resented the introduction of religion into what was plainly a political debate. When the acrimonious 1768 campaign finally ended, John Morin Scott finished last. Predictably, Philip Livingston came in first, followed by DeLancey, Walton, and Jauncey, in that order. The Livingston party suffered another blow when Robert R.—the Judge—lost his Dutchess County seat; farmers encouraged by recent rural uprisings against the great landowners and mindful of how Livingston landlords had called on British troops to put them down collected enough votes to throw out their most distinguished citizen. All was not lost, however; the Livingstons won every seat north of Westchester County, and Philip, who had strong connections to both the landed gentry and the merchants, was made speaker of the House.

Across the Atlantic another election was held in 1768 and brought John Wilkes, recently returned from exile in France, to London as a newly elected member of Parliament for Middlesex County. The king, livid over this turn of events and still fuming over Wilkes's libelous remarks in 1764, informed Lord North, the leader of Commons, "that the expulsion of Mr. Wilkes seems to be very essential and must be effected." (North collected enough votes to comply, but Wilkes ran for office twice more from jail and was twice reelected, only to be held for seditious libel and blasphemy and declared "incapable of being elected to serve in the present Parliament." He remained in prison until 1770.) The reappearance of Wilkes was cause for rejoicing and mob violence in London, and for dismay by George III and the conservative Grafton ministry, while colonials needed no reminders that the recently instituted writs of assistance bore a strong resemblance to the general warrants used to imprison Wilkes in the first place. Once again the cry "Wilkes and Liberty!" was heard in the streets of New York and Boston.

On the heels of Wilkes's incarceration, the spectral figure of William Pitt, Earl of Chatham, risen from his bed of pain, reappeared in Parliament, to inform the king that he wished to resign as lord privy seal. That brought about the resignation of Shelburne, and it became evident that the Grafton ministry was beginning to unravel.

The British capital, Benjamin Franklin wrote to a friend, is "a daily scene of lawless riot and confusion. Mobs patrolling the streets at noonday, some knocking all down that will not roar for Wilkes and liberty; courts of justice afraid to give judgment against him; coal-heavers and porters pulling down the houses of coal merchants that refuse to give them more wages; sawyers destroying sawmills; sailors unrigging all the outward-bound ships and suffering none to sail till merchants agree to raise their pay; watermen destroying private boats and threatening bridges; soldiers firing among the mobs and killing men, women, and children; which seems only to have produced a universal sullenness that looks like a great black cloud coming on, ready to burst in a general tempest. What the event will be God only knows. But some punishment seems preparing for a people who are ungratefully abusing the best constitution and the best king any nation was ever blessed with, intent on nothing but luxury, licentiousness, power, places, pensions, and plunder."

Franklin was expressing the belief of virtually all Americans that they had the best of kings and constitutions. George III was a symbol, obviously, since few colonials could possibly know him, and there was about him an aura of mystery and grandeur and power, along with a tradition going back across the centuries that people owed unquestioning allegiance to the crown and the man or woman who wore it. The faithful Anglican churchgoer attending morning and evening prayer services was instructed to beseech the Lord twice daily to bless that most gracious sovereign King George III, and that ritual, repeated year after year, generation upon generation, was bound to have the effect of sealing the bond between crown and subject.

As for the constitution, that was beginning to be another matter—the problem being that Americans believed they were entitled to the same rights that *every* Englishman possessed, whether living in Great Britain or the American colonies, and they were determined not to be deprived of them.

The Wilkes affair made it clear that the king's authority in the 1760s was enhanced by hard-liners who had taken charge, men who saw law enforcement and punishment as the answers to irregularity, whether the deviation was Wilkes or food riots or colonial discontent. The Declaratory Act was a perfect example of the rigidity they sought and indicative of their determination to keep the colonists under the Parliamentary thumb.

As relations between the mother country and colonies steadily deteriorated, three thoughtful, intensely patriotic men who had given serious attention for some years to the mounting administrative problems of an expanding

William Smith, Jr. *New-York Historical Society.*

empire came up with imaginative, workable solutions to the looming crisis. Each had benefited from the thinking of the others, with whom they were well acquainted. Best-known of the three was Benjamin Franklin, who had been thinking about this matter for a quarter century, and continued to hold to his vision of a confederation of the colonies, with a central government empowered to raise taxes and make laws that would take effect after review by the king. That was the core of the ideas he had prescribed in the failed Albany Plan of Union in 1754.

Another was William Smith, Jr., who had studied the dilemma from the vantage point of a New York lawyer and member of the Council. His ideas stemmed from a conviction that the British constitution must be more flexible, to accommodate the colonies' growing maturity and redefine their position within the empire. He recognized that the existing, popularly elected assemblies were unlikely to comprehend or appreciate imperial imperatives— notably the very real need for revenues—so he decided that the answer lay in a restructuring of institutions that would give America its own Parliament, or legislature, in tandem with a Council composed of two dozen royally appointed members, and "a Lord Lieutenant as in Ireland." This Parliament of North America would be made up of deputies chosen by the colonial assemblies and would meet in New York, as the appropriately central location. In the all-important matter of revenue collection, the king would make a requisition each year to the American Parliament, which would determine how much each colony would pay, and each colonial assembly would then decide how to raise its portion.

This would put an end to the hated taxation by Parliament, leaving that body to exercise "Legislative Supremacy, in all Cases relative to Life Liberty and Property, except in the Matter of Taxation for general Aids, or the immediate, internal Support of the American Government."

The third man, an unusual Englishman named Thomas Pownall, had first appeared on the public scene in the fall of 1753 as private secretary and chief assistant to the unhappy Sir Danvers Osborn, who killed himself six days after arriving in New York as governor, leaving Pownall to wonder what he would do in America without a job, friends, political support, or independent means. Fortunately, he had a rare gift for making friends and an inquisitive mind, and he looked on being a castaway, as it were, as an adventure and decided to make the most of being in the New World. He went first to Philadelphia, where, in four weeks' time, he met many of its notable personalities, including Benjamin Franklin, Lewis Evans, John Penn, and Governor Hamilton. He visited Alexandria, Annapolis, New York, New Haven, Providence, and Boston and joined the Pennsylvania delegation attending the Albany conference that produced the Plan of Union. There he became acquainted with such figures as Thomas Hutchinson of Massachusetts, James DeLancey, and William Johnson, plus Indians, trappers, and Albany merchants, and quickly discovered that those dealing with the Indians sought "constantly to amass a hasty fortune by every means fair and foul by which a farthing could be pickd or scrapd out of these poor defrauded people."

Over the course of the next year, Pownall devised a comprehensive plan for frontier settlement and defense which presaged that of the important land ordinance of 1785. He spent months with the cartographer Lewis Evans, and the two men concluded that a map of the disputed lands in the west was an essential adjunct to future settlement, so Pownall screened the diaries, journals, letters, and reports that came in to Evans and did much firsthand research, and when the map was published in 1755 it included a dedication to the Englishman. By May of that year, Pownall was sufficiently well known and so knowledgeable about America that the Board of Trade named him as lieutenant governor of New Jersey.

Two years later, after his appointment as governor of Massachusetts to replace William Shirley, he became deeply involved in the French and Indian War and was singled out for praise by Pitt and the king. Pownall was extremely popular with the public and with John Hancock and the leading merchants, who gave him a memorable farewell party before he returned to England in June 1760. Another admirer was John Adams, who described him as "a friend of liberty, the most constitutional governor, in my opinion, who ever represented the crown in this province." In England, in 1764, he published a book, *The Administration of the Colonies,* which was reprinted in five subsequent editions. It was a critique of the existing colonial system by a man who had been part of it and studied it carefully for a number of years, and who discussed frankly its many flaws while adding constructive ideas on how to reform the governance of the vitally important American colonies.

Pownall's hopes of achieving a proper place in English society were improved when he fell in love with and married a widow who was well connected with the aristocracy. Her interest in his career put him in touch with many important people and led to his election to Parliament in 1767. He remained in close touch with friends on both sides in Massachusetts—Governor Francis Bernard and Lieutenant Governor Thomas Hutchinson on the one hand, John Hancock on the other—and spent many hours with Benjamin Franklin in London, exchanging ideas on American affairs. Perhaps his most important contribution to a settlement of the abrasive imperial relationship was an unusually bold speech to the House of Commons in April 1769, when he moved that Parliament put an end to the Townshend duties.

Echoing colonial complaints, he condemned the Townshend measures as unjust, since the revenue they produced went for the salaries of royal governors and civil servants. He insisted that compromise was the only way to head off a collision of the hardening positions of Britain and America, and his voice was certainly a factor in changing the ministry's position.

At the time Townshend pushed through his tax program, the goal had been to raise revenue to relieve the load on British taxpayers. Now the situation was quite different. Grafton and other ministers considered the Townshend duties useless and had for a year been considering repeal, saying the small revenue they yielded couldn't possibly compensate for losses suffered by British merchants as a result of the colonial boycott. But Lord North, chancellor of the Exchequer, reflecting the king's determination, regarded repeal as an abdication of Parliament's right to tax and a defeat the colonists would surely view as weakness. "Upon my word," he said, "if we are to run after America in search of reconciliation in this way, I do not know a single act of Parliament that will remain."

North then came up with a scheme that did away with the duties on paint, lead, paper, and glass, while retaining only a tax on tea. Tea, he observed, came from India, but the other dutiable items were produced in England, and since it was not in Britain's interest to collect a customs duty on its own products, the taxes on all but tea could be repealed.

The cabinet was split on the issue, but in a five-to-four vote, the government committed itself to continuing the policy of taxing the colonies, come what may. On a single vote, so much would hinge.

Franklin, Smith, and Pownall—three men with unparalleled knowledge of colonial affairs, each with the deep conviction that something must be done to preserve a viable relationship between the mother country and her colonies—had done what they could to bring about change and convince London that the colonies were worthy of the friendliest consideration England could give them. Regrettably, no one in a position of responsibility was listening.

15

Incentive to Rebellion

James Otis had not forgotten the advice given him by the Reverend Jonathan Mayhew about communicating with other colonies, nor had his colleague Samuel Adams, and in February of 1768 the Massachusetts House of Representatives sent a letter to its fellow assemblies inviting them to join in forming a united, intercolonial front to oppose the recent harsh measures passed by Parliament. The letter, while acknowledging Parliament as "the supreme legislative Power over the whole Empire," questioned the government's right to pay the salaries of colonial governors and judges and went on to declare that no taxes, external or internal, could be imposed on Americans so long as they were not represented in Parliament. In April, Virginia approved the Massachusetts letter and sent a circular letter of its own to other colonies, reinforcing the plea for union against unlawful taxation.

As luck would have it, news of this reached London at the same time Wilkes reemerged on the scene and the Grafton ministry, faced with riots at home and resistance abroad, instructed Wills Hill, Lord Hillsborough, the new secretary of state for America, to issue "most positive Instructions" to the Americans. The Massachusetts letter was denounced as "little better than an incentive to rebellion," and Hillsborough promptly instructed colonial assemblies to treat it "with the contempt it deserves."

Hillsborough, who was regarded by Benjamin Franklin as a pompous bungler with singular lack of ability or finesse,* demanded that the Massachusetts

---

*Franklin said of him, "His character is Conceit, Wrongheadedness, Obstinacy, and Passion," but it should be noted that Hillsborough opposed certain land promotion schemes that Franklin espoused, mostly because the new colonial secretary believed that western expansion meant a continuation of Indian wars.

Assembly rescind its action or be dissolved and ordered the royal governors of other colonies to dismiss their legislatures if those bodies responded favorably to the Massachusetts request.

As one of the "King's Friends," Hillsborough had the monarch's confidence and was a close friend of General Thomas Gage, and he was thought to have a broad knowledge of the colonies and their affairs. A colonial agent in London described him as "a man of business, alert, lively, ready, but too fond of his own opinions and systems and too apt to be inflexibly attached to them; by no means so gentle and easy to be entreated as his predecessor [Shelburne]. . . ." One of his friends observed that he was not a man of vision: "His ideas are all little and confined." Whatever else he may have been, Hillsborough was determined that his policy toward the Americans would be that of a hand of iron inside a velvet glove. No weakening or backing down.

According to a disturbing report in the *New York Journal,* if America resisted Hillsborough's commands the government would "send Men of War to all trading Towns on the Continent, and stop all your trade." Not only that: the government would also dispatch "a number of Soldiers to humble you."

The first real challenge to the Townshend Act was nothing like the reaction to the Stamp Act. It came in the form of a series of letters that began appearing in the *Pennsylvania Chronicle and Universal Advertiser* on December 2, 1767, and were later published as a pamphlet titled *Letters from a Farmer in Pennsylvania to the Inhabitants of the British Colonies.* These essays, written by John Dickinson of Philadelphia, were an immediate and stunning success and were reprinted in virtually every newspaper in the colonies. As pamphlets, they appeared in Philadelphia, Boston, New York, Dublin, Paris, and London, where a preface by Benjamin Franklin was added.

Dickinson, born in 1732, was the son of a Maryland planter. Following his early education in America he studied law in the Middle Temple in London and then established a successful law practice in Philadelphia, where he was elected to a seat in the Assembly. His first letter began with beguilingly simple, just-plain-folks sentences: "I am a *Farmer,* settled after a variety of fortunes near the banks of the river *Delaware,* in the province of *Pennsylvania.* . . . My farm is small, my servants are few, and good; I have a little money at interest; I wish for no more; my employment in my own affairs is easy. . . ." Having established himself as a modest, cautious fellow with sensible views, he went on to deal specifically with New York's immediate difficulties.

His was a voice many Americans were ready to hear—that of a trusted family attorney who knew the law thoroughly and was able to guide his clients carefully and patiently through a maze of historical precedents while interpreting the British constitution for them. "With a good deal of sur-prize," he wrote, "I have observed that little notice has been taken of an act of parliament as injurious in its principle to the liberties as the *Stamp-Act* was: I mean the act for suspending the legislation of *New-York*."

This act, he went on, "is a parliamentary assertion of the *supreme authority* of the *British* legislature over these colonies in *the point of taxation,* and is intended to COMPEL *New-York* unto a submission to that authority. It seems therefore to me as much a violation of the liberty of the people of that province, and consequently of all these colonies, as if the parliament had sent a number of regiments to be quartered upon them, till they should comply." The cause of one colony is the cause of all, he cautioned his readers, and "I earnestly wish that all the rest may with equal ardour support their sister." Finally, he made the point that endeared him to moderates like the Liv-ingstons: "I am by no means fond of inflammatory measures. I detest them. . . . But a firm, modest exertion of a free spirit should never be wanting on public occasions."

Subsequent letters dealt with such issues as the Treasury's unwelcome new board of customs commissioners in Boston, charged with collecting revenues from the new duties; the granting of writs of assistance that would permit customs officers to search American homes; the creation of an American civil list to pay governors, judges, and other royal officials, removing the power of the purse from colonial assemblies; and, of course, the added duties them-selves. Dickinson argued that it mattered little whether a tax was called inter-nal or external: what was at issue was whether a tax was intended to raise revenue rather than regulate trade.

Over and over, he cautioned moderation. "Anger produces anger," he warned, "and differences that might be accommodated by kind and respectful behaviour may by imprudence be enlarged to an incurable rage." He con-demned "excesses and outrages," saying it was foolish to think that rioting would produce results. It was important that Americans' rights should be defended, not by violent action, but by constitutional means such as petitions or nonimportation. And like Franklin, he reminded his fellow colonials, "We have an excellent prince, in whose good dispositions toward us we may confide."

Many a visitor to New York felt obliged to bolster his impressions with statis-tics, and Mr. G. Taylor of Sheffield, England, was one of them. After travel-ing from New Haven in a single-horse chair, or chaise, he found lodgings at the King's Arms near the Oswego Market and in mid-September of 1768 began his tour of the growing metropolis. More than eighteen thousand souls lived here in upward of three thousand houses, he reported, and the city was "pretty well built," extending about a mile in length and half that in breadth, with "a beautiful prospect from the sea." Irregular though the streets were, they were well paved and most of the houses were constructed of brick, "in the Dutch method."

Clearly impressed by the spacious, comfortable public buildings, he listed among them the synagogue and eighteen churches, of which the Presbyterian and Methodist Episcopal (or "John Street Meeting") had been completed within the year. His walks around the city took him past what he generously termed the "Governor's Palace" inside Fort George, City Hall, the Exchange, the New Gaol, the hospital and almshouse, the troops' barracks, and five markets. Boarding the "stage-boat," he sailed up the East River to Flushing, Long Island, taking admiring note of the riverside's "beautiful plantations; and all along . . . the country houses of the City Merchants." The soil on Manhattan was fertile, he concluded, despite being so rocky.

Taylor was especially interested to see that "The Dutch, who inhabit the greatest part of this shore, come to market some twenty, some thirty miles down this river in small boats to New-York. The wives generally row the boat, while the husbands sit in an idle posture smoking. . . ." (One statistic Taylor failed to mention was that New York City had twenty-seven holidays in the course of each year—one every two weeks.)

The city Taylor visited had seen a number of changes recently. Vauxhall, formerly leased by Major James and severely damaged during the Stamp Act riots, had been extensively refurbished and had a grand opening as Vauxhall Garden, with a showy exhibit of wax figures. A Chamber of Commerce organized by twenty prominent merchants was holding meetings at Fraunces Tavern under its newly elected president, Mayor John Cruger. Earlier in the year the Assembly had voted £1,000 for an equestrian statue of George III to perpetuate for posterity "the eminent and singular Blessings received from him during his most auspicious Reign." Funding of £500 for an elegant brass statue of William Pitt had been voted earlier, in honor of "many eminent and essential Services done the Northern Colonies"—in particular his efforts in repealing the Stamp Act.

The new John Street Theatre opened at the end of 1767 with the American Company's comedy *The Stratagem,* plus a "dramatic satire call'd *Lethe.*" The building itself was not much to look at: it was made of wood, painted red, and stood about sixty feet back from the street; it was entered through a covered walkway of rough wood. But the place's appearance bothered some people less than what they found—or suspected they might find—inside. One resident wrote to the *New-York Journal* to complain that the price of tickets—£50 for a box for the season, he had heard—would work a hardship on his favorite charity. The plight of the homeless was desperate, and "The money thrown away in one night at a play would purchas wood, provisions and other necessaries, sufficient for a number of poor, to make them pass thro' the winter with tolerable comfort. . . ."

Another correspondent who signed himself "J.R." listed the evils that "this nuisance" caused: spending scarce cash for a ticket, the expense of dressing for the evening, "Obscene discourses" on the stage, "promoting a taste for dissipation, or gadding, already too prevalent among the young folks," providing "a rendezvous for many people to adjourn to the tavern," and diverting people's attention from charity. (Despite J.R., the company performed throughout the season until June, and the players were back again the following year.)

But New York's collective attention was on far more serious matters. For one thing, times were tough in the city. To the dismay of all, the boom that began with repeal of the Stamp Act had gone flat. "Never was a Country so embarrassed as this," the army officer John Maunsell complained in the early months of the depression, "our paper Curr[ency] Almost exhausted: all the Gold and Silver sent home & trade quite dead, the difficulty to live here is inconceivable, the marketts as high as ever, Labour . . . expensive. . . ." New York City had its "meaner Class of Mankind, the industrious Poor"; its homeless were increasingly evident to passersby; and an article urging people to assist these unfortunates characterized it as simple justice, not charity, to do so.* A committee appointed at a public meeting studied the situation and recommended that residents practice "Frugality and Industry," disregard the Townshend duties, and forgo a list of proscribed imports.

William Smith, Jr.—Billy Smith, as John Watts called him—had taken his father's seat on the Council and quoted the governor as saying, "The Boston People had invited the People of N York to join in a Confederacy not to send for Goods." Confiding in Smith, Moore had asked what he should do about the proposed boycott, to which Smith replied that since "our people were suspicious of Philadelphia" and since Boston was quarreling with its Governor

*Not until 1782 would a Society for Alleviating the Distresses of the Poor be established.

Bernard, Governor Moore and his Council should sit tight, do nothing, and wait for New York's merchants to accept or reject Boston's proposals.

Moore may have felt out of his depth on some of these intricate political matters. On an occasion when he and his wife had visited Philip Schuyler's house in Albany, a young Scottish lady named Miss McVickar was also a guest. Taking Sir Henry's measure, she wrote that he "had never thought of business in his life . . . spent more than he had . . . was gay, good natured, and well-bred, affable and courteous, in a very high degree." But he and Lady Moore, she continued, "were too fashionable and too much hurried to find time for particular friendships, and too good natured and well-bred to make invidious distinctions."

Now, Sir Henry Moore was understandably concerned. Less than a year earlier, Isaac Sears and some 240 New York merchants had presented him with a petition, requesting that he forward it to Parliament. The petition outlined their grievances on the parlous state of trade and the disadvantages under which they were operating and urged the government to return to the trade and navigation regulations that had been in effect for several decades prior to the French and Indian War. Moore's thanks for forwarding the petition was a severe rebuke by Hillsborough and a generally hostile reaction in Britain, including that of the Americans' friend Chatham, who called the document "highly improper" and went on to say, "What demon of discord blows the coals in that devoted province I know not; but they are doing the work of their worst enemies themselves." And so it was with the London merchants, who continued to wish the New Yorkers would "express filial Duty and Gratitude to your Parent Country."

New York merchants remained cautious. In response to the Bostonians' request they decided not to accept products shipped from Britain after October 1 if the Townshend Act was not repealed. But they attached a proviso, saying they would do so only if Boston and Philadelphia did likewise. Fortunately for the unenthusiastic New Yorkers, Philadelphia's tradesmen rejected nonimportation, but the respite was short-lived. On August 1 the Boston merchants announced their decision to stop importing British goods on January 1, 1769.

Although the Livingstons had been dealt a major setback in the '68 voting, they still held a margin of power in the Assembly and hoped to avoid a dissolution of that body, which would mean new elections. The atmosphere in the city was tense, with agitation pro and con the Massachusetts circular letter,

John Dickinson, by Charles Willson Peale. *Independence National Historic Park.*

demonstrators marching, effigies of Governor Bernard of Massachusetts and the Boston sheriff being burned, the eternal arguments over funds for quartering the troops, and merchants organizing under Isaac Sears to "ask what was become of the Boston Letters." Sears and his friends drew up a set of instructions that called Lord Hillsborough's letter "the most daring Insult that ever was offer'd to any free Legislative Body" and called upon the representatives to read the Massachusetts letter in the House and once again to take a stand against Parliament's requisition of money for quartering troops.

A majority in the Assembly rejected Moore's request for funds for quartering Gage's soldiers, addressed a strongly worded petition to the House of Lords protesting Parliamentary measures that threatened colonial trade, the jury system, and the colony's independence in general, and then outdid themselves by adopting a set of resolves that declared the Restraining Act illegal and asserted their right to correspond and consult with other colonies "wherever they conceive the rights, liberties, or privileges of the [Assembly] or its constituents to be affected."

Predictably, Governor Moore declared the resolves "repugnant to the laws of Great Britain," dissolved the Assembly, and called for new elections.

If anything, religious issues were even more blatant in the 1769 election than in 1768, voices were shriller, name-calling was louder and more abusive, fewer people went to the polls, and the DeLanceys swept the field.

When John Watts wrote to General Monckton on September 12, he reported that "Sir Harry Moore died yesterday after some days illness of a mortification of the bowels. Today Mr. Colden is expected in town once more to take upon him the administration of the Government. He fairly lives himself into office, being they tell me as hearty as when you knew him." Colden was now in his eighty-first year, and it was four years since he had left the city broken in spirit after his last stint as acting governor, four years during which his humiliation at the hands of Moore and the London functionaries had rankled. He knew he had been the king's faithful servant, yet the king's ministers never stood up for him when the Assembly refused to compensate him for his final months in office in 1765 (saying he had brought on the Stamp Act troubles by his own actions and deserved no salary), nor had they forced the Assembly to reimburse him for the loss of his carriage and other possessions. He had relished the thought of a return to power, and now that it was here he intended to get what was coming to him. A number of factors were in his favor.

For starters he inherited from Moore a Council that had only one Presbyterian (and therefore "radical") member—William Smith, Jr. For another, the DeLanceys wanted patronage and he was able and willing to oblige—for a price. He wanted his salary in full, to be paid by the Assembly when it was due, he wanted calm in the city, and he wanted money appropriated for the army. In return, the DeLanceys would get their patronage and he agreed not to dissolve the Assembly.

Writing to Hillsborough, Colden noted that he had taken the oath of office the day after Moore's funeral and while he was not yet sufficiently informed about the state of public affairs to comment intelligently, he did want to assure the earl that "it shall be my constant endeavour to keep the Province in Peace, & Tranquility." When next he wrote, he was able to inform Hillsborough that the Council and Assembly had promised to "make my administration easy to me."

What was on the assemblymen's minds, Colden added, was the long-sought approval by the king of a £120,000 paper currency bill. Hard money—sterling, in particular—was not to be had in New York, and the economy continued to suffer from the lack of it. On December 16 he wrote again, reporting that the Assembly had voted an appropriation for quartering the troops, but had not yet resolved the question of how to fund it—whether from the provincial treasury or from interest on that £120,000, which was to be issued as bills of credit. As the days dragged on with no word from London, the legislature compromised, appropriated £2,000 for the military, and decided to fund half of it from each source. Colden signed the bill reluctantly, for it ran counter to instructions in the Currency Act of 1764 prohibiting a governor from endorsing a paper money bill unless it contained a clause suspending its operation until approved by the king's Privy Council.

The acting governor was having a difficult time clarifying matters, especially the anomalies that were so evident, for his superiors in London. In one of his letters he mentioned that the Assembly—"very sensible how much it is the interest of the Colonies to have the mutual Confidence between Great Britain and the Colonies restored"—had nevertheless concurred with and adopted the resolves in the Virginia circular letter, which supported the Massachusetts plea for union against unlawful taxation. This action, Colden explained awkwardly, was taken because the New York legislators did not know whether Parliament would react favorably to their petitions. If not, they wanted to take care "not to lose their popularity" with the people of New York and the other colonies.

Colden was not the only one confused by the shifting sands of politics. The Livingstons were quick to see that a new broom was at work. Colden had promised the young Philip Livingston a job in his administration but gave it instead to Goldsbrow Banyar, a DeLancey man. The lieutenant governor also turned out the sheriffs of Westchester and Dutchess counties (Livingston appointees) and replaced them with DeLancey loyalists. In the Assembly the DeLanceys passed a bill requiring members to reside in their districts, thereby removing Philip Livingston (a Brooklyn resident) from the manor seat, and when, in the next election, Judge Livingston stood for the manor and was elected in a landslide, the Assembly voted to deny judges seats in the chamber. (For four more years the Judge ran for the manor seat and was reelected by an overwhelming margin, only to be denied membership in the legislature.) For some time he had been deeply depressed by the turn of events. "Madness seems to prevail on the other side of the water; melancholy and dejection on this," he wrote to his father, adding, "This country appears to have seen its best days."

As gloomy as the future might appear to a Livingston, the tide was about to shift during the months to come. In allying themselves with Cadwallader Colden the DeLanceys were forced to put their stamp of approval on measures that were unpopular with the Sons of Liberty, who had reorganized in July of 1769 to support nonimportation, and the Livingstons—to their considerable astonishment and frequent discomfort—found themselves cheek by jowl with Isaac Sears and the Liberty Boys. Only recently scorned, the aristocrats were once more the darlings of the popular party.

Funding in any form for Gage's army was anathema to Sears and his followers, and their determination was reinforced when South Carolina joined Massachusetts in defying the Quartering Act. When, suddenly, the DeLancey-led Assembly passed a military appropriation by a single vote, Sears and John Lamb were enraged. The next day an inflammatory broadside with the headline "To the Betrayed Inhabitants of the City and Colony of New York" appeared on street corners throughout Manhattan. (The method of secretly affixing incendiary material to the walls of buildings while concealing the perpetrator dated back to the time of the Pretender in England. This was for a man to carry a box on his back containing a small boy. While the man leaned against the wall, as if to rest himself, the boy slid open a door at the rear of the box, pasted the broadside on the wall, and shut himself up again, and when the coast was clear, the man resumed his walk.)

The opening lines of the handbill, which was addressed to "My dear Fellow Citizens and Countrymen," read, "In a Day when the Minions of Tyranny and Despotism in the Mother Country and the Colonies, are indefatigable in laying every Snare that their malevolent and corrupt Hearts can suggest, to enslave a free People . . ." and went on to detail how representatives in the New York Assembly had betrayed the trust committed to their constituents when they granted money to the troops without the consent of the people. The representatives were answerable to the people, and had failed them. Those troops were "kept here, not to protect, but to enslave us."

The Assembly's action of December 15, the handbill continued, resulted from a bargain between Mr. Colden and the DeLancey family, those "true Politicians [who] were to all Appearance, at mortal Odds with Mr. Colden, and represented him . . . as an Enemy to his Country," only to join him in order to secure for themselves the "Sovereign Lordship of this Colony" while providing Colden with his salary and offices for his children.

The scathing attack concluded with an appeal to fellow-countrymen to arise: "Will you suffer your liberties to be torn from you by your own Representatives? Tell it not in Boston; publish it not in the Streets of Charlestown!"* Finally, the author of the handbill urged them to attend a mass meeting in the Fields on Monday, December 18, after which they should go in a body to the Assembly and insist that their representatives join the minority in opposing the bill. The handbill was signed "A Son of Liberty."

Reaction in the Assembly the following morning was outrage. At the request of James DeLancey the broadside was condemned by a margin of twenty to one (Philip Schuyler of Albany cast the lone negative vote) as a "false, seditious, and infamous libel" on both the Assembly and the lieutenant governor, and a £100 reward was offered for the identity of the unknown Son of Liberty.

*That is, Charleston, South Carolina.

16

The Wilkes of America

Tuesday, January 9, 1770, was the opening day of Parliament, and throngs of angry Londoners lined the streets as His Majesty's coach made its way to the House of Lords. This was traditionally an auspicious ceremonial moment, but in sharp contrast to the enthusiastic crowds that had greeted him in prior years, on this occasion the king was hissed and booed along the route. The ugly mood of the people was easy to understand, for across England thousands of workers were idle, their families going hungry, thanks to the boycott of English goods by the American colonists. And it seemed a sign of the times that on this same day a woman was "severely whipped, from the end of Downing-street, Westminster to Whitehall," for stealing curtains and cushions from several sedan chairs.

When the doors of the House of Lords swung open to receive the king the mob pushed forward, jostling and elbowing peers of the realm who were entering the chamber. When George III in his royal robes was seated on the throne "with the usual Solemnity," the Usher of the Black Rod was dispatched to the House of Commons to command the members' attendance. The king began his speech by expressing concern over the outbreak of distemper among horned cattle, and his voice droned on, reciting the cliché-ridden phrases that had been written for him, skirting the vital issues confronting the empire and virtually ignoring the topic of America except to say that he had done his best to bring his subjects there back to their duty and to "a due Sense of lawful Authority," but in vain. Regrettably, he continued, the conduct of the colonists was "highly unwarrantable and calculated to destroy the Commercial Connection between them and the Mother Country."

When the king had finished he strode from the chamber, followed by members of the House of Commons, and as his carriage moved off slowly the mob trailed behind, shouting "Wilkes forever!" According to the report received in New York, George was seen wearing a smug smile, "considering these cries, no doubt, as more owing to the natural disposition of the people, than any possible affront meant to himself."

As soon as the Lords were called to order, William Pitt, Earl of Chatham, rose haltingly to his feet, obviously in considerable pain. He had recovered from his nervous breakdown, however, and since this was his first appearance in Parliament in more than three years, members were unusually eager to hear what he had to say and they turned out in greater numbers than anyone could remember.

He began by observing that anyone his age was entitled to retire, given his infirmities, but he found himself so deeply troubled by the alarming state of the nation that he owed it to God, his sovereign, and his country to speak out. The Lords, he said, must make the king aware of the widespread unhappiness of his subjects and the causes of their discontent. Of America, he said, "Let us be cautious how we invade the liberties of our fellow-subjects, however mean, however remote: for be assured my Lords, that in whatever part of the Empire you suffer slavery to be established . . . you will find it a disease which spreads by contact, and soon reaches from the extremities to the heart. The man who has lost his freedom becomes from that moment an instrument in the hands of an ambitious prince, to destroy the freedom of others."

But "I need not look abroad for grievances," he went on, "the grand capital mischief is fixed at home." And then, to the astonishment and dismay of his listeners, he declared that the cause of England's distress—its "notorious dissatisfaction"—was the grievous action of the House of Commons in illegally depriving an elected member of his seat. John Wilkes was his topic, and he plunged into it with all his old eloquence and gusto.

As to his opinion of Wilkes, Chatham was "neither moved by his private vices nor by his public merits." He might be the worst of men, but "God forbid, my Lords, that there should be a power in this country of measuring the civil rights of a subject by his moral character, or by any other rule but the fixed laws of the land."

Wilkes was the favorite candidate in his county, he had been fairly elected by a very great majority, yet he was denied his rightful seat by a resolution of the House of Commons and replaced with a man who had no right to be there. "No man respects the House of Commons more than I do," Chatham continued, "or would contend more strenuously than I would to preserve them their just and legal authority. Within the bounds prescribed by the Constitution, that authority is necessary to the well-being of the people; beyond that line, every exertion of power is arbitrary, is illegal; it threatens tyranny to the people, and destruction to the State. . . . Unlimited power is apt to corrupt the minds of those who possess it; and this I know, my Lords, that where law ends, tyranny begins!"

When Chatham finished his speech the nation's highest legal officer, Lord Camden, rose to state that he too believed the expulsion of Wilkes was illegal, and he expressed his chagrin that he had not opposed it when it occurred. That was too much for the king: a few days later, Camden was unceremoniously removed from office as lord chancellor. Shortly afterward, a large mob of Wilkes supporters marched on Whitehall, carrying a petition stating that Parliament no longer represented the will of the people and that the ministers, who controlled it, should be dismissed. Chatham's speech had aroused the protests of thousands of voters in more than a dozen counties, but as the cry of "Wilkes and liberty!" echoed again and again across the land, the ire and single-minded obstinacy of George III were increasingly evident in London.

Chatham had done his utmost. Burke also spoke and was "as flowry as a french parterre," while Barré was "as bold as a lion," but the court party had the votes, and eloquence came in a poor second. Before leaving for the country, Chatham declared that it was "all over." The government not only had a majority on every question but further opposition was meaningless so long as the dispute "was to be determined by the length of their purses."

On January 28, 1770, Pitt's protégé the Duke of Grafton resigned and was replaced with the man who would be, for the next twelve eventful years, the king's first minister, the man who would do his bidding. Frederick North (commonly called Lord North, his courtesy title as eldest son of the Earl of Guilford) had been in the House of Commons since 1754. He had few enemies, no particular ambitions, and an affable, easygoing personality and sly sense of humor that won him popularity and took the sting out of his remarks to opponents. He was in his element as a skilled Parliamentary manipulator and dispenser of patronage. He was a devoted husband and father, generous and loyal to his friends, and had been an able chancellor of the Exchequer.

A "great, heavy, booby-looking" individual, he was brilliantly described by Horace Walpole, who observed, "Nothing could be more coarse or clumsy or ungracious than his outside. Two large prominent eyes that rolled about to no purpose, for he was utterly shortsighted, a wide mouth, thick lips, and inflated visage that gives him the air of a blind trumpeter. A deep untunable voice which, instead of modulating, he enforced with unnecessary pomp, a total neglect of his person, an ignorance of every civil attention, disgusted all who judged by appearance, or withheld their approbation till it was courted."

The flabby, fat body was the outward reflection of an indolence that regarded hard work as intolerable and the ideas of others easier to accept than those he might form himself. He, who had been ruled by his own father, was the ideal minister for George III, who was stubborn and determined and had been searching all his life for a friend on whom he could rely. The two were complementary in every way, for their outlook and opinions on all major issues ran parallel, and North's role might be compared to that of a ventriloquist's dummy. By the time North came along, George III had finally begun to realize the political importance of patronage and the King's Friends, the immense power that was his to employ, and North became the instrument through which he would wield it. North's sloth in the coming months and years would also mean that the king was increasingly blamed for a disastrous policy that a different minister might have persuaded him not to pursue.

By now, the king and his ministers, Parliament, and the country gentlemen were as one in their determination to compel obedience by the American colonists and had embarked on a hard-nosed policy from which they had no intention of turning back.

In New York, Alexander McDougall, former privateer captain turned merchant, was keenly interested in what was going on behind the scenes as the DeLanceys and their new ally Cadwallader Colden devised a scheme to pass a currency bill, pay the military's expenses as required by the Quartering Act, and ensure Colden his salary and the quiet administration he demanded. McDougall regularly attended Assembly meetings as a visitor in late November and early December of 1769, but he was excluded from the denouement, which took place behind closed doors on December 15.

Nine days earlier the DeLancey bloc had passed a rule denying the public admission to the House gallery when the speaker was not in his chair, and when Speaker Henry Cruger was conveniently absent on the 15th of the month no outsiders were present to hear the legislators engage in a long and vehement shouting match that finally settled the dispute in the DeLanceys' favor—by a single vote. The moment the bill passed, the speaker took his seat, appointed several men to draft a military supply bill, and adjourned the session.

Alexander McDougall, by John Ramage. *New-York Historical Society.*

The immediate effect of the DeLancey victory was that Isaac Sears and John Lamb, incensed by the Assembly's submission to the Quartering Act, deserted the DeLanceys and joined Alexander McDougall in denouncing the popular party's action. It was a stunning reversal of loyalties and reunited three men who had been at odds since the Stamp Act riots four years earlier, when McDougall sided with the Livingstons in opposing the radicals' proposal to carry on business transactions without stamps. Now, by leaving the DeLanceys and joining hands with the Livingstons, Sears broke with the party most closely aligned with the merchants (of which he was one) and with the party of his religious faith, since he was a communicant of the Church of England. He had stood with the DeLanceys as long as they seemed to champion American rights, but when they abandoned that cause for fear of losing their influence in London and the prerogatives that went with it, he could remain no longer. Moreover, as he put it now, if the Livingstons "should ever lose Sight of supporting the Liberties of their Country, I shall be as ready to leave them as I have the others."

During the years of estrangement, Sears, the Anglican, had called McDougall, a Scotch Presbyterian, "a rotten hearted fellow," and the three men had drifted so far apart that on March 18, 1769, the third anniversary of the Stamp Act repeal, when the old Liberty Boys gathered to celebrate, followers of Sears and Lamb had met at one tavern, McDougall and his friends at another. McDougall tried to patch up their quarrel by proposing a toast to the other group, but it was rejected by the Sears–Lamb crowd as coming from a man not worthy to be a Son of Liberty. Several hours of serious drinking followed at both taverns, and McDougall tried again. This time the Sears–Lamb contingent debated whether to throw the messenger out a second-story window or show him the door (which they did).

A battle between the two factions erupted in the newspapers, with the Livingstons publishing a venomous attack in a series by "The Watchman," likening the DeLanceys to the hated Stuart kings, and the DeLanceys replying with the "Dougliad" articles, written by James Duane, who castigated the avaricious Livingston family and the turncoat McDougall.

Now, suddenly, the wind had shifted and the three most prominent Sons were together again. McDougall, more than the other men, had buried himself in a study of political theory, reading Locke and Montesquieu among others, and immersing himself in radical Whig ideology. Close association with the Livingstons had done a lot to convince him that the DeLancey use of public office for private gain was morally wrong and indefensible. His primary disagreement with the DeLanceys had to do with his conception of representative government—a belief that those elected to represent a constituency entered into a sacred trust to defend the people's liberties. In his eyes, a representative was answerable to his constituents and was guilty of violating the people's trust if he betrayed the people's wishes.

America had done well by McDougall. His parents, Ranald and Elizabeth McDougall, had left Scotland in the summer of 1738 with their three children and Elizabeth's illegitimate daughter, planning to settle with other Scottish families on a thirty-thousand-acre patent on the northern frontier of New York. When it turned out that they were to be tenants—little more than serfs—and not landowners, Ranald went to work on a Manhattan farm owned by Gerard Beekman. Alexander grew up in the city streets, delivering pails of milk from his father's cows.

At the age of fourteen he signed onto a ship, and he took to the sea so ably that within eleven years he was given command of an eight-gun sloop, the *Tyger.* When he set sail from New York in 1757 "on a cruise against His Majesty's enemies," it was wartime and the *Tyger* was a privateer—an armed merchant ship. He took several prizes before he was given a more important command in 1759, the ninety-ton *General Barrington,* carrying a crew of eighty and twelve guns. By now McDougall had been away from home most of the time for the last thirteen years and he was under a good deal of pressure from his wife and her family to give up his dangerous trade and come home to Nancy and their two little boys. With prize money that constituted a small fortune, he did so.

Much as he may have wanted to be a member of New York's fashionable society of old wealth, McDougall was regarded as a parvenu, a nouveau riche. A member of the entrenched Livingston family said this of him: "He gets into a privateer, and, suitable to the savageness of his clime and disposition, goes forth a hungry Scotchman as a robber of mankind. . . . He returns home weighty of purse, but unpolished in manner, rough as his profession. Mean as the meanest of [his] race."

Whatever this might suggest, McDougall was a man of substance, a pillar of the Presbyterian church, ambitious, with ideals and the courage of his convictions—a man to be reckoned with. Physically he was rugged—tall, with broad shoulders and good looks. He had dark, penetrating eyes, a hairline that was beginning to recede, and a heavy Scots brogue that was made more difficult to understand because of a bad stutter.

In 1763 his wife died, and four years later he remarried, this time to the daughter of his minister. By the time he came to public attention because of his political views he owned at least one ship, reportedly operated a "slopshop," or tavern, near the waterfront, and was an extremely active trader and successful merchant, an agent for St. Croix sugar planters, a factor and investor, and a speculator in land. He owned slaves, had a saddle horse, wore expensive (if garish) clothes, and was sufficiently interested in his sons' education to send them to the Presbyterian College of New Jersey—known later as Princeton.

The offer of a £100 reward was a powerful incentive for an Irish journeyman printer named Cummins (a "young Strippling from Cork," McDougall called him) to take revenge against his boss, James Parker, who had recently fired him. According to Cummins, who tipped off the lieutenant governor, the broadside addressed "To the Betrayed Inhabitants of the City and Colony of New York" had been printed in Parker's shop. Chief Justice Horsmanden issued a warrant on February 7, 1770, for Parker's arrest, and while the printer was being questioned by Colden and other Council members, Sheriff John Rogers walked over to Parker's place of business and brought in three young apprentices.

Threatened with jail sentences, the boys admitted that the broadside had indeed been printed in Parker's shop and that they had seen Alexander McDougall handling the proofs. When Parker was told what his apprentices had revealed, and was promised immunity, he reluctantly named McDougall as the author. The next day the sheriff arrested McDougall and brought him before Horsmanden, whose opening remark was "So you have brought yourself into a pretty Scrape."

"May it please your honor," McDougall responded, "that must be judged by my peers."

As McDougall told the story, the chief justice told him sternly that "there was full Proof that I was the Author or Publisher of the abovementioned Paper, which he called a '*false, vile, and Scandalous libel,*'" adding that McDougall must give bail or go to prison. McDougall refused bail despite his ability to pay,* and the chief justice ordered the sheriff to lock him up until "delivered by due Course of the Law."

During eighty days of incarceration, McDougall and his case became a sensation, making him a hero in the province, a leader once more in the revitalized Sons of Liberty, and a well-known name throughout the colonies. His refusal to put up bail linked him immediately in the public eye with the notorious John Wilkes, reminding them that Wilkes's imprisonment resulted from his attack on the king and his ministers, which appeared in No. 45 of the *North Briton*. That now-famous number was put to use at once to hammer home the parallel between the unpopular arrests of the two men. Visitors to McDougall's jail cell brought him a side of venison stamped "45." On February 14, the 45th day of 1770, 45 men dined with him and consumed 45 pounds of meat from a steer 45 months old. Letters appeared in the city's journals, lauding McDougall as the Wilkes of America, and in March, 45 purported virgins called on the prisoner, who entertained them with tea, cakes, chocolate, and appropriate conversation after they sang the 45th Psalm. On the anniversary of the Stamp Act repeal the Sons met at a tavern they had renamed Hampden Hall after the seventeenth-century Parliamentary opponent of the Stuart king and offered 45 toasts before marching through town with flags and a band, cheering McDougall.

What was infinitely more important than the "45" sideshow was McDougall's attitude toward his imprisonment. He rejoiced, he said, in being "the first Sufferer for Liberty since the Commencement of our glorious Struggles." Writing from the New Gaol on February 9, 1770, he said, "Let it be tried, let it be fairly tried, whether the Freedom of Speech and Freedom of Writing are not the natural Effect of the Freedom of our excellent Constitution, and whether on suppressing that Freedom, the Constitution can possibly survive." The same issue of Holt's *New-York Journal* that carried McDougall's eloquent statement reported that a fellow prisoner, when led to his cell, remarked, "Here is fine times indeed! A Son of Liberty brought to gaol, and the Liberty Pole put in irons."†

---

*One indication of his financial status is his "Waste Book," revealing his worth in 1767 as well over £7,000. This is a meticulous reckoning of his principal, income, the money owed him, and his expenses, down to a loaf of sugar, watering cans, garden seeds and "bag to put them in," tack for his horse, ladies' satin slippers, numerous articles of clothing for his daughter and nephew, and maintenance of his Negro slaves.

†An unrelated item in the same paper noted that one of John Watts's friends and correspondents was now sitting pretty. Lady Arundel, who had died the previous November, "worth near half a Million Sterling, has left her Nephew Gen. Monckton, our late Governor, a Legacy of £12,000 per Annum."

Late in April, McDougall was indicted by a grand jury. Isaac Sears had done his utmost to see that jurors friendly to McDougall were impaneled, but the DeLancey machine effectively squelched that. The archconservative Thomas Jones, who was assisting Attorney General John Tabor Kempe with the prosecution, recalled that "King Sears," who had "great influence among the rabble . . . personally applied to the Sheriff, and desired that himself and several of his particular friends might be summoned. The Sheriff took no notice of these hints [and] summoned a grand jury consisting of the most impartial, reputable, opulent, and substantial gentlemen in the city." Reputable, opulent, and substantial they may have been, but their impartiality was highly questionable. To a man, the panel of freeholders selected by Sheriff Rogers consisted of DeLancey followers, and when the jury was picked, the *New-York Gazette* learned that a healthy majority had voted for DeLancey candidates in the 1769 election.

The chief justice ruled that the jury was to deal solely with the known facts concerning publication of the broadside, so while McDougall's defense tried unavailingly to prove that his broadside was no more critical of the government than numerous pamphlets printed in prior years (including one by Colden) and attempted to show the truth of McDougall's statements, there was no denying the stories of the apprentices and that of James Parker himself, from whom the story was pieced together of how McDougall came to the shop, corrected proofs, and took away copies of the broadside, for which he paid Parker £3 for printing.

The jury, on a vote of fifteen to three, charged McDougall with being a man of "turbulent and unquiet mind," responsible for publishing a "wicked, false, seditious, scandalous, malicious, and infamous libel" antithetical to the "public peace and tranquility." He was bound over to the Supreme Court for trial, and when he appeared in court to plead his case he "made a grand show," according to William Smith, Jr. Accompanied by "an immense multitude," McDougall "spoke with vast Propriety and awed and astonished Many who wish him ill and added I believe to the Number of his Friends." The court set bail of £1,000, and this time McDougall paid half of it and two friends each provided sureties of £250.

Some six hundred people walked with him to his home, and McDougall, who was not much of a public speaker because of his speech defect, promised his admirers that they could rely on him to defend the people's liberties even at the expense of his life and fortune.

Now and later, McDougall operated on the principle that when political leaders betrayed their constituents by failing to represent them honestly, it was the people's responsibility to act, to check the irresponsible use of power and replace unworthy representatives. If necessary, street government had to be the last resort.

Describing the aftermath of the case, Thomas Jones related how Cummins, "the poor journeyman printer," was so harried and hounded with anonymous letters in the papers and handbills threatening to tar and feather him that he fled to Boston and eventually took ship to England. James Parker, the printer (as publishers were then known), was described by the devout Anglican Jones as "a rigid presbyterian, a professed hater of monarchy, and an enemy to Episcopacy, being strongly attached to the republican faction," and he remained undisturbed in the city but eventually moved to New Jersey, where he suddenly died—"not without suspicions of foul play," said Jones. With his death, the prosecution had no evidence against McDougall, and the attorney general decided to drop the charges.

Although that would seem to have put an end to the McDougall affair, in the ensuing months the city's customary bitter political infighting went on unabated, and the former sea captain was once again caught up in its toils. Control of the Assembly, the Council, and the city government put power, patronage, and perquisites solidly in the hands of the DeLancey partisans, and they made the most of their advantage, lashing out at the Livingston faction whenever they saw an opening.

An example was the jailing once again of Alexander McDougall. James DeLancey had not forgotten the attack on the DeLancey family in the broadside attributed to the former ship captain—a condemnation of himself, his family, and associates characterized in the indictment against McDougall as "wicked, false, seditious, scandalous, malicious, and infamous libel," designed to elicit "the greatest Hatred, Scandal, Contempt, and Infamy" against the DeLanceys.

So, although the case against McDougall had been officially dropped, DeLancey arranged for the Assembly to question the former captain about his authorship of the tract "To the Betrayed Inhabitants." McDougall refused to answer. To do so, he argued, constituted double jeopardy, since the legislature had condemned the broadside as libelous and he was still technically under grand jury indictment as the author. He succeeded only in angering members of the House, one of whom suggested that torture might be a way to extract a confession from him, and at one point McDougall raised his fist and declared that "rather than resign the rights and privileges of a British subject, I would suffer my right hand to be cut off at the bar of this House." That tore it. Some irate legislators shouted that he should be jailed for his defiance, saying he had shaken his fist at them, and when McDougall refused to leave the chamber with the sergeant-at-arms, demanding that the Assembly order his arrest, he was taken at his word and hauled off to prison, where he remained until Governor Dunmore prorogued the Assembly almost three months later.

This time, unfortunately for McDougall, few rallied to his defense and no more was heard of his martyrdom as the "Wilkes of America." The public had its mind on what it considered more important matters than trial by jury, free speech, and freedom from peremptory arrest. But McDougall's stand had impressed a number of liberal thinkers—among them Benjamin Franklin, who wrote him that "we have for sincere Friends and Wellwishers the Body of Dissenters, generally, throughout England . . . who from various Motives join at applauding the Spirit of Liberty. . . ." In New York, as in England, those whom Franklin called Dissenters lacked the political muscle to alter the course of events, yet Alexander McDougall's ordeal was instructive. His troubles began as a simple protest against the Quartering Act, but by the end of his second confinement the causes for which he stood embraced the rights of free speech and freedom of the press, trial by jury, and immunity from arbitrary arrest. His unwillingness to yield to the power of the DeLancey faction suggested that he was unlikely to cave in to that of the crown in the months and years to come.

17

Battle of Golden Hill

Writing to Lord Hillsborough in January of 1770, Lieutenant Governor Colden tried to dispel any idea the ministry might have that New York was a hotbed of dissent. Meetings of the Sons of Liberty were poorly attended and of little consequence, he said: "People in general, especially they of property, are now aware of the dangerous consequences of . . . riotous and mobish proceedings." Yet Colden had to admit that "the supply of the Troops is unpopular, both in Town and Country."

Indeed, the very presence of Gage's soldiers was like a festering sore in the city; the redcoats knew it, resented it, and were eager to make their tormentors pay. The focus of the military's anger was the Liberty Pole, and with the beginning of the new decade they made plans to destroy it. On Saturday evening, January 13, sentries were posted on all streets leading to the site so as to screen the activities of some forty enlisted men from the barracks, who launched an attack, planting gunpowder in a hole bored in the pole. Two pedestrians, seeing what they were up to, ran to Montagne's tavern, where a few Liberty Boys were hanging out, and gave the alarm.

Rushing outside, the Sons shouted "FIRE!" to attract attention, but just then the fuse fizzled out and failed to ignite the charge. By now spectators had collected and were jeering and laughing at the frustrated troops, who responded by charging Montagne's public house "with drawn swords and bayonets," insulting the customers, beating the waiter, and threatening Montagne's life. They smashed eighty-four of the inn's windowpanes, plus lamps and bowls, before running off and retreating to barracks. Three soldiers were arrested, but that did little to quiet the hue and cry of citizens, and on Tuesday the 16th, after two more unsuccessful attempts on the Liberty Pole, a broadside signed "Brutus" was posted on street corners throughout the town.

It was a summons—probably written by McDougall—to a public meeting the following day. Taking to task those people who employed soldiers to work for them instead of hiring the city's desperately needy poor, "Brutus" reminded people that "the army is not kept here to protect, but to enslave us." And this while New Yorkers' tax money—one-third of the total for all the colonies—went to furnish troops with lodging and supplies. Was it not enough that their taxes went for billeting and supporting the troops, but also for "a poor tax, to maintain many of their whores and bastards in the workhouse"? "Experience has convinced us," he went on, that "good usage makes soldiers insolent and ungrateful; all the money that you have hitherto given them, has only taught them to despise and insult you." All friends of liberty should meet at the Liberty Pole at noon on Wednesday the 17th.

This message incensed the men of the 16th Regiment, who arrived in the dead of night and finally managed to cut down the pole and saw it in pieces. When the Liberty Boys arrived on the scene the next morning they found the remnants of their pole thrown helter-skelter in Montagne's doorway.

On the 17th an estimated three thousand people gathered where the Liberty Pole had stood and heard a speaker appeal for unity in support of their liberties, at which the crowd adopted with roars of approval several resolutions condemning the soldiers and the Quartering Act. When someone in the throng suggested that a nearby house, a derelict building that served as a barracks, be pulled down, soldiers overheard him, drew cutlasses and swords, and dared the people to try. Fortunately, several magistrates intervened and violence was averted, but the encounter was a portent of trouble ahead.

As "A.B."* wrote in Holt's *Journal,* the events only confirmed the fears of people about the soldiers' presence in town: ". . . if they behave thus, under the Controul of strict Discipline and good Officers, what have we to apprehend if they should be under bad ones? What would they be ready to do at the Word of Command? The present Disposition on both sides seems to forbode ill Consequences, unless timely prevented."

As tension mounted, sailors moved in gangs along the docks, forcing all the soldiers they found working on merchant ships or in shops to return to

*"A.B." was one of William Livingston's pseudonyms.

their barracks, and the redcoats began posting their own handbills, one of which attacked the Sons of Liberty as "the real enemies of society"—phony patriots who "thought their freedom depended on a piece of wood." The Sons, it stated, had nothing to boast of but their "flippancy of tongue" and stirring up sedition, while the soldiers "watched day and night for the safety and protection of the city and its inhabitants," suffering from the scorching heat of summer and winter's freezing, snowy nights.

Yet another of the 16th Regiment's handbills contained this bit of doggerel:

God and a Soldier all Men doth adore
In Time of War, and not before:
When the War is over, and all Things righted,
God is forgotten, and the Soldier slighted.

When Isaac Sears and a friend, Walter Quackenbos, collared a couple of redcoats posting these broadsides, a fellow soldier drew his bayonet and threatened them. For some reason, Sears had a ram's horn in his hand, and he threw it at the man and hit him in the head. At that the remaining soldiers ran toward the barracks to sound the alarm while Sears and Quackenbos marched their captives to the mayor's office and demanded their arrest. All this commotion attracted a crowd of townsfolk, and at the same time a score of soldiers—some with bayonets in hand—ran up, shouting for the release of their comrades. The civilians made ready for a fight, grabbing wooden rungs from nearby sleighs just as the mayor and Alderman Elias Desbrosses came outside and ordered the soldiers to return to barracks. The troops filed off, but instead of going the way they had come they trotted past the Fly Market and through the narrow streets near the East River that were lined with down-at-heel tenements and workrooms.

More people fell in with the crowd pursuing the redcoats, and others blocked their path, pushing and shoving, and when the soldiers tried to break through they were attacked with fists, clubs, and rocks. Immediately the fracas became a real riot, and as the badly outnumbered, near-desperate servicemen struggled up a small rise known as Golden Hill, another squad of redcoats appeared, more citizens joined the fight, and an officer in mufti shouted, "Soldiers, draw your bayonets and cut your way through them!"

"Where are your Sons of Liberty now?" soldiers taunted, and "fell on the citizens with great violence, cutting and slashing" with their deadly weapons, according to a bystander. The townsfolk, mostly unarmed except for a few men with sticks or clubs, backed off in panic. One hapless fellow, a Quaker named Francis Field, was standing in his doorway watching the fighting and was badly wounded on the cheek by a cutlass. Other victims were a tea-water man, a fisherman who lost a finger, and a sailor who was cut on the head and hand. Another sailor was fatally stabbed; a young boy going into Mr. Elsworth's house for sugar was wounded; and a soldier lunged with a bayonet at the woman who was answering the door.

A former militia captain named Richardson, who had been one of those defending the mayor's house against the soldiers, was assaulted by two red-coats with swords and managed to hold them off with a stick until someone handed him a halberd, a weapon with an axlike blade and steel spike mounted on a long shaft, with which he drove them off. John Targe came out of his house to see what was happening and was driven inside by three soldiers; he reached for his halberd and went after them, swinging the wicked weapon at his tormentors.

While the battle raged on Golden Hill (so called for the golden grain that once grew there), another contingent of troops appeared, calling to the out-numbered redcoats to cut their way out. They would meet them halfway, they yelled. More fighting had broken out by the Fly Market now, where John White, an unarmed citizen, was running for his life, pursued by a soldier with a bayonet. Fortunately the attacker tripped over the gutter and fell sprawling just as he was about to stab White, allowing the intended victim to escape.

Several soldiers on Golden Hill were badly bruised and one had a serious wound, and finally a group of officers, alerted to the fighting by aldermen who had come from several districts, appeared in time to disperse their men before the situation got completely out of hand. Even so, ugly incidents con-tinued: that evening soldiers assaulted a lamplighter and pulled the ladder out from under another while he was lighting a lamp. On Saturday a soldier tried to stab a woman coming from the fish market and narrowly missed wounding her when he ran his bayonet through her cloak and dress.

A fight erupted between soldiers and sailors, and the mayor and some aldermen tried in vain to break up an attack by fifteen soldiers who had cor-nered two sailors at the new Presbyterian meetinghouse. The mayor finally despaired of quelling the riot and started to leave to summon officers from the barracks, but townspeople begged him to stay. By this time a huge crowd had gathered, having heard that the soldiers "were slaughtering the inhabi-tants in the Fields," near the New Gaol. Yet another detachment of twenty men from the lower barracks arrived. The crowd fell back and let them pass, but one soldier snatched a stick from a bystander, took a sword from another, and a new fight broke out with both sides slashing with weapons.

The soldiers realized they were greatly outnumbered and in real danger. As they headed for their barracks, they were pursued, scuffles erupted, two citizens were wounded in the face, and a soldier was badly cut on the shoulder. When the fighting finally sputtered out, the crowd dispersed, and an uneasy quiet returned to the deeply divided city. One New Yorker wrote to a friend in London, "We are all in Confusion in this City. . . . What will be the end of this, God knows."

What did General Gage have to say about the street brawling that went down in history as the Battle of Golden Hill—the first battle of the Revolution as New Yorkers liked to call it? Judging from his letter to Hillsborough on February 21, it was something of an annoyance, but nothing to concern the ministry. "Endeavours were not only used to Set the People against the Bill for quartering, but also against the Soldiers, and provoked them to a Quarrell. The Minds of the soldiers were at length so sowered, as to become alarming, and to require uncommon Care to restrain them from Excess. But thro' the Diligence of the Civil and Military Powers, Harmony and good Order was soon restored."

Cadwallader Colden, in a lengthy letter to Hillsborough, put the blame squarely on the city's troublemakers, consisting of "a violent Party [that] continue their assiduous Endeavours to disturb the Government by working on the Passions of the Populace, and exciting Riots. . . ." Only "the prudent conduct of the Magestrates and officers of the Army" had quelled this recent outburst. "An ill humour had been artfully worked up between the Towns People & Soldiers, which produced several affrays, and daily, by means of wicked Incendiaries, became more serious."

At the root of the disturbances, he said, were persons of "inferior Rank," aided and abetted by "some Persons of distinction in this Place" and perhaps "encouraged by some Persons of note in England." They were chiefly Dissenters, he added, among them "Independents from New England, or Educated there, and of republican Principles." Behind all these allusions, of course, one could read Sears, Lamb, McDougall, and others of their ilk, who were dismissed as persons of inferior rank; the Livingstons, persons of distinction (though of the wrong religion) who had strayed from the righteous path; Chatham and others of his persuasion in England; and, of course, the evil rabble-rousers from New England, notably Yale alumni.

Whether Gage and Colden discussed in advance what they would tell Hillsborough is impossible to say, but each played down the fighting and gave credit to the other for putting a stop to it. And there matters stood when Isaac Sears, Alexander McDougall, and several others requested the mayor's permission to erect another Liberty Pole near the barracks, "as a Memorial to the repeal of the Stamp Act." The proper place for it was where it had always stood, they said, but they were willing to locate it near St. Paul's Church, as an alternative site. Mayor Hicks quickly passed the request on to the Council, where it was denied by a nine-to-five vote, but with the curious statement that the City Corporation "would not have objected, or been displeased, if the Pole had been erected without any fresh Application to them." In other words, put it up—just don't tell us.

To avoid any possible dispute about ownership of the site, Isaac Sears purchased a small plot of land near the former location, and there,* on February 6, 1770, the fifth Liberty Pole was erected. And an awesome piece of work it was. Dragged through the streets from Crommelin's wharf by six horses decorated with ribbons, with three flags flying, accompanied by three thousand cheering New Yorkers, the pine mast was nearly sixty feet long. The first forty feet were encased in iron bars, laid lengthwise and riveted in place. Over the bars were half-inch iron hoops, and above these were more, laid not so close but riveted and hooped in the same manner, with the exposed wood filled with nails. It was raised, the newspaper account stated, "without any Accident, while the French Horns played God save the King." Once the pole was in place in a twelve-foot hole, secured by timber, huge stones, and dirt, a twenty-two-foot topmast was fastened to it, and the crowning glory was a gilt vane bearing a single word: LIBERTY.[†]

Gates's officers had been warned that this was to take place and were there to see that nothing happened, and although many soldiers were also present, they "neither gave nor received any Affront."

On February 22 the *New-York Journal* published a letter from a Londoner to a friend in the city: "You have a new Governor appointed, Lord Dunmore; he has the Character of being a good temper'd honest Man; a Soldier, brave and generous. . . . I hope you will be as happy in him as in his Predecessor." The city was quiet now, but fear still stalked the streets, and Dunmore, who was scheduled to arrive in the spring, would need all the qualities attributed to

*In the present City Hall Park.
[†]And there it stood until 1776, when British troops took possession of the city and tore it down.

him if he was to carry out the king's wishes in his new post. (In fact, Dunmore's furniture arrived on July 7 and Colden moved to his country house. On August 18 the new governor was still expected daily, but he never did arrive until October 18, and the inevitable dispute began, with Colden claiming the perquisites of office for the period until Dunmore actually took office.)

Increasingly, New York was being split into different factions. On the one hand the imperial quarrel was dividing people into those who opposed the ministry's policies and those who favored them. Many of those who took sides chose the DeLanceys or the new combination of Livingstons and Sons of Liberty, and the comments of partisans reveal the depth of the divide: ". . . party runs very high," wrote James Rivington, the printer; "the Republicans [i.e., the Liberty Boys] grow vastly troublesome to the friends of government." And James Duane, a Livingston supporter, put his finger on what had become the real dilemma. New York, he said, is "run mad with Faction and party, not in defence of our Common Right, but against each other." Party feuding had so obscured the main issues that people who should have been shoulder to shoulder were squabbling over what were often picayune matters.

The Sons of Liberty had split into two opposing forces—one led by Sears and McDougall, claiming to be the *real* organization, the other composed of DeLancey followers, such as Joseph Allicocke, who said they were the *true* Sons. Nor did the schism stop there. The DeLanceys were Anglican partisans, the Livingstons Presbyterians and Dissenters, so it had been something to marvel at when Isaac Sears, a Church of England man, left the DeLancey forces and joined the Livingstons. And now a feud broke out in the pages of the *New-York Journal* during April—a shouting match between "Watchman" and "Americanus."

The latter defended the DeLancey adherents in a dissertation that traced the argument with Livingstons back to 1755, accusing "Watchman" of distorting the facts concerning the Militia Act of that year. The reply by "Watchman" included a personal attack on the late James DeLancey, referring to his affection for cockfighting , horse-racing, and women, castigating Oliver DeLancey and his followers' "preaching, crying, canting, lying, and many other Jesuitical qualifications, whenever they can promote their political schemes."

By late April and early May the two were regularly trading insults—with "Americanus" describing "Watchman's" "most inhuman, barbarous, and scandalous manner"—while "Americanus" attacked Isaac Sears and his current allies—men who had previously opposed him at every opportunity.

· · ·

The idea of nonimportation had been around for a long time and since petitions had had no visible effect on the government in London, it was generally
regarded as the only way to put a stop to the ministry's taxing policies. In January of 1765, Evert Bancker had written to a fellow merchant saying that four
hundred New York merchants had signed a resolution warning that unless the
Stamp Act was repealed they would sell no more European goods shipped
after January 1, 1766, either on their own accounts or on consignment, and
that they would soon countermand all their former orders. While the ensuing
boycott had taken its toll on British merchants, the damage was also severe in
America, and by 1770 the fervor of New York's merchants had waned along
with their tumbling profits.

James Rivington, a bookseller and printer, expressed the attitude of opponents to the hotheads of Massachusetts, who kept demanding an end to
imports. Writing to Moses Hays, Rivington said that "our inhabitants are . . .
afflicted at the terms they [in Massachusetts] are on with the English, they
want all to import, but wait like lurchers* upon each other, for an infraction
of the foolish nonimportation measure. The dirtiest subjects of the English
Realm are at the bottom of this association. It would be of eminent advantage
to the General Good were the third George to send warrants over to decimate
these vagabonds and weed our community."

He was not sanguine of success, however, believing that the "pusilanimous
merchants" of New York would take pity on the "Laboring people" who could
not support their families unless they had access to a variety of articles obtain-
able only in England.

The effect of nonimportation was most evident in the financial value of
imports from England. In 1768 they amounted to £2,153,000. In 1769 they
decreased to £1,332,000, and in New York alone the decline was precipitous—
from £482,000 to £74,000. Even so, nonimportation was losing support in
New York. In the first place, merchants large and small were wearying of lost
opportunities and mounting losses, and they deeply resented stories that
rivals in other colonies were cheating. In March, for example, a London
tradesman wrote his correspondent in New York that the reason the Townshend Act had not been repealed was the fault of the Bostonians, who had
ignored nonimportation and received no less than £150,000 in English goods.

*A crossbred dog used by poachers—thus, a sneak thief.

Another, equally important reason for the lack of enthusiasm was that New York, Boston, and Philadelphia—the three most important commercial centers—had markedly different interests that were causing them to part company. And finally, resistance to the Townshend duties lacked the magnetic appeal that had brought down the Stamp Act and failed to elicit the strong organizational movement that resulted in appeal.

The fading interest in the boycott of English goods was a great disappointment to many thoughtful men throughout the colonies, who had hoped it would provide a real spur to domestic manufactures. George Washington and George Mason of Virginia were prime movers in that province's nonimportation association, and Mason felt that too much had been expected of the boycott in the short run: the stagnation of British trade was bound to take more time. If the merchants lacked the patience and resources to hold out, however, he argued in favor of a partial boycott, at the very least. If Americans would only refrain from importing "articles of luxury and ostentation," it would encourage a fair amount of colonial manufacturing.

Speaking of the agreement that had been in effect, George Washington said, "I wish it to be ten times as strict." He was thoroughly conversant with the subject and wrote to Mason that as long as Parliament was determined to deprive Americans of their freedom, "it seems highly necessary that something should be done to avert the stroke and maintain the liberty which we had derived from our ancestors." The manner of doing it was the question. And then he added a sentence indicating how strongly he felt and how willing he was to take the ultimate step in resistance.

"That no man should scruple, or hesitate a moment to use a-ms in defence of so valuable a blessing, on which all the good and evil of life depends, is clearly my opinion; yet A-ms, I would beg leave to add should be the last resource. . . ."

In contrast to Washington's willingness to resort to arms, Mason claimed, "There are not five men of sense in America who would accept of independence if it was offered." But while Americans recognized the government of Great Britain, "we will not submit to have our money taken out of our pockets without our consent. . . . We owe our mother country the duty of subjects; we will not pay her the submission of slaves."

In London, Benjamin Franklin was longing for a continuation of nonimportation, in the belief that "we shall reap more solid and extensive Advantages from the steady Practice of those two great Virtues [industry and frugality] than we can possibly suffer Damage from all the Duties the Parliament of this Kingdom can levy on us."

While Sears and McDougall worked tirelessly to arouse public opinion to force continuation of the boycott, the tide was running against them. A committee of merchants, initiated by the DeLanceys, undertook a house-to-house poll in the city collecting signatures of those opposed to the boycott, and in June informed the merchants of Boston and Philadelphia that New York planned to end the boycott, except for tea. The Liberty Boys, caught off guard, belatedly conducted a poll of their own, but they were clearly out of step with the community and were outvoted. Boston and Philadelphia angrily rejected New York's proposal, but it was evident that nonimportation was over in Manhattan, thanks largely to the DeLanceys.

The fact that the colonists retained a boycott on tea might seem curious, but it was a direct response to a decision made in Parliament in March of 1770. After Lord North emerged from the debate on the Townshend Act as the strong man of the cabinet, Grafton resigned, and North replaced him as first lord of the Treasury and took the reins of government.

Two months into the new decade, North was ready to deal with the Townshend Act. The utter failure of those duties, which were supposed to resolve the question of raising a revenue from the colonies and alleviate the tax burden on the British citizenry, had been revealed in a letter published by the London *Public Advertiser* on January 17, 1769, and later reprinted in the *Pennsylvania Gazette*. Total revenues received from the duties amounted to no more than £3,500. At the same time, the colonies' nonimportation resolve had cost Britain some £7,250,000 in lost business.

The letter, which was almost certainly written by Benjamin Franklin, ended by warning that the Townshend program, if continued, might well lead to a revolt by the three million inhabitants of the colonies. To deal with that, the writer continued, would require an army of 25,000 men, supported by the fleet, and would take at least ten years to put down. It could cost as much as £100 million, and who could say how much loss of life it would entail or how much hatred it would engender in the aftermath of war?

Whether North was influenced by that letter is not known, but in March of 1770 he took up repeal of the Townshend duties—all, that is, except the tax on tea. The king had been quite specific in his instructions, saying he was willing to abandon the tariff on paper, paint, lead, and glass, but "I am clear that there must always be one tax to keep up the right, and as such I approve of the tea duty." It was, as members of Commons were to hear repeatedly,

Lord North, studio of Nathanial
Dance. *National Portrait Gallery,
London.*

"a wise and proper Duty," and must be preserved for "the Honour and
Dignity of Parliament."

In the ensuing debate, Thomas Pownall moved that *all* the Townshend
duties should be rescinded, but North had the whip hand. On Monday,
March 5, 1770, Commons voted to repeal the other duties while retaining the
tax on tea.

On that same Monday, in Boston, an event occurred that was to worsen
permanently the deteriorating relations between Britain and its American
colonies. A year and a half earlier, the thunder of cannon had saluted the
arrival of warships of His Majesty's Navy, bringing troops to the notoriously
unruly town to "overawe" the citizens, as General Thomas Gage put it. After
the troops debarked they formed up and marched to the accompaniment of
drums and fifes to the Common, led by officers who carried drawn swords,
looking for all the world like conquerors. Unfortunately Gage had selected
the 29th Regiment of Foot for the job—an outfit noted for poor discipline
and bad acting in New York—and as the months passed the army began to
dominate the life of the city, from early morning, when citizens awoke to the
tattoo of drums and the shrill of fifes, to midday, with soldiers swarming in
the markets and shops, to nightfall, when redcoats challenged men on the

streets, walking home to their families. It was increasingly and maddeningly clear to Bostonians that their community had been occupied by an alien force, and the Sons of Liberty, led by Sam Adams and James Otis, made propaganda capital of the presence of these "invaders."

Writing to Hillsborough, General Gage told him how townspeople constantly insulted and harassed the soldiers, lying in wait for them in alleys to knock them down, so that it was unsafe for officers and men to go out after dark. Rowdy gangs of young boys collected, jeering and whistling at the despised redcoats, calling them "bloodybacks," "lobsterbacks," yelling "Lobsters for sale," and throwing snowballs and chunks of ice at them. Several ugly fights between soldiers of the 29th and workmen at John Gray's ropewalk were followed a week later by what Gage called "a general Rising on the Night of the 5th of March."

On top of the accumulated snow of winter, piled high everywhere, a fresh snowfall covered the icy streets that night, and the new moon rose on shadowy figures gathering on Brattle Square, most of them carrying "Clubs, Bludgeons . . . some of them with Musquets." It was clear that they were out to attack the soldiers. Someone rang the fire bell, and more people poured into the streets and began provoking the soldiers to come out of barracks. Finally the mob confronted the lone sentinel at the Custom House, taunting and threatening him, pelting him with chunks of ice. He dodged as best he could while shouting for help, and Captain Thomas Preston, the duty officer, hearing his cries, sent a sergeant and twelve men to his aid. When they formed a semicircle around him the crowd began attacking them with bricks, stones, ice, and snowballs, yelling, "Fire if you dare!"

Preston arrived and tried to calm the citizens, saying his men would not shoot them, but one soldier received a violent blow and fired his weapon. Someone swung a club at Preston's head, but the officer was turning around to see who had shot and the blow hit his arm. Now the mob, seeing that no damage had been done and figuring that the soldiers had only loaded with powder to frighten them, attacked more violently. Fearing for their lives, and hearing shouts of "Fire!" all around them, the panicked troops began to shoot into the crowd.

When the thick black smoke cleared, five men lay on the icy street—three of them dead, the other two dying. Gage added, "Captain Preston and the Party were soon delivered into the hands of the Magistrates, who committed them to prison," which was the only place they would have been safe that night. In the days that followed the troops were removed from the city and sent down the harbor to Castle William, where the general remarked that they could be of no use whatever, so he planned to remove them from the province entirely.

The sobering lesson, Gage reported, was that "the People were as Lawless and Licentious after the Troops arrived as they were before. The Troops could not act by Military Authority, and no Person in Civil Authority would ask their Aid. They were there contrary to the Wishes of the Council, Assembly, Magistrates, and People, and seemed only [to offer] Abuse and Ruin. . . ." The general grimly concluded that "Government is at an End in Boston."

The shocking tragedy was immediately memorialized by Paul Revere, a local silversmith, engraver, and ardent Son of Liberty, who titled the prints of his engravings "Fruits of Arbitrary Power, or the Bloody Massacre Perpetrated in King Street."

Blood had already been spilled in the streets of New York. Now Boston's turn had come.

18

Coercive Measures

In the wake of the Boston Massacre in 1770, three local men—James Bowdoin, Samuel Pemberton, and Joseph Warren—were appointed by town authorities to compile the facts about "that execrable deed" and send them to Catharine Macaulay in England. The hope was that this version would arrive in London before General Gage and Governor Thomas Hutchinson submitted reports giving their own views of the event. Mrs. Macaulay was chosen for several reasons: she had recently published several volumes of her history of England, which John Adams characterized as a work "calculated to strip off the false Lustre from worthless Princes and Nobles and Selfish Politicians . . ." and she was known as a true friend to American patriots. Her history was replete with a republican ideology drawn from a study of the Greek and Roman states, and in it she described the corruption of British liberties by royal power.*

Her brother John Sawbridge was a member of Parliament as well as an outspoken advocate of "the American Cause," and the three-man committee forwarded the "humble and fervent Prayer of the Town and the Province in general that his Majesty will . . . order the said Troops out of the Province," in

---

*Along with Adams, other American Whigs who corresponded with her were John Dickinson, Richard Henry Lee, and Mercy Otis Warren. Mrs. Macaulay's first husband, George Macaulay, died in 1766 and twelve years later her marriage to the twenty-one-year-old William Graham caused a scandal because she was forty-seven. The two of them visited America and stayed with George Washington, with whom she had struck up a close friendship.

hopes that Mrs. Macaulay and her brother might somehow convince the king that the safety of Bostonians was at risk as long as British soldiers were present.

George III, predictably, chose instead to listen to his first minister and to the man who commanded his armed forces in the colonies, and the troops were not withdrawn but instead were reinforced by four fresh regiments. Unhappily, Lord North was no man to bridge the deep divide between the British and Americans that had opened in 1765 with the Stamp Act protests and widened after the Boston Massacre five years later. As John Watts put it, "The affairs between the Mother Country and this have been strangely conducted indeed, tho' I believe it scarcely possible that [they] could have been conducted worse than the affairs of Brittain itself . . . all instability & confusion, what will be the end. . . ." As for the future, he observed ruefully, "the prospect is not very enchanting."

American feelings in general were difficult to quantify. Many colonials remained deeply devoted to their king and to what they called "home," many others lacked the same degree of affection, but were nevertheless dead set against any real change in the status quo. But the hostility of a growing number of people toward the existing system had hardened and, consciously or not, was coalescing into what could be described as a national kinship.

Regulations and restrictions that once had been merely the cause of grumbling now became punitive and unacceptable, and the relationship between Britain and her colonies was at best an uneasy and uncertain truce, crying out for moderation, goodwill, and patience on both sides. Unfortunately, the indolent, hopelessly impercipient Lord North handled matters in such a way that he seemed to be willfully antagonizing the colonists at every opportunity, and his Tea Act of 1773 was the latest in a series of blunders that exacerbated the worsening imperial relationship.

When William Pitt came to office in 1766 one of his primary objectives was to put a rein on the high-flying British East India Company. The firm— which had been chartered as a joint stock company on New Year's Eve, 1600, by Queen Elizabeth—was conceived as a mercantile venture to tap the riches of the Orient. But as British merchants moved aggressively into the Indian subcontinent and built trading stations and forts to protect them, the enterprise grew and prospered mightily; it was raising its own armed forces; and by the eighteenth century what was known as the "John Company" (presumably for John Bull) had become a sovereignty ruling over a vast territory. It was the chosen instrument of British government in India and the darling of many prominent Britons, who were shareholders.

Its East Indiamen, constructed in its own yards on the Thames, were quite simply the best merchant ships afloat. Their size made them awkward, but what they lacked in maneuverability they made up in armament, carrying enough powder and shot to outgun pirates or most other potential enemies. Trading with China was restricted to the *hongs* of Canton, and the East India Company had a virtual monopoly there, challenged only sporadically by Dutch, French, and Portuguese. Its wealth, preeminence, and power were reason enough for those rivals, consumers, and smugglers alike to loathe it.

In addition to the profits derived from trading of all kinds, including, after 1758, control of the illicit opium trade with China, the company took in more than a million pounds sterling each year, and Chatham, as Pitt was then called, was determined to lay hands on some of that booty to ameliorate the enormous debts caused by the Seven Years' War. He wanted to avoid taxing America, to give the colonies a breathing spell, and chose to look to the east, not the west, as a source of revenue.*

His investigation into the affairs of the East India Company, requiring an accounting of revenues and expenditures, and inspection of its charters and agreements, had the blessing of George III, but some members of the cabinet felt otherwise and their opposition surfaced at the same time Chatham's health went into a precipitous decline. With his complete collapse in 1767 the inquiry lapsed and several months later Parliament took an easy way out and limited the company's dividend to 10 percent. Unfortunately for the American colonies, that half-hearted measure, along with a reduction of Britain's land tax, made it certain that additional taxes would be levied and that America, not the East India Company, would bear the brunt of them.

As the eighteenth century wore on, tea became the most important export from Asia to Europe; as a socially acceptable, stimulating drug, it had become a virtual necessity in England and its American colonies. By 1775, more than ten million pounds of tea were being shipped every year to England alone,† and it was estimated that the company took as its cut an override of at least one-third the cost of the tea, or about £100 per ton on the five thousand or

---

*By coincidence, Chatham's grandfather had established the family fortune by buying a fabulous diamond when he was a commercial adventurer in India, and selling it to a French nobleman at a staggering price.

†The tea ships needed ballast and about a quarter of it was made up of Chinese porcelain, known loosely as "china." Before 1780 it was cheaper than ordinary pottery and one offshoot of the tea trade was that even the most modest English households might possess some of the world's finest porcelain.

more tons that went to Britain. Because of the duty charged on imported tea, the American market for the leaves was almost entirely in the hands of smugglers, who bought it from Holland and sold it to the colonists below the price of tea shipped from England.

The government insisted that the East India Company pay it £400,000 annually, starting in 1767, and that drain on its finances, coupled with war in India, famine in Bengal, and the company's insistence on raising its dividends to stockholders, created a crisis in the tea trade, making the company's fiscal condition precarious. In 1772—the year of a financial crash—Parliament again investigated the enterprise, only to discover that it was on the edge of collapse, and decided to place it under direct governmental control while loaning it £1.4 million and forgoing the annual payments. When the company's stock plummeted, bankruptcies followed, fifteen banking houses in Amsterdam failed, and Benjamin Franklin attempted to use this situation as leverage for repealing the one remaining Townshend tax—the duty on tea. In the company's warehouses, he pointed out, were tea leaves worth £4 million, and if the tax were lifted, the American market would suddenly open up— delighting American housewives and relieving East India Company investors.

Alas, Franklin had not reckoned with the intractability of the king and his prime minister, who were determined to maintain the tea tax as symbol of Parliament's right to levy taxes on the Americans. In short, it was a matter of principle, and Lord North took what he regarded as an irresistible proposition to Commons in April 1773. The East India Company, which had been required to sell its tea exclusively at auction in London, would now be permitted to export and sell it directly to the colonies without the duties customarily paid in Britain (which averaged about two shillings sixpence per pound), but still subject to the Townshend tax of threepence a pound in America. North reasoned that a colonist would pay less for his tea than a smuggler charged for it but in doing so he would be tacitly admitting the right of Parliament to raise a revenue from his purchase. A further provision of the Tea Act was the appointment of certain individuals as the exclusive company agents in America—"another Species of Stamp Masters," was William Smith's derisive term for them.

According to a letter from England published in Holt's *Journal,* the tea would be sent to New York, Philadelphia, and Boston, where it would be stored in warehouses and sold by the agents, or factors, four times a year. The letter (or, just possibly, the editor) then offered some advice: "It is hoped the Americans will convince Lord North that they are not yet ready to wear the Yoke of Slavery, and suffer it to be rivetted about their Necks, but that they will send back the Teas from whence they came."

When New Yorkers read the terms of the Tea Act in the *New-York Gazette* of September 6 they were aghast. Not only was the continuation of one of the Townshend duties abhorrent, but they could see that the East India Company would have a monopoly on tea, and a monopoly on one commodity could quite easily become a monopoly on another . . . and another. Isaac Sears, John Lamb, and Alexander McDougall went to work immediately, rallying the Sons (who were formally reorganized in November), and dispatching urgent messages to their network of allies in other colonies. Three weeks later the *Lord Dunmore* docked at the wharf and bystanders were told that the East India Company planned to ship 600 chests of tea to the city—no one could yet say when.

On October 13, 1773, William Smith wrote in his diary that "A new Flame is apparently kindling in America." Holt's *Journal* printed letters from London, one writer observing that the Tea Act was "a Scheme of Lord North" to trick Americans into tacit acknowledgment of Parliament's right to tax them, adding the hope that "the Yorkers will stand their Ground." Another said he had warned officials of the company that the tea and the ships would be burned, that New Yorkers would "never suffer an Act of Parliament to be crowded down your throats, for if you do it's all over with you."

The Liberty Boys' goal was to unite the merchants, tea smugglers, and the Sons in opposition and McDougall launched the campaign in an incendiary broadside entitled "Alarm No. 1," which—with subsequent issues—was published in John Holt's *Journal*. (Holt, Sears noted appreciatively, "made it a point to insert everything that wou'd have the least tendency to promote the cause of Freedom in this Country.")

At a well-attended meeting, thanks were given by the crowd to the city's ship captains whose "prudent Conduct in refusing the freight of the East India Company's Tea merits the Approbation and Applause of every well wisher to the Liberties of this or any other Country." It was the first American demonstration of resistance to the Tea Act and Sears and McDougall followed up by doing what they could to discredit the three factors chosen to distribute the tea in New York—Henry White, Benjamin Booth, and Abraham Lott (the provincial treasurer who had done his best to be appointed a stamp master in 1765). On the following day, Philadelphia merchants threatened that anyone approving or abetting the East India Company's plan to bring its tea into America would be regarded as an "Enemy to his Country."

In the same week that "a considerable large whale" was seen in the Hudson and East rivers, and an earthquake, "preceded by violent rain, and immediately succeeded by very awful lightning and tremendous peals of thunder," shattered china and glassware in the city, William Tryon, who had replaced Lord Dunmore as governor in October of 1770, wrote to Lord Dartmouth, describing New York's reaction to news of the impending shipment of tea. He reported the appearance of several publications that were "calculated to sow sedition and to support and make popular the cause of those who are deepest concerned in the illicit trade to Foreign Countries."

On November 5, 1774, a number of New Yorkers met at the home of Captain Thomas Doran and appointed a committee to ask Messrs. White, Booth, and Lott about their intentions—whether they indeed planned to serve as factors. The three replied carefully that they had received no appointment from the East India Company, but if the tea was shipped to them they would not execute their commission, and—true to their word—when the packet arrived on November 30 carrying their appointments, they announced, "the Tea *will* come, liable to the American Duty; and agreeable to their former Promise [the agents] have declined receiving it and selling it." Their resignation presented Governor Tryon with the knotty problem of what to do with the tea ships' cargo when it arrived in New York.

The hue and cry continued, with more broadsides and public meetings stirring up public concern, along with a warning against anyone so foolhardy as to think he could land or store the tea. This was signed "The Mohawks"— a label that was to appear in Boston less than three weeks later, strongly suggesting that the Sons of Liberty in the two cities were keeping in close touch with each other.

It was probably no accident that the three putative tea factors announced their decision not to take custody of the shipment just four days after the Mohawks issued their threat, and one day after Sears and McDougall called for mobilizing the Association of the Sons of Liberty of New York while launching a drive for signatures of those who would be members.

On Tuesday, December 7, an express rider from Boston trotted into town, bearing letters addressed to Samuel and John Broome (both Presbyterians and Livingston allies), Philip Livingston, Isaac Low, Isaac Sears, and Alexander McDougall, informing them that the Town of Boston had resolved that any tea arriving there would be sent back to London in the same ship, without being landed. The decision had delighted John Adams. Writing to Catharine

Macaulay, he informed her that the latest ministerial maneuver had aroused a more determined resistance than ever and that "a few more Such Experiments will throw the most of the trade of the Colonies into the hands of the Dutch, or will erect an independent Empire in America—perhaps both." At this juncture, he added, "Nothing but equal Liberty and kind Treatment can secure the Attachment of the Colonies to Britain."

The New York Liberty Boys may not have realized it, but their determination to fight the Tea Act was largely responsible for the Bostonians' reaction. In the Massachusetts town Sam Adams and his fellow propagandists had tried in vain to break their compatriots of the tea habit, warning that it weakened "the tone of the stomach, and therefore of the whole system, inducing *tremors and spasmodic affections,*" while transforming healthy adult males into "weak, effeminate, and creeping valetudinarians." Their efforts had accomplished little, however, and when New York and Philadelphia took the lead in opposing the landing of tea Adams decided that the only way Boston could keep pace was to strike a real blow at the government. "Our credit is at stake," he announced, "we must venture, and unless we do, we shall be discarded by the sons of liberty in the other colonies." The result was the decision described in the letters that arrived in New York on December 7.

It appeared to William Smith that the message from Boston stiffened the resolve of Sears and the others not to allow tea to be unloaded in New York, yet he knew the Sons would be taking a chance. As matters stood, precious little tea was in the merchants' warehouses and the public appetite for it could bring about a change of heart, with people demanding that East India Company tea be brought ashore upon arrival. Isaac Low—a DeLancey man— argued that it was a mistake for the governor to consider it his duty to deal with the tea—that was a job for the merchants. If landed, it might not be safe; and the impact of their actions on the other colonies had to be considered. "If we land it here," he said, "they will elsewhere, & we can't be sure it will not be vended, & immense animosities may arise from it."

Sears and his cohorts sought out Smith in his capacity as adviser to the governor and insisted that the tea ships be ordered to return to England as soon as they arrived—*without* unloading any tea. Smith worried about this scenario: he could visualize thousands of people massed at the wharf, fights breaking out, soldiers firing into the crowd. Low and Livingston sympathized with his view; Sears and McDougall did not. The latter blurted out, "What if we prevent the landing and kill the Governor and all the Council?" Livingston was appalled by the remark and so, presumably, was Smith, who was one of the councillors.

When Smith reported all this to Tryon the governor listened and then made up his mind. He would allow the tea to be landed but would not facilitate the process with military force. "I will use no Arms until after they have abused & disgraced their Govr. & themselves," Smith quoted him as saying. "I will run the risk of Brick Batts & Dirt and I trust that you & others will stand by me."

When a summons to a meeting of the utmost importance at Town Hall on December 17 appeared on the streets, everyone in authority was aware that this could have ugly ramifications, and behind the scenes the governor and the councillors debated how to handle it. The question was "What is to be done?" and Smith's notes convey something of the confusion and uncertainty of the governor's advisers. Someone made a "cold sluggish reply." One man ventured a suggestion, another offered a "different evasive" response. No one present knew who was behind this summons to the public and the question was asked, "Is their Meeting lawful?" One councillor predicted that nobody would attend. When someone proposed that the governor issue a proclamation much arguing ensued and Smith stayed out of it for a while, and then objected strenuously. It would exasperate New Yorkers and be despised here, he said. Furthermore, if it catered "to the Taste of the Populace it would expose [us] to censure at Home, & perhaps be imputed to Fear here." That led to his recommendation that if a large number of people attended the meeting, the governor should go and speak to them. On the other hand, "if they were a contemptible Handful," he was certain they would sink "into Despondency" at their inability to rouse the city to violence."

The discussion dragged on and on until Smith urged the governor to appear at the meeting and explain his reasons for storing the tea, but other councillors argued that it would not be proper for Tryon to address the meeting, that he should dictate his message to the Recorder, who would transcribe it for the mayor, who would speak to the crowd. The clock ticked on until three o'clock while the governor sat "cold & silent" until Mayor Hicks finally appeared.

At the Town Hall between two and three thousand people assembled and listened while John Lamb read letters from Boston and Philadelphia announcing their decision to reject tea shipments. After they elected a Committee of Correspondence that included Sears, McDougall, and several other Sons of Liberty, Mayor Hicks spoke, informing them that the governor was duty-bound to prevent the destruction of the tea "even if it was the property of aliens." Tryon had no intention to use force, he added, and would employ civilians to land the tea in broad daylight. Hicks was treated with respect, but the temper of the crowd was definitely "against the landing."

Smith was disappointed at the outcome: he complained later that Tryon had not been sufficiently explicit in his instructions to the mayor; but Sears and McDougall were jubilant. They were elated by the presence at the meeting of a number of prominent merchants—including Leonard Lispenard, Abraham Walton, Francis Lewis, Isaac Low, and David Van Horn—who had been elected to the Committee of Correspondence. Although they declined to serve, the very fact of their presence signified to the public that they favored the Sons' position. As a confident McDougall later informed Smith, if the governor attempted to land the tea, three-quarters of the citizens would resist it.

New York's newly formed Committee of Correspondence had its origins in the Virginia House of Burgesses. There, in March of 1773, Thomas Jefferson and Richard Henry Lee had persuaded their fellow legislators to approve a standing committee of eleven members—all of them anti-British Whigs, it might be noted—to serve as a committee of correspondence. Within a year, all the colonies but Pennsylvania had such committees, having discovered that even if their assembly was prorogued by the governor, a standing committee could continue to act.

Thanks to these groups, like-minded men in the disparate provinces began to feel a sense of unity and common purpose and, of course, whenever a crisis appeared on the horizon, they were capable of setting action in motion. Because they were initiated to unify the protests of widely separated communities and arouse the people, they proved to be extremely effective channels of republican propaganda. Among Tories they naturally had an unenviable reputation. Governor Hutchinson of Massachusetts once remarked of Boston's organization, "Some of the worst of them one would not choose to meet in the dark—Three or four at least of their Correspondence Committee are as black-hearted fellows as any upon the Globe."

On December 21 Paul Revere rode into town with the startling tidings that Boston "Mohawks"—three companies of fifty men, their faces blackened, carrying hatchets, and dressed as Indians—had marched down to Griffin's Wharf, clambered aboard three tea ships, and dumped 342 chests of tea valued at £18,000 into the dark waters of Boston Harbor. What Revere called "this interesting act" had occurred on December 16, the night before the mass meeting in New York, and even though the "Indians" were well fortified with rum, they had accomplished their mission "without the least injury to private property." As one of the participants described the occasion, it was understood by all that each individual would keep his own identity and that of others secret. In about three hours the chests were broken open and thrown overboard, and although British naval vessels were anchored nearby no attempt was made to resist the Mohawks. It was, he said, "the stillest night . . . that Boston had enjoyed for many months."

Although Revere was to make a name for himself as a courier, a bearer of important messages, he was a man of many parts. A superb silversmith, he was also one of Boston's most politically active citizens. In fact, he and Joseph Warren were members of more of that town's seven revolutionary organizations than anyone else—even including Samuel Adams. So when Paul Revere came to town he was recognized as more than an ordinary post rider—he was as knowledgeable as any man alive of what was going on in Boston and what the Whigs there were planning.

The *Essex Gazette* declared that Sam Adams and his Liberty Boys were in "a perfect Jubillee" after the tea party. Thomas Hutchinson saw the affair accurately as "the boldest stroke which had yet been struck in America." Across the country, enthusiastic Whigs rejoiced while Tories lamented how the Sons "thought they could not be friends to their Country unless they trod in the same Steps, and imitated the Example of the Bostonians."

On January 4, 1774, Tryon wrote to Dartmouth, saying he had hoped temperate measures would be pursued, but in view of the events in Boston he had concluded that "the landing, storing & safe keeping of the Tea when stored could be accomplished [only] under the Protection of the Point of the Bayonet and Muzzle of the Cannon. . . ." (Dartmouth responded icily, wondering why on earth New York's people could have been influenced by the "audacious Insult" at Boston to the authority of the kingdom.)

William Smith described New York's reaction: "The Boston News astonished the Town," as well it might. On top of that came word from Charleston of the South Carolinians' determination to send back any East India tea shipped to them, all of which greatly influenced New Yorkers and convinced William Smith that they would definitely not permit any tea to be landed. Philadelphia's Liberty Boys were also active. In a broadside circulated in the city they put a question to the Delaware River pilots who would bring the expected tea ships into port: "What think you, Captain, of a Halter around your Neck—ten Gallons of liquid Tar decanted on your pate—with the Feathers of a dozen wild Geese laid over to enliven your Appearance?"

Beyond that, they planned to send burning rafts into the tea ships when they appeared in the river.

Understandably, fear of violence spread in New York, stoked by a letter signed "Tom Bowline" (a nom de plume used by Isaac Sears), which appeared in newspapers, calling on his "worthy messmates, the renowned sons of neptune" to be ready when the tea ships entered the harbor. The last time the "Sons of Neptune" had been heard from was immediately prior to the Stamp Act riots, when a letter signed in that manner urged residents to ignore "peaceable orators" and attack Fort George. While radicals huddled over tables in coffeehouses, looking conspiratorial as they planned their reception for the tea ships, the governor and Council members held endless discussions about how to deal with the growing probability of violence.

According to Smith, Tryon was determined to be popular in New York to counteract a reputation for lack of prudence he had acquired in North Carolina, and was relying on Henry White, a councillor and one of the three merchants chosen as factors for the tea, to act for him in the present crisis. In that way Tryon could remain out of sight and avoid the appearance of caving in to the mob. Having now concluded that the only way to save the tea was to send it back to England, he had White approach William Smith—who was known to be on good terms with leaders of the Liberty Boys—to see if a deal could be struck so as to avoid trouble.

When Rivington's *Gazetteer* was distributed on December 23 the public learned that a decision had been made to return the tea to England without landing it in New York. What they were not told was that a three-way secret agreement was responsible. For his part, Tryon promised that he would not permit the tea to be landed and would withdraw his instructions to the navy to watch for the ships' arrival. The tea factors vowed that they would not accept the tea and would order the ship captains to sail without unloading their cargo. And finally, the Sons pledged that if the ship captains complied, they would see that the vessels were provisioned for the return voyage to England.

William Smith drafted a letter to be delivered to the captain of any tea ship entering the Narrows, and it was a message calculated to throw a scare into the boldest of men. The recipient was warned "of the Danger of bringing your Ship into Port while there is a Way of Escape," and advised that "The whole Continent is thrown into a Ferment by the last Act of Parliam't authorizing the East India Company to send Tea in America." Thus far, at least, the New York mob had been neither "violent nor tumultuous," but the situation was highly charged. The letter explained carefully that agents were not ordering the ship to return to England, only stating that they could not vouch for the safety of the tea after what had happened in Boston. In the opinion of the agents, landing the cargo "can not be attempted but with a certain Prospect of exposing the Lives of your Crew as well as your Ship to Destruction by an exasperated and irresistible Multitude."

Governor Tryon was sufficiently worried about the arrival of tea in New York that he wrote Dartmouth, telling him that opposition to the East India Company's monopoly and the duty was so formidable that while it might be possible to land, store, and protect the tea from harm, it could be accomplished only under the protection of the guns of the Royal Navy. It was not a promising prospect.

As if William Tryon did not have enough trouble, the governor's house burned to the ground on the night of December 29, and he and his family barely escaped with their lives. Had it not been for the snow on neighboring roofs, the whole southeastern section of town might have gone up in flames. As it was, one of the Tryons' maidservants—sixteen-year-old Elizabeth Garret—lost her life, another survived only by jumping from a second-story window into the snow, Lady Tryon lost some £2,000 in jewelry, and the governor had only enough time to throw on a vest, overcoat, and two unmatched stockings and dash from the house without his shoes. Providentially, the great seal of the province was finally found and raked out of the rubble—coated with ashes, but intact.

The General Assembly voted £5,000 (later amended to £12,000) to compensate the governor for his personal losses, plus £6,000 for the house. The discussions about rebuilding the house provoked a sour letter to the *New-York Journal,* noting that since the ministry in London had ruled that royal governors were henceforth to be independent of the citizens and no longer dependent on them for their salaries, "with what Propriety can the People be taxed to provide a House and furnish it with Fire and Candle for the Accommodation of a Governor?"

As the weeks passed with no news of the tea ships the New York Liberty Boys grew increasingly restive. Now it was their turn to prove their mettle and they were eager for any opportunity whatever to share honors with their colleagues in Boston and Philadelphia. In the latter city, a tea ship heading for port had been turned back, and after learning that the ships destined for New York had been delayed by contrary winds, the New Yorkers wrote to Boston, saying, "We have long & impatiently waited the arrival of our tea Ship, that we might have the satisfaction to Cooperate with our Sister Colonies in defeating the pernicious project of an Arbitrary Ministry; a Project that was Pregnant with the ruin of this free Country." To be certain that nothing escaped their notice, the Sons planned to hold a special meeting every Thursday at Jasper Drake's tavern.

By April, when Governor William Tryon was due to leave for England, the tea ships were still at sea. (It turned out that the *Nancy* had been driven off course to Antigua and on her passage back to New York she met with rough weather, lost an anchor, had her mizzenmast carried away, sprung her topmast, and was thrown on her beam ends. In the terrible storm some eighty Scots passengers died.)

Tryon informed the Council and the Assembly in January that the king had commanded him to return for a short visit to discuss various matters, and he was hopeful that a rest would help him regain his health, for he had been ailing for months. On the morning of April 7, 1774, the governor and his family boarded the Falmouth packet and an emotional departure it was. Mrs. Tryon was "dissolved in tears" and her husband was deeply affected by the immense crowd that had come to see him off, with people waving and cheering from every window along his route to the wharf. When the last line was cast off and the crowd gave him three thunderous cheers, Tryon's voice failed him and he turned away to wipe his eyes as the packet slipped out into the bay, saluted by guns from the battery, HMS *Swan,* an independent artillery company, a battery on Long Island, and Captain Lashar's company of Royal Grenadiers, while many ships in the harbor hoisted their colors.

Robert R. Livingston had sent a long farewell letter to Mrs. Tryon, filled with gallantry and flattering words for her husband, calling him the best hope New Yorkers had for composing the differences with the mother country. But it would require "lenient measures" by the ministry to achieve that, he said: anything less "must either terminate in the utter ruin of the Colonies or their total independence—events which are equally to be dreaded both by Great Britain & America."

William Smith observed that Tryon's departure was the first public parting for a governor in the colony of New York and gloated that "The DeLanceys distinguished themselves in their Coolness toward the Govr. & sank into Contempt."

At noon on that day Cadwallader Colden was once again sworn in as acting governor of the province. He was now eighty-six years old.

. . .

On the night of April 18 the *Nancy* finally arrived off Sandy Hook, where the letter drafted by Smith was handed to Captain Benjamin Lockyer. Naturally enough, Lockyer protested, until he was informed that the entire town had been summoned to meet and voice "their detestation of the measures pursued by the Ministry and the India Company." Several days later he was afforded a glimpse of what might have occurred had he ignored the warning.

On April 22 the *London* entered the Narrows, picked up a pilot, and the captain, James Chambers, assured him that no tea was on board his ship. Unfortunately for the captain, New York's Liberty Boys had learned from their allies in Philadelphia that "18 boxes of fine tea" were in the *London's* hold, and when the ship docked at Murray's Wharf members of a citizens' committee came aboard and questioned Chambers. He denied having any tea, but when they threatened to open the hatches and conduct a search he admitted that some tea was indeed aboard and that he, not the East India Company, was the owner. The tea had been shipped on his own account.

Now Chambers was a respected old-timer, who had been sailing between New York and London for years, and somewhat ironically, it was he who had brought the hated stamps to the city in 1765, and he who had refused to carry the East India Company's tea the previous summer, for which he received the thanks of the town. But he had chosen a bad time to do his profiteering. The Mohawks decided they would pay him a visit that night, but the townspeople beat them to the job. Hundreds of people gathered on the docks and in the early evening stormed aboard the *London,* located the cases of tea, and dumped them overboard. Captain Chambers was nowhere to be found.

The triumphant crowd was finally dispersed by the ringing of the town's bells but a huge number of people—"the greatest number . . . ever known in this city," according to Rivington's *Gazetteer*—assembled at eight the next morning in and around the Coffee House. A band was present and, incongruously, was ordered to play "God Save the King" as Captain Lockyer was led out by the Committee of Correspondence. Loud cries went up for Captain Chambers—"Where is he? Where is he?" But Chambers had vanished. Meanwhile, Lockyer was escorted to a pilot boat and followed to the *Nancy* by committee members who waited until the ship got under way and stood out to sea to be absolutely certain that none of the ship's cargo was unloaded.

If Captain Lockyer didn't already think the contents of his hold were a Jonah he may have done so when he caught a number of his crew who had put together a raft and tried to jump ship rather than return to England. After several days it was determined that Chambers, "not without some risk of his life," had escaped to the *Nancy* and returned aboard her to England.

Understandably, these events contributed to a growing sense of uneasiness among conservatives. Writing to Pennsylvania's governor John Penn, Gouverneur Morris warned, "The heads of the mobility grow dangerous to the gentry; and how to keep them down is the question." Those in the DeLancey party worried increasingly about the threat to their power, the merchants were deeply troubled about their ability to trade freely and profitably, and Sears and McDougall—the "heads of the mobility"—personified the dangers facing them.

In late January 1774, news of Boston's tea party reached London and was greeted with profound shock and anger. It was recognized immediately as a lawless affront to the government, which could neither be ignored nor papered over. Clearly, the "licentious Bostonians" were preparing to rebel and must be punished for their wanton assault and taught respect for the authority of England.

Whatever else men called it, the tea party was the agent that unleashed the pent-up forces that had been gathering strength in America and would lead to war between the colonies and the mother country. A furious George III reacted immediately. Sending a message to Parliament deploring "the violent and outrageous Proceedings at the Town and Port of Boston"—a subversive act that was clearly designed to obstruct the commerce of his kingdom and undermine the constitution—he laid the matter before the two Houses, confident that they would enact measures to put an immediate halt to "the present Disorders" and ensure the dependence of the colonies on the crown and Parliament. It was no longer a question of upholding Parliament's right to tax America, but whether Boston's mobs would be allowed to roam the streets at will, unpunished, while defying the king's authority and destroying the commerce of the empire. This time the monarch demanded vengeance.

The news could not possibly have arrived at a worse time.

Benjamin Franklin, who had been agent for Massachusetts since 1770, had written a Boston churchman that same year conveying his views on the imperial relationship between colonies and mother country. Those entities were "distinct and separate States," he maintained, joined only by the same "head, or Sovereign, the King." What was more, the provinces—which he called "States"—had "equal Rights and Liberties" and were connected in the same manner as Scotland and England had been before the union of Great Britain in 1707. As a result, he continued, Parliament had no jurisdiction over the separate states in America and had, in fact, "usurp'd an Authority" when it made laws governing it in the past.

Now this was heretical, revolutionary stuff, made more incendiary when the Massachusetts legislature adopted Franklin's doctrine in a dispute with Thomas Hutchinson. The governor, apprehensive that he had a potential crisis on his hands, addressed the legislature in January of 1773, giving members his considered views on the constitution of the empire. For more than a hundred years, he reminded them, the laws of the "supreme and subordinate authority were, in general, duly executed," but now the assembly had denied the authority of Parliament to make and establish laws for the province.

"I know no line that can be drawn between the supreme authority of Parliament and the total independence of the Colonies," he said. "It is impossible that there should be two independent Legislatures in one and the same state, for although there may be but one head, the King, yet two legislative bodies will make two Governments as distinct as the Kingdoms of England and Scotland before the Union."

Quite right, the assembly replied, delighted to have the opportunity to agree. Exactly so. And in a response skillfully edited by John Adams, the members accepted Hutchinson's premise, saying, "If there be no such Line, the Consequence is, Either that the Colonies are Vassals of the Parliament, or, that they are totally independent." Since the parties surely had no intention of reducing the provincials to the condition of vassals, the conclusion must be that they were independent.

By this time Hutchinson was convinced that Franklin was behind a move to assemble delegates from all the colonies at a general congress, which the Massachusetts governor saw as a formidable barrier to reconciliation between England and its colonies. When he informed Dartmouth of his fears, they fell on receptive ears; the king and his ministers had already concluded that Franklin's views were treasonable and for some time they had been intercepting and reading the old man's letters.

For years Boston's Sons of Liberty had had it in for Hutchinson and had tried to besmirch his reputation. This campaign was instrumental in the destruction of Hutchinson's home during the Stamp Act rioting, and Hutchinson, who was lieutenant governor at the time, and Andrew Oliver, the colony's secretary, were shocked by the violence and began corresponding with an associate of George Grenville named Thomas Whately in England. Their letters were relatively innocuous—complaining mainly of the trend toward "licentiousness" of the Boston mobs. Franklin somehow came into possession of them and sent them to one of the patriot leaders in Boston, instructing him not to copy them and not to make them public.

But Samuel Adams soon got wind of the letters, read them, and saw a golden opportunity to inflame the public against Hutchinson and Oliver, who were now governor and lieutenant governor, respectively. He edited the letters so subtly that it was impossible to tell whether the authors or Adams was speaking, and had them printed and sent to all the towns in Massachusetts and all Sons in the other colonies. God, said Adams, had revealed a plot laid by "malicious and invidious Enemies," and he persuaded the legislature to take action. In June of 1773 the Massachusetts assembly petitioned the king, via Franklin, to remove Hutchinson and Oliver from office for plotting "to overthrow the constitution of the province." Those two villains were responsible for "all that Corruption of Morals in this Province and all that Misery and Bloodshed" that were the result. (It was no help to Hutchinson that when the names of the five Massachusetts tea factors were announced, two were his sons, one was his nephew, and two were his friends.)

John Adams, writing to Catharine Macaulay, said the Hutchinson letters "have broken the charm in this Province. They have furnished full Proof of what was suspected by many and fully believed by a few here before, that all our calamities have originated in the cruel, rapacious Breasts of some of our own Countrymen—God grant them their reward!" The only thing that would bring peace and harmony, he went on, is "to be restored to our old Situation."

He hoped she would not think him ill-tempered, "but really, to see a continent, an Empire, danced for seven years like Puppetts upon the wires of two mean Americans [Hutchinson and Oliver, of course] for no Purpose in the World but to build up their own Families excites more indignation in me than I can well restrain."

Franklin presented the Massachusetts petition to Dartmouth on August 21, 1773, but a hearing at Whitehall was not scheduled until January 29, 1774. By that time Hutchinson had informed the ministry that the plot against him had been contrived in England, obviously at the instigation of Benjamin Franklin. London gossip had it that William Whately, the brother of the man to whom the letters had been written, had allowed them to become public. Whately not only denied this, but accused John Temple, a friend of Franklin, of releasing the documents, and the result of this contretemps was a duel with pistols and swords between the two men, in which Whately was wounded and both men emerged dissatisfied. When Franklin learned of the duel he confessed that he had indeed acquired the correspondence and sent it to

Boston. Unfortunately for him, news of the tea party had arrived in London a few days before the hearing and feelings were running high against the agent and Massachusetts.

Alexander Wedderburn, the solicitor general and a close friend of the late Thomas Whately, confronted Franklin at a hearing in the Cockpit,* before the Privy Council's Committee for Plantation Affairs and about three dozen mostly unfriendly spectators, who included Lords Dartmouth, Hillsborough, and Sandwich. A forty-one-year-old Scot, Wedderburn had worked diligently to get rid of his brogue, and was a formidable debater with an acid tongue. Ambitious, unscrupulous, and a thoroughly nasty man, he launched into a scathing attack on Franklin that was described as "gross, brutal, and vulgar." He began by accusing Massachusetts of fomenting rebellion and condemning Franklin, as its agent, who had been "so long possessed with the idea of a great American Republic that he may easily slide into the language of the minister of a foreign independent state." He was an "incendiary," the "first mover and prime conductor" of Boston's Committee of Correspondence. Wedderburn even lashed out at him in Latin: *Nunquam . . . amavi hunc hominem* (I never liked the man). He had obtained the letters of Hutchinson and Oliver "by fraudulent or corrupt means, for the most malignant of purposes; unless he stole them from the person who stole them . . . I hope, my lords, you will mark and brand this man."

Throughout the violent, abusive tirade against him, during which the great majority of "their lordships seemed to enjoy highly the entertainment and frequently burst out in loud applauses," as Franklin put it, the sixty-eight-year-old victim—dressed in a suit of brown velvet† and wearing an old-fashioned, full-bottomed wig—stood stock-still, without the least change of expression, never giving Wedderburn the satisfaction of knowing he had hit home.

Writing about his experience to Thomas Cushing, speaker of the Massachusetts House, Franklin commented that "the favourite part of [Wedderburn's] discourse was levelled at your agent, who stood there the butt of his invective ribaldry for near an hour." Wedderburn's speech was considered so

---

*During the reign of Henry VIII, when Westminster was a royal palace, the king built a pit here for cockfighting. In later years it was built over and the cockpit became a Parliamentary committee room.

†Franklin never forgot his humiliation, and four years later, on the occasion when Louis XVI of France greeted him at Versailles after news of the American victory at Saratoga convinced France to declare war against Britain and side with the American revolutionaries, he wore this same suit.

good, he added, that it was printed; "but the grosser parts of the abuse are omitted, appearing, I suppose . . . too foul to be seen on paper."

Since the General Assembly and Franklin had little but the questionably provocative letters as grounds for their petition, the administration threw out the charges against Hutchinson as "groundless, vexatious, and scandalous," created for the "seditious purpose of keeping up a spirit of clamour and discontent" in the province of Massachusetts Bay.

Evidently Franklin had heard how upset the Massachusetts governor was by the furore, but doubted that the government would console him much. Franklin wrote his son William, saying, "I do not wonder that Hutchinson should be dejected. It must be an uncomfortable thing to live among people who he is conscious universally detest him. Yet I fancy he will not have leave to come home, both because they do not know what to do with him, and because they do not very well like his conduct."

The immediate upshot of the incident was that Franklin, the unofficial voice of America in England (he was also the agent for Pennsylvania, New Jersey, and Georgia), was censured, discredited, and dismissed from his position as deputy postmaster-general in America, a job in which he had done as much as any man alive to tie the colonies together. Franklin had blundered seriously in passing the letters to friends in Massachusetts, but the resulting ordeal at the hands of Wedderburn had revealed the arrogance and vindictiveness of the king and the men who ran the government. Sadly for Franklin, it was the end of his dream of a united America within the empire and the failure of his efforts to bridge a gap that was as wide as the ocean that separated England from her colonies.

More than anything else, the debacle of the Hutchinson–Oliver letters was an indication of the way relations between England and America were collapsing. The Boston tea party, not the letters, created the real political crisis. In March 1774, when the ministry had the king summon Parliament to consider the grave situation in America, it was not only the administration that had turned against the colonists, but much of the British public as well. Edmund Burke described the mood in a letter to the New York Assembly: "The popular current, both within doors and without, at present sets sharply against America." And he cautioned against optimism. Be assured, he told them, "that the Determination to enforce Obedience from the Colonies to Laws of Revenue, by the most powerful means, seems as firm as possible, and that the Ministry appears stronger than ever I have known them."

Edmund Burke, by Sir Joshua Reynolds. *National Portrait Gallery, London.*

Even America's friends were aggrieved. Chatham called destruction of the tea as "certainly criminal." Rockingham said, "The conduct of the Americans cannot be justified." And Benjamin Franklin, observing that dumping the tea "seems to have united all Parties" in London against the Bay Colony, argued that since unknown persons were responsible for the incident the town of Boston should pay compensation. It was at this time that General Gage spoke with the king and informed him that if the government was resolute, the Americans would "undoubtedly prove very meek," and that four regiments of troops stationed in Boston would easily control that unruly town. George III, like many of his government officials, was convinced that "fatal compliance" in 1766—the repeal of the Stamp Act—had emboldened the colonists "annually to encrease their pretensions" of independence. In the past, leniency had encouraged further disobedience. What was needed now were strong measures, not compromise.

Nothing stood in the king's way, not even the French. Across the Channel the old king lay dying. Louis XV, once known as *le Bien-Aimé* (the Well-Beloved), had been on the throne for fifty-nine years and with his passing the British had little cause for concern that France—deeply troubled by the poverty and misery of its people—would give them any trouble. Franklin, who was a keen observer of that country, had noted that the water works of Versailles were out of repair, its brick walls shabby, its windows broken, and, like Paris, it revealed "a prodigious mixture of magnificence and negligence."

A further source of comfort for Britain was that the Well-Beloved's successor would be his grandson, twenty years old and said to be indolent and unsure of himself, while his wife was the frivolous, luxury-loving Marie Antoinette, known contemptuously as *l'Autrichienne* (the Austrian woman, with the emphasis on "*chienne*," the word for "bitch") and cordially despised by France's increasingly restless lower classes.

On the same day that Benjamin Franklin was being humiliated by Wedderburn, Britain's cabinet met and decided that the government must take steps "to secure the Dependence of the Colonies on the Mother Country." The methods to be employed were contained in four bills presented to Parliament between March and May of 1774—known to the government as the Boston Port Act, the Massachusetts Government Act, the Act for the Impartial Administration of Justice, and the Quartering Act.

Edmund Burke, who began serving the province of New York as its agent following the death of Robert Charles, saw the acts for what they were— "coercive Measures" designed not only to bring Boston and Massachusetts, that "refractory Town and province into proper Order," but to hold out "an Example of Terrour to the other Colonies."

In America, they became known for good reason as the Intolerable Acts.

19

An Act of Tyranny

As the consequences of retaining the tea tax began to emerge, Lord North suffered an attack of severe melancholia, a debilitating disorder that was to plague him again and again during his ministry, and he was prevented from resigning only by a firm and fervent request from the king. Even so, he seemed to lack the physical and mental will to support Dartmouth's program for the Americans. Four years earlier, Thomas Pownall had warned North against retention of the tax as a symbol of Parliamentary authority: it was as foolish as it would be unproductive, he had said, and would be seen by Americans as a yoke around their necks—a yoke that could become a millstone for Englishmen if it led to revolt or civil war. And so it was to prove.

Neither North nor his half brother William Legge, Earl of Dartmouth, had the stomach for military coercion, and they hoped at first to confine any harsh punitive measures to Boston, the perpetrator of this latest outrage. But the two were virtually alone in their sentiments, and with the rest of the cabinet—and, increasingly, public opinion—solidly arrayed against them, they were about to be pushed down a road from which there would be no turning back. It was to be a retaliatory program that offered only two choices: submission or suppression. North admitted that he wanted to punish Boston, the ringleader of violence and opposition, and emphasized that this was no longer about taxation. It was, plain and simple, about who was in charge. "If they deny authority in one instance," he said, "it goes to all. We must control them or submit to them."

The first of the so-called Coercive Acts closed the port of Boston, effective June 1, 1774. No vessel could enter the port after that date; after June 14 none could leave except coastwise craft engaged in carrying food or fuel to the town. The Custom House was transferred to Marblehead, the capital to Salem. This meant that Boston would cease to be the political and mercantile heart of Massachusetts until the East India Company was fully reimbursed for damages sustained and until the king proclaimed that peace and obedience to the laws were restored and trade safely carried on, with the customs duties duly collected. According to Dartmouth, who had proposed the port bill at the suggestion of Thomas Pownall's brother John, his undersecretary for America, the resulting economic distress would bring Boston to its knees. Dartmouth, along with just about everyone else in government except Chatham, was convinced that none of the other American colonies would come to the rescue of their unruly neighbor.

Later in the session, the cabinet met constantly to discuss what further measures would be employed. A second bill, as North described it, was "to take the executive power from the hands of the democratic part of government." It altered the province's sacred 1691 charter, replacing members elected to the governor's Council by the lower house with men chosen by the crown. Jurors were to be selected by sheriffs appointed by the governor. With a few exceptions, town meetings—those "hotbeds of sedition," as George III termed them—could be called only with the governor's consent. And the governor was no longer to be a civilian, but General Thomas Gage, who also retained command of the army and was expected to demand "full and absolute submission" to Parliament's authority. Gage, having served more than seventeen years in America without any vacation, had requested a leave of absence, which was granted. He had accumulated a respectable estate, he had six children with another on the way, and he and his wife wanted to spend time at Highmeadow, the Gage estate, while renewing acquaintance with old friends and family. In the early summer of 1773 he had sailed for England, but he was not to remain there for long.

In London the following winter, he informed the king that the discontented colonists "will be Lyons, whilst we are Lambs, but if we take the resolute part they will undoubtedly prove very meek." Sending four regiments to Boston, he continued, would be ample force to "prevent any disturbance." Now Lord North and the cabinet had decided to send him back to the increasingly unruly Boston to try out his theory.

A third bill—the Administration of Justice Act—authorized the governor to change the venue of a trial of any crown official under indictment to another colony or to Britain. The fourth measure, a new Quartering Act, required the colony to provide accommodations for British troops when no barracks were available.

These measures, North said in summing them up for the members, were "not cruel nor vindictive, but necessary and efficacious." And since temporary distress requires temporary relief, he explained, the bills were to be in effect for only three or four years. Members should realize, he added, that "every thing we have is at stake; and the question is very shortly this: Whether they shall continue the subjects of Great Britain or not." Finally he warned the colonies that the ministry would "not suffer the least degree of disobedience to our measures to take place."

At the same time, the British made plans to use force. Dartmouth ordered Gage to use his troops "with effect, should the madness of the People on the one hand, or the timidity or lack of Strength of the peace officers, make it necessary to have recourse to their assistance." By now, Dartmouth realized, the crisis was so far advanced that little hope of a peaceful settlement remained.

Before Parliament was prorogued on June 22, 1774, a Quebec Act was passed. Mistakenly, the colonists regarded this as yet another Intolerable Act, though it had no relationship to the other coercive measures other than timing. In the eyes of many Americans, however, it was as bad as, if not worse than, the others. It redefined the boundaries of the province of Quebec southward from the Great Lakes to the Ohio River, giving Canada an enormous new region that appeared to nullify Virginia's claims and those of New England. Inflamed public opinion—especially a host of outraged land speculators—saw it immediately as a move to re-create the French and Indian threat along the frontier. Worst of all, its inclusion within Quebec meant that a Roman Catholic bishop had jurisdiction over it. Militant colonial dissenters were enraged at the thought that popery would run amok in territory they thought had been promised to them. According to the *New-York Journal* the Anglican bishop of London was so incensed about "giving popery and arbitrary power a legal establishment" in one of the British dominions that he refused to vote for the bill.

New York's new agent, Edmund Burke, confirmed his clients' worst fears about the Quebec Act when he reported that the ministry's goal was to restrict westward expansion and keep the colonies supine and weak—a message that was to influence their decision to align themselves with the other colonies. Even so, Burke was convinced that "American affairs will not come to any crisis sufficient to rouse the [British] public from its present stupefaction."

Although the Earl of Chatham was greatly disturbed by Boston's conduct, he argued that the ministry's method of forcing the people there to behave was "diametrically opposite to the principles of sound policy." By blocking up the harbor, he argued, "you have involved the innocent trader in the same punishment with the guilty profligates who destroyed your merchandise." Adopt some lenient measures, he urged, measures that might "lure them to their duty," and then "proceed like a kind and affectionate parent over a child whom he tenderly loves." Then, returning to his old and passionate theme that Britain had no right to tax its colonies, he offered a prayer for America's welfare: "Length of days be in her right hand, and in her left riches and honour; may her ways be ways of pleasantness, and all her paths be peace!"

Ever supportive of America's welfare and constantly seeking intelligence on colonial affairs, Chatham had recently met an unlikely informant. She was a fifty-year-old Quaker widow from America named Patience Wright who, with her sister, had become well known for the portraits she fashioned in wax. The two women traveled extensively in the colonies to execute their commissions and had two permanent exhibition rooms—one in Philadelphia and the other in New York. On a visit to Boston, Mrs. Wright met Benjamin Franklin's sister, Jane Mecom, who wrote a letter of introduction to the great man in London, and in 1772 the sculptress sailed for England, leaving behind her sister and four children.

There in the capital she sought out Franklin at once, taking with her his sister's letter and a wax bust of Cadwallader Colden, whom he knew. Very quickly she became something of a rage, meeting the actor David Garrick, John Wilkes, Horace Walpole, and many other notable people, and she modeled busts of Lord North, Thomas Pownall, Catharine Macaulay, and others. Her method was to mold the wax likenesses, or bustos, as they were called, in her lap while she conversed with the sitter. Benjamin West, the painter, is thought to have obtained an interview with the king for her, which resulted in bustos of George III and the queen in 1773—and, not so incidentally, a request from His Majesty for information on American affairs, which she was only too happy to supply.

Patience Wright was not only a talented artist, she was also a gossip, trading news for news, and she circulated widely in both pro- and anti-American camps in London, raising speculation as to whether she was a spy. In any case, she passed along much of what she had heard where it would be of maximum benefit to the American cause. Through Franklin she met the Earl of Chatham, and her enthusiasm can only be imagined. She wrote to all she knew who might be helpful, and shared their identities and thoughts with Chatham in conversation and in letters, which were notable for their appallingly bad handwriting and highly imaginative sentence structure. From her the earl learned that Robert Murray, a New York merchant now in London, had gone to Lord North with three other merchants trading with Boston, offering to pay the East India Company for its losses in hopes that the ringleaders of the Tea Party could be brought to justice. (North was not interested.)

From Mrs. Wright the man she called America's "guardin angel" discovered in late June of 1774 that the Continental Congress planned to threaten the West Indies with a boycott unless the islands agreed to nonimportation of English goods. Closing that letter to Chatham, she sent hopes that "Providenc [would] Keep your Life Long a Blessing to your Contry and a Patren of wise Counsil and the name of Pitt be remembred for Ever is the hearty Prayr of P. Wright."

She remained in London throughout the Revolution but in 1781 moved to France, stayed a year, and returned to England, where she died in 1786.

Unfortunately for P. Wright and America, the "guardin angel" was part of an increasingly lonely minority these days, and his efforts at appeasement were made no easier when Bostonians, in no mood to seek the leniency of Parliament, had boarded another tea ship on March 9, 1774, and destroyed thirty more cases of its cargo.

The vagaries of weather were evident when the *Concord* reached New York on the night of May 11, having taken six weeks for the crossing from Liverpool, followed the next day by the *Samson,* a mere twenty-six days out of London. Both vessels brought news of the Boston Port Bill, as it was generally called in the colonies, which had been signed by the king on March 31, along with the announcement that General Gage was to be the new governor of Massachusetts. "This intelligence was received with Great abhorence & indignation by the Sons of Freedom," Alexander McDougall wrote, adding that Parliament's assurance that no action would be taken against New York or the other colonies was preposterous. Quite apart from indignation, it presented the Liberty Boys with an acute dilemma. McDougall and Sears agreed that an immediate renewal of nonimportation was the logical weapon to use, but they were keenly aware of the difficulty of selling that to the merchants—particularly the DeLancey crowd. A further risk was that it would divide the colonies, which could be fatal. They had been alerted by an ally in England that the ministry was determined to pit Americans against each other, making it imperative that they "bear with every Infirmity among yourselves, that like a Bundle of tender Rods you may not be separately broken to Pieces." Unless the other colonists stood together with the Bostonians, the friend wrote, "you must fall the easy Victims of Tyranny and become the most abject Slaves of the Earth. . . . The times are growing dangerous, and I know they would be glad to have my Head, therefore you will excuse my not writing my Name—you know my Hand. . . ."

The friend's warning was not the only inducement. On Sunday, May 15, the two former ship captains ran into James Duane and talked over what was to be done about the Port Bill. According to Duane, Lord North was said to have admitted that if the colonists had stuck with nonimportation for another six months, the last of the Townshend Acts would have been repealed. That was enough for McDougall and Sears: they met with a number of merchants and Liberty Boys and agreed to hold a meeting the following evening at Fraunces Tavern "to determine on a nomination of a Committee of Correspondence, to bring about a Congress."

They also decided to notify Boston's Sons immediately of the news from England, in case they had not yet heard it, and Sears and McDougall then sat down to write a letter of support to be carried by the courier to Boston. Stating that "a great number of our citizens wish our port to be in the same state with yours," they implied that their proposals were approved by a majority of New Yorkers, which of course they were not. Even so, it was a message of exceptional importance. Without discussing their intentions with anyone, they took the responsibility for reassuring the Bostonians, adding that the "Act of Tyranny" was aimed not only at their city but at all Americans.

Urging their Massachusetts friends to bear the burden as bravely as possible and not capitulate to the ministry by complying with the act by paying for the tea (which would bring on "a more general Calamity"), they proceeded to set forth a plan of attack. Having taken the pulse of New Yorkers, they had summoned the city's merchants to a meeting to adopt both a nonimportation and a nonexportation agreement. The latter was a bold new idea: they proposed to ban all exports to the British West Indies in order to deny the West Indies interests—"our Enemies in the House of Commons"—their commissions on the produce of the islands, their interest and debt payments from the islands, and the valuable cargoes of at least two hundred ships, at the same time depriving government of all those lucrative duties.

The two New Yorkers said they would write to friends in New Haven, Philadelphia, Charleston, Georgia, and North Carolina to enlist support for the scheme, while asking the Bostonians to sound out "the Minds of the Sea Port Towns" in New England east of New Haven. Although their letter was written in great haste, it was extremely cogent and significant because it was the first call made by a public body for a continental congress to deal with the crisis brought on by the Intolerable Acts. By early Sunday afternoon it was in the hands of an express rider, who galloped off on the post road to Boston. Sears and McDougall knew they were going out on a limb by not sharing the letter with their colleagues, but as the latter wrote, "As no time was to be lost, we judged it unnecessary to detain the express till the other members of our Committee signed it. At 2 pm . . . ye express set off."

By then, of course, the Boston Sons had dispatched Paul Revere to New York and Philadelphia to appeal for their support, and would send off a proposal to all the colonies for a "Solemn League and Covenant" shutting off all trade with Britain. When Samuel Adams received the New Yorkers' letter he honored the request of the authors that their names be kept secret, and then turned over an edited version of the document to the *Boston Gazette*. Curiously, he omitted any reference to the general congress they had proposed, perhaps because he did not want the New Yorkers to get credit for the idea, or possibly because he felt it unlikely that a unified front on this question was practicable.

When the news from the *Concord* and *Samson* reached the streets, Billy Smith noted, "A General Consternation and Disgust works among the People," particularly since some of the newspapers and letters carried by the ships accused the colonists of being rebels, which only "increase our Disaffection & excite a Contempt of Government." Smith lamented, "I fear we shall lose all that Attachm[en]t we once had to so great a Degree for the Parent Country." He was infinitely saddened by what he saw going on—the ministry's absolute refusal to consider a moderate course, which only drove radicals and moderates alike to dig in their heels and resist further.

William Smith seemed to sense intuitively what would result from the North ministry's Coercive Acts. Boston's appeal for support could not be ignored by her fellow colonists, and it was as though a line had been drawn in the soil, demanding that people take a stand on one side or the other and face up to the issue of loyalty to Great Britain for the very first time. They found themselves forced to answer the unthinkable question.

A wave of sympathy for Boston was immediate, and by June 1, when the port was to be closed, spontaneous demonstrations had erupted in villages and towns across the land, shops closed their doors, bells tolled, and, along with promises of solidarity, donations of foodstuffs were sent off to the beleaguered city. Only in New York was the reaction cautious and equivocal.

. . .

Smith sought out McDougall and pleaded with him to "postpone Operations" and act prudently. Let us avoid the use of force at all costs, he continued, and do no more than complain, in hopes the British will feel sorry for us. He agreed, however, that the best move was to call a congress and to "shoot no Bolt" that would expose colonial weakness. Remember, he said, the government has more to fear from a congress than nonimportation, and might be afraid that the colonies were seeking help from a foreign power.

Both men realized that the Port Bill changed the dynamic from persuasion to coercion, but McDougall and his partner Isaac Sears remained hopeful that nonimportation—which had worked before—would work again now. But the odds were against them. While Oliver DeLancey announced that he "would rather spend every shilling of his Fortune than that the Boston Port Bill be complied with," neither he nor other members of his party had any intention of supporting a nonimportation agreement. (Andrew Ludlow declared "openly and insolently" that he would not go along with any such nonsense.) The DeLancey group's resistance became more evident on Monday, May 16, by which time the Liberty Boys had persuaded some of the merchants to support their program forbidding imports from England and exports of lumber to the West Indies. The DeLanceys would have none of that, and suddenly the breach between New York's two political forces was out in the open for all to see.

For years these implacable foes had been at sword's point over every issue, no matter what the excuse—the college, their faith, class, friends, associates, even the library. But something altogether different had entered the equation. Hitherto, loyalty to the mother country was a given, with neither side questioning a relationship that had always been taken for granted. Now, ever so gradually, those associated with the Livingstons, Sears, and McDougall were beginning to doubt the validity of that relationship, wondering if the rights they sought and were willing to struggle for could be achieved within the framework of the British Empire in its current form.

On one side of the divide were the DeLanceys, who had chosen all along to pin their hopes on support from the crown and America's special place within the empire. Theirs was the party of elitism and special privilege, the Church of England, and business as usual, predicated on a prosperity that came to the most prominent and deserving merchants as a result of their alliances with England. It all had to do with who you knew and what they could do for you. While no man was better informed than James DeLancey

on the legitimate grievances that troubled so many Americans, it was clear to
him that if he and his supporters addressed those problems and endeavored to
come to terms with them, they would very likely play into the hands of the
radicals, involuntarily lending support to the mobs that were taking over the
city's streets.

On the other side of the divide and at the other end of the political and
social spectrum were Sears, McDougall, and a host of largely faceless, name-
less "leather aprons" and seamen who could be counted on to rally round
whenever the call for action went out. But joined with them, albeit grudgingly and uncomfortably, were wealthy folk such as the Livingstons, who had
slowly awakened to the realization that public support was the essential ingredient of political power and the only means by which they could take it away
from the DeLanceys.

The widening gap and the disdain each side had for the other was evident
in how they described their antagonists. Alexander McDougall, speaking of
the DeLancey faction, referred to them as "the old enemies of Liberty," occasionally as "the DeLancey Junto," or—more inclusively—as "Enemies and
Luke warm friends to America." Cadwallader Colden castigated the New
York radicals, or Patriots as more and more of them now called themselves, as
"hot-headed People," or "the lower Rank and all the Zealots of those call'd the
Sons of Liberty," while characterizing those who had his approval as "cool
prudent Men" or "the principal People" or "Gentlemen of Property and principal Merchants." (Referring to the disputants in the New Hampshire Grants,
he termed the New York claimants "his Majesty's peaceable Subjects" while
labeling the squatters "a Lawless set of Men . . . a dangerous Body of Ban-
ditti . . . Fugitives from all Parts . . . and the worst of Men.")

The waspish archconservative Thomas Jones was careful to distinguish
loyalists from Whigs (the worst of whom were "flaming" republicans and
"demagogues of rebellion") while sneering at the "rabble" and describing how
Sears and company "paraded the town with drums beating and colours flying
(attended by a mob of negroes, boys, sailors, and pickpockets)." Jones despised William Smith, Jr., calling him "a rigid Presbyterian [Jones, of course,
was a staunch Church of England man]—a factious republican—a hater of
monarchy—an enemy to Episcopacy, a leveller in principle, and a sly, arch,
hypocritical ringleader of sedition."

Smith himself, who took pride in being a middle-of-the-roader, but in
truth tended to lean philosophically in the direction of the Livingston–Sears–
McDougall group, nevertheless spoke regularly of their more rough-hewn
followers as "the lower classes" and drew a line between "the People of Prop-

Thomas Jones and Ann DeLancey Jones, from paintings by R. Arnold.
Author's collection.

erty" and "the lower sort," while referring to his opposition on the Council as
"Knaves or Fools—or both."

In like manner these men had decidedly different versions of what happened that spring and summer. McDougall made careful notes of daily occur-
rences throughout the month of May; Smith kept track of events in his diary;
Colden wrote frequently to Dartmouth and Tryon in London; and all three
saw events in a different light.

On the morning of May 16, when McDougall posted a notice intended only
for merchants, urging them to attend a meeting at Fraunces Tavern that
night, the DeLanceys immediately set to work to ensure that their followers
would be present and in the majority. James DeLancey knew that most of his

merchant associates would oppose nonimportation, but he had to be sure the mechanics and artisans who had been with him for years, for reasons of self-interest or loyalty, would not be carried away by the emotions of the moment.

This was the first in a seemingly endless string of meetings, announced by handbills and newspaper notices, day after day, week after week in numbing succession until the end of July, so that hardly a day passed without one or even several assemblies. That first evening some three hundred people—more than the tavern could accommodate—were redirected to the Exchange, and wrangling erupted between the DeLancey faction and the outnumbered and badly outmaneuvered Liberty Boys. A number of councillors attended—including Oliver DeLancey, James Cruger, Thomas Jones, John Watts, and Isaac Low—all of them endeavoring to persuade the crowd that payment for the tea would open the port of Boston and there the problem would end. They argued that a decision on nonimportation should be delayed until the "sense of the other colonies should be known," and when a vote on a committee of correspondence was called, the DeLanceys managed to fudge the issue and focus on the number and makeup of the group. The Sons of Liberty preferred a small, workable number, but were outvoted, and the number of members was set at fifty, with fifteen to constitute a quorum.

Isaac Low, serving as chairman,* appealed for an end to party divisions, asking those present to remember that what was at issue was "the preservation of our just rights and liberties. . . . Zeal in a good cause is laudable," he pontificated, "but when it transports beyond the bounds of reason it often leaves room for bitter reflection." As he called for nominations from the floor, Low recognized DeLancey men again and again, with only an occasional nod to the Liberty Boys. Somehow James Jauncey was put on the list without a vote, and McDougall immediately reminded the crowd that Jauncey had accused the Bostonians who opposed the landing of tea of being guilty of treason or rebellion, but he was elected nonetheless. A majority of those present voted for John Lamb and Francis Lewis—both of whom supported nonimportation—yet neither man's name made it to the list. And so it went, to the dismay of McDougall and his friends. Most of those elected were merchants or lawyers who were attached either to the DeLancey or Livingston factions. Of the total, twenty-six were definitely allied with the DeLanceys, fifteen with the Livingstons, and ten were men whose loyalties are not known. At a later

*The *New-York Mercury* of May 23 stated that Low was appointed, but McDougall indicated that he assumed the chairmanship without being asked.

meeting the radical Lewis was inexplicably added and the organization became known as the Committee of Fifty-one.

Reporting to Dartmouth, Colden wrote that "the Gentlemen of the Council and others of weight in the City" [i.e., the DeLancey faction] were committed to "prevent the hot-headed People from takeing Measures that might endanger the Peace and Quiet of the Colony." These merchants and the "principal Inhabitants" saw to it that the Committee of Fifty-one included "the most prudent and considerate Persons of the Place," who— although they knew the proceedings were illegal—decided to participate so that the business of the meeting would not "be left in . . . rash hands." As for siding with the Bostonians, he went on, these cool prudent men could be counted on to "keep Measures in suspence."

As confident as he was that DeLancey's followers would prevent the radicals from taking control, Colden allowed a note of doubt to creep into his report. He had heard about a move to invite the colonies to send deputies to a general meeting "to deliberate upon some Plan whereby the Jealousies between Great Britain and her Colonies may be removed." He was assured by those he called the "Intelligent People" that these unauthorized assemblies were illegal and might be dangerous, "but they deny that they are unconstitutional when a national grievance cannot otherwise be removed." He had to admit it was a puzzling situation and, writing to Tryon, said that while he was sure New York would not comply with the request of Boston, "what they will do I cannot as yet say."

Not only an instinctive fear of mob action but a very practical concern over the potential loss of profits on their exports kept the merchants and landed aristocrats coming to the seemingly endless series of meetings in the city. Some insisted that New York should ignore Boston's problems. Others, including many wealthy landowners, who were angered by the ministry's treatment of Massachusetts and wanted to do something, nevertheless opposed nonimportation or other extremist measures and settled on a congress as a lesser evil—one they might be able to control. But the deep concern of most of them was expressed by the merchant John Thurman in a letter to London: "We are very uneasy & don't know but Parliament mean to drive us to measures w[hi]ch may prove destructive to Great Brittain & her colonies. Every good friend to both will wish for a lasting union & I am sure it is the desire of every good American to wish Great Brittain may forever Remain our Head & Ruler tho never to impose Internal Taxation."

At a meeting on May 19, the DeLancey people again got out the vote while the turnout of the republicans was disappointing. McDougall, who was ill, did not show up, which left matters in the hands of Sears. The purpose of the gathering was for townspeople to approve the slate of fifty-one or select alternatives. This was triggered by the decision of a committee (largely Sons of Liberty) calling themselves Mechanics, who had met the night before and chosen twenty-five candidates—all but two of them from the list of fifty-one, and a majority of them Livingston allies. The meeting turned into a battle between the two Isaacs—Sears and Low—with Sears demanding that Low read a letter from the Boston committee which had just been delivered by Paul Revere, Low refusing, Sears attempting to read it himself and being shouted down by the DeLancey people. And so it went, with nothing whatever being accomplished.

On the following day, Smith met with Sears and McDougall and persuaded them to abandon the idea of a smaller committee and settle for the list of fifty-one—all in the interest of demonstrating to the outside world that New Yorkers were united. Further, he cautioned them, do not push for a nonimportation agreement: that would only affront the merchants. And above all, avoid the use of force: time will do everything for us, he predicted, "if we maintain our Firmness without Violence." The two men took his advice, and at their urging, the Sons of Liberty agreed to accept the list of fifty-one. But they were still a long way from convincing conservative committee members to aid the Bostonians and give them the kind of moral support they were receiving from other colonies.

On May 22, Paul Revere stopped off on his way home from Philadelphia and disclosed that city's resolves in response to the Bostonians' appeals. According to McDougall, "Capt Sears and I advised the express to wait till next day for an answer from our Comm[itte]e to the Letters he brought. . . ." The radical leaders were confident that the first meeting of the Committee of Fifty-one would produce the results they wanted, and at the Coffee House the next day, with forty present, McDougall was all smiles and conciliation, voicing the hope that past disputes and hard feelings would be set aside in an effort to present a unified front and promising that his own future conduct would convince members of his sincerity. After the letters from Boston and Philadelphia were read, Isaac Low, James Duane, John Jay, and Alexander McDougall were appointed members of a subcommittee to draft a letter to Boston. The group went to work at once, and Duane took the results of their work home with him "to furbish it up."

At eight o'clock that evening the finished draft letter was read to the committee. Acknowledging that the town of Boston was suffering in "the common cause," the letter proposed that a congress of deputies from the principal colonies is of the utmost moment; that it ought to be assembled without delay, and some unanimous resolution formed in this fatal emergency, not only respecting your deplorable circumstances, but for the security of our common rights.

Along with that, it offered a pledge of cooperation "with our sister colonies in every measure which shall be thought salutary and conducive to the public good." If the Bostonians approved the congress, the letter concluded, "we may exert our utmost endeavours to carry it into execution."

The reading produced an immediate reaction from four DeLanceyites—William Bayard, Theophylact Bache, Charles McEvers, and Charles Shaw—who objected strongly to the suggestion of a congress ("it was too soon to propose it," they said) and wanted to delete the statement that the Bostonians were suffering in the cause of American liberty. That brought James Duane to his feet to reply that "if the Boston People were not suffering in the cause of American Liberty we should cast them off and not write to them." With that stinging rebuke to the conservatives and a single change—substituting "Colonies in General" for "Principal Colonies"—the draft was overwhelmingly approved, and it was delivered to Paul Revere the following morning.

As it happened, Revere did not leave New York until ten in the morning on May 24, and along with the committee's letter he carried an urgent plea from McDougall that was too controversial to include in the written message—a request that the Boston committee settle at once on a time and place for the congress to meet. That was the goal Sears and McDougall wanted above all else.

20

The Mob Begin to Think

The best way to describe the scene in New York in the weeks that followed is in William Smith's words: "The political Sky at this Place is Cloudy." Describing the makeup of the Committee of Fifty-one as "jarring Members," he told Philip Schuyler that ten or a dozen had left the committee in protest against that body's failure "to join the common Voice of the Continent." Word had come from Boston at last that Massachusetts (along with Rhode Island) had chosen delegates for a congress, and Sears and McDougall took that as a signal to push New York to follow suit. At their prodding the Committee of Fifty-one debated the question at several sessions and finally agreed to put forth a slate of five men to represent the city. Sears immediately took the floor and nominated Isaac Low, James Duane, Philip Livingston, John Morin Scott, and Alexander McDougall. The last two were too much for the conservatives to swallow, and they insisted on replacing them with John Alsop and John Jay. That was on July 4, and the committee voted to submit these candidates for the citizens' approval at a meeting at the Town Hall on July 7.

Once again the radicals pushed their luck by calling a meeting in the Fields on July 6. A packet was leaving for England the next day, and they wanted it to carry a strong message to their friends there. In the belief that a statement of purpose was more important than the choice of delegates (who would have to follow instructions), they persuaded the assembled crowd to ratify a number of resolutions. They condemned the Boston Port Bill, called an attack on one colony an attack on all, endorsed nonimportation and nonexportation as the most effective means of nullifying Parliament's attacks, instructed the delegates representing New York to seek common agreement on these measures, promised that New York would honor and support the goals, sought aid for Boston's poor, and instructed the Committee of Fifty-one to carry out the resolutions. John Holt took a copy of the document, set it in type, and printed it in his paper in time to put copies aboard the packet.

Unfortunately for Sears and McDougall, at the scheduled meeting on July 7, conservative members of the committee condemned the rump session in the Fields, rejected their scheme out of hand, and voted to censure their activities. Just when the meeting was about to break up, Charles McEvers, who knew what Sears and McDougall were up to, demanded that the proceedings of the committee repudiating the radicals' actions be recorded and "accompany [Holt's] paper wherever it went." This so angered the two former captains and nine of their friends that they stormed out of the hall in a rage, ordered their names struck from the list of members, and ran "bawling along the streets 'the Committee is dissolved—the Committee is dissolved!'" From that moment on, neither side ever trusted the other again.

As Smith observed, it was "Strange that the Colony who had the first Intelligence of the Parliamentary Measures is behind all the rest." In stark contrast to New York's waffling, "The whole Province of South Carolina acted in the Appointment of Members for the Congress & bind themselves to perform what they may resolve at Phila the 1 of September next, & the

View of Harlem from Morrisania. *Stokes Collection, Iconography of Manhattan, New-York Historical Society.*

Merchants agree to suspend their commerce in the interim." Throughout the colonies the motives of New Yorkers were beginning to be questioned: how sincere was their support for the cause of liberty?

During the summer of 1774, which Cadwallader Colden spent at his place on Long Island, members of the Council obliged the old man by holding many of their meetings at the ferry landing on his side of the river in order to spare him the trip across the water. The lieutenant governor had announced his intention of distributing lands in the New Hampshire Grants even though the crown had forbidden any further activity there, and while William Smith objected to Colden's practice at every meeting, on grounds that it was con- trary to the king's instructions and would only exacerbate the situation and kill any hope of settling the civil conflict, his was the lone voice in opposition. Smith had learned that Colden planned to grant petitions for land "regardless of the last Instructions & without the Council" and noted in his diary, "Observe this well."

In mid-June the Council prorogued the Assembly until August 3 and then proceeded to hear more petitions for lands. "Never did People act more absurdly," Smith grumbled, while arguing that "the King alone was the proper Judge of the Equity" of such petitions. But "All in vain."

In a letter to his friend Philip Schuyler, Smith posed an interesting ques- tion. Reminding Schuyler that Colden was granting lands in the face of instructions to the contrary, Smith said he had been offered land between Lake Champlain and the Connecticut River for a mere eighteen pence per acre. He intended "to sport away about £1,000 as I suppose it will be the last Chance. The Lands are remote but remember that the Country settles fast." In other words, he would be buying lands that he had opposed granting to anyone, and his question was "Have I not discharged my Duty when I voted ag[ains]t a Petition in which I was myself concerned?" As for Schuyler, he should "apply soon, for the next Packet may close the present Scene in which the Kings Property is to be disposed of agt. his Will—Let all this be a Secret."

Land speculation was a long way from the thoughts of Isaac Sears and Alexander McDougall, whose fortunes had suddenly taken a turn for the better. On July 19 the reduced Committee of Fifty-one had met to appoint delegates to the congress and, as William Smith put it, "approve certain pusil- lanimous Resolves," but the conservatives' planned program went badly awry, with the result that "we had Proofs of the Rise of the Popular Pulse for

Liberty." John Morin Scott made a fire-eating speech, the conservatives' resolutions were rejected, and the public appointed a new committee of fifteen, which included both Sears and McDougall.

Finally, on July 28, after the committee pledged not to import goods from Great Britain until America's grievances were settled, Philip Livingston, Isaac Low, John Alsop, James Duane, and John Jay were named as delegates to the congress. Grudgingly, Thomas Jones offered a few lukewarm words of praise for four of the nominees. Livingston, he wrote, "though a republican, [was] not one of the most inflammatory kind." Duane and Jay were both "gentlemen of eminence in the law, had each a sufficiency of ambition, with a proper share of pride," and both, he added approvingly, were strong Episcopalians and staunch supporters of the British constitution. (Jones did not say so, but Duane and Jay were DeLanceyites who had married into the Livingston family, and Duane was the anonymous author of the "Dougliad" letters criticizing McDougall and the "greedy Livingston family.") Alsop was "an honest, upright, wealthy merchant, had knowledge enough for a man in his way," but was not cut out to be a politician. He was, to his credit, a steady churchman and "loved Bishops as well as Kings."

Low was another case altogether. He belonged to the Church of England, but was "unbounded in ambition, violent and turbulent in his disposition, remarkably obstinate, with a good share of understanding, extremely opinionated, fond of being the head of a party, and never so well pleased as when chairman of a committee, or principal spokesman at a mob meeting."

New York's loyalists thought themselves safe with these men, Jones added, and instructed them to seek a redress of grievances and a firm union based on constitutional principles between Great Britain and America. Time would tell how successful they might be.

What outlying areas of the province might do about naming delegates to the congress was an open question, but Colden, writing to Dartmouth earlier in July, observed, "The present political zeal and Frenzy is almost entirely confined to the City of New York." From what he could gather, all but one of the other counties in the province had declined the New Yorkers' invitation to appoint committees of correspondence and, unlike the city, were "perfectly quiet and in good order." To Tryon, he added, "Except in the city of New York, the People in the Province are quite Tranquile, and have declin'd takeing any Part with the Citizens." If a nonimportation agreement was forthcoming, however, and the government retaliated by turning away American exports, the picture could change: that was a possibility "the Farmers clearly see will be ruinous to them."

One man whose family would be affected by any halt on exports to the West Indies was Gouverneur Morris, who had been raised as a provincial aristocrat on the manor at Morrisania. A graduate of King's College, he studied law under William Smith, Sr., became a member of the New York bar at the age of nineteen, and now, aged twenty-two, had a highly successful practice. In his view, the growing power of the common people was alarming, and how to control them was the question. Here they were, corresponding with the other colonies, calling and dismissing popular assemblies, making resolves to bind the conscience of mankind, and bullying poor printers, and although the aristocrats held the reins of power, they were in danger of losing them. "The mob begin to think and reason," he wrote. "Poor reptiles! It is with them a vernal morning, they are struggling to cast off their winter's slough, they bask in the sunshine, and ere noon they will bite, depend on it. The gentry begin to fear this."

Many New Yorkers who sympathized with Morris's views regretted having gone along with so much of what the radicals wanted and wished they had "an opportunity to throw off the mask, to join with the friends of government." That, as one correspondent wrote in the *New-York Journal,* might be the only way to end "all disputes between us and our mother country, [so] that trade and commerce might flourish again. . . ." Morris himself, in his present state of mind, concluded that immediate reconciliation with Great Britain was the sole answer, since it would deprive the radicals of the opportunity to rouse the public and take America down a road into uncharted territory. As always, religion entered the picture. Another letter that appeared in the *New-York Journal* stated, "I am no friend to Presbyterians. I fix all the blame . . . upon them," since they "always do, and ever will act against government, from that restless and turbulent anti-monarchical spirit which has always distinguished them every where and whenever they had, or by any means could assume power, however illegally." The Anglicans, he went on righteously, acting from truly loyal principles, had done everything in their power to "stop the rapid progress of sedition, which would have gone much further lengths if it had not been for them."

After the interminable haggling, the vituperative struggles for ascendancy, and a great deal of tough bargaining, the radicals had some reason for satisfaction over what they had accomplished. It was by no means all they had hoped for, but at least Massachusetts had called for a congress to meet in Philadelphia early in September and New York City had chosen five delegates—pledged to nonimportation—to attend. More, the DeLancey-led faction in New York had reluctantly conceded that it would abide by any decisions made by the congress. Nevertheless, what came to be called the Continental Congress was of profound importance to the New York Sons of Liberty. They had done all they could on the local scene; now it remained to be seen if the meetings in Philadelphia would advance or negate their hopes of seeing New York provide meaningful support to Boston.

In early August, Colden mailed a report to Tryon, informing him of the death of Sir William Johnson and urging Tryon to lobby for Guy Johnson to be appointed the successor to his father for Indian affairs. Then, turning to the local scene, he noted ruefully that the citizens "have been in continual ferment of Division among themselves upon their political Measures, which at bottom arises from their local Party views—they have all an eye to the next Election, more than any thing else." Speaking of the appointment of delegates to the forthcoming congress, he suggested that they might accomplish something positive if they pursued "only such prudent Measures as are calculated to remove the destructive Dissensions which subsist between Great Britain and her Colonies. . . ." Even though the meeting was illegal, it might do some good, he added moodily.

As Colden told Tryon, a major effort had been made to induce residents of other counties to appoint delegates to the congress, but the lack of interest was painfully disappointing. Albany, Dutchess, Westchester, and Ulster supported the New York City nominees; Orange, where twenty voters turned out, elected two men; Suffolk elected a single delegate; and Kings selected two—by a vote of only two men, one of whom nominated himself.

In Boston, General Gage was writing to Dartmouth about Sir William Johnson's death—a heavy loss, he said, since Virginians were slaughtering Indians "so wantonly and cruely that we might reasonably expect every Tribe would rise upon us. . . ." Only Sir William's influence had restrained them until now. As for matters closer to hand, Gage was all confidence. The effects of the Port Bill he passed off as a joke. Bostonians' hopes were kept alive by the promise of assistance from other colonies, but that amounted to little. South Carolina had sent some rice, and sheep had arrived from another source, but supplies of this sort were too precarious to depend on and the local folk were beginning to realize that "carrying Molasses & Rum twenty eight miles by land is found not to answer as well as it was expected it would."

Boston's hopes rested on the same tired and unlikely measures, he observed—a union of the colonies, nonimportation, the assistance of their friends in England, and a general clamor from merchants and manufacturers. The latter might prove serious if they could rally those two groups, "but the rest is Talk and Noise only, and Nothing better."

On August 20, several of Gage's Boston tormentors arrived in New York. Thomas Cushing, Robert Treat Paine, Samuel Adams, and John Adams were on their way to the Philadelphia congress, and Alexander McDougall took them under his wing for a tour of the city and introductions to some of the prominent political figures. Very likely, John Adams and his fellow Bostonians were as curious about their hosts and Manhattan as the New Yorkers were about them. After all, New York's importance was self-evident. At the beginning of 1774 the population of the province was 182,247, of whom 161,098 were whites, with the remaining 20 percent blacks (most of them slaves). The city of New York, with 25,000 inhabitants, was the second-largest in the colonies—behind Philadelphia's 40,000, but well ahead of Boston, which had 16,000. (Charleston's population was 12,000, and at least eight other towns, including New Haven, Baltimore, and Newport, had more than 5,000.)

More important than its population figures was New York's wealth, its geographical position as the link between New England and the other provinces, and its status as one of the busiest seaports on the continent. In 1770, moreover, thanks to massive lobbying efforts by the DeLanceys, New York had abandoned nonimportation and the other colonies had gone along. If New York should decide to repudiate the congress at this juncture, it could doom the cause of liberty in America.

John Adams kept a diary, and in it he set down his impressions of the various New Yorkers he met. Looking down his long Puritan nose at them, he sized them up as an unimpressive, unattractive lot, saying that "there is very little good Breeding to be found. We have been treated with an assiduous Respect," he admitted, "but I have not seen one real Gentleman, one well bred Man, since I came to Town. At their Entertainments, there is no conversation that is agreeable. There is no Modesty, no Attention to one another. They talk very loud, very fast, and alltogether. If they ask you a Question, before you can utter 3 words of your Answer, they will break out upon you again—and talk away."

Individually, he had kinder words for some of them. McDougall, his unofficial host, who squired the Massachusetts men—as well as the delegates from Connecticut and New Hampshire—around the city, Adams considered a "very sensible Man, and an open one. He has none of the mean Cunning which disgraces so many of my Country men." He obviously had a thorough knowledge of politics and told the visitors in some detail about "the two great Families in this Province, upon whose Motions all their Politicks turn . . . the DeLanceys and the Livingstones. There is Virtue and Abilities as well as fortune, in the Livingstones, but not much of either of the three in the Delanceys, according to him."

McDougall took them on a grand tour of the city, showing them the fort and the battery and a prospect of the two rivers. What particularly impressed Adams was "a beautiful Elipsis of Land, railed in with solid Iron, in the Center of which is a Statue of his Majesty on Horse back, very large, of solid Lead, gilded with Gold, standing on a Pedastal of Marble very high." Their next stops were the old church and the magnificent new church, the prison, the barracks, the college and the new hospital, the shipyards, and finally the Merchants Coffee House, where they met John Morin Scott, among others, and stayed until eleven o'clock having "much Conversation."

Adams found the streets far more regular and elegant than those of Boston, the houses "more grand as well as neat"—almost all of them painted, brick buildings as well as frame.

On Sunday, August 21, McDougall led Adams and Paine to morning and afternoon Presbyterian meetings and introduced them there to William Smith, who made a strong impression on Adams. He was "a Gentleman a little turn'd of forty—a plain composed Man," who very politely invited them to tea. When they told him they had another engagement, he said he would call on them. Before then, Adams learned that Smith was one of the "triumvirate"—"all of them Children of Yale Colledge"—that had figured in battles against the Church of England and had written *The Independent Reflector.* Scott and Livingston, he heard, were lazy, but Smith "improves every moment of his time."

Before their visit ended, the Massachusetts contingent met most of the important people in New York, and when the time came to introduce them to the conservative faction, McDougall warned them to be careful of what they said—especially to members of the "powerfull Party here, who are intimidated by Fears of a Civil War. . . ." Temporarily, at least, that group had been mollified by assurances that danger was not imminent and that "a peaceful Cessation of Commerce would effect Relief." Another faction consisted of men who were intimidated lest "the levelling Spirit of the New England Colonies should Propagate itself into N. York." Yet another group that was suspicious of the New Englanders was the Episcopalians. Then, of course, there were the merchants, who feared the whole idea of nonimportation, nonconsumption, and nonexportation. And lastly, the visitors should be wary of those who looked to the government for favors. There was no end, it seemed, to the complex array of prejudices in New York.

Curiously, Adams made only one brief reference to Isaac Sears, one of the few local notables he did not attempt to characterize in some fashion. On the evening of Thursday, August 25, he noted that "several Gentlemen came to our Lodgings and among others Mr. Sears." Either Sears failed to impress him in any way or, what seems more likely, he went out of his way to conceal the identity of those "several Gentlemen" and make no mention of what they—and Sears—had to say.

At subsequent meetings the Massachusetts attorney found William Smith even more to his liking: he "has the Character of a great Lawyer, a sensible and learned Man and yet a consistent unshaken Friend to his Country and her Liberties." That was high praise indeed coming from John Adams, who was keenly interested to hear what Smith had to say about Massachusetts's new governor, Thomas Gage. Smith professed to have a high personal regard for the general—he knew him as a good-natured, peaceable, and sociable fellow—but considered him "altogether unfit for a Governor of the Massachusetts . . . he would lose all the Character he had acquired as a Man, a Gentleman, and a General and dwindle down into a mere Scribbling Governor, a mere Bernard, or Hutchinson."

Among others introduced to the New Englander was Isaac Low, who professes "Attachment to the Cause of Liberty but his Sincerity is doubted." (Several days later Adams met Low's brother Cornelius, a wealthy merchant, whose lady, he wrote admiringly, "is a Beauty.") Another lawyer he met was the twenty-six-year-old John Jay, who was a "hard Student and a good Speaker." Philip Livingston was "a down right strait forward Man . . . a great, rough, rappid Mortal." There was "no holding any Conversation with him; he blusters away." Livingston told Adams that if Britain should turn its colonies adrift they would "instantly go to civil Wars among ourselves [over] which Colony should govern all the rest." "Seems to dread N. England—the Levelling Spirit &c.," Adams noted, and he made several references to the Goths, the Vandals, and the Quakers who were hanged in Massachusetts.

Adams assessed John Alsop as "a soft, sweet Man" who was lacking in ability and perhaps "unequal to the Trust" of being a delegate to the congress, while James Duane was "very sensible . . . and very artful . . . with a sly, surveying Eye, a little squint-Eyed." Duane quoted Edmund Burke and friends in England who said that Americans could no longer depend on support of any kind from Britain, particularly from the merchants, after their tea ships had been turned away from colonial ports.

These candid and often caustic comments probably reflected the views of other New Englanders, but the most important consequence of the meetings was that they and the New Yorkers now had a tangible sense of who they were dealing with and could put a face and an overall impression to each name.

The Bostonians also met Peter Van Brugh Livingston (sensible and a gentleman, who had become rich in trade), Philip Livingston, and other aristocrats, including John Morin Scott, who entertained them at his sumptuous country home overlooking the Hudson River.* There Adams was received by Scott, his wife and daughter, and the latter's husband in a fine airy anteroom before they sat down to breakfast. "A more elegant Breakfast, I never saw," he noted, "rich Plate—a very large Silver Coffee Pott, a very large Silver Tea Pott—Napkins of the very finest Materials, and toast and bread and butter in great Perfection"—followed by peaches, pears, plums, and muskmelon. Scott, he had been told, was "one of the readyest Speakers on the Continent," and he was quite knowledgeable about the New Hampshire Grants, where James Duane had "unhappily involved almost all his Property" by purchasing patents and claims amounting to 100,000 acres.

From another source—the conservative members of the Committee of Fifty-one—they heard in no uncertain terms exactly what the congress should do and what the New York delegates should try to achieve. One extremely unwelcome opinion was that paying for the tea dumped in Boston's harbor would undoubtedly open that port to normal commerce. Trade relationships with the mother country should be broken off only in the most extreme circumstances, they were told, and should that step be taken, then nonimportation would have to be effectively and universally enforced and include "importation of every European commodity from all parts of the world."

The New Englanders climbed into the steeple of the new Dutch church for a bird's-eye view of the city; visited Ebenezer Hazard, who was beginning his compilation of documents relating to the early history of America ("he is a Genius," Adams wrote); paid a call on Holt, "the Liberty Printer"; went to Trinity and St. Paul's churches and the college, City Hall, the Supreme Court's quarters; and finally departed by the ferry from Paulus Hook. All things considered, it had been quite a visit.

---

*It stood in what is today West 43rd Street, between Eighth and Ninth avenues.

. . .

Early on Monday morning, August 29, John Jay set off for Philadelphia alone
and unnoticed and was followed on Thursday by the other three delegates,
who left to great fanfare. Isaac Low was escorted to the Paulus Hook ferry by
a large crowd "with Colours flying, Music playing, and loud Huzzas at the
end of each Street." Six admirers accompanied him and his wife across
the river while a band played "God Save the King." About half past nine the
others were honored with a similar procession from the Coffee House to the
wharf near the Exchange, where they embarked after James Duane gave an
affectionate and moving talk, thanking the crowd for the honor they had con-
ferred on the delegates and promising, "Nothing in their Power should be
wanting to relieve this once happy, but now aggrieved Country." Duane left
with a heavy heart: as most people knew, only three weeks earlier his eldest
child and namesake, a little boy of five, had fallen from the wharf at Livingston Manor and drowned.

As the delegates waved goodbye, cannon at the Battery fired round after
round and were answered by the guns at St. George's ferry while the citizens,
in the words of the *New-York Gazette,* "bid them go and proclaim to all
Nations that they, and the virtuous People they represent, dare *defend their
Rights* as PROTESTANT ENGLISHMEN." Nor was that the end of it.
Before the delegates had vanished from sight, much of the crowd, lingering at
St. George's ferry, drank "many loyal, constitutional, and spirited Toasts,
sealed with frequent Discharges of Cannon" and followed with a solemn declaration that each of those present "would support at the Risque of every
Thing sacred and dear, such Resolutions as our Delegates in Conjunction
with those worthy Gentlemen of the other Colonies, should think necessary
to adopt for the Good of the common Cause."

It was said by many that they dated the salvation of the colonies from that
hour, and at the last they joined in singing "God Save the King."

21

Blows Must Decide

On September 1, 1774, the people of Boston were roused from sleep by the unmistakable sound of marching men. In the predawn darkness a detachment of Thomas Gage's redcoats tramped over the cobbled streets toward the Long Wharf, piled aboard thirteen waiting boats, and disappeared into the gloom at 4:30 A.M. Proceeding up the Mystic River, they landed at Temple's farm, marched to the powder house in Cambridge, and quickly seized the entire store of powder—some 250 half-barrels that belonged to the province—which they took back to the magazine in Boston. That brief march aroused the entire countryside around Boston, and within twenty-four hours the town was ringed with armed men.

By now the feelings of confidence and well-being General Gage had felt in July had deserted him; the jocularity and sense of superiority were gone. Having returned to America with the unenviable assignment of enforcing the Port Bill in Boston, he found himself longing for the relative sanity of New York, where everything was quiet, the people in general moderate and "well affected to all Measures but Taxation." He had been to the Bay Colony's new capital at Salem and found matters much worse than he had imagined. Newly appointed Council members had fled from their homes to take refuge in Boston, where they could be protected by the king's troops. Sensible gentlemen, men remarkably firm and not to be intimidated, had abandoned their homes to the mercy of the people. At least six councilmen had resigned. The Superior Court met but could get no jurors to serve; the judges, in fact, had told the general it was impossible to carry on the business of the courts in any part of the province. Gage ordered General Haldimand to secure the magazines at Fort George in New York and dispatch troops from that city and Philadelphia to reinforce him in Boston. As he assured Dartmouth, he wanted to avoid a bloody crisis as long as possible, but he needed a "very respectable Force" to handle the worsening situation. He would have that, for certain: by the time his reinforcements arrived, there would be one soldier on the streets of town to every five inhabitants.

He had just received a note from Andrew Oliver, the lieutenant governor, pleading with him not to dispatch any troops to Salem—the situation there was out of hand, with "a Vast Concourse of People assembled . . . from various Parts." The worst of it, Gage told Dartmouth in a message that sounded almost frantic, was: "Nothing that is said at present can palliate. Conciliating, Moderation, Reasoning is over. Nothing can be done but by forceable Means. . . . Tho' the People are not held in high Estimation by the Troops, yet they are numerous, worked up to a Fury, and not a Boston rabble but the Freeholders and Farmers of the Country. A Check any where wou'd be fatal, and the first Stroke will decide a great deal."

Gage was taking other precautionary measures. Fearing that open warfare might break out at any time, he had begun fortifying the Neck, a narrow strip of land that connected the town of Boston to the mainland. He had also begun building barracks for his troops, and these two measures led John Adams and other delegates to the congress in Philadelphia to suppose that Gage "means to act only on the defensive." In every hamlet and town in Massachusetts the talk was of restoring the provincial government to what it had been before the Intolerable Acts. Those freeholders and farmers were drilling on village greens, collecting arms and ammunition—even some artillery—wherever and however they could. In Worcester, Gage informed Dartmouth, they "openly threaten Resistance by Arms, have been purchasing Arms, preparing them, casting Ball, and providing Powder, and threaten to attack any Troops who dare to oppose them."

In some respects the most frightening sign of the times was a series of resolves by the Suffolk County Convention, which had been called to discuss how to circumvent the prohibition of town meetings. Those resolutions went far beyond what Gage described as "fixing a plan of Government of their own." They called for the use of force to prevent the "attempts of a wicked administration to enslave America," attacked the present government as "tyrannical and unconstitutional," and urged the people to "acquaint themselves with the art of war as soon as possible" and to hold military drills at least once a week. When the Continental Congress received the resolves and astonishingly voted to approve them, Joseph Galloway observed unhappily that "the foundation of military resistance throughout America was effectually laid." When they were published in London, a shocked Dartmouth told Governor Hutchinson, "Why, if these Resolves of your people are to be depended on, they have declared War against us. . . ."

While the congress deliberated in Philadelphia, Gage appealed yet again to the administration, citing his desperate need for reinforcement, urging the hiring of Hanoverian and Hessian mercenaries if none of the king's regiments could be spared. On top of everything else, he and Admiral Graves had to contend with an increasingly disturbing number of desertions from the army and navy. Advising London that "these provinces must be first totally subdued before they will obey," he said that unless the government was prepared to do just that, it should suspend the Coercive Acts. That proved to be a fatal suggestion—an apparent sign of faintheartedness which George III and the cabinet never forgave or forgot. Meanwhile, the general worried quite sensibly about security: he learned that James Bowdoin of Boston had somehow obtained a copy of Gage's instructions from London; in addition, the road between Boston and New York was so insecure that the military could not risk sending mail over that route to be conveyed to England by the packet.

Whether Gage suspected it or not, the cabinet was not about to give him anything like the support he needed: three ships of the line and about six hundred men were to be the extent of it. This caution had its roots in a divided cabinet and in a contest over grand strategy between Lord Sandwich, first lord of the Admiralty, and William, Viscount Barrington, secretary at war. Sandwich and Barrington agreed on one thing: France was the real menace the nation faced, and the armed services must be beefed up to counter an attack by the Bourbons. But Sandwich wanted soldiers sent to America while the navy was strengthened in European waters, and Barrington believed the coming conflict in America could and should be resolved by the navy while he kept his troops in England, ready to repel an invasion.

Barrington, to his credit, foresaw a real quagmire on the American continent—a protracted land war that would be ruinously expensive to conduct and all but impossible to win, given the vast distance between the British Isles and America and the staggering problem of supplying and supporting an army, with every article of clothing and equipment having to be transported across three thousand miles of ocean, where the westerly passage could take as long as three months. Immensely costly, it was also appallingly wasteful. Ships sank or were blown off course, food supplies spoiled, animals perished en route. Worst of all, men died too (eventually an average of about 11 percent of the troops were lost on these crossings). Beyond that was the prospect of waging guerrilla warfare in a vast wilderness that was unfamiliar, hostile, and unsuitable for soldiers trained in entirely different tactics. Defeating the colonists militarily, one of his colleagues observed morosely, was "as wild an idea as ever controverted common sense." "It is true," Barrington said of the Americans, "they have not hitherto been thought brave; but enthusiasm gives vigour of mind and body unknown before." But even should Britain win, Barrington added, the cost of maintaining the colonies in a state of subjection would be staggering.

Barrington wanted Gage's troops out of Massachusetts, "where at present they can do no good, and without intentions, may do harm." If those men were transferred to Canada and Florida, where they could be more usefully employed, a tight naval blockade might persuade the colonists to "submit to a certain degree." After all, he said, the issue facing the government was merely a point of honor, a point that could easily be resolved if only "we for the future abstain from all ideas of internal taxation."

Barrington had gone to the heart of the problem, noting that even some of the cabinet members, while believing they were right, nevertheless doubted "the equity of such taxations." But Barrington ignored his monarch's view of exactly that point of honor, which was that the supremacy of Parliament *must* be maintained at all costs. "The New England Governments are in a State of Rebellion," the king announced; "blows must decide whether they are to be subject to this Country or Independent."

While it seemed obvious that Britain's vaunted sea power was the best means of controlling the upstart colonials, the navy was simply not prepared to undertake major commitments simultaneously in European and American waters, and the blame could be laid directly at the feet of Lord North. In 1772 the prime minister had intimated to the House that some £1,500,000 might be made available for reducing the public debt, and at the same time informed Sandwich that some of that money—as much as £600,000 of it— would have to come from a decommissioning of certain ships. Sandwich argued vehemently that the uncertain foreign situation did not warrant reducing naval power, and he and his allies in Parliament forced North to give up his plan, but the minister—fearful of offending France—squelched a much-needed increase in funding for the fleet.

Economy measures did not end there. By 1774, when reports that France was fitting out a fleet at Toulon reached England, the king himself became alarmed over the possibility that the French might react aggressively to any overt military mobilization, saying that "the conduct of our Colonies makes Peace very desirable." Emboldened by this pronouncement, North resurrected his plan to pay off some of the national debt and foolishly undertook to do so by reducing the number of seamen by 4,000 and restricting the army to 17,500 men. Ignoring the significance of the congress in Philadelphia and still refusing to believe that the other provinces would side with Massachusetts, he declared that "the forces now demanded were sufficient, unless from the conduct of the other colonies it should be judged necessary to extend the line with respect to them."

At the same time, North's secretary of the Treasury, John Robinson, had completed a study of what could be expected if the administration called for new elections, and North reluctantly agreed to dissolve Parliament in the expectation of enlarging his already comfortable majority. In stark contrast to the colonies, where voting eligibility for adult white males ranged from 50 to 80 percent (and something close to 100 percent in certain communities), in England—where the franchise was the most liberal in Europe—no more than 15 percent could vote.

As North knew well, an election campaign meant endless bargaining over the purchase and sale of seats in Parliament. Of some 558 House members, 322 held titles in England, Scotland, or Ireland or were related to a titled person, and while a number of them might oppose the North ministry, their votes could often be ensured by the award of pensions, appointments, or other favors. Another seventy-three members held government or court appointments or some sort of contract entitling them to stipends or honoraria, but, like the titled members, they were not likely to stray from the path laid out by leaders of the majority when favors were in store for those who remained loyal. In short, North could likely count on 395 votes out of the 558, but since voting attendance in the House was usually about 400 and occasionally went as low as 150, it is easy to see how his ministry held on to its majority in Commons for such a long time.

The opposition, having no government patronage to offer, was up against enormous odds, and the composition of the new House of Commons, which was to serve until 1780, revealed how much the government of the country was in the hands of a small and cohesive upper class. Horace Walpole observed that the Rockingham party, recognizing that they had no chance of prevailing unless the situation in America became desperate, never even came to London until Parliament opened "and even then found the merchants asleep and not disposed to stir on the grievances of America. The Dissenters, still more threatened, were as supine. Wilkes was squabbling in the Court of Aldermen . . . and attended to nothing else."

With a ministry committed to punitive measures and unwilling to compromise, an attitude of defiance by the Continental Congress could only strengthen the resolve of North's majority.

In Philadelphia, two differing points of view emerged on the opening day of the congress on September 5 and persisted until its adjournment seven weeks later. The New York delegates quickly aligned themselves with the moderates and conservatives, voting to support Joseph Galloway's choice of the State House as a meeting place, out of respect for him as speaker of the Pennsylvania Assembly. For secretary, they favored Silas Deane of Connecticut over the radical Charles Thomson of Pennsylvania. In both instances they were defeated: Carpenters' Hall was selected as being "highly agreeable to the mechanics and citizens in general," while Thomson was preferred by the more liberal delegates.

Sixty-four men from twelve colonies (Georgia did not attend) were a good cross section of the prominent political figures in America in 1774, and their collective state of indecision was probably a reasonable facsimile of how their constituents back home felt. Behind their every discussion was the question of whether ties to the mother country would be broken and if so, to what extent. The Virginia firebrand Patrick Henry broached the issue at the outset, when he proposed that voting should be proportionate to population (slaves to be excluded). In an emotional outburst, he shouted, "Government is at an End. All Distinctions are thrown out. All America is thrown into one Mass." The presence of fleets and armies proved that "Government is dissolved," and that "We are in a State of Nature."

John Jay. *Library of Congress/ American Heritage Publishing Company.*

John Jay of New York rose immediately to disagree. Recalling that voting in the Stamp Act Congress was one vote per colony, he replied that even if they had assembled here to frame an American constitution, instead of correcting the faults in an old one, "I can't yet think that all Government is at an End. The

Measure of Arbitrary Power is not full, and I think it must run over before We undertake to frame a new Constitution."

One reason Jay's proposed one vote per colony was approved was that the Massachusetts delegation, despite its radical bias, was aware that "Absolute Indepen[den]cy etc.," as John Adams put it, "are Ideas which Startle People here," and he and his colleagues were determined to avert a split in the congress, lest nothing be accomplished. The pessimistic Patrick Henry believed that the government's policies would lead to war. Eliphalet Dyer of Connecticut said that the British "have drawn the sword" and predicted that "the next summer will decide the Fate of America." Yet war was not something these delegates wished to contemplate, and independence—as they all recognized—would certainly result in an armed struggle.

The real debate in Congress centered on Joseph Galloway's "Plan of Union"—a concept reminiscent of Benjamin Franklin's 1754 Plan of Union. (In fact, this Continental Congress was the latest in a number of steps toward colonial unity that had commenced twenty years earlier in Albany and gathered strength with the Stamp Act Congress and the Sons of Liberty network, followed by this meeting in Philadelphia.) Galloway, a good friend and protégé of Franklin's, had been close to him ever since he first entered Pennsylvania politics in the 1750s and had kept in frequent touch with him during his years in London. Essentially what Galloway envisioned was a system in which the colonies would remain part of the empire, governed by a president general (appointed by the king), and a grand council (chosen by the provincial assemblies) that possessed the same rights as the House of Commons. The colonial legislative body and Parliament would each approve laws passed by the other.

How this strange hybrid might have worked is hard to guess, but it went down to defeat by a single vote—thanks largely to the opposition of Richard Henry Lee and Patrick Henry of Virginia, who managed to win the support of a majority of delegates. As for the New Yorkers, James Duane seconded the motion for adoption of the plan, while Isaac Low argued, "We ought not to deny the just Rights of our Mother Country. We have too much Reason in this Congress, to suspect that Independency is aimed at. I am for a Resolution against any Tea, Dutch as well as English." Jay observed that Galloway's proposal offered the colonies much that was desirable while taking away nothing, and hoped it would be adopted. Curiously, the records of the First Continental Congress contain no mention whatever of Galloway's plan or the vote on it.

The most significant action of the congress was the formation of a Continental Association, a nonimportation, nonconsumption, nonexportation

agreement that was to be enforced by local committees of inspection throughout the colonies. In taking this course, Congress was boldly denying Parliament's supremacy—insisting that it could no longer tax the colonists—and
the question that haunted moderates was whether that meant Parliament
could no longer legislate for them. Inevitably, they figured, the next step was
independence.

Of New York's delegates, all but Philip Livingston seemed at the outset
of the Philadelphia meetings certain to be Tories, but while two of the
others opposed all talk of independence, their experience in the First Continental Congress saw them veer decisively in the direction of the patriot
faction. John Jay, a grandson of a Huguenot refugee, was as well connected to
the conservative/moderate establishment as it was possible for a New Yorker
to be, given his relationship to Van Cortlandts, DeLanceys, and Stuyvesants,
plus marriage to a daughter of William Livingston. He was eloquent, with a
sharp mind and great ability in the practice of law, and from the time he was
elected to the Committee of Fifty-one he moved slowly but surely toward a
liberal position. After he drafted "An Address to the People of Great Britain,"
which was read to an enthusiastic Congress on October 29 by his father-in-
law, William Livingston, a New Jersey delegate, he was thrust into the first
rank of Whig propagandists. His "Address" accused the British of installing "a
system of slavery" after 1763 and reminded his fellow Englishmen that Americans were entitled to the same rights they had, including trial by jury and a
fair trial guaranteeing the accused the right of adequate defense. What's more,
he said, "no power on earth has the power to take our property from us without our consent." Minimizing the Boston Tea Party as a "trespass committed
on some merchandise," he urged Britons to ask themselves if that was adequate grounds for suspending the Massachusetts charter and altering its constitution. Finally, he warned, "We will never submit to be hewers of wood or
drawers of water for any ministry or nation in the world."

His was a tough stance, yet it was also conciliatory, and his appeal to the
Englishman's sense of fair play was made in the hope that harmony and
friendship would be restored. Jay was far from being an independence man,
however, as he indicated in a letter to a friend at this time: "God knows how
the Contest will end. I sincerely wish it may terminate in a lasting Union with
Great Britain."

James Duane was another prosperous lawyer in the city who, through his
marriage to Maria Livingston and, after her death, to Gertrude Schuyler, had
a position not unlike Jay's in New York society. The son of a wealthy Irish
merchant and landowner, he had a handsome town house, a country estate,

and 36,000 acres west of Schenectady, where more than two hundred tenants operated his mills and made potash.

Duane hated the mobs, worried that his Livingston in-laws might suffer for their association with the Sons of Liberty, and was heard to say, "God forbid that we should ever be so miserable as to sink into a Republick!" Yet in Congress he advocated and worked hard for a statement on American rights and upon his return to New York played an active role on the committee that enforced the Continental Association. There, at the insistence of the Mechanics, the Committee of Fifty-one was replaced by a sixty-member Committee of Observation, and at a public rally on November 22 its members were confirmed—half of them being members of the patriot, or popular, party.

Jay and Duane were exemplars of what was occurring in New York City politics. Curiously, despite the apparent hostility between the moderate or conservative patriots on the one hand and confirmed Tories on the other, the difference in political philosophies was often a fine line indeed. Both groups had the same distaste for London's venal politicians, the ministry's unreasonably harsh measures, and its obstinate unwillingness to comprehend and ameliorate the colonists' concerns, not to mention a growing fear of tyranny and disgust over the corruption that was rampant throughout government. Although Thomas Jones believed that those who became Tories had gone to Philadelphia because they wanted "a redress of grievances, and a firm union between Great Britain and America upon constitutional principles," the fact was that the other side went with the same objectives in mind. The difference was that the Tories thought they got a declaration of war instead of a firm union.

Ideologically they may not have been far apart, these basically moderate or conservative gentlemen, but elements of class, religion, or wealth set the hard-core loyalists, who were essentially elitist and aristocratic, apart from patriots of all stripes. Fear of anarchy, fear of independence, abhorrence of equality, or "leveling"—all played a part in the Tory attitude. Placemen feared for loss of their jobs and perquisites, merchants feared a loss of their economic links throughout the empire, others were unwilling to abandon the political ties to the DeLancey party they had had for years.

A majority of the royalist families were probably affluent, yet they came from many walks of life, including merchants, crown officials, newly arrived English immigrants, and Anglican churchmen. The latter, like President Myles Cooper of King's College, or Samuel Seabury and Thomas Bradbury Chandler, were unrelenting advocates of having an Episcopal bishop in America.

Yet Anglicans were not the sole sectarians to side with the loyalists. They were joined by some members of the Dutch Reformed Church, Methodists, and Lutherans—many of them driven by their distaste for Presbyterian dissenters.

New York was filled with rich men and women whose money came from huge landholdings or trade or advantageous marriages. It was also the home of numerous privileged royal officials—civilian and military—not to mention Anglican ministers convinced of their superiority over dissenters of all kinds, whose attitude toward the "lower sort" was that they lacked intelligence and were incapable of governing themselves or others. By and large, the city's Church of England communicants were loyalists, whereas almost all Presbyterian ministers and a majority of the Dutch Reformed had strong patriot ties.

From the moment the enforcers of the new Continental Association began to nose into the affairs of businessmen and landowners, investigating rumored violations of import or export sanctions, questioning citizens' attitudes toward the Continental Congress or the association itself, even going so far as to insist that people swear allegiance to the organization, a large number of New Yorkers decided that their opponents had gone too far and had to be stopped before it was too late. What had been a relatively thin ideological gap between the two factions suddenly became a chasm.

The bizarre aspect of all this—as evidenced by both Jay and Duane—was that each of New York's social groups had members with conflicting views, wide areas of agreement or disagreement. By late 1774 the complex mix that constituted New York had begun to break into the three factions that John Adams identified long after the Revolution—Whigs or revolutionaries on the one hand, Tories or royalists on the other, and, between them, a much larger group of people who were uncommitted. Many of the latter wished a pox on the other two; they simply wanted to be left alone to get on with their lives or preferred to wait and see what the future held in store before taking sides.

Geographically, the three counties facing New York City across the bay and the East River were Tory strongholds—deeply distrustful of radicalism, especially the New England variety. Kings, Queens, and Richmond, astride New York's agrarian perimeter, had for years been solidly involved in the city's commerce with the outside world, but as the city grew, their prosperity was increasingly reflected in rising land values as well as their income from trade. Their populations were steady, slow-growing, and unlike counties on the Hudson River north of New York, they had a dearth of extreme wealth or dire poverty. Beyond Kings and Queens on Long Island was Suffolk, invulnerably republican because of its traditional ties to New England.

Upriver counties that evinced the strongest radical tendencies were more populous than those facing New York, having experienced steady population growth over the years. Westchester, Albany, and Dutchess were integral parts of an international trading network that saw the wheat that was often ground into flour in their own mills shipped in their own Hudson River sloops to New York and then on to customers on the Atlantic rim. The same markets purchased lumber from their mills and iron from their furnaces. These were also counties where the range of wealth and poverty was extreme, where classes were at opposite ends of the scale with not much in the middle.

In the province as a whole, intractable loyalists probably made up less than 20 percent of the population, but in locales where they outnumbered the patriots they were vociferous in their defiance of Congress and the new Continental Association. In New York City the wealthiest merchants—John Watts, John Cruger, the DeLanceys, and a majority of their well-heeled fellows— sided with the crown, while the less affluent mercantile crowd, like Alexander McDougall, John Lamb, and Isaac Sears, tended to be republicans.

22

Affairs Grow Serious

The lines of division were hardening. Express riders were thundering along dusty roads throughout the colonies bearing dispatches from committees of correspondence in Boston, Hartford, New York, Albany, Philadelphia, and Charleston to and from little towns across the countryside, all with resolves, addresses to freeholders and freemen, reports of hastily convened meetings, all carrying the same sense of alarm, the warning that America was in mortal peril.

"The Affairs of this Country grow very serious," wrote William Smith, whose worries about the possibility of civil war were heightened by the people's sudden change in attitude toward the king. "Instead of that Respect they formerly had for the King, you now hear the very lowest Orders call him a Knave or a Fool. . . ." Writing to his nephew, who was secretary to General Gage, Smith predicted that the first "Act of Indiscretion" by citizens or soldiers that resulted in bloodshed would "light up a Civil War."

The merchant John Thurman, a political moderate who had written in May to a London friend, mentioning his membership in the Committee of Fifty-one and saying it would do its utmost to keep peace and order, could not fathom the government's policies, which were laying the foundation for civil war and eternal separation. "United in Love & friendship to Great Britain, we are a Happy People," he said, but if the ministry pursued its acts of oppression, "God only knows what will be the end." Now, writing another Londoner, he called himself a true friend to the liberties of America and a sincere lover of Great Britain, but he had to wonder if she was so weary of her greatness and prosperity that she had to "Turn her Voracious desires on Plundering America, her best friend." Much as we dread the consequences of a civil war and fighting with our best friends, he added, that dreadful prospect seems at hand. He warned, "There is not a Man born in America that does not Understand the Use of Firearms . . . and should you drive America into a Rebellion you will in my Opinnion find it Easier to Conquer France than to subdue them."

For all the political commotion and malaise, life in the city went on and signs of sanity, progress, and occasionally even humor were reported. Someone estimated that New York's three thousand houses each had a fire burning in one room daily, the year round. Some two-thirds of those dwellings also had a parlor fire burning, and a number of larger homes burned three or four fires daily from November to April. The news item citing this information made no mention of air choked with smoke, but noted that ample opportunity existed for chimney sweeps.

In February a lottery was proposed to raise £6,000 for a Bridewell—a commodious building for vagrants, the dissolute, and the idle, which was essential because of the "great number of vagrants daily sculking about this city from every part of the continent." Another much-needed improvement was launched thanks to the efforts of one Christopher Colles, who finally convinced the Council that the city needed a reservoir and the means of delivering potable water to its citizens. He reminded them that until now the only wholesome drinking water had come from the "Tea Water Pump" at Chatham and Pearl streets, and was peddled by carts. Although water from wells was also in use, it was generally so bad that horses refused to drink it.

The governor signed several useful bills into law. One was for a tax on dogs, the proceeds to be used as a bounty for making tile for roofing. Another was "for better preventing of excessive and deceitful Gaming," though whether this had to do with the reopening of the old race course at Harlem was not apparent. Yet another stipulated the procedures to be followed for sweeping the streets by the public scavenger.

Newspapers were filled with the usual advertisements and announcements—rewards offered for runaway slaves and indentured servants, notices of the arrival and forthcoming sale of imported goods, properties being sold to clear up the estate of the recently deceased, paste for preserving teeth from scurvy and making them beautifully white, notices of insolvency, store openings and closings, ship arrivals and departures.

Along with the ceaseless messages from or about local political figures came snippets of news from abroad. Among them in an August newspaper was a comment from Paris to the effect that France's last two kings had reigned for a combined total of 131 years—from 1643 to 1774. "Lewis XIV," as his name was Anglicized, had come to the throne at the age of five and died at seventy-seven. His successor was his great-grandson, "Lewis XV," whose grandfather, father, and elder brother had all died within the space of one year, before old Louis XIV, the Sun King, passed away and left the throne open for a boy who was not quite six years old and who lived until 1774.

From England came a story about the death of one Adam Garley, a coal merchant, who was laid out in his coffin ready for burial on a Friday. On Thursday night, however, while the bereaved family was at supper, footsteps were heard coming downstairs and Garley suddenly appeared in his shroud, "having only been in a trance." When the family members recovered from the shock "they put him in a warm bed, gave him some comfortable things, and he is now in a fair way of doing well."

Early in September some of the New York merchants refused the use of their ships for transporting troops and military supplies to Boston; local carpenters declined to travel to that town to construct barracks for Gage's men; local pilots were warned not to assist any ships involved in helping Gage's army; and one reason for their cooperation was apparent. A notice in the *New-York Journal* warned, "should any sordid miscreant . . . aid the enemies of this country to subvert her liberties, he must not be surprised if that vengeance overtakes him, which is the reward justly due to parricides." At the same time, voices of moderation were heard. In a broadside, someone calling himself "Humanus" counseled citizens not to deprive British soldiers of food and clothing, which would make every man of them an enemy and could result in skirmishes, if not general hostilities. These matters were of such importance, he said, that they should be left to the Continental Congress to decide.

Once again the DeLancey machine swung into action and the merchants attending a meeting at the Coffee House censured the radicals who were meddling in what they called a businessman's private affairs. Early in October, Colden reported that "the Merchants go on completing their orders without farther Interruption," and a few days later ships carrying artificers sailed for Boston unmolested. That occurred just before Congress adopted the Continental Association, however, which imposed stiff restrictions on the merchants, with those who failed to cooperate boycotted and considered enemies to American liberty.

The president and secretary of the congress had kept busy after its sessions ended, sending letters to speakers of all the provincial assemblies, to the people of St. John's, Nova Scotia, Georgia, and East and West Florida who had not had delegates representing them, and to the colonies' agents in London, enclosing copies of the congress's petition to the king, with its list of grievances. Neither petition nor list was to be released to the public until George III received them, but the recipients were urged to furnish John Jay's address to the people of Great Britain to trading cities and manufacturing towns throughout the United Kingdom. Agents were also to ask for the assistance and support of those noblemen and gentlemen who were known to be favorably disposed to the colonies.

The rationale for this was clear: "So rapidly violent and unjust has been the late conduct of the British administration against the colonies, that either a base and slavish submission, under the loss of their ancient, just and constitutional liberty, must quickly take place, or an adequate opposition be formed."

Another congress was scheduled to take place on May 10, 1775, and in the meantime, the message concluded, "We pray God to take you under his protection, and to preserve the freedom and happiness of the whole British empire."

The November 24 issue of Holt's paper, the *New-York Journal,* reported the ominous news that eleven regiments of regulars, plus artillery, were now quartered in Boston, and on the same day this story broke, a pamphlet appeared with what Holt labeled a "false, arrogant, and impudent title, viz, 'Free thoughts on the proceedings of the continental congress held at Philadelphia. . . .'" Published by James Rivington, known as the Tory printer, and signed "A. W. Farmer," the pamphlet was addressed to the farmers and other inhabitants of North America—and to those of New York, in particular. Holt condemned the work as "one of the most treacherous, malicious, and wicked productions that has yet appeared, from the implacable enemies of the British colonies and nation," and said the author's reasoning was contemptible, his conclusions absurd. As for his screed, it was "committed to the flames," some of the copies being burned at Mr. Rivington's door.

A. W.[estchester] Farmer was, in fact, Samuel Seabury, a forty-five-year-old, American-born Church of England priest who ministered to communicants in Eastchester and Westchester. A big, husky man, Seabury had the beefy, well-fed look of a bishop* about him—self-assured, commanding, with

---

*A title which was to become his in fact. Eventually elected a bishop by Connecticut's Anglican clergy in 1783, he was denied consecration in England on grounds that the United States might consider this to be meddling in its internal affairs. He then received consecration from the Episcopal Church in Scotland and thus became the first American bishop in 1785.

one eyebrow arched in a manner suggesting that he was about to ask a difficult question. He was a confirmed activist who had involved himself in the
great struggle between the Anglican Church and the Dissenters from the time
he returned to America from Edinburgh and London, where he had first been
trained in medicine and then ordained by the bishop of London. One of his
first battles had been to counter the series of articles in *The Independent
Reflector,* by William Livingston, William Smith, and John Morin Scott, who
opposed the establishment of King's College as a sectarian institution.

For years the Anglican clergy had agitated unsuccessfully to have bishops
appointed for the colonies, and in the late 1750s New York and New Jersey
formed a convention to further this effort and Seabury was chosen as secretary. The appearance of "An Appeal to the Public in Behalf of the Church
of England," supporting an episcopacy, once again pitted Seabury against
Livingston and his colleagues, who wrote in a series of articles called "The
American Whig" that the Anglicans desired a "modern, splendid, opulent,
powerful prelate" and argued that "such a Bishop would be one of the worst
commodities that can possibly be imported into a new country, and must
inevitably prove absolute desolation to this." One of Livingston's articles predicted that it would cost £293,780 to establish a bishop in New York, and the
salaries of his retinue would be nearly £22,000.

Seabury and several other Episcopal clerics took on the task of defending
their position in a year-long succession of articles for Gaine's *New-York
Gazette* and Parker's *Gazette or Post-Boy,* accusing the Whigs of casting "injurious Reflections upon the other Denominations, as seditious Incendiaries,
and disaffected to King and Government." But the 1774 pamphlet "Free
Thoughts . . ." was the work of Seabury alone and it was written in a plain,
straightforward style about practical matters that were calculated to appeal to
an agricultural audience. He focused his readers' attention on the effects of
Congress's prohibiting the export of flaxseed and sheep.

Most of New York's flaxseed was shipped to Ireland, and if Congress
thought the Irish would give up making and selling linen because their source
of flaxseed had been withdrawn, it had better think again, Seabury wrote—
flaxseed was readily available from Holland, the Baltic countries, and Canada.
Not only that: the loss of income from flaxseed for a single year would cost a
farmer more than paying the three-penny duty on tea for twenty years.

As for halting the importation of wool, "You want Woollens for your
winter clothing [but] there is not wool enough on the continent, taking all
the colonies together, to supply the inhabitants with stockings." Congress's
ban on the export of sheep to the West Indies was ludicrous. Obviously the

Samuel Seabury, by Thomas Duche, Jr.
Trinity College, Hartford.

congressmen knew nothing about sheep husbandry, since they had forbidden the sale of wethers, or castrated rams, so as not to lose that source of wool. "But let me ask you, my brother farmers, which of you would keep a flock of sheep barely for the sake of their wool? Not one of you. . . . They are not worth keeping for their wool alone."

Voicing an argument that farmers have used over the centuries, he decried the way people in general "treat us *countrymen* with very undeserved contempt. They act as though they thought that all wisdom, all knowledge, all understanding and sense, centered in themselves, and that we farmers were utterly ignorant of every thing but just to drive our oxen and follow the plough." The day exports were stopped, the ruination of farmers would begin—they could not sell their produce, they could not pay their bills, their farms would be worthless, and since it was said that all legal processes except criminal cases were to be halted, how could the farmer collect the money he is owed? "The farmer that is in debt will be ruined: the farmer that is clear in the world will be obliged to run in debt to support his family: and while the proud merchant and the forsworn smuggler riot in their ill-gotten wealth, the laborious farmers, the grand support of every well-regulated country, must all go to the dogs together.—Vile! Shameful! Diabolical Device!

"Tell me not of Delegates, Congresses, Committees, Riots, Mobs, Insurrections, Associations—a plague on them all."

The loyalists rejoiced in A. W. Farmer's pamphlet, but a more significant consequence was the appearance on December 15 of a reply entitled "A Full

Vindication of the Measures of the Continental Congress," which appeared in Rivington's *Gazetteer* without attribution but was later discovered to have been written by an eighteen-year-old student at King's College named Alexander Hamilton. Only one or two of the young man's classmates knew he had written this remarkable rebuttal, in which he refuted Seabury's arguments in general and then directed his comments to farmers. This dispute, he said, was not an argument between Great Britain and America over a three-penny-a-pound tax on tea: it concerned the far more important principle of "whether the inhabitants of Great Britain have a right to dispose of the lives and properties of the inhabitants of America or not?" and "whether we shall preserve that security to our lives and properties, which the law of nature, the genius of the British Constitution, and our charters afford us; or whether we shall resign them into the hands of the British House of Commons, which is no more privileged to dispose of them than the Grand Mogul?"

He charged that A. W. Farmer was in fact no farmer (though in this he erred—Seabury had cattle and raised hay and corn on his land) and was an agent of the British ministry whose claim to be a tiller of the soil was a fraud. But his main arguments were that the farmers of America were well represented in Congress, where their interests would be protected, and that restrictions on trade—not petitions or dissuasion, which had failed to get the Stamp Act repealed—were the only measures that would work.

By January of 1775, A. W. Farmer had published four pamphlets, each one more strongly worded, more critical of his unnamed antagonist, each endeavoring to persuade his readers that their property and their liberties would be taken from them by congresses and associations "chosen by the weak, foolish, turbulent part of the country people." Back and forth went charges and countercharges from Seabury and Hamilton, and finally, in early March of 1775, Hamilton published a carefully reasoned argument entitled "The Farmer Refuted . . ." in which he stated that the title of A. W. Farmer's most recent publication promised remedies, "but the Box itself contains Poisons."

How influential Seabury's pamphlets were is hard to judge, but it is worth noting that the New York Assembly rejected the resolves of the Continental Congress and, instead, petitioned the king and Parliament for relief of its grievances. On the other hand, the Liberty Boys and their followers were moving boldly ahead with their own program, with results that were already discernible. On December 11, 1774, James Beekman was writing to the Messrs. Marsh, Hudson & Streatfield in London, bemoaning the fact that he could not send them an order for merchandise to be sold in the spring. He had been prevented from doing so "by the unhappy misunderstanding that at present subsists between Great Britain & the Colonies, which has brought us to the disagreeable necessity of entering into a Non Importation agreement, untill proper redress of American Grievances is obtained. . . ."

On Monday, October 31, the Massachusetts delegates to the Continental Congress passed through town on their way home from Philadelphia. They had come by way of Princeton (where they found Nassau Hall deserted because the college president, Dr. Witherspoon, was away), Brunswick, and Elizabeth Town, where John Adams celebrated his thirty-ninth birthday, and then boarded two ferry boats in which they "Sail'd or rather rowed, Six Miles to . . . Staten Island." After a brief stop at a tavern for refreshments, they crossed the bay to New York, arriving about ten o'clock at night.

The next day they visited with McDougall, Sears, and Scott, among others, went to see the new hospital, which Adams called "a grand Building," and spent the evening at a local tavern. The Sons of Liberty, Adams observed after talking with them, "are in the Horrors here. They think they have lost ground since We passed thro' this City." Although Sears and McDougall were pleased with the actions taken by the Continental Congress, they realized they had difficult days ahead, given the conservatives' anger over that body's decisions. Thomas Jones wrote that the New York loyalists were "totally disappointed in the proceedings of the late Congress" and horrified to find their delegates transformed "into fixed republicans." As a consequence, he said, the DeLanceys resolved to oppose sending delegates to any future congress.

To the astonishment and delight of the Liberty Boys, the New York delegates to Congress appeared to have had a change of heart; as William Smith observed, they had become "Converts to the prevailing Sentiments" they found in Philadelphia and now that they were home again they were instrumental in doing away with the Committee of Fifty-one and replacing it with a new group—the Committee of Sixty, known also as the Committee of Observation. As might be expected, the new committee had a much larger number of Livingstonites, Mechanics, and Liberty Boys than its predecessor. The result, according to Smith, was that conservative members of the Fifty-one "who formerly dictated all their Movements have retired outwitted and disgusted and as they think, betrayed."

Outside the province, many observers continued to have doubts about New York's intentions. The fact that many moderates remained on the committee was suspect, and in New England rumors spread that New York's merchants had repudiated the Continental Association and that the unthinkable had happened: King Sears had become a Tory. When this charge appeared in a letter to him from Thaddeus Burr of Connecticut, Sears was stunned and showed it to McDougall, who replied to Burr immediately, defending his old friend. Noting that he had been intimately involved with Sears for the past six years, McDougall said, "I can with great Truth assure you that he has been and now is very Steady in his principles, Uniform, and active in opposition to the Parliamentary System of Enslaving this Country." Besides, he continued, it was "high time for the Known Friends of the Country to have more confidence in Each other." At this very moment, he added, Sears was aboard a boat near the Narrows, observing the actions of the ship *Beulah,* just arrived from London, to make certain her cargo was not landed. He was enforcing the Continental Association's order that no goods were to be landed after February 1.

The *Beulah* was owned by two Quakers, Robert and John Murray, who pleaded with the Committee of Observation to allow their ship to land and its cargo be unloaded. But as Peter R. Livingston wrote his father, "the People in general are determined she shall go back." Under terms of the association, the Murrays were required to reship the cargo, and to ensure that the rule was observed, the committee's sloop kept the ship under constant surveillance until she finally sailed. That night the weather turned foul, forcing the surveillance sloop to head for shelter near Sandy Hook, but in the meantime the Murrays hired a crew to transport their cargo to safety in New Jersey.

Sears and McDougall learned of this and confronted the Murrays, who confessed. The two republican leaders were fearful that lenience would fuel suspicions that New York was not enforcing the association, so they were inclined toward severe punishment—banishment from the province, it was said. This prompted Robert Murray's heartbroken wife to write the two, pleading for mercy, and when McDougall showed the piteous letter to William Smith, the latter advised him to respond "in the tenderest Terms."

It was a case requiring judgment and extreme sensitivity, and it had attracted considerable interest. General Gage, for instance, wrote Colden to say he was waiting with "Impatience to hear the Fate of the Beulah. If she lands her Cargo it will be the means of inducing other Ports . . . to do the like." The radicals decided on caution, with the result that John Jay was able to write the New Haven committee, telling them that although the *Beulah* had gone to Halifax, which was not in the New Yorkers' power to prevent, the episode proved that "we have no Reason to apprehend a Defection of this Colony, whose Inhabitants are as sensible of the Blessings of Liberty as any People on the Continent. . . ."

The *Beulah* incident was by no means the only one to create friction between radicals and the authorities. Late in December, customs officials seized a quantity of firearms and gunpowder from the *Lady Gage,* just arrived from London, whose cargo was addressed to a merchant named Walter Franklin. Quickly a crowd gathered, took the munitions from the customs officers, and carried them away. Andrew Elliot, collector of customs, ran to the Merchants Coffee House and told the patrons there what had happened; they helped him recover the arms and put them on board a British warship.

A group that signed themselves "The Mohawks and River Indians" tacked up a broadside at the Coffee House on October 19 informing Elliot that his seizure of the firearms was illegal, since the ship had cleared customs in London on October 15, predating the king's proclamation of October 19 prohibiting the export of weapons. Another message declaring Elliot to be "an inveterate enemy to the liberties of North-America" said that the Mohawks would demand these arms from him whenever they were needed. For his own safety and that of his associates, they warned, he should see to it that the arms were not sent away: revenge would be swift.

Elliot's dignified and restrained reply, claiming that as long as he had the honor to act as collector of the port of New York he would "exert the same attention and firmness" that had characterized his work for the past ten years and had "enabled him to give satisfaction to his superiors . . . and to live happily among the inhabitants of this city." Predictably, this did not sit well with the Mohawks, and with "PLAIN ENGLISH" in particular, who lashed out at Elliot in a broadside rich in hyperbole: "At a time when slavery is clanking her infernal chains, and tyranny stands ready with goads and whips to enforce obedience to her despotic and cruel mandates . . ." he urged the people of New York to "throw off your supineness; assemble together immediately, and go in a body to the Collector, insist upon the arms being relanded . . . there is no time to be lost."

The upshot was that a group of merchants rallied round and safeguarded Elliot against intimidation and the crisis simmered down. As James Duane observed, the people of New York were in general agreement that peaceful persuasion must prevail, that violence was the last resort. And in this McDougall agreed, telling William Cooper in Boston that he was morally certain that the citizens of New York would not take up arms unless the British troops attacked the Bostonians, or unless New Yorkers were provoked by the other colonies to do so. "Sure I am," he said, "we shall be the last of the Provinces to the Northward of Georgia that will appeal to the Sword."

Yet another incident that had the lieutenant governor, his councillors, and the merchants in fits was the arrival of the Scottish ship *James* on February 2. Captain Montagu of HMS *Kingfisher* told the lieutenant governor and his Council that he had put men aboard the incoming vessel, but that a sloop carrying armed men (led by Isaac Sears) was close by. What should he do? The councillors equivocated, Colden hemmed and hawed and refused to make a decision, and that evening the *James* made her way to port, trailed by the surveillance vessel. The ship's master, Captain Watson, came ashore and was outraged when told that he could not land his cargo, but the angry mob sent him back to his ship in a boat.

Next morning, to the consternation of Colden, Watson appeared at his office, asking for protection. The councillors, fearful of the spirit that "last Night struck Terror," now blamed the captain for not leaving town. Oliver DeLancey stormed into the Merchants Coffee House, pointed to the Scottish ship, and called to Philip Livingston and Francis Lewis, "What does that damn'd Rascal come up here again for? Why don't he quit the Port?"

Finally, Watson went on board the *James* at the urging of merchants named Buchanan, who were among the intended recipients of the *James*'s cargo, and who arranged for clearance from customs, saying the *James* would sail the next day, weather permitting. As a disgusted William Smith described the incident, it was Colden's "design to do nothing, & yet cast the Blame upon his Council."

Colden was, in fact, performing a high-wire act these days, doing his best to reassure the administration and avoid censure while keeping things on something resembling an even keel in New York. His goal, and that of the DeLanceys, was to prevent the Assembly from endorsing Congress and supporting its plans. The lieutenant governor had decided, after the delegates returned home in October, that he would not call the legislature into session until he could assess the way it would vote. Unfortunately for him, the patriots had a trick up their sleeves: if he did not convene the Assembly, they would summon a provincial congress, which was the last thing Colden wanted. So he set January 10, 1775, as the day on which the session would open.

Before then the Council—minus William Smith, who had not been notified when they were to gather—met to draft Colden's opening speech to the Assembly. When Smith arrived belatedly and read it he gave the others nine or ten arguments against it, the burden of which was that it was too harsh and would force the assemblymen to take hard and fast positions. They relented, Colden said he would draft an address himself, and they agreed to meet again several days later. Before that time, however, Smith discovered what was behind what he called the "violent speech" written by the councillors. It turned out that the DeLancey faction had arranged it, figuring that a tough, partisan address would trigger an intemperate response by the Assembly and give Colden an excuse for dissolving the session before members voted on the association or delegates to the next congress. If things had gone according to plan, no action would have been taken on Congress and the DeLanceys would not be held responsible. Their scheme had been foiled by Smith's timely intervention, but it was more apparent than ever that they would do anything possible to prevent New York from backing the popular cause.

23

The Sword Is Drawn

For weeks, rumors were rife that the ministry in London was planning to bribe New Yorkers to remain loyal to the crown. The province was, after all, central to Britain's plans—with a great port second to none, which the Royal Navy could enter or leave at will, where troops and munitions and stores could be unloaded, where the Hudson River formed a 140-mile-long water barrier between New England and the colonies to the south while providing the British with access to the interior. And unlike any other province, New York had a powerful, active, and reliable loyalist front, though if it was to remain useful in the months or even years to come it must be nurtured. Cadwallader Colden regularly informed his London superiors that the radical "frenzy" was an urban aberration, fostered by a relative handful of the "lower sort," and his optimistic view of the situation was confirmed from time to time by such visitors as Governor Josiah Martin of North Carolina, who informed Dartmouth that the spirit of loyalty was stronger in New York than in any other colony. Echoing Colden, Martin urged the American secretary to send a substantial number of troops there—a show of strength that would not only boost local morale but have a powerful psychological effect elsewhere on the continent.

So it was natural that stories of financial and other inducements to strengthen loyalist ties should circulate. Coffeehouses in London were full of such talk; so were the provincial newspapers. James Duane wrote to New York's attorney general, John Tabor Kempe, saying rumor had it that Kempe had assured the ministry that if it supplied him with £100,000 he would undertake to buy off all the patriots in the province. General Gage, it was said, was armed with a rich purse to offer leading colonials, especially those in New York. A Londoner wrote that Tryon, soon to be returning to New York, "has the command of money to bribe," and that Major Philip Skene had boasted to the ministry that he could purchase "all the Members of the Continental Congress." According to the letter writer, "The ministerial plan is undoubtedly to reduce every American to the most degraded state of bondage and servitude," to use force and violence in New England, and "bribery and other artifices to divide the rest of the Colonies from the common cause." Nor was money to be the only inducement. President Myles Cooper of King's College was to get a bishopric, Parson John Vardill a deanery at least. In mid-March word came that Lord North "still looked for a Defection in New York & that money was to be given or Promises to be made to effect it."

Nor were these the only rumors. A gentleman from New York, writing to a friend in Boston on April 3, relayed the suspicion that British troops might march five or ten miles into the countryside "in order to compel you to commence hostilities first." As if to confirm that view, on the same day it was written Lord Percy actually did lead a brigade about four miles out of Boston.

In London, the recent discovery that muskets, lead, and gunpowder had been smuggled into New York aboard the *Lady Gage* proved to the ministry "how necessary our precautions were," Dartmouth wrote to Colden, and the timely intervention of merchants to rescue Elliot, the collector of customs, was an example of how a resolution not to submit to the tyranny of mobs would soon "restore vigour and tranquillity to Government"—especially if the Assembly adopted prudent, conciliatory measures. Colden's mail these days was filled with compliments and glowing words from officials in London and from Gage, so positively and confidently had he described his own efforts as well as those of the Council and Assembly to hold the line against the radicals. Surprisingly, though Colden had expected endless machinations and mischief from the "restless spirits," the Assembly proved remarkably resistant to pressure from the radicals.

By a narrow margin the legislators—led by James DeLancey—refused in February to endorse the actions of the Continental Congress, and several weeks later, by a larger majority, they voted against sending delegates to its forthcoming meeting in May, prompting Colden to predict that New Yorkers would daily provide more evidence of their loyalty and affection for their gracious sovereign. Westchester seemed to prove him correct: there, when a vote was taken to determine whether delegates would be chosen to represent them at a provincial congress, they "peremptorily disowned all Congressional Conventions and Committees . . . declared themselves already very ably and effectually represented in the General Assembly . . . by Isaac Wilkins, Esquire," and, for emphasis, sang a chorus of "God Save the King," followed by three cheers. On Staten Island, as well, the assembled citizens agreed not to send deputies.

Yet somehow things were not working out the way the lieutenant governor imagined they would. Writing to Dartmouth he expressed remorse that the Assembly's actions had not put an end to the Continental Association's nonimportation measures, which continued to be rigorously enforced. Ships from Glasgow and London had been turned away with their cargoes still packed in the hold. Not only that: the "Enemys of Government" continued to spread the malicious rumor that the ministry would relent, as it had after the Stamp Act riots, and now these "Mischeivous Folks" were busily engaged in convening a provincial congress—a completely new legislative body that would bypass the Assembly, which was a prospect Colden dreaded. He regretted that "It is not in the Power of Government to prevent such Measures." As indeed it was not.

A month after Colden shared his fears with Dartmouth, the Committee of Observation delivered a notice to the *New-York Journal,* signed by Isaac Low, urging freeholders and freemen to assemble at the Exchange at noon on Monday, March 6, to select delegates to the next congress. Despite the efforts of opponents, who held a meeting chaired by John Thurman at the Widow De La Montagne's tavern, what Thomas Jones described as a "motley assemblage . . . of the most violent republican partizans" paraded through the streets and around the docks and wharves, "with trumpets blowing, fifes playing, drums beating, and colours flying; by this means collecting all the boys, sailors, negroes, New England and Jersey boatmen that could be mustered." (These poor fellows were Jones's favorite cast of villains, the objects of his derision: boys, sailors, Negroes, and boatmen appear regularly in his memoirs when he mentions a parade of the radicals.) Led by Isaac Sears and several of his friends, they first hoisted a Union flag with a red field on the Liberty Pole and about eleven o'clock began marching to the Exchange, accompanied by a band. Two standard-bearers carried a large Union flag with a blue field, on which were the words GEORGE III REX AND THE LIBERTIES OF AMERICA. NO POPERY. On the reverse side was the inscription THE UNION OF THE COLONIES AND THE MEASURES OF THE CONGRESS.

According to Jones, the radicals were armed and the two opposing forces almost came to blows. According to the *New-York Journal,* "some Confusion arose, but subsided without any bad Consequences." Whatever the truth of the matter, Low first called for a vote on whether they would approve the election of deputies to a provincial assembly on April 20, at which New York's delegates to the Continental Congress would be chosen. Next, he asked them to authorize the Committee of Observation to nominate eleven deputies to attend the April 20 meeting—these deputies to be approved by a poll in New York City. The ayes had it on both questions, and by a substantial majority, the newspaper observed, adding that the victors "are supposed to have been the most numerous and respectable ever known in this City on the Decision of any public Proposal." When the day's business was settled, the "Friends of Freedom paraded thro' one of the principal Streets of the City to the Liberty Pole, and there dispersed, in the most quiet and orderly Manner."

Not surprisingly, Tories condemned the vote as indecisive, saying these people were not entitled to the franchise—they were "rabble which may always be collected by the pageantry of a flag and the sound of drum and fife." And shortly after the vote, Isaac Low announced that he would not be a delegate even if chosen, because he had "long been weary of Politics, which appear . . . to be too much influenced by Melevolence and Faction."

By now it was apparent that these outdoor gatherings, to which the public was invited and which attracted large crowds, almost always enthusiastically endorsed the republican position. Indoors, however, in the Assembly and the Council meetings, the conservatives won almost all the votes, each with an increasing margin as their supporters arrived from the outlying districts. Yet although they prevailed on every issue, it was as if a door were slowly closing on the DeLanceys and their friends, shutting them into a chamber from which there was no escape, while outside a whirlwind was gathering that would sweep away their familiar world, transforming it into a land that would be forever alien to them.

Another sign of how the wind was blowing occurred in early April over the question of whether to send nails—and, indeed, "implements of war" and other necessities—for use by Gage's troops in Boston. The brothers Ustick, William and Henry, who had been purchasing spades, shovels, bill-hooks, and pickaxes, as well as nails and other items for the army, were denounced as "inveterate foes to American freedom." Angrily, the two denied the charge, while questioning what right some "paltry sons of mischief" had to deprive them of the trade by which they earned their bread. Several meetings, chaired by Marinus Willett and John Lamb, were held at Philips's Beerhouse, at Bardin's, at the Liberty Pole, and finally at Van Der Water's, where new foes were denounced—Ralph Thurman, who had been packing straw, and Robert Harding, who was purchasing boards, all bound for Boston.

Thurman was no man to take this attack lying down, and after announcing that no enemy of peace and order was going to tell him what to do, he said that if the civil authorities were incapable of handling these "arbitrary Sons of Discord," he would defend his freedom even if it cost him his life. Prompted by Mayor Hicks and Brigadier General Robertson, to whom Thurman made his complaint, the Council voted to investigate the matter, but Hicks misunderstood the request for more information and instead issued arrest warrants for Sears and Willett. When arrested, Sears—unlike Willett—refused to put up bail on grounds that it was a violation of his liberty, and he was unceremoniously hauled off to jail. Word of this flew through the town, and Sears's partisans immediately rallied to his support, rescued him at the jail door, and led him in triumph through the Fly Market, Wall Street, and Broadway to the Liberty Pole. At six that evening, King Sears mounted a platform in the Fields, from which, "like the Devil in Milton, 'By merit raised to that bad eminence,'" he gave a long account of his past and present achievements before the question was put to the huge crowd: "Whether a Son of Liberty ought to give bail or not?" To no one's surprise, this was carried in the negative, followed by three huzzas led by Captain Alexander McDougall.

"Anti-Licentiousness," whose letter appeared in Rivington's *Gazetteer* on April 19, 1775, the day of Sears's arrest, insisted that he was "determined to contend against the tyranny of the British Parliament and Ministry," but pleaded with people not to be deluded when the cry of liberty was used as an excuse for violence, nor to permit "the sway of a mob, which includes despotism, the most cruel and severe of all others." The restraints of the law, he reminded readers, are the security of liberty.

On that same date Samuel Auchmuty, rector of Trinity Church, wrote to Captain Montresor, the engineer, who was now serving with Gage's army in Boston, telling him about the "rascally Whig mob" that had accomplished nothing beyond the rescue of "Sears, the King" at the jail door. New York's magistrates did not have the spirit of a louse, he continued, but in spite of their faintheartedness he predicted that his notorious parishioner Sears would soon be "handled by authority."

Sears may not have been overly concerned by the comments in Rivington's paper, but he was deeply troubled by Ralph Thurman's innuendo that Sears and his son-in-law, Paschal Nelson Smith, had been supplying Gage's army with provisions. That sort of charge, if it stuck, could destroy the credibility of the Sons' efforts. On April 24, 1775, an affidavit signed by Isaac Sears and Paschal N. Smith appeared in Gaine's *New-York Gazette; and the Weekly Mercury* stating that neither of them, nor anyone acting for them, had "supplied or caused to be supplied, the army at Boston with any manner or kind of provisions whatsoever. . . ."

The unrest was by no means confined to the city. In mid-July of 1775, Robert R. Livingston wrote to John Jay saying that many of his tenants at Clermont had refused to sign the Continental Association. They would stand by the king, they declared, "in hopes that if he succeeded they should have their Lands." But now that troops had been raised in the province and two of his brothers had received commissions in the new army, they changed their tune, asserting that they could not engage in the controversy, since their leases were not for life and if they were killed their families would lose everything. To solve that, the Judge's father, old Robert Livingston, Sr., assured them that a new lease would be given to the family of every man killed in the service and his wife (who owned considerable land in her own name) had promised to do likewise. But the tenants remained restless. As Henry B. Livingston of the upper manor wrote to Robert R., "The Tenants here are Great Villains. Some of them are resolved to take advantage of the times & make their Landlords give them Leases forever."

On March 10, Colden had showed his councillors a letter Dartmouth wrote on January 21, "commanding him to use his utmost Power to prevent Delegates going to the next Congress," which the American secretary labeled an illegal convention. But as William Smith perceived immediately, "This is an Instance of Ld. D's Weakness. How could he expect obedience to *his* Letter when the Continent are opposing the whole Legislature of Gt Britain!" In his opinion it revealed a lack of judgment on Dartmouth's part. The New Englanders would undoubtedly publish the letter and "it will inflame the Continent. It could have no other Tendency."

Wednesday, March 22, was the day on which delegates were to be chosen for Congress, and the Council agreed that Colden should show Dartmouth's letter to members of the Assembly, as a reminder that the congress was forbidden by North on account of George III's keen displeasure. Once that news was out, Smith noted, within two hours it "was in every Man's Mouth," and the public at large, which strongly supported participation in the Continental Congress, grew increasingly restive. Despite Colden and the Council, however, delegates were chosen and included Philip Livingston, John Jay, James Duane, John Alsop, and Francis Lewis—all of New York City—as well as Philip Schuyler of Albany, George Clinton of Ulster, Robert R. Livingston, Jr., of Dutchess, Lewis Morris of Westchester, and several others. So pleased with the choice of delegates were the friends of liberty that they held an ox roast in the Fields to celebrate.

In the meantime the General Assembly was trying to hammer out a final version, based on James DeLancey's draft, of grievances to be presented to the king. When the document was finally published late in March, the compromises that had been reached in order to ensure its adoption were immediately evident. "Inviolably attached to your Royal Person and Government," it read, "We mean not to become independent of the British Parliament; on the contrary, we cheerfully acknowledge our Subordination to it as the grand Legislature of the Empire. . . ." Those words of subservience were followed by something entirely different—a recitation of grievances: no taxes without representation, no extension of admiralty courts "beyond their ancient limits," no sending colonials to England for trial, on and on through a total of four printed pages. What the Assembly called a "humble, firm, dutiful, and loyal" petition was carried on board the sloop *Charming Peggy*, bound for Bristol, on March 30.

Colden wrote to Dartmouth expressing pleasure that this appeal to the king, plus a memorial to the Lords and a remonstrance to the Commons, had been expressed in moderate, decent style, but any discerning reader could have predicted the reaction. His Majesty George III may have been pleased to hear expressions of regard and attention, as well as of warm regard for the authority of the parent state, but as Dartmouth informed Governor Tryon, these blandishments had unfortunately been "blended with Expressions containing Claims which made it impossible for Parliament, consistent with its Justice & Dignity to receive them."

One reason for this failed effort was a misguided hope on the part of the New York legislators, most of them loyal subjects of George III, that the opposition—their friends in England, notably Chatham, Fox, Burke, and Pownall—would stand up for their rights and ultimately prevail over the wicked ministry. On the other side of the Atlantic the reverse held true: the king, Lord North and his ministers, and their followers in Parliament all counted on support within the colonies from what they believed to be a host of loyalists, and no small blame for that false optimism belonged to the man who repeatedly misled them as to the strength of the "friends of government"—Cadwallader Colden. The behavior of each side, in other words, was based on erroneous assumptions, and the consequences were catastrophic.

With General Gage now in Boston instead of New York, and without a commanding naval presence nearby, Cadwallader Colden decided to insinuate himself into the role of military strategist. The old lieutenant governor wrote on February 20 to Admiral Graves in Boston, sending the letter unsealed via Gage, asking that he approve it and pass it on—saying, "We have among Us a sett of violent Spirits of the lowest rank and desperate Fortunes," aided and abetted by a few "of superior Condition," all of them looking for any excuse to "raise Mobs and excite Sedition." On the side of government were the moderate men, however, and it only seemed reasonable that they be afforded as much protection as possible. Since the colonies to the southward were threatening New York and pledging to join Massachusetts, he reminded the admiral that the Hudson River had to be passed before any large body of men could reach Massachusetts.

Since the river was navigable in at least twenty-four feet of water for a hundred miles above New York, and could be traversed by a ship of six hundred tons, why not send a large warship to the city—a ship large enough to put two or three hundred men on shore—plus small vessels to obstruct passage on the river?

Military preparedness was not the only topic on the old man's mind. Once again the nettlesome, seemingly insoluble question of the New Hampshire Grants demanded attention. He of course bore much of the responsibility for this, having decided to make grants of land to relatives, friends, and those who might do him good politically despite the crown's ban on such transfers. Here as elsewhere, religion was an ingredient in the witches' brew: some years earlier, Governor Benning Wentworth of New Hampshire had had the foresight, when making grants of his own in the area, to set aside in each one a glebe for the Church of England and another for a school. No such provision had been made by the governor of New York, and the king had ordered (on pain of his "highest displeasure") that no further grants be made by that official. More recently, the Board of Trade—hoping to calm the conflicts in the Grants—had forbidden the governor of New York to distribute any more lands there. But Colden had taken it upon himself to ignore the ruling and was handing out grants freely, undeterred by William Smith's lone opposition in the Council.

In Cumberland County, the lieutenant governor informed Dartmouth, "a dangerous Insurrection" had erupted, fomented by rioters from Massachusetts and New Hampshire. The county—bounded on the east by the Connecticut River and on the south by the northern border of Massachusetts—was a strip of land about seventy-three miles deep and averaging about twenty-four miles wide.* A mob had taken control of the courthouse; the sheriff and a posse showed up and opened fire on them, killing one man and wounding several others; and the next day a huge crowd gathered, overpowered the law officers, seized a judge, the sheriff, the court clerk, and others, and dragged them off to jail in Massachusetts. Colden had requested funds from the Assembly "to bring those attrocious offenders to punishment," but the opposition in the legislature forced the majority to appropriate a stingy amount, which prompted the lieutenant governor to appeal to General Gage.

No sooner had that letter gone off than Colden learned the Bennington rioters were at it again, and he decided the only way to ensure their obedience was by force. This uprising had nothing to do with land disputes, he fumed. It was all part of the "contagion spread from Massachusetts Bay," and the way to cure that was for Parliament to "support . . . authority and punish some of the rebellious Leaders in America."

For their part, a large number of those who lived on the east side of the Green Mountains had declared that they were in great danger of having their property "unjustly, cruelly, and unconstitutionally taken from them" by the hated Yorkers and voted to renounce and resist the leaders of that province until they could lay their grievances before His Majesty George III, in hopes that he would permit some other colony to annex them or, better yet, incorporate them as a new one.

In the meantime, there was an almost universal foreboding that a clash of some kind was imminent. Describing conditions in Massachusetts, Gage wrote the governor of North Carolina saying a "new-fangled Legislature, termed a Provincial Congress . . . seem to have taken the Government into their hands" and radical leaders were doing everything in their power to bring about a confrontation. A Virginian received from England a letter saying, "The sword is drawn here, and the scabbard thrown away. . . . It is determined to put you to the trial; and every thing that is dear to us depends on your firmness. . . . The very existence of liberty on the face of this earth," the writer continued, depended on America. A correspondent to *The Gentleman's Magazine* observed, ". . . there is a malignancy discernible in the leaders of

---

*The western boundary ran roughly along a line through present-day West Dover, Mount Tabor, East Wallingford, and Rutland, Vermont.

the contending parties that will not easily be subdued on either side. From this observation it needs not the gift of second sight to foretel that no plan of reconciliation will ever be formed that will content the present Ministry and the present continental Congress. The preparations on both sides for shedding blood is alarming to a very high degree. . . ."

In Taunton, Massachusetts, parties of so-called "minutemen" from every town in the county turned out on April 10 to round up Tories who had signed up with the king's troops, took their muskets, powder, and bullets, and sent eleven men who refused to mend their ways to work in the Simsbury, Connecticut, mines. (The eleven were "sufficiently humble before they had got fourteen miles on their way" and were brought back home, where they signed documents promising to mend their ways.)

Two men from Ridgefield, Connecticut, showed up in Wethersfield and noisily praised Ridgefield's disapproval of the Continental Congress and its doings. This did not sit well with the Wethersfield Liberty Boys, who ushered the unwelcome visitors out of town "amid the hisses [and] groans" of a considerable throng and "the beating of a dead march." The republicans justified their action by citing an old law prescribing the treatment of strolling idiots and lunatics.

At about the same time, one New Yorker glimpsed a horror that might be in store for others in the city. Hearing a strange noise outside his window early one morning, he saw a supposed informer who had been thrown into a cart, where rowdies were coating him with tar and feathers. "He was carted almost round the Town before the magistrates could collect," the onlooker said, but fortunately they managed to rescue the poor devil and see that two of his persecutors were jailed.

This and similar incidents came about after April of 1775, when a system of sorts was in place throughout the colonies for administering the pledge to support the Continental Association. Unfortunately people were often victimized by local committees (often self-appointed) that interpreted loosely their authorization by the Continental Congress to observe people's conduct, detect conspiracies, and take action when appropriate. A refusal to pledge support was more often than not the criterion for determining whether an individual's heart was in the right place. Transgressions ranged from the serious—passing information to the British or recruiting or spying for them— to the trivial, such as drinking tea or name-calling. Neighbors reported on conversations they had overheard and reported them to local committee members, who summoned supposed offenders to explain or recant or face the charge of being inimical to America. In many locales the result was bullying,

intimidation, whippings, or the tar-and-feather treatment, delivered by neighborhood strong boys.

Letters from abroad brought word that eleven regiments from England and
Ireland had embarked aboard transports, that fifteen thousand tents and
other field equipment had been shipped from the Tower of London, while a
seventy-four-gun man-of-war, two frigates, and two sloops were fitting out at
Woolwich with the utmost dispatch. A Londoner informed a friend in New
York that 285 members of the House were being paid to rubber-stamp whatever Lord North proposed, that the king read and approved the schemes
brought to him by an inner circle (which was in cahoots with Hutchinson,
Colden, and other "lying spirits" who were betraying the colonies), and that
Lord North's motion to promote peace with the colonies had been made only
to deceive them. Bostonians, he added, were to be declared rebels; Hancock
and Adams were to be seized. And worst of all, "the King is your greatest
enemy. Be not deceived by his low cunning. . . . The King is his own Secretary; he gets up at six o'clock every morning, sends off his box with remarks
on a bit of paper tied round each order; four of the ablest lawyers are constantly with him . . . to advise and search for precedents, to screen his head
and throw the blame on Parliament. Two millions have been squandered in
bribery and corruption."

William Legge, Earl of Dartmouth, was a pious man, an earnest one, and
at heart a sincere friend of the colonies, but he was surrounded by colleagues
whose disapproval of his American views led them to be contemptuous of
him and do what they could to undermine his policies. In fact, his one supporter in the cabinet was the first minister, Lord North, but even he did not
always agree with Dartmouth. By January of 1775 the American secretary was
feeling intense pressure from the king and his friends in office to get tough
with the colonists and force them to submit. Making things more difficult for
Dartmouth was the mail from General Thomas Gage in Boston, three thousand miles away, whose frequent letters continued to insist that coercion
could not be employed unless he had sufficient force at his disposal. More
men, more munitions was the continuing, annoying message, and by now the
king and his coterie were fed up with what they saw as Gage's timidity and
caution, his irresolution and inactivity. Yet the king, for all his determination
to force colonial compliance, had a soft spot for Gage and was unwilling to
have him dismissed, so the bizarre decision was made to send three major
generals—William Howe, Henry Clinton, and John Burgoyne—to assist him.

William Legge, Earl of Dartmouth, by Matthew Hone. *Hopkins Museum, Dartmouth College.*

The upshot of all this was that Dartmouth sat down on January 27, 1775, and dictated a long letter to Gage telling him repeatedly to move decisively. Labeled *Secret,* the letter stated firmly that an "actual revolt" existed and therefore "The King's Dignity, & the Honor and Safety of the Empire require that, in such a Situation, Force should be repelled by Force." He reminded Gage that he presently had almost four thousand men available, that a detachment of marines had been sent in October, that substantial reinforcements were to embark immediately, and surely such numbers would enable the general to play a more active and determined role. Gage's earlier estimate that it would take twenty thousand men to effect a conquest was out of the question: after all, he was dealing with "a rude Rabble without plan, without concert, & without conduct," and a smaller force would certainly suffice.

Having told Gage in no uncertain terms that he was to act forcefully, Dartmouth added the caveat that "this is a matter which must be left to your own Discretion to be executed or not as you shall, upon weighing all Circumstances, and the advantages and disadvantages on one side, and the other, think most advisable." The American secretary was covering himself and the ministry nicely: if all went well, the credit would be the government's; if not, well, that was Gage's problem.

Although this was written during the waning days of January, it was not sent until February 22. For one thing, the cabinet wanted to be certain the House of Commons approved this course, which it did despite eloquent

Whig appeals for conciliatory measures—notably from Chatham and Edmund Burke. For another, Dartmouth was apparently attempting *sub rosa,* through intermediaries, to get Benjamin Franklin to set forth whatever terms might make possible a last-minute accord between mother country and colonies. When nothing came of this, the secret dispatch was put aboard HMS *Falcon* and a duplicate copy entrusted to Captain Oliver DeLancey of the 17th Light Dragoons, who was to sail to Boston aboard HMS *Nautilus* on a mission to buy horses for his regiment.

On April 14 the *Nautilus* reached Boston, and DeLancey went immediately to Gage's headquarters with the sealed, secret dispatch. The general knew the red-faced, stocky captain, of course, as he had known all the wealthy, powerful DeLancey clan during his years in New York, and Oliver was also a cousin of Gage's wife. In fact, the young man looked rather like his father, Oliver DeLancey, Sr., a rakish, ill-tempered man. The son, who had been educated at Eton before a commission in the army was purchased for him, was about to become Gage's aide-de-camp, joining several other relatives by marriage that the general had chosen for his intelligence staff.

Before taking any action now, Gage waited until he had in hand the original of Dartmouth's dispatch, probably to avoid making a misstep in the event that discrepancies existed between the two documents. When the original arrived aboard the *Falcon,* two days later, on April 16, the season for campaigning was approaching, and he solidified the plans he had been formulating to strike a quick, decisive blow at the rebels. He determined that Lieutenant Colonel Francis Smith would lead a task force to Concord, marching by the Lexington road, and seize a large store of gunpowder thought to be there, plus other munitions.

The fuse that ignited a revolution in America was about to be lit.

At this same time—on April 15—Lord Dartmouth wrote Gage another letter, this to be delivered by Major General William Howe, who, with Major Generals Henry Clinton and John Burgoyne, was sailing from Portsmouth aboard the *Cerberus.* It was clear now, Dartmouth stated, that all forts in North America that might afford any advantage to the rebels must be secured by garrisons of British troops or be dismantled and destroyed, and that all small arms, cannon, and other military stores be seized and safeguarded. Gage was given the power to issue a proclamation "offering a reasonable Reward for apprehending the President, Secretary, & any other of the Members of the provincial Congress, whom you shall find to have been the most forward & active in that seditious meeting. . . ." Further, those who had opposed the law but who now surrendered themselves and took the oath of allegiance and promised obedience might receive "His Majesty's gracious Pardon for all Treasons they have committed." That letter was not received by Gage until May 25, 1775, five weeks after the event that began one of the most fateful wars in history.

24

You Must Now Declare

Somewhat surprisingly, Paul Revere did not carry the news of fighting from Massachusetts to New York. He had been to Manhattan at least six times during the past sixteen months on important missions, but on this occasion he was unavoidably detained. He and dozens of other patriot riders had been out during the moonlit night of April 18, warning the countryside that the British army was on the march. After leaving Boston at 10 P.M., Revere headed for Lexington, but before he reached the village he and another rider were captured by a party of British officers. Later he was released, after which he spent the rest of the night spreading the alarm. By the time he and his cohorts had done their job, so many militiamen had gathered to harass Gage's troops that it seemed to one eyewitness "as if men came down from the clouds." The credit was due Revere not only for the heroic ride he—and others—took that night, but for the advance planning that made possible the incredible assembling of men within a very short time. He had prepared for this contingency well in advance, establishing contacts with other Whigs, known town leaders—churchmen, physicians, lawyers, military commanders—each with an assigned task, plus "expresses" who could be counted on to carry a message quickly and accurately to a carefully chosen destination.

Before dawn the exhausted Revere was urging John Hancock and Samuel Adams to make their escape from the Clarke parsonage in Lexington and then, with a friend, located Hancock's massive wooden trunk, loaded with important papers, in the Buckman Tavern, where Hancock had been staying. They carried the trunk out the front door, looking for a place to hide it, and saw British troops approaching in the half-light. Staggering under the weight of their burden, the two men passed through the ranks of Captain John Parker's militiamen, who were running onto the Common to form up, as drummer William Diamond beat the call to arms. Revere and his friend, struggling with Hancock's precious trunk, crossed the road at the far end of the Common and were heading for the woods when they heard, first, a single shot, then what Paul Revere described as "a continual roar of musketry." Where Revere spent the rest of that day is not known: he had not been to bed since the night of April 17 and one hopes he got some rest. But by evening of the 19th he was somewhere in the neighborhood of Cambridge and Watertown, and the following morning he met with the Committee of Safety, whose members were dealing with the enormous and uncharted problem of organizing a military effort against the might of Great Britain.

Because Paul Revere was otherwise engaged, it fell to twenty-three-year-old Israel Bissell to carry the news of the fighting at Lexington to the west. Bissell was a regular post rider who happened to be in Watertown on the morning of April 19 and on orders from the Committee of Safety he set out at ten o'clock to follow the Boston Post Road and spread the news to every town along the way to Connecticut. So hard did he ride that his horse died of exhaustion as he arrived in Worcester. Remounted, he galloped on, reaching Brooklyn, Connecticut, at eleven on the morning of the 20th.

The first accounts of an action between the king's troops and the inhabitants of Boston reached New York on Sunday morning, April 23, by ship from Providence, Rhode Island, but no one believed them. Then, about twelve noon, an express arrived with what was considered to be more reliable news. The message, dated Watertown, Wednesday morning, "near 10 o'clock, 19th April, 1775," was signed by T. Palmer of the Committee of Safety and addressed "To all Friends of AMERICAN Liberty." The report stated that a brigade of about a thousand or twelve hundred British regulars had landed at Cambridge and marched to Lexington, where they found a militia company under arms and fired on them "without any provocation," killing six men and wounding four others. What may have been most credible to New Yorkers was Palmer's grim statement: "I have spoken with several who have seen the dead and wounded."

Before Palmer finished writing this message an express rider reached him with news that another thousand-man British brigade was on the march from

Boston, and Palmer called on all persons who read his letter to furnish the bearer, Israel Bissell, with fresh horses as required. If more corroboration of the fighting were needed, it came from Ebenezer Williams in Fairfield, via express to New Haven, from which it was sent on to New York, whence it was forwarded at once to Philadelphia by Isaac Low. This second account spoke of a retreat of the first British brigade, which had been continuously harried by some four thousand Americans, and the landing of a second party of regulars, equipped with artillery. The provincials were determined to prevent the two from joining forces. Some British had reached Concord, it was said, where they had burned the courthouse and seized two cannon. There was a fight at Concord Bridge, where "many on both sides were soon killed." A postscript added that fifty Americans were killed and 150 of the redcoats, as near as could be determined. Meantime, "It will be expedient for every man to go who is fit and willing."

It seemed as if this staccato recital was the news Isaac Sears and John Lamb had been waiting to hear (Thomas Jones, for one, said they had "wished for it for a long time"), and they went into action immediately. The two of them, accompanied by a half-pay British officer, paraded the town with the "rabble" regularly mocked by Jones, "inviting all mankind to take up arms in defence of the 'injured rights and liberties of America.'" What Jones did not seem to comprehend was that the former sea captain was taking command of the military situation in New York before anyone else could act. Sears's first action was to lead his men to the docks and, with Lamb, supervise the unloading of two sloops ready to sail to Boston with provisions for the army. Then he ordered the detention of all ships preparing to ferry supplies to Gage's troops. As night began to fall, he led his followers to the town hall and demanded the key, and when he was refused, had the armory door battered down. Inside were some five hundred muskets, numerous cartridge boxes, and bayonets, and before anyone was the wiser he took possession of all that and twelve hundred pounds of gunpowder from the city's magazine on the edge of town.

On Monday the 24th, the lieutenant governor, councillors, and judges met with the mayor and militia officers to try to decide what must be done. The consensus was with Mayor Hicks's gloomy statement that "the Magistratic Authority was gone." As indeed it was. Judge Livingston reported that all was quiet in Dutchess County, and Judge Jones said the same was true in Queens, but the fact was, as William Smith said, "We were thus unanimously of Opinion that we had no Power to do anything & the best mode of proceeding for private Safety and general Peace was to use Diswasion from Violence."

. . .

A man in Wethersfield, Connecticut, writing to a friend in New York, made no bones about a matter that was on the minds of many Americans. After recounting in considerable detail the story of what had happened in Massachusetts, he added, "We are all in motion here, and equipt from the Town, yesterday, one hundred young men, who cheerfully offered their service." They were all well armed and in high spirits; his brother was one of them; men "of the first character and property" in his and neighboring communities had shouldered their arms and marched off to the scene of action. By nightfall several thousand Connecticut men would be on their way to Boston. Then came the message, and a stunner it was.

"The eyes of *America* are on *New-York;* the Ministry have certainly been promised by some of your leading men that your Province would desert us. . . . It is no time now to dally, or be merely neutral; he that is not for us is against us, and ought to feel the first of our resentment. You must now declare, most explicitly, one way or the other, that we may know whether we are to go to *Boston* or *New-York* . . . our men will as cheerfully attack *New-York* as *Boston;* for we can but perish, and that we are determined upon, or be free."

Always there had been bad blood between New York and New England, and that some substance was behind this threat was apparent several weeks later, when Colden informed Dartmouth that two or three thousand Connecticut men were camped at Greenwich, and "The declared Purpose of this army is to keep this [New York] Government in awe and prevent any defection Here. . . ."

The remarkable speed at which the news of Lexington and Concord traveled from one colony to another testifies to how well organized the committees of correspondence were by this time. The message Isaac Low received in New York at 2 P.M. on Sunday, April 23, was dispatched immediately to Philadelphia, arriving there the next day. Two days later, on the 25th, another bulletin arrived from Boston, via Connecticut, and was sent to Elizabethtown, Woodbridge, and New Brunswick, New Jersey, that same day, arriving at the latter place at midnight. The next day at 3 A.M. it was in Princeton, at Trenton at 6:30, in Philadelphia by noon, and then on to Chester, New Castle, Christiana, reaching Head of Elk in Maryland sometime after midnight, when one S. Patterson sent it on with the curt note "Night and day to be forwarded." At night on April 27 it was in Baltimore; in Annapolis on the 28th; then Alexandria, Fredericksburg, Williamsburg on May 2, New Bern on May 6, finally reaching

Charleston, South Carolina, sometime on May 10. It was a truly extraordinary feat, given travel conditions over rough, winding roads that were often no better than footpaths, rivers that must be crossed by ferry, streams that had to be forded more often than not, and in uncertain weather. While there is no telling what the true mileage was, considering the way roads meandered, it must have been at least nine hundred miles from New York to Charleston, which meant that the message was traveling sixty miles or more each day.

On May 10, Rivington's *Gazetteer* printed the names of American casualties at Lexington and Concord—forty killed, nineteen wounded, and two missing. A week later—along with news that John Livingston had married a Miss LeRoy, "a young lady of great beauty and merit, with a handsome fortune"—the paper published an account of the capture by "provincials from Connecticut" of two important forts, Ticonderoga and Crown Point. Commanding the attackers was Colonel Benedict Arnold (who may have seen to it that neither Ethan Allen nor his Green Mountain Boys shared in the credit). Colden, however, had another view of the matter. It was a "wanton Act of Treason," and the culprits, he told Dartmouth, were "that set of lawless people whom your Lordship has heard much of under the name of the Bennington Mob," who were joined by a party from Connecticut and another from Massachusetts.

The news reached London in a manner that did General Gage little credit. On April 22, 1775, he addressed a letter to Lord Barrington, His Majesty's secretary at war. After a brief routine paragraph acknowledging several promotions and the appointment of a hospital staff for America, he played down the news of recent events, saying with extraordinary sang-froid, "I have now nothing to trouble your Lordship with, but of an Affair that happened here on the 19th Instant." And with that he began his report, describing his own decision to destroy military stores in Concord and the dispatch of grenadiers and light infantry that had led to the battles, the astonishing reaction of the Americans, and the "continual Skirmish for the Space of Fifteen Miles," when his troops were "receiving fire from every Hill, Fence, House, Barn," before being ferried over to Boston from Charlestown. With the letter he enclosed a somber list—the return of the known killed and wounded.

The general gave this dispatch to a naval officer, Lieutenant Nunn, but made the mistake of ordering him to take passage on the first available vessel, which proved to be the brig *Sukey,* a poky two-hundred-ton ship heavily loaded with a cargo for London sent by the merchant John Rowe.

On April 22, three days after the battle, the Massachusetts Provincial Congress was sitting at Concord and voted to take depositions from eyewitnesses so that a full record of Gage's foray into the countryside could be prepared. These men were fully aware of the propaganda value of telling your story first and telling it the way you wanted it to be heard. The evidence was to be sent to London by the first ship from Salem, making all possible speed and with the sailing orders kept "a profound secret from every person on earth." As it happened, the Salem shipmaster Captain Richard Derby, who was a member of the Provincial Congress, owned an exceptionally fast schooner called the *Quero,* which he offered to dispatch on the mission. Because the ship was small, it was an easy task to prepare her for sea, she required few hands, and since his son Richard would fit her out and another son, thirty-four-year-old John Derby, was to command her, maintaining secrecy would be no problem.

The messages on board the *Quero,* which were to be delivered to Benjamin Franklin for London's lord mayor, John Wilkes, and the city's aldermen and common council, who were known to be sympathetic to the colonists, included a letter from Dr. Joseph Warren to the "Inhabitants of Great Britain" and copies of nearly a hundred depositions. Although the *Quero* departed four days after the *Sukey,* she sailed in ballast and made excellent time, crossing in twenty-nine days. The details of Derby's landing are shrouded in mystery, but the likelihood is that he was rowed ashore on the Isle of Wight, leaving his first mate in command of the *Quero,* went to Southampton, and took the stage to London.

The capital was anxious for news of America. As Horace Walpole reported, the stock market began to grow a little nervous, and when an unknown American sailor—a man Walpole called the "Accidental Captain"— suddenly appeared on the scene, having arrived in a manner he did not explain, he had the ear of everyone. Derby took lodgings in London on Sunday evening, May 28, and immediately gave his accreditation papers to Arthur Lee, who had succeeded Franklin after the latter sailed to America. He then delivered to the Lord Mayor copies of the Salem *Gazette* for April 21 and 25, the letter from Warren, and the affidavits, presenting the facts as Boston wanted them to be known and creating a sensation, which the government was unable to confirm or discredit for two weeks. Within a week every paper in England had published the news.

Former Massachusetts governor Thomas Hutchinson noted Derby's arrival in his diary on May 29, saying he was sure that Gage's account—when it came—would be different. Hutchinson brought the news to Dartmouth, who published a notice on May 30 that "no advices" had yet been received from General Gage—the implication being that what Londoners had heard from Derby was merely propaganda, which Gage's report would contradict.

On June 1 a Londoner wrote to an American friend to say that the ministers "have not as yet formed any plan in consequence of the action of April 19. They are in total confusion and consternation and wait for General Gage's despatches. . . ." On June 3 the historian Edward Gibbon wrote from London, "No news from Gage," and went on to say that although Derby's vessel "cannot be found, it is pretty clear that he is no impostor. . . . He is now left town and is gone, it is said, on a trading voyage to purchase ammunition in France and Spain." Meantime, other vessels were arriving from America, all with news confirming what Derby had brought, but still no sign of *Sukey*. On June 4, Hutchinson entered in his diary, "Wind still easterly and no intelligence."

Finally, on June 9, the *Sukey* arrived and Lieutenant Nunn delivered Gage's report. Dartmouth, who received much the same account as Gage had given Barrington, responded with a long, frosty letter indicating the damage that had been done by the intelligence "sent by the Enemies of Govt on purpose to make an Impression here," and telling Gage that in the case of future events of importance, he would be well advised to make use of "one of the light Vessels of the Fleet." The unkindest cut came from a London newspaper, which had compared the accounts carried by *Quero* and *Sukey* and stated that "the facts, in every material circumstance, precisely agree." In the ultimate rebuke, the editor observed that Gage's account, "as a literary composition, is a disgrace to the Kingdom."*

Gage had other reasons for concern. He had five companies in New York City under Major Isaac Hamilton of the 18th Royal Irish Regiment of Foot—some one hundred men who were no earthly good unless attached to a larger force, and their ranks were thinning with each passing day. Writing to Hamilton on May 7 the general said he had received accounts of "the Commotions in New York" and concluded that the situation there must be critical. He wanted the major to confer with the lieutenant governor and decide what was the best course of action, but from a distance, Gage added, it seemed prudent for Hamilton to get his men on board the *Asia,* where they would be safe.

---

*When he returned to America, Captain John Derby gave General George Washington an account of how he took news of the outbreak of war to London. Eight years later, in 1783, by incredible coincidence, it was his good fortune to bring home from Paris in the *Astraea* the first news of the peace that ended the war.

Hamilton followed orders and informed Colden that in spite of "the most tempting baits" only four of his men—the worst of the lot, he was glad to say—had deserted, but in the past three days he had lost as many more and was apprehensive that all the rest might vanish unless he acted quickly.

The sixty-four-gun man-of-war *Asia* dropped anchor in the East River on May 26, and Captain George Vandeput immediately informed Colden that he was there to assist in any way possible. Colden should know that he had intended to send the *Kingfisher* to Boston with dispatches, but had received so many accounts of rebel vessels carrying arms and ammunition up and down the coast that he had found it advisable to keep Captain Montagu's ship on patrol to intercept them.

By June 5, Major Hamilton was nearly at wit's end. By then his losses from desertion were so great that Captain Vandeput had to agree to take the five companies on board the *Asia,* but he said he could not accommodate the women and children. Would the lieutenant governor permit them to camp on Governors Island until such time as General Gage could send a ship to transport the men and their families? And could he instruct the barrack master to lend some blankets and utensils for use by officers and men who were unable to board the man-of-war immediately?

At that point all might have gone smoothly had it not been for Marinus Willett. Thirty-five years old, Willett was the great-grandson of an English trader and sea captain who had arrived in Plymouth colony in 1630. Born at Jamaica, on Long Island, Willett had spent most of his life in New York, where he attended King's College and subsequently became a successful merchant. He had fought in the French and Indian War, as a lieutenant in Oliver DeLancey's regiment when Abercromby made his disastrous attack on Ticonderoga in 1758, and with Bradstreet when he captured Fort Frontenac. More recently he had become an active member of the Sons of Liberty and was evidently present when Sears led a number of them to seize the arms at the town hall. Those arms, Willett recalled, were distributed among the most spirited Sons, who formed themselves into a corps of volunteers and "assumed the Government of the City." Subsequently a Committee of One Hundred was chosen to restore order and to serve until some sort of guidance was forthcoming from the Continental Congress.

A good many Sons, Willett among them, regarded the Royal Irish Regiment with unvarnished hatred, and when they learned that the outfit was ordered to join Gage's forces in Boston, decided to assist the Massachusetts brethren by doing what they could to eviscerate the regiment. About ten in the morning on June 6, a fine sunny day, Major Hamilton's men formed up

Marinus Willett, by Ralph Earl.
Metropolitan Museum of Art, bequest of
G. Willett Van Nest.

and began their march to the wharf. Willett and half a dozen of his fellow Sons were at the public house near Beekman Slip kept by Isaac Sears's father-in-law, Jasper Drake, when they got wind of this and learned that the troops were taking with them cartloads of chests filled with arms. Willett was one of many who had argued in favor of taking them prisoner, but this had been discouraged by the many loyalists on the Committee of One Hundred. The "timid disposition of the Committee Caused them to suppose this could not be effected without the loss of a number of lives," Willett grumbled, and they "agreed to let them depart with their arms and acoutraments without Molestation." Believing that the committee's permission did not extend to taking spare arms with them, the little group at Drake's tavern decided to act, and began by spreading the alarm throughout the city.

Willett's route took him past the coffeehouse on the corner of Wall and Water streets, where he told the customers what was happening, then through Water Street to the Exchange at the lower end of Broad Street, where he saw the troops marching down Broad. He ran toward them and saw several carts loaded with chests of arms, guarded by only a few men. Quickly he stopped the first horse in the procession, which halted the whole line of march, and when the commanding officer rode up to inquire what was going on, Willett informed him that the permission granted by the committee did not extend to the troops taking with them any arms other than those they carried.

At this juncture Mayor Hicks appeared (a man, Willett noted, "whose tory principals were well known to be opposed to Congersenal measures"), and as he argued with Willett numerous citizens began to collect, and Willett somehow managed to divert five carts loaded with arms from the line of march and sent them up Broadway to John Street, where Abraham Van Dyck—"a good Whig"—had a large yard. That was not the end of his work: he leaped onto one of the carts, shouting to the British troops that if they wanted to "Join the Bloody business which was transacting near Boston," he and others were ready to meet them on the battlefield, but if any of them "felt a repugnance to the unatural work of sheding the blood of their Countrymen," they could keep their arms and receive the protection of the citizens. That, apparently, was enough to lure several soldiers, who were received with open arms and loud huzzas by the assembled crowd. At the end, Willett recorded, "The troops marched to the river and embarked under the Hisses of the citizens."

When Colden heard the full story he was outraged, and wrote at once to Major Hamilton and Mayor Hicks to express his "shagreen and Uneasiness" over the insult and outrage to His Majesty's troops. Hamilton had been assured by the magistrates that his men would be well treated, instead of which their baggage was taken from them, trunks and packages broken open and strewn about, their contents examined, and more than one hundred stand of arms taken, along with the officers' personal fusils.

This was all of a piece with a report the merchant John Alsop, who was in Philadelphia as a delegate to Congress, received from a colleague in New York. "The City is not behind hand in its martial spirit, for they are continually exercising in every corner of the town, in short every man bears arms. . . ." Hardly a day passed that Alsop did not hear from his constituents—most of them importuning him to have his fellow delegates assist New York's troubled mercantile community. From one man he heard that "Markets would be much Quicker if we had Vessells. I never knew so few in the Harbour as at present. What few does come in are loaded Imediately." These were anxious times, financially, and his associate Christopher Smith, reporting that "Matters appear Very Serious & Wears a different Aspect than when you left us," wanted guidance on just about everything, from whether Alsop wanted to ship a quantity of wheat to London aboard the *Polly,* which Smith had just engaged for that purpose, to how New Yorkers should cope with some two thousand British troops who were supposedly arriving two or three days hence. If Congress did not want the soldiers to land, they would be opposed, he stated with assurance, for New York was still hearing "the Old Story of Backwardness"—its reputed reluctance to support the cause of liberty.

Smith had purchased a sloop and outfitted her with a new mast, and he proposed to load her with salt for London. But should he have the captain sell the sloop with the salt and bring the money home? "In these Troublesome times I cannot think it safe in London." What did Alsop think about the store Smith was building? The foundation would be laid by next week, but should he finish it or let it stand as is until they had more news from England?

Another insistent query that came to Alsop from Smith and others concerned tea. Peter Keteltas put the matter bluntly. What was the Continental Congress going to do about the tea languishing in the merchants' warehouses? After all, they had purchased it legally, before Congress decided to prohibit its consumption, and surely it was not the intention of Congress to ruin people—which would be the case if they did not permit the tea to be sold. Here was the Committee of Safety in New York, determined to raise £10,000 for arms and ammunition, and, as Alsop knew, they would lean hardest on those merchants who customarily imported arms as well as tea.

"The Congress," Keteltas wrote, "ought not to look with so evil an Eye on those Persons whom in contempt they call Smuglers." Were it not for them, no English tea would have entered the city. By the same token, smuggling was the only way to obtain arms, which meant that these people who skirted the law were those who had to be dealt with.

Keteltas undoubtedly reflected the sentiments of most merchants when he urged Congress to petition the king again—this time "in a soft strain, and abate their demands rather than Involve the Continent in a Cruel War. . . . You know the pride of the Mother Country, they cant bear to be talked to in a High Strain—for my part I think with Solomon—that soft Words turn away Anger."

Almost all the ships in the harbor had departed, he continued, and the country was still full of flour and wheat. What an amazing change this was from four or five years ago. In other news, the Anglican minister Thomas Bradbury Chandler, Myles Cooper of King's College, and others had fled to England, and Rivington, the printer, was still on board the *Asia,* where he had sought safety after threats were made on his life for articles published in his paper.

James Beekman, writing to the Messrs. B. Pomeroy & Son in London, told them, "The present State of our Public Affairs has put a total Stop to Trade, as also to collecting in Debts, which renders it extremely difficult & next to impossible for our Merchants to make Remittances Home. On which account I am prevented making that Payment, which was my intention &

which I should otherwise have done." He went on to express his hope that the "Disturbances & Animosities" would quickly subside, for "we are so intimately connected, that whatever affects one Part, must inevitably affect the whole. . . ."

Of the twelve men selected to go as delegates to the Continental Congress, three were members of the Livingston clan—Philip, the lord of the manor's brother; James Duane, the proprietor's son-in-law; and their cousin at Clermont, Robert R. Livingston, Jr., son of the Judge. All of them, as well as their elders, were leery of the topic that was bound to surface almost immediately in Philadelphia—independence. Describing New York in the wake of Lexington and Concord to his wife, the Judge said the city was in "a continual Bustle," and joked that the people were "perfectly Fearless, I mean the Wiggs and the Tories turn Wigg so fast that they will soon be as much united as they are in the Massachusetts Bay." Unity, as the Judge well knew, was hardly plausible in New York, given the deepening divide between the two disputing factions. Writing to his son, he admitted his feelings of ambivalence: "Every good man wishes that America may remain free: in this I join heartily; at the same time I do not desire she should be wholly independent of the mother country. How to reconcile their jarring principles, I confess I am altogether at a loss." Duane, writing to his father-in-law at the manor, said, "I sincerely join with you in dreading a separation from Great Britain, which can be acceptable to very few." He was quite right: it was a fear shared by the great majority of colonists.

In another letter to Margaret from New York, Robert R. Livingston reported "continual confusion," with Sears and Lamb "calling out the people almost every day to the liberty pole." Meanwhile an alarming report had been received from Philadelphia to the effect that Oliver DeLancey and John Watts "had wrote Letters Home very unfriendly to the Liberties of the Country," with the result that some men actually loaded their guns and were prepared to shoot them. That "ferment was allayed and now has quite subsided," he added with obvious relief, noting that thanks to guidance received from the county committee and the Provincial and Continental congresses "we are got now into a regular kind of Government and the Power of our Demagogs are at an End."

Then, anticipating what he knew to be her questions, he wrote, "You'll say, what have you to do with all this? Why do you not write of your own affairs? Why don't you come up?" and responded matter-of-factly, "I have large accounts to pay and want to receive some Money." He was talking to a potential buyer of some water lots, he added, and didn't see how he could get away until Saturday—three days hence. He hoped she was not uneasy in these troublesome times (though he obviously knew she was), and tried to reassure her by saying that "we are in the hands of God, to him let us trust all our concerns. He that places his confidence in him He will not forsake."

Margaret Beekman Livingston soon had reason to wonder if the Lord had forsaken her, for a curse seemed to have been laid on the family. First had come the drowning of James Duane's little boy. Robert of Clermont, her father-in-law, died at the age of eighty-seven, shortly after learning of a big battle at Bunker Hill, and his final words were "What news of Boston?" That autumn Margaret was summoned to Rhinebeck to the bedside of her own aged father, who was terminally ill, leaving her husband at Clermont, suffering with a cold and fever. When her father rallied she headed for home, and on the way a messenger rode up to her carriage with the shattering news that her beloved Judge was dead of apoplexy at the age of fifty-seven. Nine days after his funeral she was back in Rhinebeck, where her father lay dying, and when she returned once more to Clermont it was to learn that her daughter Janet's husband, General Richard Montgomery, who was second in command to General Philip Schuyler, had fallen in the American attack on Quebec.

25

The Proposition Is Peace

In October of 1774, according to the *New-York Journal*, Benjamin Franklin had booked passage for Philadelphia and was on the point of departure when he was summoned by the Earl of Chatham, who persuaded the American to remain in London until after the next session of Parliament, when Chatham intended "to make the most vigorous efforts in favour of this country."

In the aftermath of the Boston Tea Party a dejected Benjamin Franklin had written to Thomas Cushing, "I suppose we never had since we were a people so few friends in Britain." Following Wedderburn's attack on him in January of 1774 he had ignored the ministry, maintaining "a cool, sullen silence, reserving myself to some future opportunity." He did indeed attend the House of Lords to hear Chatham's speech, which incorporated many of his own ideas and proposed that the king withdraw the troops from Boston, only to see that the address was "treated with as much contempt as they could have shown to a ballad offered by a drunken porter." No wonder: Chatham lost his temper and his attack on the king's friends cut too close to the quick. "Were I disposed," he told them, "I could demonstrate that the whole of your political conduct has been one continued series of weakness, temerity, despotism, ignorance, futility, negligence, blundering and the most notorious servility, incapacity and corruption."

By now Franklin knew that his own time in England was being spent to little avail, and when he learned that his wife had died suddenly he determined to leave by the first ship to Philadelphia. One of the last things he heard was a British general's remark "that with a thousand British grenadiers he would undertake to go from one end of America to the other and geld all the males, partly by force and partly by a little coaxing." To the very last day he continued to hope that America's friends in and out of Parliament might collect enough strength to throw out the North ministry, but that was obviously out of the question at this late date. On March 19, he spent several hours with Edmund Burke, who gave his great speech on conciliation just three days later (four weeks to the day before the fighting at Lexington and Concord):

> The proposition is peace. Not peace through the medium of war; not peace to be hunted through the labyrinth of intricate and endless negotiations. . . .
> It is simple peace, sought in its natural course and in its ordinary haunts. . . .
> We cannot, I fear, falsify the pedigree of this fierce people, and persuade them that they are not sprung from a nation in whose veins the blood of freedom circulates. . . . An Englishman is the unfittest person on earth to argue another Englishman into slavery.

Then he warned the members that "a great Empire and little minds go ill together."

On Franklin's final day in London he was with Joseph Priestley from morning until night, reading to him from American newspapers, unable to keep the tears from his eyes, saying that if war came it would be a long one— perhaps ten years—and while America would win, he would not live to see the end. On March 21, 1775, he and his grandson Temple boarded the packet for Philadelphia, and six weeks later, after a fine voyage during which he lowered a thermometer into the water for hours every day to prove his contention that a ship made better time sailing east to west if it crossed the Gulf Stream directly instead of running against it for days, he arrived on May 5.

As soon as his ship docked he learned of the bloodshed at Lexington and Concord, and the next morning he was told that the Pennsylvania Assembly had selected him as one of its deputies to the Second Continental Congress, which was to meet in Philadelphia four days hence. Franklin was not only the oldest man in the Continental Congress, he was almost a generation older than half the delegates, but he was also one of the boldest, despite his age, and was as reserved as was George Washington. Thomas Jefferson remarked that during the period he served with Washington in the Virginia legislature and with Franklin in Congress, "I never heard either of them speak ten minutes at a time, nor to any but the main point which was to decide the question. They laid their shoulders to the great points, knowing that the little ones would follow of themselves."

On May 8 a letter from a Philadelphian was published in New York, reporting on Dr. Franklin's return and his remarks, including the statement that "we have no favours to expect from the Ministry, nothing but submission will satisfy them. . . ." Said to be elated that his countrymen were arming and preparing for the worst, he believed a spirited opposition would be the means of America's salvation.

In a curious way, things had come full circle for Franklin. Two decades earlier, in 1754, he had done his utmost to structure a union of the colonies within the empire. More than any other leading participant in imperial affairs, his was a vision of a peaceful, prosperous, political marriage in which the unified colonies would be partners, not servants, of the crown. He had done his utmost to avert a break in the relationship, counseling caution, patience, and reason. Nonimportation, not violence, was as far as he was willing to see the ties stretched, but despite his wish for harmony he was a realist and knew that if it came to blows, as had seemed more likely with each passing month, the colonists would have a desperate need for the arms and accouterments of war. Muskets, balls, powder, bayonets, cannon, blankets, clothing, hundreds of other necessities, and, above all, money were sorely lacking in America. During his travels in Europe, Franklin had built up a relationship with businessmen in Britain and on the Continent—a network of merchants with whom he negotiated clandestinely the purchase of weapons. In addition, his friendship with ship captains in Boston, Philadelphia, and London—men with an uncanny knowledge of the numerous openings and hidden coves along the vast Atlantic coastline, men versed in smuggling, who winked at the navigation acts passed by Parliament while evading British customs officials and naval vessels—had made it possible for him to arrange periodic shipments of contraband to America.

Even more essential than the logistics and matériel of war, however, was the imperative need for colonial unity and cooperation that would bring together the separate provinces and enable them to sustain a prolonged conflict. Except for a few instances of cooperation, such as their resistance to the Stamp Act and the Townshend duties, the colonies had never shown a real determination to forge a union. Now that was the paramount issue, and it remained to be seen if they could set aside their differences for the sake of their common beliefs. The ultimate irony would be if the colonies at last came together as Franklin had always hoped, but this time outside—not within—the empire.

Benjamin Franklin realized that a new world had made new men of the Europeans who came here. Ever so gradually, they had become Americans, and as the semifeudal relationship with Great Britain eroded, they came to resent their subordinated role in trade and the English view of them as second-class citizens. The British, who wanted to preserve that subordination, believed they could do so through taxation. But taxation without even a semblance of legislative representation was anathema to Americans, and a reactionary king and a puppet Parliament, angered by America's resistance, turned to ever harsher measures. By 1775, both sides were armed or arming.

Taken by surprise by the outbreak of hostilities in America, the British were slow to act. Several factors were at work here. Henry Howard, Earl of Suffolk, was in the process of organizing a "war party," and in this he was supported by Lord George Germain, soon to enter North's ministry and replace Dartmouth. Suffolk, as northern secretary, was already negotiating (unsuccessfully, as it proved) for twenty thousand Russian mercenaries, believing they would be "charming visitors at New York and civilize that part of America wonderfully." Germain was pressing for coercion, as was the king, and faced with these and other demands for action to crush the rebellion, whatever hopes North and Dartmouth had of avoiding hostilities looked to be futile. In fact, North's obvious reluctance to commit to war with the colonies was a source of major discontent in his cabinet, threatening to upset a fragile balance of power. Warned that several members were "surly in their Language, sulky in their Conduct, and ill-disposed to your Administration," he finally accepted the fact that they, the king, and the British people in general expected rigorous action.

On February 2 he moved in the Commons that New England be declared in rebellion, and despite fierce resistance from Fox, Burke, and others, the motion passed there and in the Lords. An increase in military forces was approved, as was a bill restraining New England's trade and closing the Newfoundland fisheries to those colonies. Then, suddenly and without notice, on February 20, North moved a Conciliatory Proposition, which declared that any colony that contributed its share to the common defense and provided support for the civil government and the administration of justice would be relieved of paying taxes or duties except those necessary for the regulation of commerce. It was the first crack in the rigid edifice established by the Declaratory Act, but it came too late. Chatham labeled it "mere verbiage" that would be spurned by America and laughed at by her friends.

What North seemed unable to fathom was that the dispute had gone far beyond taxation and that the very principle of parliamentary supremacy was now at issue. He undoubtedly hoped that his Conciliatory Proposition might provide a wedge that would frustrate colonial unity, but on the other side of the Atlantic, as Chatham predicted, there was no trusting the ministry now. Speaking for many of his countrymen, Samuel Adams characterized the proposal as "an insidious Manoeuvre calculated to divide us."

For a week after news of Lexington and Concord reached New York it was "impossible to describe the agitated State of the Town," according to William Smith. "At all corners People inquisitive for News—Tales of all Kinds invented, believed, denied, discredited." Old-timers said they had never seen so few vessels in the harbor. Taverns were crowded with customers at night, and little business was done during the day; few jurors or witnesses showed up in court; men with weapons roamed the streets, summoning others to come and learn the manual of arms. James Beekman reported an almost total stagnation of every kind of business, adding that all ranks of people were buying guns—many of them patronizing the well-known gunsmith Gilbert Forbes, a short, stocky fellow whose shop, the Sign of the Sportsman, was on Broadway, not far from Bowling Green.

The city's merchants, Smith said, were amazed and humbled by the sudden outbreak of violence, and they confined whatever complaints they had to sighs or whispers, for "They now dread Sears's Train of armed Men." Sears had gone to the polls like a little dictator and ordered them to accept the list of candidates proposed by the Committee of One Hundred, enraging moderates—Whigs and Tories alike—who promptly called for a committee of their own.

William Smith, who liked to call himself "Patriotic Billy," had a plan for achieving peace, and on May 16 he sent a letter to Philip Schuyler, who was then with the Continental Congress at Philadelphia. The moment was at hand, Smith said, at which "the greatest Blessings may be secured to our Country," and Schuyler must urge Congress to act at once. "Could you wish for a better Opportunity to negotiate? You have the Ball at your Feet. For Heavens Sake don't slip so fair a Prospect of gaining" by counting on a change in the ministry. They hoped to divide the colonies, he reminded his friend, but the very existence of the Continental Congress demonstrated that this had become impossible for them to achieve. Either the ministry must change policies or it would be driven from office, and now was the time to strike.

If he were a delegate to Congress, he went on, he would propose that the ministry be told that peace was possible, but only if it assured the colonies that no taxes would be raised without their consent and that religion be a matter for the colonial assemblies to decide—that is, no established church. And, to avoid commercial ruin, America should insist that taxes be paid into the colonies' treasuries, or if the money *did* go to England, that it be credited to the colonies. If the British objected to this scheme on grounds that it delayed their receipt of revenue too long, an American Parliament would be authorized to determine the amount of money to go to the mother country and set a quota for each colony.

"This simple Proposal if adopted will make Peace," he said confidently, "for the whole System of our Grievances will then fall like Scaffolds" after a building has been raised. What's more, the men who passed the offensive acts against America would be spared humiliation and a proud Britain would not have to haggle over a long list of prerequisites to peace.

Continuing, Smith said he had just learned of Dr. Franklin's arrival from England and was alarmed. The trouble, candidly, was that Franklin—a man of considerable influence in Congress—had allied himself with Lord Chatham, a situation Smith viewed with dread. Chatham would exempt the Americans from internal taxation, all right, but Schuyler should look back at all Pitt's speeches and "then judge whether with the Sceptre in his Hand and the Nation at his Heels you have not more to fear from him than from a Ministry that are trembling before you"—a ministry seeking a way out of its dilemma by switching policies, not cabinet officers. Besides, Franklin would never want to keep a set of men in office who had "deplumed him and who detest him." Look at it this way: what difference does it make to our country whose ambition is flattered as long as we are saved?

Smith was almost certainly right in one respect, for when it came to the supremacy of Parliament over the colonies, Chatham was as much a hard-liner as the toughest of North's ministers. But whether North and his cabinet were trembling before the Americans or had the slightest interest in changing their plans was highly questionable.

On May 4, 1775, a jittery Cadwallader Colden wrote to both Lord North and Lord Dartmouth to apprise them of the present "state of annarchy and Confusion into which this Province has run since the actual Commencement of Hostilities." In particular he wanted them to know that several "warm Friends to Government" had resolved to go to England in hopes of avoiding bloodshed and the calamity of civil war. In fact, so many informed people were boarding the outgoing packet that the noble lords would have an unparalleled source of eyewitness testimony to "the total prostration of government" in New York.

With his customary shading of the facts to please his masters in London, Colden put the best face on the refugees' departure, implying that they were sailing in order to convey information to the authorities. That may have been one element of the travelers' intention, but the real reason they were leaving was terror—fear for their lives and for unknown horrors that might lie in store. The ship embarking on May 4 was the first available packet after the news of Lexington and Concord reached New York, and these wealthy, prominent individuals, whose names were household words because of their positions, associations, and loyalist views, knew they were marked men.

One of them was Lieutenant Colonel Maunsell, a retired British officer on half pay who had lived in the city for the past eleven years; he was carrying Colden's dispatches to Dartmouth and hoped to obtain an interview with North. Without a word to the Council about their plans, two of its members—John Watts and Roger Morris—arranged at the last minute to depart on the packet *Harriet*, bound for Falmouth, and with only a few hours to spare, threw together some clothing and important papers before boarding ship. At the time New York received news of the fighting in Massachusetts, Watts had two sloops loaded with flour for the British troops in Boston, and they had been unloaded by an angry crowd. He was also painfully aware of the story that he and DeLancey had written letters inimical to the patriot cause which had given the Liberty Boys the idea of coming after him. That ugly rumor seems to have originated in a letter from London, published in Bradford's *Pennsylvania Journal*, whose author reported that fresh British troops were being sent to Boston and New York and that those bound for the latter place had been requested "by DeLancey and his band of traitors, [Myles] Cooper, [Henry] White, Colden, and Watts, to aid them in securing New-York for the Ministry." (With James Rivington, these were known to local Liberty Boys as the "Odious Six.") White had a broadside printed, declaring on his oath that assertions that he had written letters urging Britain to send troops were utterly false, but this did him little good.

Manhattan, the London writer claimed, was to be headquarters for the British army and a buffer to prevent assistance from Pennsylvania, Maryland, Virginia, and other southern colonies from reaching New England. Another letter, signed "Three Millions," was addressed to James DeLancey and the other four, accusing them of calling for a civil war "and all the calamities of towns in flames. A desolated country, butchered fathers and weeping widows and children now lie entirely at your doors. . . . Fly for your lives," "Three Millions" warned, "or anticipate your doom. . . ." John Watts obviously took the threat seriously, and shortly after arriving at Bristol he wrote to Sir John

Johnson, the husband of his daughter Polly, saying, "I really could not stand the cruel injustice done me after so many years of faithfull service, from which I call God to witness I have never deviated to this present hour, nor would anything tempt me to turn Traytor to the Country that gave me a Being. . . ." Many years later, in a deposition applying for recompense for his financial losses, Watts less emotionally gave his reason for leaving America in 1775. Hostilities had commenced, he said, and all government was dissolved, while the "many groundless Charges and menaces" he received convinced him that it was "adviseable to embark for Eng^d [at] an advanced time of life, leaving his Family, property and Connexions behind him."*

Another dignitary departing the city, his going unnoticed and unremarked, was James DeLancey. Sometime after the fighting broke out at Lexington, he quietly slipped out of town, journeyed to Fort Stanwix and down the St. Lawrence, and sailed to England from Quebec. DeLancey had done everything in his power to overcome the radicals, but he knew when he was beaten. After the First Continental Congress convened, he and his conservative allies in the New York Assembly were determined to outmaneuver the republicans and petition the king on their own terms. DeLancey was a member of the committee of correspondence that wrote to Edmund Burke in 1774, protesting actions of the government. He was on a committee of grievances and personally drafted the resolution sent to the king and Parliament— the message that acknowledged the colonies' subordination to the authority of Parliament. Surreptitiously, he had been reading all the letters sent to James Rivington for publication in his *Gazetteer*, altering them in such a way "that everything might be expunged which were thought likely to do hurt to the Cause of Government." Perhaps his most important act, and the last of any real significance, was to mastermind the narrow defeat of Philip Schuyler's motion in the Assembly that would have approved the proceedings of the Continental Congress—a move, he admitted later, that aroused more animosity toward him than anything else he had done.

At the end, he met with a number of friends and supporters to assess the possibility of uniting New York's loyalists against the supporters of Congress, but not receiving enough encouragement, he thought it fruitless to pursue that plan, and soon afterward quitted New York. He and his friends were

---

*During 1775, Sir John Johnson was continually harassed by the rebels, and the next year, when he was away from home, a detachment of troops plundered Johnson Hall, stole his slaves, livestock, carriages, and papers, and forced his wife, Polly—seven months pregnant—to ride in a carriage to Albany, some forty miles away, accompanied, Thomas Jones wrote, by a former cobbler, now a lieutenant, who was wearing the clothes he had stolen from Johnson's closet.

convinced "they could have mastered the disaffected in New York," but feared they would be overpowered by the radicals in New Jersey and Connecticut. It was then he realized that he could do no more.

He left behind his wife and children, presumably because he expected order to be restored in the province, at which time he would come back, yet he must have had some anxious moments, wondering if they would be safe in the meantime. Also at risk was a fortune in real estate holdings that had made him the wealthiest man in the colony, with the possible exception of Frederick Philipse. His home at Broadway and Thames Street with property fronting the Bowery* was a large brick mansion that compared favorably with any residence in America. The DeLancey farm lay north of Division Street, extending from the Bowery Lane to the East River and north to lands of Peter Stuyvesant. Most of his income came from rentals of property on the East Side of the city, and with the surplus he had for years been acquiring land elsewhere. In the New Hampshire Grants he and his boyhood friend James Duane held a patent for lands on both sides of Otter Creek,† and his properties included major holdings in New Jersey, Pennsylvania, New York's Cherry Valley, and other locations in Albany and Tryon counties.

As in the case of John Watts's decision to go to England, DeLancey surely sensed what lay ahead for him in the present climate of hatred and violence. They may have planned to return to America, but neither man did.

Several Church of England men found themselves in jeopardy. On April 20, James Rivington announced the coming publication of another pamphlet by "A. W. Farmer"—one more reply to Alexander Hamilton—but when news of the fighting in Massachusetts arrived and the Liberty Boys took over the local government, Samuel Seabury vanished, and Rivington never published the pamphlet. For a time Seabury holed up—perhaps in the massive chimney in Isaac Wilkins's home where he and other loyalists had concealed themselves the previous autumn—but he then retired to his Westchester parish. The Sons of Liberty knew he was there and harassed him continuously, he said, going miles out of their way to do so on their travels between New York and New England. On November 22, 1775, the day before Isaac Sears and a troop of Connecticut horsemen rode into New York to destroy Rivington's printing office, they seized Seabury and took him to New Haven, where he was held until December 23. There he pleaded not guilty to the charges

---

*The house, approached along a semicircular entrance drive through a row of magnificent shade trees, was bounded by the present Christie Street, between Delancey and Rivington streets.
†In the present towns of Rutland and Pittsford, Vermont.

against him and was released. On his return home he found his school van-
dalized and his pupils gone. Finally, he moved his family into New York City
and remained there throughout the war.

Another refugee was the Reverend Myles Cooper. In August, according to
Thomas Jones, "a mob, or rather a select party of republicans," gathered at a
pub and "after swallowing a proper dose of Madeira, set off about midnight
with the full design of seizing the Rev. Dr. Cooper, then President of King's
College, in his bed, of shaving his head, cutting off his ears, slitting his nose,
stripping him naked, and turning him adrift. . . ." Luckily, one of Cooper's
students overheard these threats, raced off on a shortcut to the college, and
warned the president. He was just in time: Cooper threw on some clothes and
crawled out a rear window just as the mob entered the front door. He
escaped, half-dressed, over the college fence, took refuge in a friend's house,
and the following night was conveyed to the *Kingfisher* in the harbor. Two
weeks later he sailed to England aboard the *Exeter*. In a tribute to his friend
Cooper, Jones commented on his love of good company, adding, "He loved
God, honoured his King, esteemed his friends, and hated rebellion." Thanks
to Cooper's extreme unpopularity, however, the college was unfairly believed
to sympathize with his views and the Committee of Safety demanded that it
cease operations. The buildings were surrendered for military purposes, and
the library and scientific apparatus dispersed.

When letters from another loyalist to the clergyman Samuel Auchmuty
were intercepted and published, resulting in threats to Auchmuty, a New
Yorker wrote to a friend in London, saying, "Our Worthy and Reverend Pastor, DOCTOR FAT-DUCKS (the name A——y goes by, from his having a
particular relish for those birds, when well-dressed and in high perfection),
hath been secreted on Staten Island for some weeks past. . . . He is at present
sequestered in his own house, and as he affects to be very sorry for his
ungrateful conduct, it is probable he may escape the tar and feathers."

Colden wrote a separate letter to Dartmouth about Isaac Wilkins, a member of the Assembly who represented Westchester and "opposed Congresses
and Committees, and all their Plans of Violent Resistance," as a consequence
of which he was the target of deep resentment. The people's rage against him
ran so high, Colden said, that "his situation is really dangerous and he was
very soon obliged to seek security last Evening by flying from his House and
Family." An inflammatory broadside had been posted on street corners, offering a reward for apprehending Wilkins so he could be sent to a prison camp
in Massachusetts:

STOP HIM! STOP HIM! STOP HIM!
One Hundred Pounds Lawful Money Reward!
A Wolf in Sheep's Clothing!
A TRAITOR!

Wilkins sailed on the packet, but he differed from his fellow passengers in that he left behind a letter, published in Rivington's *Gazetteer* of May 11, explaining his reasons for abandoning his homeland.

"My Countrymen," he began, "Before I leave America, the land I love, and in which is contained every thing that is valuable and dear to me, my wife, my children, my friends, and property; permit me to make a short and faithful declaration, which I am induced to do neither through fear, nor a consciousness of having acted wrong."

All he had done or said during the unnatural dispute between Great Britain and her colonies "proceeded from an honest intention of serving my country." Her welfare and prosperity were paramount in his thoughts; they would remain so when he was in England; and he prayed to God that Britain and America would soon be reunited and continue "a free, a virtuous, and happy nation to the end of time."

"I leave America, and every endearing connection," he wrote, voicing the feelings of many a loyalist, "because I will not raise my hand against my Sovereign—nor will I draw my sword against my Country; when I can conscienciously draw it in her favour, my life shall be chearfully devoted to her service."

Andrew Elliot, collector of customs for the port of New York, had as much reason for alarm as most other loyalists, but he tended to be philosophical and fairly relaxed about his situation. Writing his brother, Sir Gilbert Elliot, in England, he reported that the situation in New York was the same as in other colonies and would be even if it had twice as many "Friends to Government." Some seventeen hundred Connecticut men were camped about three hundred yards from his house, and "They are a Civil quiet sett, very ignorant, awckward, lazy, well-looking young men, they trample down my ground but do no other meschief altho under no sort of command." They had no more than a "Country Education," he added, but he hoped they would not stay in town long enough to improve their minds. They had come to keep the Tories in order, he had been told, but he didn't see how they could be kept long in a camp. "I'm very Civil to them, give them milk & Greens &c, & divert myself with them. Three weeks ago I trembled at their name &

woud still have done so had I, like many, run off with my Family. I'm the only one in the Neighbourhood that stayd." Having seen these lads and gotten to know them, he decided that others must be the same. They are really handsome men, he observed, and were probably courageous, but their total lack of subordination must make them bad soldiers. He longed for the day when matters were happily settled and hoped that Congress would come up with a solution to the dilemma.

In contrast to New York City, in areas where Tories greatly outnumbered patriots, the latter were having a tough time of it. Charles Pettit, a merchant in Amboy, New Jersey, who also had a job with the provincial government, realized that his sentiments were so different from those of his neighbors that he avoided socializing with them whenever possible and had no one with whom to share his anxieties. He had been told that a person with his political views had no business holding any government office and fully expected that he would be forced to resign. He was beginning to think he was "in almost the only spot of Ground in America where a Friend to American Liberty is a disgraceful character." But he added that his situation stiffened his resolve.*

Gouverneur Morris and Robert Morris, by Charles Willson Peale. *Pennsylvania Academy of the Fine Arts.*

*Pettit later served as aide to William Livingston and as assistant quartermaster general.

As people began taking sides, not only did friends and business acquaintances find themselves opposed to each other, but families were driven apart, their loyalties divided. Perhaps the most prominent example was the break between Benjamin Franklin and his natural son William, governor of New Jersey. In the case of the Livingston family, three brothers of Robert, third lord of the manor, were active patriots, as was he, but his brother John was a loyalist. Philip and William Livingston were both members of the Continental Congress, and Philip signed the Declaration of Independence.

The Morris family of the two-thousand-acre Morrisania was another sad example of a divided household. Lewis Morris, third lord of the manor, was a delegate to the Continental Congress and a brigadier general of the Westchester County militia, and in 1776, while British warships were within cannon range of his home, he signed the Declaration of Independence. His half brother Gouverneur was another distinguished Whig. Their sister Isabella, however, married Isaac Wilkins, and their mother was a staunch loyalist who remained within British lines during the war. Three sons of Lewis served in the Continental Army, while his brother Staats was a British officer and member of Parliament.

26

Full Exertion of Great Force

On Saturday, the day after the *Harriet* sailed down the bay carrying the handful of heartsick, worried loyalist refugees to England, a large crowd of the "principal gentlemen" of New York rode a few miles out of town in carriages and on horseback to greet New England's delegates to the Second Continental Congress, who were en route to Philadelphia. These triumphant arrivals included John Hancock, Thomas Cushing, Robert Treat Paine, and Samuel Adams of Massachusetts Bay and Eliphalet Dyer, Roger Sherman, and Silas Deane of Connecticut, and the welcome they received testified to the support Congress had from the people of New York. Not until Sunday evening was John Hancock able to write his betrothed, Miss Dorothy Quincy, and tell her about the exciting events of the past thirty-six hours.

He had arrived at King's Bridge, he said, shortly before three in the afternoon, to find the other delegates and the New York gentlemen waiting for him. Off they went, the egotist Hancock wrote, with "the Carriage of your humble servant, of course, being first in the Procession." Within three miles of the city a grenadier company and the New York militia met them—a thousand men under arms plus thousands of civilians on foot, "the Roads fill'd with people, and the greatest Cloud of dust I ever saw." When they got within a mile of the city, Hancock's carriage was stopped and a group of men carrying harnesses began to take the horses out of their traces so they could pull his carriage themselves. Deeply embarrassed and "not being fond of such Parade," Hancock talked them out of this, but farther along the same thing happened and only after he asked "the Leading Gentlemen" in the procession to intercede for him was he able to travel on, drawn by his horses, "amidst the Acclamations of Thousands," to Fraunces Tavern. Despite their fatigue, the delegates were obliged to stay up till eleven that evening talking with visitors, when they finally went "to Capt. Sears's (the King here) and lodged." Hancock's dear Dolly was not to worry: the grenadier company would be under arms during his stay in New York; they had posted a guard "Night and Day at our Doors," and when they crossed at the ferry a guard would accompany them. "I cant think they will dare to attack us," he assured her, though it was not exactly clear who "they" might be.

On Sunday, June 25, the city's divided loyalties were revealed for all to see. For on that day George Washington, who had been named commander in chief of the new Continental Army on June 15, was scheduled to pass through town en route from Philadelphia to Cambridge, Massachusetts, where he was to assume command. At the same time—indeed, quite possibly at the same hour—William Tryon, who had spent the past fourteen months in England, was returning to his post as royal governor of the province. In the words of William Smith, it was a "Singular Event." The city's dilemma was acute not only because of the expected conjunction of these two stars, but also because New York was so small that it couldn't possibly handle simultaneously two very important receptions, accompanied by parades, the gathering of dignitaries, speeches, an honor guard of soldiers, and all the ceremonial niceties that would normally be lavished on either one of these gentlemen.

Washington had been to New York fairly recently, when he brought his stepson to King's College, but that was a brief visit and he was known only to a few of the residents. So everyone—friend or foe of the Continental cause—was eager to see the man who was likely to play a huge role in their destinies.

Tryon was something of an enigma. He had not wanted to be governor of New York—in fact, he had no particular wish to be in America. His ambition was to get an important military post. But despite that, he had done a good job as chief administrator of the province and was then and now very popular. Poor health had taken him home to England, and he had returned to the colonies only because he was ordered to do so, and it is hard to imagine that he had much enthusiasm for what lay ahead. Somewhat curiously, in August the king promoted him to be a major in the 1st Regiment of Foot Guards, which would have given Tryon a way out of his predicament, but he did not take it, probably because he knew Dartmouth wanted him in New York as governor.

The Assembly, wanting to do right by both distinguished visitors, decided to hold Washington's welcome party uptown and the reception for Tryon downtown, and in order to achieve this goal dispatched a four-man committee to meet Washington and his party before they crossed the North River and steer them beyond Paulus Hook Ferry to the Hoboken Ferry, which would deposit them about a mile above the town. In a masterly compromise they ordered Colonel Lasher to send one of his battalion's ten companies to meet Washington and another the incoming governor, while the other eight companies held themselves ready "to receive either the general or the Governor Tryon, whichever shall first arrive."

Now Washington was traveling with two major generals—Charles Lee and Philip Schuyler—several aides, servants, and a uniformed company of Philadelphia Light Horse as escorts, so it was quite a cavalcade. Fortunately, Tryon got word of the situation while still aboard the *Juliana,* in the harbor, and tactfully postponed the proposed time of his landing from 4 to 8 P.M.

Crossing the Hudson, Washington could see the elegant homes distributed along the river's edge, fronted by well-tended lawns and gardens, and at one of them a large collection of milling people that looked for all the world like the crowd at a country fair or racetrack, figures in bright costumes and uniforms, men on horseback, bands playing. When the general stepped ashore, he noticed how eager the sober welcoming committee seemed to be to complete the opening ceremonies, and when he was taken inside Leonard Lispenard's handsome mansion a few hundred yards from the ferry landing, he discovered why. Someone handed him a sealed dispatch from the Massachusetts Provincial Congress, addressed to John Hancock of the Continental Congress, and urged him to open it. The New York committeemen assumed it to be an accurate account of the fighting on Charlestown Neck a week earlier, and since only fragmentary reports had been received to date, expressed the opinion that this might affect the general's plans. Reluctantly, since it was Hancock's mail, Washington broke the seal and read.

A bloody battle had in fact occurred on "a small hill, south of Bunker's Hill," where the Americans had built a small redoubt and repulsed two frontal British attacks before they ran out of ammunition and were driven from their little fort. The town of Charlestown had been "laid in ashes" and Breed's Hill, Bunker Hill, and the whole peninsula were in the hands of the enemy. The American loss was sixty or seventy killed and missing, with perhaps a hundred wounded. The only bright spot was that "The loss of the enemy is doubtless great"—which indeed it proved to be. Equally bad was the news that Massachusetts had little gunpowder left, prompting the New Yorkers to say that they had shipped a thousand pounds of powder—almost all they had—to Massachusetts three days earlier. This meant that New York's continued existence depended on whether or not the commanding officer of the *Asia* decided to level the city with his sixty-four guns and ample stores of powder and shot.

After a round of speeches and a heavy dinner at Lispenard's, the parade formed up and began the march into town—the New York companies in the lead, followed by members of the Provincial Congress, the major generals, then Washington, in his blue uniform with a purple sash, his hat with a fancy plume. After him came the Philadelphia Light Horse and the cheering crowd, more of them, it was said, than had ever assembled in town—and noisier. Janet Livingston, daughter of the Judge and wife of General Richard Montgomery, said that "the whole town was in a state of commotion. All the militia was paraded, bells ringing, drums beating." Quite a different view was expressed by Thomas Jones, who remembered with sour distaste "the repeated shouts and huzzas of the seditious and rebellious multitude" and the "tumultuous and ridiculous" behavior of the marchers. The parade finally disbanded at Hull's Tavern—the best hotel in the city, run by a man named George Burns—and Washington retired to his room at almost the same moment William Tryon came up the steps onto the wharf at the foot of Broad Street, a few blocks away, and was greeted by a respectful crowd.

While at sea the *Juliana* had been hailed by a ship from Maryland and given news of the fighting at Lexington and Concord, so Tryon was aware that hostilities had begun. William Smith noticed that he appeared grave and said little as he walked, followed by an enthusiastic crowd (many of whom had hurried over after honoring Washington), up Broad Street and on to the home of Hugh Wallace, a councillor, where he was to stay. After he had eaten, he received callers, one of whom was Oliver DeLancey, described by Smith as "neglected & sullen at Times & vexed," humming a tune as he always did when in a vile temper and unable to speak his mind freely. The odd aspect of this meeting was that DeLancey, as a member of the Council, had quarreled frequently and heatedly with the governor, who—when he first arrived in New York—made it clear that he intended to govern the province himself, without taking orders from the powerful DeLancey family. So it was interesting, to say the least, that DeLancey should humble himself now and pay his respects (he had pointedly stayed at home, rather than seeing him off, when Tryon departed for England). Obviously, a drastic change in the political climate had induced DeLancey to make his peace with the governor.

The arrival of Tryon presented Washington with a problem. If the governor were to take any action, military or otherwise, that threatened the patriot cause, what was to be done? Here Washington turned to Philip Schuyler, who was not only a great landowner in the province, but an important political figure and a man with twenty years of military experience, who was to remain in the divided city and "take command of all the troops destined for the New York department." Schuyler was plagued with a frail constitution, but he had a tough, aristocratic, no-nonsense look about him. He was also one of the most conservative of patriots—a man whose actions were likely to offend only the most reactionary Tories. On the other hand, he had a notoriously hot temper, which could create grave problems in this matter; Tryon had a lot of friends, and precipitate action might alienate them and damage the patriot cause.

To Schuyler, Washington gave his first orders as commander in chief. Recognizing the possibility that the governor might begin to arm the loyalists, Schuyler might have to arrest him. This, clearly, was "quite a new thing and of exceeding great importance," and Schuyler must consult Congress before taking such action. If Congress was not in session, however, Schuyler should not hesitate to take the necessary action on his own. Certain matters required swift decisions and action, and in such cases Washington wanted no delay.

Whether Washington gave any thought at this time to the risks he faced is impossible to know, but he was certainly conscious that his position obliged him to make decisions that put him in grave jeopardy. Like other prominent patriot leaders—even more than most of them—he was in danger of losing a great deal more than his property or his freedom. His uncertain future held the probability of death at the hands of the hangman, for by his actions he would be judged a traitor.

On the following morning, Isaac Low and William Morris called on Washington, saying that the Provincial Congress wished to present an address and asking what would be the most convenient time for him to receive it. Much as the general wanted to leave for Cambridge, he could hardly refuse this, and members of the Provincial Congress showed up at the appointed hour of two-thirty and handed him a courteous, neatly crafted message that said, in effect, that as loyal subjects of His Majesty they deplored the calamities of the divided empire but rejoiced in the appointment of Washington. They wished him every success "in the glorious struggle for American liberty" and were certain that when the contest was decided by an accommodation with the mother country, Washington would "cheerfully resign . . . and reassume the character of our worthiest citizen."

Washington was prepared. In equally gracious terms he expressed gratitude for their consideration, said that he and his associates would bend every effort to reestablish peace and harmony with the mother country, and then spoke the words they wanted to hear: "When we assumed the soldier, we did not lay aside the citizen; and we shall most sincerely rejoice with you in that happy hour when the establishment of American liberty, upon the most firm and solid foundations, shall enable us to return to our private stations in the bosom of a free, peaceful and happy country."

It was after three o'clock when he and his fellow officers, the New York militia companies, and the Philadelphia Light Horse got underway at last. They rode to King's Bridge and spent the night there before leaving for Connecticut and points north and east. Six days later, on July 2, Washington arrived in Watertown, Massachusetts, to assume command of the Continental Army.

Some time after the commander in chief's departure, Philip Schuyler was staying at the home of his friend William Smith, Jr., while making preparations for an expedition against Canada. According to Thomas Jones, Schuyler was "under great obligations to Mr. Tryon," and since the governor was renting a house directly across the street, the American general thought it proper to call on him. But Schuyler, Jones continued, "had the impudence to dress himself in the regimentals of rebellion, go to the Governor's, and send in word that *'General'* Schuyler would be glad to see him. The Governor, with his usual spirit, returned for answer *that he knew no such man*," and that was that.

In the city, life went on, but it was increasingly apparent that the people had arrived at a fork in the road and each individual had to decide which route to follow. The radicals among them took a rough, untried track leading to a destination that was impossible to imagine, much less discern. The conservatives followed the familiar, well-trodden route lined with known, comforting landmarks. As the travelers moved along, the roads diverged farther and farther, and the radicals had to find their way through *terra incognita* by trial and error, trying to unravel the mysteries of running the city's affairs at the same time they were expected to create an army from scratch. Conservatives, who abhorred the Whigs' desire for equality, tried to hew to the old ways, met, discussed, argued, and met again, only to find that there was little point to it, that they were powerless, struggling in a vacuum, going nowhere, and realizing at last their incapacity to accomplish anything at all.

Recognizing its urgent need for a military force in being, Congress had told each colony how many men it was to contribute to the Continental Army. New York's quota was four regiments, each to have four companies of "able-bodied and sober men of good reputation," making a total of about three thousand officers and men to be raised. Immediately the difficulties became apparent. Few men were qualified to be officers. Few men wanted to volunteer for service in the ranks. And since few of what Colden persisted in calling "the better sort" expressed much interest in becoming officers, most ranking members of New York's regiments were radicals—men like Alexander McDougall, a newly appointed colonel, and two of his sons.

Fighting almost certainly lay ahead, and while no one had an inkling how long it would last, it seemed certain that the trouble that had begun in Massachusetts would come to New York before long. Yet even a cursory glance revealed that just about everything needed in a war was lacking—trained soldiers, uniforms, cannon, muskets, bayonets, gunpowder and balls for the guns, money to pay the troops, tents to shelter them, and blankets to cover them. The list was long, and every week's newspapers produced evidence of the efforts being made to remedy the deficiencies. In the meantime the *Asia* and other naval vessels were turning away boats carrying iron or any cargo that might be useful to rebel troops; only those loaded with food were permitted to land.

Along with the usual advertisements for clean flaxseed and Irish linens, the availability of a wet nurse "with a good breast of young milk," a pair of handsome dark bay horses, and a twenty-six-year-old Negro woman who could do all kinds of housework, plus her female child twelve months old, appeared announcements by the Provincial Congress that since no gunpowder was available in the city and almost none in the colony, a bounty would be paid for every hundredweight of powder manufactured in the province, and a £20 bonus for every one hundred good muskets. Inhabitants were reminded to furnish themselves with arms and ammunition and to "perfect themselves in the military art." One S. Patrick informed the public that he had a furnace and could cast iron balls of any given dimension for £15 per ton, delivered anywhere on the North River. A committee was appointed to find someone interested in casting brass field pieces. McDougall informed the Provincial Congress that since tents and other necessities for his men were lacking, he proposed to lodge them in the city's barracks for now. Calls went out for blacksmiths to make gun barrels, bayonets, and iron ramrods; good locksmiths to make gunlocks; and ten shillings were offered to every man who joined up and brought his own musket. On August 8 the first contingent of McDougall's troops sailed for Fort Ticonderoga, followed two weeks later by a second lot, but the colonel remained in New York, presumably busily recruiting.

Residents began noticing that all the young men seemed to have disappeared from the city, and since almost none of these boys had any knowledge of warfare, let alone the wilderness to which they were bound, it remained to be seen how they would cope with fighting on the frontier.

The Continental Congress had resolved that the Hudson River highlands—between Peekskill and West Point—must be fortified to deny the British navy passage up the river, and New York was given the task of executing this. Elaborate plans were discussed by the Provincial Congress, and when the subject of cannon came up, Isaac Sears reminded members that twenty-one guns were sitting idle in front of Fort George and suggested that these be removed and taken upriver. A vote was taken and Sears's motion passed. These were British naval cannon of various sizes, each one weighing a ton or more, mounted on small wheels and not made for overland travel, but on the night of August 23 a good many enthusiastic citizens and men from Lasher's battalion and John Lamb's artillery company dragged them off the ramparts and began pushing and tugging them up Broadway. As it happened, Governor Tryon had heard about the plan and told Captain Vandeput, who dispatched a boat with sailors to keep a lookout. The action onshore created a good deal of commotion, and about midnight the boat pulled close to shore and fired a shot at Lasher's men, who were protecting those who were removing the guns.

Lasher's men returned the fire, one man on the boat was killed and others wounded, and after the boat pulled out of range, heading for the *Asia,* the man-of-war fired several rounds. No one onshore was hurt, but residents who had no idea what was happening panicked. Some ran to their cellars, others came out into the streets to see what was going on, still others packed precious belongings and headed for the ferries. Strangely, the firing stopped. As Vandeput later explained to city officials, it was his duty to protect the king's property and he had fired those shots as a warning. Several hours passed and suddenly, about 3 A.M., the *Asia* let go again, this time with a full broadside, thirty-two guns that seemed to shake the city to its foundations and lit up the night sky. This time the roofs of Roger Morris's house and Fraunces Tavern were hit, each with an eighteen-pound ball, and other houses and outbuildings in the vicinity of the Battery were damaged. Vandeput realized that his initial warning had not stopped the removal of the guns, but the broadside did. A diarist recorded that the city was thrown into the greatest consternation and distress, "And next day Multitudes of Women and Children were removed."

Among the distressed was Governor William Tryon, who had been visiting friends on Long Island and was appalled to see terrified refugees fleeing the city when he came rushing back to town. Five days later the exodus still went on. Pastor William Shewkirk recorded in his diary, "The Moving out of the Town continues, & the City looks in some Streets as if the Plague had been in it, so many Houses being shut up." The Provincial Congress was chagrined at the effect of its decision to remove the guns and embarrassed by the sight of eleven cannon sitting abandoned on the Commons. For his part, Governor Tryon recognized the difficulty of getting the guns back to the fort and agreed that they could be left where they were as long as they were moved no farther.

For most of the spring, James Rivington, bookseller and publisher of the *Gazetteer,* had been in hot water, thanks to his outspoken brand of loyalism. Angry Whigs in Newport, Rhode Island, where his paper circulated, resolved to have no further dealings or correspondence with him, and several communities in New Jersey and upstate New York followed suit. The fact that he had been appointed His Majesty's Printer for the Province of New York—an honor that carried with it an annual stipend of £100—did nothing to endear him to the republicans. In March the Continental Association called Rivington to task for printing a false and groundless statement about the committee, and when asked what authority he had for his comment, the printer replied that it was common knowledge—an admission the committee found unacceptable.

A month later the *Gazetteer* published a story reporting that "some of the lower class inhabitants" of New Brunswick, New Jersey, had hung up an effigy of Rivington, causing the editor to state that his only mistake was to exercise freedom of the press. Several weeks afterward he printed an apology for giving offense to many of his readers: his concept of a free press and his duty as a printer were responsible, he said, but he would henceforth be more careful. That apology was not enough for his enemies, however, and on the night of May 10, the mob, whose plan to capture the Reverend Myles Cooper had been foiled, came after Rivington, who was rescued by a number of his friends and taken aboard the *Kingfisher* in the harbor, where he remained for a month, editing his paper from his quarters aboard the ship.

From the *Kingfisher* he sent an apology to the Continental Congress, stating that he had always tried to do his duty as a servant of the public and had opened the pages of his paper to all parties, with the result that "many of the best pieces that have been written . . . in favour of the American claims" had been published by him. (Richard Henry Lee of Virginia was sufficiently impressed by Rivington's penitential attitude to suggest that he be forgiven.)

On June 7 the New York Provincial Congress, satisfied that he would mend his ways, resolved that he could return safely to home and family and was not to be molested again. And there Rivington's trials might have ended, had it not been for Isaac Sears.

The *Gazetteer* was the leading paper in New York. It appeared every Thursday and had a circulation exceeding 3,500—more than any of its competitors. It contained more news (especially foreign) and was well-written, amusing, and typographically superior to other local journals. Editorially, it was pro-British and against the new association, which was why patriots considered it an abomination. Rivington was well aware that his livelihood depended on the goodwill of New Yorkers, who paid for advertising, circulation, job printing, and the sale of books and pamphlets from his ground-floor bookstore in a building at the corner of Wall and Queen streets, and that accounted for his several public apologies.

Rivington was popular, amusing, the life of many a New York party, and something of a clown when he was in his cups delivering recitations to admiring audiences. Unfortunately for him, he had chosen Isaac Sears as a favorite target for his humorous insults in print, calling him a "laughing stock of the whole town" and making fun of his big ears.

Now Sears was not the man to take criticism of this sort. He was tough, he was something of a bully, and for a decade and more he had been the most visible political agitator in the province—a man feared and despised by many. Recently, however, he had lost some of the prestige his pugnacity had brought him, and he was almost certainly conscious that some of his former colleagues were now embarrassed by his strongarm tactics. Recently elected to the Provincial Congress in New York, Sears suddenly appeared in Connecticut, recruited some horsemen in New Haven, and on November 22 led them to Westchester, where he planned to kidnap the Reverend Samuel Seabury. The clergyman was not at home, but that did not deter Sears and his band from terrorizing his wife and children, threatening one of the girls with a bayonet when she refused to reveal her father's whereabouts, breaking furniture, and rifling Seabury's papers for incriminating evidence that he was "A Westchester Farmer." After pilfering some loose change, the minister's beaver hat and silver-handled whip, and two silver spoons, they rode off to his school and took him prisoner.

After spending the night in Westchester, they took the Post Road to Kings Bridge, where some hundred or more New Yorkers—most of them regulars in Sears's mob activities, Liberty Boys, sailors, and drinking companions—awaited them. From here they followed the Post Road to Bowery Road and on to Queen Street, which took them to Rivington's printing establishment, which they proceeded to destroy. They smashed the presses, trashed his files, and filled crocus sacks with his precious imported fonts of type, which were irreplaceable in America. All this while a crowd looked on, cheering from time to time as the *Gazetteer's* existence came to a violent end. Whether anyone wondered why a New York legislator should lead a band of Connecticut soldiers to prey on a New York business is not known, but several patriot leaders were appalled by Sears's actions. As John Jay put it, "The late valorous Expedition against Rivington, gives me Pain. I feel for the Honor of the colony. . . ."

Rivington, unable to replace the type Sears's men had taken and thrown away, and unable to afford new printing presses, sailed for England in January of 1776, unsung by any of the city's remaining newspapers—all of them advocates of the patriot cause, and none of them the equal of the *Gazetteer*.

The New York Assembly had not convened since March, when it sent off its petitions to the king and Parliament and promptly adjourned. In its place, in City Hall, sat members of the Provincial Congress, an earnest, hardworking lot of men who probably didn't realize how powerful they were at this juncture. Certainly Governor Tryon thought they were forceful, and was inclined to think that they had usurped his power.

Although the giant *Asia* and her sixty-four guns loomed menacingly over the harbor, most British troops had been withdrawn from the city, and Governor Tryon was understandably concerned about his own security. Isaac Sears revealed to Philip Schuyler that he planned to take Tryon prisoner and jail him in Connecticut. Sears had talked with some members of the Continental Congress about this and they were all for it, but Schuyler protested that the scheme was "rash and unjustifiable," and added that he had written orders from General Washington against any such action. Members of the Provincial Congress heard about the scheme, but most refused to believe it: the governor was a widely admired man who seemed unlikely to throw his weight around or upset the fragile political balance of the city. While Schuyler did not inform Tryon of Sears's plan, the governor got wind of the plot—someone said from James Duane's butler, who had once worked for him—and ordered Captain Vandeput of the *Asia* to open fire on the city if he was seized. Tryon's gout was acting up, he was increasingly testy, and he informed Mayor Whitehead Hicks that he contemplated leaving his quarters and would seek safety on board one of His Majesty's ships in the harbor.

Hicks and the other magistrates were firmly opposed to Tryon's removal, but the governor replied that it was his duty in this alarming situation not to remain onshore unless city officials could guarantee him protection. Isaac Low, enlisted to persuade the governor to stay put, told the magistrates that neither he nor other councillors had the least fear of danger to his person or property.

Tryon found that assurance insufficient, left the city on October 19, and first boarded the *Halifax* and later the *Duchess of Gordon*. The latter was a merchant ship that afforded Tryon several advantages: it was far more comfortable than a man-of-war, and unlike a naval vessel, it permitted him to receive visitors and carry on what passed for an office. He even entertained friends at dinner parties, and surprisingly the Provincial Congress had no objection to any of these arrangements, although republican members must have known that certain of Tryon's guests would supply him with information that might better have been kept from him.

In the meantime, the governor's letters to Dartmouth could have afforded that gentleman small comfort. "Oceans of blood may be spilt," Tryon wrote, "but in my opinion America will never [accept] Parliamentary taxation." America's hatred of being taxed was at the heart of its resistance—a feeling shared even by loyalists who were now torn between "dread of Parliamentary taxation and the tyranny of their present masters."

The city had changed in so many ways. Tempers were quick to flare in the charged atmosphere. Tension mounted every day with reports of open hostility within and without the town. Arguments that once were no more than heated exchanges now had an ugly, threatening edge to them, with business rivals often at sword's point, and lurking in the background was the ever-present, dreaded specter of the mob.

No matter how many Americans might profess loyalty to the crown, it had become clear that a revolution had, in fact, already begun. A powerful current now, it had begun as a trickle that had been set in motion and slowly gathered strength since 1760—not overtly, but in the hearts and minds of people who finally came to believe that they had been betrayed. The reasons were many, but most people considered that they had been shaped in London, in the blinding stupidity of a series of administrations with utter disregard for the needs and wishes of the colonists, their mulish determination to exact revenue from Americans without giving them any say in why or how it was to be spent, their refusal to listen to those like Benjamin Franklin or William Smith or a host of others who wanted desperately to preserve the empire with America in a partnership—not a subservient—role.

Finally, of course, there was the king. As he would declare the following spring, in a speech closing Parliament, no price was too much to pay for preserving the rights and interests of the whole empire. But then, in the next two sentences, he revealed the rationale for an unrelenting attitude and an unwillingness to grant any of those rights to certain members of the empire. He continued to hope that "my rebellious subjects," whom he clearly regarded as naughty, wayward children, "may be awakened to a sense of their errors" and voluntarily return to their duty. Only in that manner could they bring about his favorite wish, which was the restoration of harmony. But if a due submission was not forthcoming, "I trust that I shall be able, under the blessing of Providence, to effectuate it by a full exertion of the great force with which you have intrusted me." The extended hand wore a glove, and within it was a fist of iron.

To a businessman of some substance, a large landowner, a person of consequence in some field, whatever it might be, loyalty to the mother country was an insurance policy, in addition to less tangible advantages. It meant security—knowledge that his investments in goods or property or specie were safe. The laws of the country were there to protect him and his family and his fortune.

But loyalty went beyond that for many of these people. It was something intangible, not easy to express in words—a feeling in the heart that they and their forebears had had for generations. The tradition of loyalty, or fealty, had existed for centuries, and the idea that kings ruled with divine approval was a persistent one. The Church of England, moreover, taught that loyalty to George III was a matter of religious duty. It was true that the man who wore the crown, for all of his robes trimmed in ermine, the jewels and other trappings of royalty, was in the flesh a rather unattractive-looking, pop-eyed man whose immediate predecessors—his Hanoverian grandfather and great-grandfather—cared little for their adoptive land. Yet that was beside the point. Some thousands of transplanted Englishmen revered George III for the simple reason that he personified the tribal leader of old, whom it was your duty to follow with no questions asked, if the tribe was to survive and prosper. The origins of the concept might be lost in the shrouds of time, but it remained a powerful and vital goad, nonetheless.

Everyone had heard the dark joke that made the rounds during the winter just past, about a man at the dinner table inquiring of another guest: "Pray, what is a Tory?" To which the answer was: "A Tory is a thing whose head is in England and its body in America and its neck ought to be stretched."

By no means did all Tories have a feeling approaching reverence for their king. There were, after all, many hundreds of civil servants, placemen—toadies, many of them—the receivers of favors large and small, for whom the king was simply the man at the top of the pyramid, who had the power to bestow the blessings of the caste system on you and yours, even the power to ennoble you at the touch of a sword.

The loyalists, whatever their rank, had everything to lose—and quite possibly nothing to gain—if they elected to stay in New York with a wait-and-see attitude. Yet many who did so were confident that the American rebels couldn't possibly stand up against what was considered the most powerful armed force in the world. True, the king's soldiers were greatly outnumbered now, but more were on the way, and the rebels were largely untrained, undisciplined, unskilled in the rudiments of European-style warfare, and almost totally lacking in money and other resources, arms, and experienced leaders.

More to the point, few loyalists were willing to sacrifice all the capital they had built up in America—their position in the community, their home, their land, their business connections—for the likes of an Isaac Sears, or worse. Those who fled out of fear for one reason or another were not frightened by such people as James Duane, John Jay, or the Livingstons, although they may well have been outraged by their foolhardy undermining of government and have considered them deluded or misguided or even traitorous, at worst. They undoubtedly worried about Sears and McDougall for the trouble they might brew. But it was the followers of those two who terrified them—the brutish mobs, the rabble from the docks and city slums, bristling with envy and hatred of all forms and degrees of wealth, the elegant homes and fancy clothes, the aristocratic manners, the jewelry and walking sticks, the snobbery. It took very little imagination to guess what the "lower sort" might do if they got out of control, for evidence was already at hand.

Instances had been reported—had even been seen by some—of the tar-and-feather treatment—the unspeakable, humiliating agony of having your clothes torn off and then being slathered with hot tar from head to foot and covered with feathers before being forced to straddle a fence rail while ridden around town, jeered and pelted with sticks and stones by a howling mob.

Already in 1775 some Tories were in hiding, concealed in swamps, forest, barns, hollow trees—some of them in the pine barrens, some sailing by day in small boats in Long Island Sound, landing at night to sleep in the woods. The former speaker of the Assembly John Harris Cruger, who had written James Duane in July of 1775 assuring him that he was "a *warm & sincere friend* to the liberties of all America," and that "the greatest interruption to the restoration of harmony in the place is the old private politics," was, later that hot summer, forced to hide out in a hay mow in a farmer's barn for three weeks with Jacob Walton. Augustus Van Cortlandt hid in the cow barn of a Dutch loyalist, who brought him food and drink. According to Thomas Jones, "The Loyalists were pursued like wolves and bears, from swamp to swamp, from one hill to another, from dale to dale, and from one copse of wood to another." Many were captured, some wounded, and a few murdered, and prisoners were taken without a hearing to different parts of New England where, if they were not jailed, they were released on parole and restricted to certain areas, where they suffered constant abuse and insults.

As time went on, more and more loyalists learned to their dismay that New York was no safe place to be, even after British forces occupied it in 1776. One night in November of 1777 a band of rebels, bent on vengeance, crossed the Hudson from New Jersey and broke into Oliver DeLancey's home at Bloomingdale, about seven miles north of the city. While they were plundering the house they insulted Mrs. DeLancey, who ran out into the night and hid under the stoop until the raiders left the house. The men hit her sixteen-year-old daughter, Charlotte, several times with a musket, set fire to the house, and tried to wrap Charlotte's friend Elizabeth Floyd in a burning sheet. Fortunately she broke loose, but as she ran down the stairs she narrowly avoided a flaming sheet thrown at her by one of the rebels. The two girls, dressed only in nightgowns, ran through the fields to a swamp, where they remained until the next morning, up to their knees in mud and water. There they were discovered by friends and taken to the nearby home of Charles Apthorp. Somehow Charlotte had managed to pick up her brother Stephen's infant child and carry it with her. Both girls had lacerated feet and legs from the briers, and Miss Floyd was unable to walk for three weeks.

An older daughter, the wife of John Harris Cruger, also escaped and tried to reach a British encampment about two miles away, in order to alert the troops, but in her confusion and fright she lost her way and wandered off in the wrong direction. Finally the exhausted, distraught woman reached a house about seven miles from her father's place and was taken in by a farm family. Her experience, and that of her mother and sisters, was the ultimate degradation of a family that had led New York for two decades.

On June 15, 1775, preparing for the worst, Congress had named George Washington commander in chief of the American army. Yet even after the bloody battle for Bunker Hill, fought two days later, the moderates in Congress had enough strength to make a final try for peace, which took the form of a last-ditch petition to the king, an "Olive Branch" proposal. A collaboration between one of New York's delegates, John Jay, and John Dickinson, who drafted the final version, the fiercely debated document assured George III of the American people's attachment to him, expressed hope that harmony would be restored, and urged the king to prevent further hostile actions until a reconciliation could be effected. Benjamin Franklin, who knew the character and temper of George III and his ministers better than any other American, was certain that this appeal was futile. But he did not oppose it, and on July 6, 1775, the petition was adopted and sent off to the king.

Four months later, the Continental Congress had the king's answer. His Majesty George III had refused even to accept the petition, let alone read it or respond. In New York, the Council received from John Pownall, deputy secretary to Lord Dartmouth, a copy of the royal proclamation, dated August 23, 1775, for suppressing sedition and rebellion in America.

There would be no discussion, no negotiation, no reconciliation. The king had made his decision. It was to be war.

EPILOGUE

The outburst of fighting at Lexington and Concord in the spring of 1775 soon became a war in earnest, and in July of the next year General William Howe landed on Staten Island with 9,300 British troops. By the time German and additional British soldiers joined them, the total invasion force swelled to more than thirty thousand.

In late August of 1776, Howe landed two-thirds of his force on Long Island and decisively defeated Washington's men, but he failed to capitalize on his victory when he allowed the trapped rebels to escape. Moving to Manhattan, his army quickly seized Fort Washington on Harlem Heights, took three thousand rebel prisoners, and all of Manhattan Island was in British hands.

General Charles Lee, a former British officer who chose to fight with the Americans, had assessed the daunting task facing the rebels in New York. "What to do with the city, I own, puzzles me," he observed in February of 1776. "It is so encircled with deep navigable waters that whoever commands the sea must command the town." He was right, of course, and since Britain's naval superiority was unchallenged by the Americans, New York remained in enemy hands throughout the war, although almost one-third of the city was destroyed when a disastrous fire broke out on September 21, and, fanned by high winds, consumed so many houses that no one could count them, but the number was estimated at somewhere between five hundred and twelve hundred, plus many public buildings, including Trinity Church.

Peter Van Schaack.
New-York Historical Society.

Thanks to the British army's presence, New York City became a haven for loyalist refugees from elsewhere in the states. When the war ended with Britain's defeat, thousands of them fled to Quebec, Ontario, Nova Scotia, and New Brunswick to begin a new life. Many journeyed to other states, a number settled in Great Britain (though nowhere near as many as emigrated to Canada), and an indeterminate number eventually returned to New York.

From the very outset, the war of the Revolution was also a civil war, cruelly dividing families and friends, and during its course loyalists who lacked the protection of the British army suffered personal indignities, sometimes prison and torture, and the hatred of fellow Americans who had chosen the other side. One factor in that hatred was more personal than political—the age-old divide between the haves and the have-nots, between the privileged few and those who lacked influence or well-placed friends. Particularly in those areas where loyalists were in a minority, Tory-baiting was a popular sport, and a resort to violence was often carried out by rioters who relished their ruthless persecution of the defenseless. Mob action frequently led to outrageous behavior and flagrant disregard of the law. Chief Justice Oliver in Massachusetts found it too hazardous even to attend his brother's funeral, where a mob was chanting and yelling at the gravesite. In his diary he wrote, "never did cannibals thirst stronger for human blood."

You had two competing cultures in the same society at war with each other, and thousands of ordinary, moderate, middle-of-the-road Americans were caught up—many in spite of themselves—in the revolutionary fervor that was sweeping the country, almost like a religious revival, in its power. These people had in common the very real fears and doubts that accompanied their figurative vote for or against that swelling tide. What the consequences of that vote might be, no one could foresee. But the consequences could be terrifying—the potential loss of reputation, friends, family, business, property, even life itself. As time passed, fewer places of refuge were open to the uncertain—to those who honestly saw some merit on both sides of the argument.

Whether a person owed loyalty to king or country was the question that seemed to be at the heart of the division, yet the first allegiance of most loyalists was not to the king, nor to England, but to America. Those in exile continued to think of themselves as Americans, not English or Canadians. Uprooted from home, and some from family as well, those who fled to Britain had to endure the hazards and hideous discomforts of a long sea voyage, only to be confronted with strange new surroundings, straitened means, no occupation, and the sorrow that their children would never know America or have any feeling for the land they loved. Only slowly, as the likelihood of British victory waned, did they begin to comprehend the long-term consequences of exile and their agonizing personal plight.

After the war the British government established a commission that examined 4,118 loyalist claims for restitution and ultimately authorized payment of £3,300,000 to applicants. But the amounts paid seldom came close to the exiles' losses,* and many were forced to live in penury until they finally received payment. Few, if any, were satisfied with the settlements, and some were envious of the amount received by others. John Watts's daughter Ann— Mrs. Archibald Kennedy—wrote to her brother that John Tabor Kempe, onetime attorney general of the province of New York, was "much dissatisfy'd with what Government has done for him," adding that she had no patience with such people. Kempe had lost a fortune, nearly all of it in some 168,000 acres of land, which he valued at £65,656, and for which he was awarded £5,546, plus £1,500 for loss of income, and a pension of £640.

Ann Kennedy argued that if he had remained in New York he would have received nothing—and then "what would his Lands have brought him?" Continuing, she complained, "I think we are much worse off. What remittances do we get? . . . They wont give us a Six pence for what the British troops have

---

*Examples of some large claims were those of Frederick Philipse III, who reckoned his losses at £155,328 and received £51,660; Sir John Johnson, £103,182, received £38,995; General Oliver DeLancey, £78,066, received £23,446.

demolished. I wish our estate had been forfitted. We should then have got as [much as Thomas] Jones, [who] has thirty thousand. . . ." That much, she added, would have given their children good estates "when we are call'd away."

Those who went to England—most of them in greatly reduced circumstances—were dismayed by the high prices of everything. Since a majority of these exiles had no English friends, they stuck together, feeding off gossip and rumors from America, restless and depressed, leading aimless lives, wishing when they died to be buried in the country they loved. Yet it was unavoidable that many would harbor a hatred against Americans for the harsh treatment and persecution they had suffered, particularly those "popular" leaders like Sam Adams and Isaac Sears, whom Judge Samuel Curwen of Salem described as "unprincipled men who run riot against all the laws of justice, truth, and religion."

On October 22, 1779, the New York legislature, sitting at Kingston, in Ulster County, passed "An Act for the Forfeiture and Sale of the Estates of Persons who have adhered to the enemies of this State, and for declaring the Sovereignty of the People of this State, in respect to all Property within the same."

This was the notorious Act of Attainder, by which the estates of certain loyalists were confiscated. A long list of individuals was "hereby . . . convicted and attainted." These unfortunates included such eminent figures as two former governors of the province of New York, the Earl of Dunmore and William Tryon; John Watts and eight other merchants; Oliver DeLancey; John Harris Cruger; the former attorney general John Tabor Kempe; Judge Thomas Jones; Frederick Philipse the elder and the younger; Sir John Johnson; David Colden; Beverly Robinson, his wife, and his son; Roger Morris and his wife; and many others. Fifteen of those named were former governors of King's College.

Their entire estates, real and personal, were forfeited, and they were "for ever banished from this State." Worse yet, if at any time they were found anywhere in New York, they would "suffer death, as in cases of felony, without benefit of clergy." This vengeful statute was enacted only after the sort of fierce arguments and infighting that were characteristic of New York's partisan politics. The document was drafted by John Morin Scott, at the instigation and with the enthusiastic participation of John Jay's brother James, who had old scores to settle with the former King's College governors.

After the bill was passed in the House, one member of the Senate sought reasonably but unsuccessfully to remove the names of those attainted who were "not known to have taken up arms against us, or been guilty of high

Treason." It finally reached the Senate, where it passed by one vote, but was then reviewed and vetoed by a council headed by Robert R. Livingston, Jr. The council declared that it gave powers to the commissioners "which No free State ever entrusted to any Man, or body of Men whatsoever, viz., An absolute and uncontrolled Right to deprive the good Subjects of the State of their Possessions, to turn them and their families out of their Houses, and to oblige them to contend by course of Law for the Inheritance of their Ancestors. And this too, not upon a solemn Trial by Jury (to which the [British] Constitution entitles them) not upon a cool dispassionate Examination of Evidences, not even upon a reasonable presumption. . . ."

All to no avail, as it turned out. Subsequently the bill was passed by both Houses, with no record of the votes pro and con, and then, even more curiously, approved by Livingston's council with no comment.

Even after the preliminary treaty of peace was signed in November 1782, followed by an armistice with Great Britain in January 1783, and even though the articles provided that no future confiscations would be permitted and that former loyalists could travel anywhere in the thirteen states and remain unmolested in their efforts to obtain restitution of their estates without hindrance, local individuals and committees disregarded these terms. Too much envy, hatred, and desire for vengeance was abroad in the land, and the infamous act was put into effect and the confiscation of loyalist estates proceeded. A New York loyalist wrote: "The Rebels breathe the most rancorous and malignant Spirit everywhere. Committees and Associations are formed in every Colony and Resolves passed that no Refugees shall return nor have their Estates restored." All this, he continued, while Congress looked on tamely, lacking either the will or the power to halt this travesty of justice. "In short," he said, "the Mob now reigns as fully and uncontrolled as in the Beginning of our Troubles. . . ."

In every colony but Georgia and New Hampshire, Tories were executed, some without a trial, some by court-martial, some killed by a mob. New York's Provincial Congress decreed the death penalty for anyone who owed allegiance to the state who was convicted of waging war against New York or of adhering to the king or other enemies of the state or giving them comfort. It was a bloodthirsty time: Gouverneur Morris, writing to Alexander Hamilton, called for "a few more executions." Nothing, he said, "can be more efficacious."

One man who disagreed with him was Cadwallader Colden, Jr., who had taken no active part on either side of the controversy, but was nevertheless detained and sent by boat with a number of other prisoners to Kingston.

There, in jail, he befriended one of the several men condemned to death and, while trying to prepare the fellow for what awaited him, wrote to John Jay asking that he delay the execution at least for a few days, to give the poor devil some time with his wife and children. Jay was for several months a member of New York's Committee for Detecting and Defeating Conspiracies, and Colden pleaded with him as an old friend for whom he had a particular regard not to take the lives of his fellow creatures: "Depend upon it," he said, "the Hanging of them will not make one Man Change his Sentements in Your favour, But the Very Reverse." Despite Colden's plea the sentence was carried out.

Peter Van Schaack and John Jay were good friends. They attended King's College together and went on to practice law in New York, where both were members of the Debating Society, which met for four hours every Thursday evening in 1768 to debate controversial issues of the day. That and the Moot, to which they also belonged, were excellent training for young lawyers, and they saw each other frequently at the Social Club, a long-standing group that met at Fraunces Tavern and included Gouverneur Morris, John Watts, Jr., Robert R. Livingston, Jr., and other prominent young blades.

When Van Schaack eloped with Elizabeth Cruger, daughter of the merchant Henry Cruger, in the autumn of 1765, Jay was amused. "Credere Pastores levibus nolite Puellis," he commented to his friend Robert Livingston— "Shepherds, put not your trust in fickle maids." Van Schaack, a punctilious lawyer, had a shepherd's calm, quiet, unassuming manner and did not wear his sentiments on his sleeve. Unfortunately for him, he was one of those people who saw the two sides of a question and often empathized with both, and when he was forced to take a stand on the burning issue of the day he was incapable of making a decision. In ordinary times that might have made no difference, but in late 1776 the newly declared United States were fighting for their lives and anyone who equivocated was suspect. As Van Schaack's son described his father's dilemma, "Although he decidedly condemned the conduct of the Home government, he was yet opposed to taking up arms in opposition to it." As a result, he was ordered to appear in Albany for interrogation by the Committee for Detecting and Defeating Conspiracies. And who should be there as a member of the committee but his old friend John Jay.

When Van Schaack refused, on grounds of conscience, to take the oath of allegiance to the State of New York and fight the British, he was treated as if he were a dangerous threat to the state and was sent to Boston, where numerous men found guilty of disloyalty were incarcerated. Later he was called back for questioning by the Provincial Convention in Kingston and paroled for two years at his home in Kinderhook.

In the early spring of 1776 he lost the sight of his right eye, and shortly thereafter he was elected to membership in the Albany County Committee of Safety, only to be expelled after the first meeting for refusing to sign the association pledging to take up arms against the king. That August his wife became terminally ill with consumption, as tuberculosis was called, and Van Schaack was forbidden to take her to New York for treatment by a well-known English physician. In 1778, after refusing once again to swear allegiance, he was sentenced to perpetual banishment by his former law student Leonard Gansevoort, sent inside British lines, and threatened with death if he returned. Soon afterward he took ship to England, leaving his motherless children behind. His son was about to enter Yale, and Van Schaack told him he hoped he would not come to England—he wanted him to have an American education.

Like many another exile, Van Schaack had few financial resources and requested help from the British government, citing the loss of his property and profession. (He had been disqualified from practicing law for failing to support American independence.) He was granted £100, only to have it reduced to £60 when a Treasury official discovered that he had been living on that paltry amount while in England.

When peace finally came, Van Schaack learned that his old friend John Jay was in Paris and he sent him a cautious note, asking for news. The two had been in touch occasionally during the war, and Jay now replied promptly and warmly to say that while their views had differed, he had never blamed Van Schaack for following his conscience, nor had he ever ceased to be his friend. Not knowing what his financial situation was, Jay generously offered help to him and his family: "While I have a loaf, you and they may freely partake of it. If your circumstances are easy, I rejoice; if not, let me take off their rougher edges."

Money was not what Peter Van Schaack cared about. He wanted only to return to his home in America. Reconciled now to Britain's defeat, he said, "My heart warms whenever our country (I must call it my country) is the subject, and in my separation from it I have dragged at each remove a lengthening chain." He had learned to his sorrow during his time in England that "corruption pervades every channel of power," and he now had no difficulty making up his mind to be a loyal citizen of the new republic.

After nine years of searing hardship and trial, it was 1785 when the ship carrying Peter Van Schaack sailed through the Narrows and into the great beckoning harbor of New York. John Jay was standing on the dock to greet him. He came aboard, took him by the arm, and led him off to call on the governor and chief justice of the state, who were waiting to welcome the exile to his beloved America. Peter Van Schaack was home at last.

PRINCIPAL CHARACTERS

John Adams (1735–1826). A Boston lawyer, he gained prominence as a patriot for his legal arguments against the Stamp Act. A delegate to the First and Second Continental Congresses and initially fearful of separation from England, he came to see it as inevitable and supported the Declaration of Independence in 1776. During the war he served on diplomatic missions in Europe and negotiated, with Benjamin Franklin and John Jay, the Treaty of Paris ending the Revolutionary War. He was the first American minister to Great Britain after the war. He was Washington's vice-president, and after being narrowly elected to the presidency in 1796, he served a single term.

Samuel Adams (1722–1803). A distant cousin of John Adams, he was tax collector in Boston before organizing resistance to British colonial policy. He helped organize the Sons of Liberty and created the first committee of correspondence in Boston in 1772. He was involved in the Boston Tea Party and arranged a controversial publication of letters by Governor Thomas Hutchinson. After running unsuccessfully for the U.S. Congress after the war, he served Massachusetts as lieutenant governor and governor.

*Joseph Allicocke.** New York merchant, perhaps born in Ireland, perhaps of African-American descent. A partner of Isaac Sears, he and John Lamb married sisters. He was a leader of the Stamp Act riots, but then joined the DeLancey faction and actively supported British measures. In 1776 he was tried for supplying British troops with provisions and fled to Antigua. He returned to New York in 1777 and departed again in 1782. Returning to England, he was captured and imprisoned by the French. Eventually he settled in England and received compensation for his losses.

*Where birth date and/or death date are not included, they are not known.

John Alsop (d. 1794). A prosperous New York merchant, a conservative, and according to John Adams "a soft, sweet man," he resigned from the New York delegation to Congress when independence was voted, saying that since the door to reconciliation was closed, he could no longer serve. When the British occupied New York, he withdrew to Middletown, Connecticut, where he sat out the war, returning to the city and his business when it was over.

Samuel Auchmuty (1722–1777). Anglican rector of Trinity Church in New York, he favored an American episcopate and was an ardent loyalist. He died not long after the loss of his church and house in the great fire of September 1776. His son, Sir Samuel Auchmuty, fought with the English and later became a general in the British army.

Goldsbrow Banyar (1725–1815). Emigrated to America as a young man and between 1746 and the outbreak of the Revolution held various colonial offices, including deputy secretary of the colony, and enriched himself by land speculation. During the war he moved to Rhinebeck, and by the 1790s he had settled permanently in Albany, where he was known as the wealthiest man in the area. He was a director of the Bank of Albany and collaborated with Philip Schuyler on developing navigation along the Mohawk River.

Isaac Barré (1726–1802). Born in Ireland of French parents, he became a British soldier and fought with Wolfe at Quebec, where he was wounded. A member of Parliament, 1761–1790, he opposed the North ministry and taxation of the colonies. His surname is the eponym of Barre, Vermont, and, with that of John Wilkes, Wilkes-Barre, Pennsylvania.

Sir Francis Bernard (1712–1779). Colonial governor of New Jersey, and of Massachusetts, 1760–1769. Although willing to support the commercial interests of colonials in the face of Parliament's demands, he found it increasingly difficult to act as mediator and was removed from office after the Massachusetts legislature charged him with corruption. He was cleared of the charges, but returned to England and spent his remaining years in retirement.

Edmund Burke (1729–1797). British statesman, eloquent writer and orator, born in Ireland. At first supportive of Parliament's colonial policy, he later espoused the colonies' interests and delivered two important speeches on taxation and conciliation in 1774 and 1775. After the American victory at Saratoga in 1777 he deplored further attempts to hold the colonies by force. He denounced the use of Indians by the British in the war and eventually forced the resignation of Lord North.

John Stuart, third Earl of Bute (1713–1792). A Scottish favorite and trusted adviser of George III. Prime minister from 1761 to 1763, he played an important role in winning back political influence for the Tories after years of isolation. He opposed repeal of the Stamp Act and was reviled in America and Britain as a symbol of corruption of parliamentary government. He was often depicted in satirical cartoons as a boot.

William Pitt, Earl of Chatham (1708–1778). English statesman known as "the Great Commoner," he entered Parliament in 1735 and soon gained renown for his oratory. After some rocky years in opposition, he was given full control of military affairs in 1757, and his vigorous prosecution of the Seven Years' War brought about French defeat in Canada, India, and Africa. He opposed efforts to tax the American colonists, favored repeal of the Stamp Act, and supported conciliation with the colonies. His effectiveness in his last years was greatly hampered by mental illness.

Cadwallader Colden (1688–1776). Born in Ireland of Scottish parents, Colden emigrated to Philadelphia, then to New York in 1718. Appointed surveyor general, he repeatedly sought higher office and finally obtained the lieutenant governorship on the death of his political opponent James DeLancey. A distinguished scientist in botany, medicine, and physics, he conducted a wide correspondence with colleagues on both sides of the Atlantic, but these talents were obscured by the resentment he aroused by his political activities. A loyalist, he was burned in effigy during the Stamp Act riots, but narrowly weathered the crisis by handing over the stamps to the city's mayor. Ousted from office in 1776, Colden retired to his home on Long Island, where he died.

Peter Collinson (1694–1768). English naturalist and merchant who traded extensively with the American colonies. He was a fellow of the Royal Society and corresponded with Benjamin Franklin, Cadwallader Colden, and other Americans on scientific matters. He strongly advocated the development of American agriculture.

Henry Seymour Conway (1721–1795). A cousin and close friend of Horace Walpole, he had a distinguished military career, but was temporarily deprived of his regiment and income in 1764 for speaking in favor of John Wilkes and contesting Grenville's American policies. As secretary of state in Rockingham's administration he proposed repealing the Stamp Act and in 1767 was against suspending the New York Assembly's legislative power. He disapproved the use of force in America and from 1773 on attacked North's administration.

Myles Cooper (1737–1785). Anglican clergyman and president of King's College, New York. Educated at Oxford, he was a loyalist who favored an American episcopate. Frequently accused of writing loyalist tracts, at the news of Lexington and Concord he barely escaped a mob, fled for protection on a British ship, and soon afterward sailed to England, where he held various church livings and received a pension from the crown.

John Cruger (1710–1791). The son of a merchant who was New York's mayor, Cruger himself became a popular mayor (1756–1765) who handled the Stamp Act crisis diplomatically. Closely connected through family ties with the Tories, Cruger spoke out against British colonial policy. He left the city during the British occupation but returned after the war ended. His nephew Henry Cruger went to Bristol in 1757 to learn the family business and eventually was elected to Parliament.

William Legge, Earl of Dartmouth (1731–1801). British politician. As first lord of trade in 1765–1766 he voted to repeal the Stamp Act, gaining credit with the colonists, but as secretary of state for America in North's administration he upheld Parliament's supremacy over the colonies and in 1776 advocated the use of force against them. He gave his name to Dartmouth College, founded in 1769.

James DeLancey, Sr. (1703–1760). Well connected in England, where he trained in the law, DeLancey rose quickly to prominence on his return to New York. He replaced Lewis Morris as chief justice of the Supreme Court, and by 1753, when he also took office as lieutenant governor, the "DeLancey party" was on the way to dominating New York government. A year later he signed the charter for King's College, raising Presbyterian opposition from the "Livingston party" to his family's Anglican position. Upon his sudden, unexpected death in 1760, Cadwallader Colden became acting lieutenant governor.

James DeLancey, Jr. (1732–1800). Born in the family home that became Fraunces Tavern, he was the eldest son of James DeLancey, Sr., and after his father's death sought to entrench the Tory-Episcopalian interest against the Livingston Whig-Presbyterian faction. He disapproved of all republican activity and in 1775 sold his famous horse stables and quietly left for England. He was attainted, lost his estate, and after the war served as agent for New York loyalists claiming compensation. He died at Bath.

James DeLancey (1746–1804). A loyalist, he was the nephew of James DeLancey, Sr., and grandson of Cadwallader Colden. From 1770 to 1776 he was sheriff of Westchester and during the Revolution participated in acts of banditry and cattle-raiding in the "neutral ground" north of New York City. Proscribed by the Act of Attainder of 1779, he moved to Nova Scotia in 1782.

Oliver DeLancey (1718–1785). Merchant, politician, and loyalist soldier. The brother of James DeLancey, Sr., whose political aims he supported, he joined General Howe on Staten Island in 1776, raised three loyalist battalions, and served as commanding officer on Long Island. His property was confiscated and his mansion plundered. He left New York in 1783 and died in England.

John Dickinson (1732–1808). Philadelphia lawyer, educated in London. A conservative, he argued against violent resistance, supported nonimportation, and published influential pamphlets against British policy (the most widely known being *Letters from a Farmer in Pennsylvania to the Inhabitants of the British Colonies,* denying Parliament's right to tax the colonies). He drafted petitions to the king and was still advocating conciliation in 1776, when he voted against the Declaration of Independence.

He retired to his Delaware estate during the war, supported the federal Constitution in 1787, and retained an interest in public affairs until his death.

James Duane (1733–1797). The son of a New York merchant, Duane became a lawyer and was associated with the DeLancey political interest until his marriage to Maria Livingston in 1759, when he changed sides. He was at first dubious about independence but served in the Continental Congress and supported the nonimportation agreement. The first mayor of New York after the British occupation (1784–1789), he was later district judge of New York State.

John Murray, fourth Earl of Dunmore (1732–1809). After serving in Parliament as a Scottish peer, he was briefly governor of New York in 1770 and then governor of Virginia, where by 1775 he was openly hostile to most people in his colony. He lost several battles against the patriots in 1775 and 1776, when he returned to England, and in 1787 was appointed governor of the Bahamas.

Andrew Elliot (1728–1797). Born in Scotland, he was the brother of Sir Gilbert Elliot, known as a "king's friend" in the House of Commons and treasurer of the navy. He succeeded Archibald Kennedy as receiver-general and collector of customs in New York from 1764 until the end of the Revolution. In 1774 he was threatened with violence for seizing firearms sent to a city merchant. He remained in New York through the war, serving as lieutenant governor (1780–1783) and acting governor from April 1783 until the British evacuated the city.

Lewis Evans (c.1700–1756). A surveyor and mapmaker, he was born in Wales and traveled through the colonies collecting observations for unusually detailed maps. General Braddock used one of his maps during the French and Indian War, and they remained in print as late as 1814. A protégé of Governor Thomas Pownall, Evans died while under arrest for slander against Pennsylvania governor Robert Hunter Morris.

Benjamin Franklin (1706–1790). A native of Boston, he left for Philadelphia at an early age and set up as a printer. Dividing his time between politics, business, and science, he became the best-known of all American colonists. He was deputy postmaster-general of the colonies (1753–1774), proposed the plan of union at the Albany Congress of 1754, helped draft the Declaration of Independence, and was sent to negotiate peace with Great Britain after the war. His natural son, William Franklin, was the last royal governor of New Jersey.

General Thomas Gage (1721–1787). Born in Sussex, he entered the military and served in America under Braddock (1755), Abercromby (1758), and Amherst (1760). Appointed commander in chief in North America, he was headquartered in New York from 1763 to 1773, when he was sent to Boston as governor (the last royal governor of that province, as it turned out). The expedition he sent out to seize rebel supplies precipitated armed hostilities at Lexington and Concord. After the battle for

Bunker Hill he resigned and returned to England. He was commissioned a full general in 1782.

Joseph Galloway (1731–1803). Lawyer, loyalist, and colonial statesman. As speaker of the Pennsylvania Assembly (1766–1775) he favored conciliation with England. At the First Continental Congress his plan of union for an American congress sharing power with Parliament was rejected. During the British occupation of Philadelphia he was civil administrator, and then fled to England. His American estates were confiscated and he was refused permission to return to Pennsylvania. His last years were devoted to religion, the aid of fellow American exiles, and writing.

George I (1660–1727). The son of the elector of Hanover and Sophia, he became king of Great Britain and Ireland in 1714 by the Act of Settlement (1701), which required a Protestant successor to Queen Anne. He spoke no English and was unpopular at first, but garnered Whig support after the 1715 attempt to restore the Catholic Stuart monarchy. Though George disliked Robert Walpole, he was forced to accept him as his first minister after Walpole allied himself with the king's son. The divorce and imprisonment of his wife, Sophia Dorothea, for adultery caused scandal and contributed to alienating his son (the future George II) from him.

George II (1683–1760). Born abroad, he was educated from childhood for his role as British monarch, and began his rule in 1727. After quarreling with his father, George I, in 1717, he set up a rival court at Leicester House, and here began his close association with Robert Walpole, who was to become his principal, or prime, minister. During George II's reign, Lord Halifax initiated the policy of more stringent control over the colonies, and under William Pitt's guidance Britain was victorious in the French and Indian War, ending France's North American empire.

George III (1738–1820). The grandson of George II. His accession to the throne in 1760 brought an end to Whig control of government. His favorite, Lord Bute, replaced Pitt, and was soon followed by a succession of unfortunate choices whose colonial programs precipitated the American Revolution. Finally George III found his man in Lord North, a pliant agent whose ruinous policies led to revolt and the loss of the colonies. Some years after the war he suffered a series of mental attacks and went blind, and after 1811 he was permanently deranged.

August Henry Fitzroy, Duke of Grafton (1735–1811). After serving in several ministries, Grafton was first minister from 1768 to 1770. He was friendly to the colonies and advocated repeal of the Townshend duties, but was finally outvoted in his own cabinet over the American tea duty and resigned under attack.

George Grenville (1712–1770). As first lord of the Treasury and chancellor of the Exchequer he proposed a budget in 1764 that included duties on colonial commerce, plus stamp duties. He also supported establishing a standing army on American soil.

The king, who detested him for his tedious, overbearing manner, finally got rid of him, after which Grenville—satirized in the press as "Greenvile"—defended the American duties and the Stamp Act with considerable eloquence.

George Montagu Dunk, third Earl of Halifax (1716–1771). An uncle of Lord North, he was president of the Board of Trade and Plantations (1748–1761) when trade with America began to flourish. Sometimes called "Father of the Colonies," he did his best to tighten imperial control to produce more revenue for the crown. Halifax, Nova Scotia, was named for him.

John Hancock (c. 1736–1793). Merchant and politician who became, in his twenties, the wealthiest Bostonian of his generation through inheritance. After his ship *Liberty* was seized for smuggling activities in 1768, Hancock's name became closely tied to anti-British protest. Following the Boston Massacre in 1770, he worked closely with Samuel Adams. He was president of the Provincial Congress and delegate to the Second Continental Congress, and his is the largest signature on the Declaration of Independence. He was elected the first governor of the state of Massachusetts in 1780; he resigned five years later but was elected again and served until his death.

Whitehead Hicks (1728–1780). Born on Long Island, he was a successful lawyer, clerk of Queens County in the 1750s, and was appointed mayor of New York City by Sir Henry Moore in 1766. He served in that office for ten years, and then as judge of the New York Supreme Court until his death.

Wills Hill, first Earl of Hillsborough (1718–1793). More courtier than statesman, Hillsborough was secretary of state for the colonies in 1768 and ordered Francis Bernard to dissolve the Massachusetts Assembly should it continue to protest taxation and communicate with the other colonies. Shortly afterward he ordered General Gage to station troops in Boston. A resolute opponent of conciliation.

John Holt (1721–1784). Virginia-born printer and journalist. He was a partner of James Parker before founding the *New York Journal; or, the General Advertiser* in 1768. An Anglican, he was also a patriot, and fled New York during the British occupation, but continued printing from various locations throughout the war. On his return to New York he published the *Independent New-York Gazette*.

Zacharias Hood. Maryland stamp master whose home in Annapolis was destroyed by a mob in 1765, after which he fled to New York hoping to find safety in Fort George. The New York Sons of Liberty captured him and forced him to resign his office.

Daniel Horsmanden (1691–1778). After settling in New York in 1731, he allied himself with the DeLancey faction and secured a series of government offices, including a place on the supreme court. Stripped of these offices by DeLancey's foe Governor George Clinton, by 1755 he was restored to the court, and in 1763 he became chief justice. He was irreverently called "old Horsey" by William Smith.

Thomas Hutchinson (1711–1780). Born in Boston, he served in the House of Representatives, was a delegate to the Albany Congress in 1754, and by the 1760s was leader of the court party and lieutenant governor of the colony. Though he opposed the Stamp Act, he believed in the subordination of the colonies to the mother country and aroused such enmity that his home was burned by a Boston mob. In December 1773 his letters advocating strong measures against colonial resistance were made public, and soon afterward he left Boston for England, where he died in exile.

Major Thomas James. British officer in the Royal Artillery whose acid comments on the Sons of Liberty led to a threat that he would be buried alive. During the Stamp Act riots he prominently defended Fort George, and the mob then ran to Vauxhall, the estate he was renting, trashed it, and destroyed many of his belongings.

James Jauncey (d. 1790). A wealthy New York merchant who was a member of the Assembly and a stalwart of the DeLancey party, even though he was a Presbyterian. In the course of the war he was imprisoned in Connecticut with his wife and son. His property was confiscated and he died in England.

James Jauncey, Jr. (1747–1777). He was related by marriage to Sir Gilbert Elliot and Andrew Elliot, collector of New York customs. In 1775 he replaced the recently deceased Sir William Johnson as a member of the Council. Jailed with his father and mother in Connecticut, he applied to George Washington for his release, was referred to Congress, and died while awaiting an answer. He is buried in Trinity Churchyard in New York.

Samuel Johnson (1696–1772). Clergyman and philosopher. After his conversion to the Church of England from Congregationalism in 1722 he was appointed a missionary in Connecticut. Initially mistrustful of America's resistance to Britain, he came to see the interests of American Anglicans as different from those of the British. In 1753 he became the first president of King's College in New York City.

Sir William Johnson (1715–1774). A poor Irish immigrant, he became a huge landowner in the Mohawk Valley. While engaged in the fur trade he developed close ties with the Six Nations of the Iroquois Confederation, learning their language and adapting to their life, and became the enormously influential superintendent of Indian affairs. He played a key role in driving the French from North America. His home, Johnson Hall, was the scene of numerous Indian conferences. His son Sir John Johnson and son-in-law Sir Guy Johnson were loyalist leaders in the Revolutionary War.

Thomas Jones (1731–1792). A jurist from Long Island, he was attorney for King's College. He married a daughter of James DeLancey, Sr., and in 1773 was appointed to the Supreme Court. During the Revolution he was arrested and released repeatedly, and the scars of that experience are manifest in his bitter *History of New York During the*

Revolutionary War, the best-known loyalist account of the conflict. He was attainted, his estates were confiscated, and he left America in 1781, never to return.

John Tabor Kempe (1735–c. 1790). The last royal attorney general of New York. Born in England, he arrived in New York in 1752, where his father was attorney general before him. In 1775 he fled with Governor Tryon to a British ship in the harbor, and he remained in the city, and in office, during the British occupation. When his wife was captured by patriots an exchange was made for the wife of Francis Lewis. The couple left the city in 1783; he was attainted in New York and New Jersey, and their property confiscated.

Captain Archibald Kennedy (d. 1794). A Royal Navy officer who married, as his second wife, John Watts's daughter Ann. He built an elegant mansion at No. 1 Broadway and when, prior to the Stamp Act riots, Lieutenant Governor Colden announced that he would transfer the hated stamps to a warship, Captain Kennedy refused to accept them, presumably fearing what would happen to his home if he did. The house was spared, but that decision led to his recall by an angry king. In 1792 Kennedy succeeded a cousin as eleventh Earl of Casillis.

John Lamb (1735–1800). The son of a reputed burglar who had been transported to the colonies and became a successful mathematical instrument maker, Lamb went into the liquor trade. He was fluent in Dutch and German, was a good speaker and writer, and was of real use to the Sons of Liberty. With Isaac Sears, he took charge of the city's arsenal when news of Lexington and Concord reached New York. He was commissioned as an officer in the war, and served under Montgomery and Arnold in the attack on Quebec. After the war, he became collector of New York customs, and was a vocal anti-Federalist leader. He died impoverished, having sold most of his property to replace a sum of money embezzled by a clerk from the customs office.

Margaret Beekman Livingston (1724–1800). Wife of Judge Robert R. Livingston. She had eleven children by him.

Philip Livingston (1686–1749). The son of Robert Livingston ("the Founder") and Alida Schuyler Van Rensselaer, he was born in Albany, entered his father's business, and became involved in local politics, law, and land titles. After his father's death he became second lord of Livingston Manor, an estate he greatly enlarged.

Philip Livingston, Jr. (1716–1778). A successful New York City merchant, he was one of the first to advocate founding of King's College. He sought to unite merchants and gentry against British colonial policies, but was ousted from the conservative New York Assembly in 1768. He publicly opposed the Stamp Act, was a member of the Continental Congress, and signed the Declaration of Independence, although he did not favor revolution.

Robert R. Livingston, "the Judge" (1718–1775). Helped organize opposition to the Stamp Act, but hoped for conciliation with Britain. His wife, Margaret Beekman, brought him powerful connections and increased his wealth. As justice of the Supreme Court he antagonized Cadwallader Colden, and when the Assembly denied him his seat in 1768 he was outraged and continued to fight for it until 1774.

Robert R. Livingston, Jr., "the Chancellor" (1746–1813). Son of the Judge, he was an early supporter of colonial liberties and was one of the five-man committee that drafted the Declaration of Independence. He was the first U.S. secretary of foreign affairs and, as chancellor of New York State, administered the oath of office to President Washington in 1789. As minister to France he negotiated the Louisiana Purchase. His interest in steam navigation led him to back Robert Fulton and his steamboat, the *Clermont,* named for Livingston's Hudson River estate.

William Livingston (1723–1790). One of the liberal, Presbyterian "triumvirate" with William Smith, Jr., and John Morin Scott, he was the guiding spirit behind *The Independent Reflector* and then and later conducted a press war against the DeLancey party and worked to oust them from government in the 1760s. He was a delegate to the Continental Congress, fought in the Revolution, and as governor of New Jersey steered that state through ratification of the Constitution.

Catharine Macaulay (1731–1791). Her history of England from the accession of James I to the 1750s was infused with republican ideology and describes the corruption of British liberty by royal power. She corresponded with a number of patriots in America.

Jonathan Mayhew (1720–1766). The pastor of West Church in Boston and a liberal in religious doctrine, he denounced plans for an episcopate in America and participated in a lively controversy on church matters. A friend of Otis, Quincy, and Samuel Adams, he dedicated one of his last sermons to William Pitt after repeal of the Stamp Act.

Alexander McDougall (1732–1786). A member of a Scottish family that emigrated to New York, he delivered milk from his father's cows to residents, went to sea at an early age, and became a privateer in the French and Indian War. Later a successful merchant, he was an active Son of Liberty and during his imprisonment for writing a controversial pamphlet became known as the "Wilkes of America." He served as a general under Washington, commanded at West Point after Benedict Arnold's treason, and was a member of the Continental Congress in 1781–82 and 1784–85.

James McEvers (1755–1829?). A New York merchant who was appointed stamp master for the province and resigned after hearing how Bostonians had treated their stamp distributor.

General Robert Monckton (1726–1782). During the French and Indian War he helped expel the French from Nova Scotia, and at Quebec he was one of General Wolfe's three brigadiers (along with Lord George Townshend and James Murray), all of whom loathed their commander. Monckton was severely wounded there, with a musket ball through the lungs. Appointed governor of New York and commander in chief in 1761, at the end of the year he was sent to conquer Martinique. He returned to England two years later to restore his health and did not return to America.

Captain John Montresor (1736–1799). British army engineer who followed in his father's footsteps to become "chief engineer in America." He served with the Braddock expedition and others in the French and Indian War and was engaged in building or repairing various works in the colonies, including Fort George in New York. He was a manager of the famous "Mischianza"—a celebrated ball in Philadelphia honoring Sir William Howe on his departure for England. He purchased a little island near Harlem known as Montresor's and later as Randalls Island.

Sir Henry Moore (1713–1769). Born in Jamaica, he was lieutenant governor of the island and was made a baronet after suppressing a slave uprising in 1760. As governor of New York from 1765 until his death in 1769, he annoyed Colden by partially dismantling Fort George and refusing to enforce the Stamp Act. His attempt to establish a playhouse in 1766 alienated the Presbyterians and increased their opposition to the Quartering Act.

Lewis Morris (1726–1798). An aristocratic New York landowner who sided with the Livingstons against the DeLanceys, he was a delegate to the Second Continental Congress and signed the Declaration of Independence. After serving in the war he restored his famous estate, Morrisania, which the British had plundered. His half brother Gouverneur helped draft the federal Constitution.

Lord North, courtesy title of Frederick, second Earl of Guilford (1732–1792). He entered the House of Commons at the age of twenty-two and was chancellor of the Exchequer from 1767 to 1782. His opposition to Wilkes and his support of American taxation made him unpopular at home and in the colonies. A pliant agent of the king, he was largely responsible for the Boston Port Bill and Restraining Acts of 1775. He resigned in 1782.

James Otis (1725–1783). As a brilliant Boston lawyer, in 1761 he argued against the use of writs of assistance, general search warrants, to enforce the Sugar Act. A prolific pamphleteer with the reputation of an extremist, he argued that man must be "free from all taxes but what he consents to in person, or by his representative." He was a delegate to the Stamp Act Congress and afterward suffered frequent attacks of insanity and eventual mental decline.

James Parker (c. 1714–1770). Publisher of the *New-York Gazette or, the Weekly Post-Boy* from 1747 to 1773. A patriot, he brought out his paper in mourning during the Stamp Act troubles. When he printed McDougall's broadside signed "A Son of Liberty," both men were arrested. Parker died before the case was settled.

Thomas Pownall (1722–1805). Secretary to Sir Danvers Osborn, who arrived in New York as the new governor and committed suicide a few days later. Pownall later became governor of New Jersey and of Massachusetts, where he offended conservatives by siding with popular leaders of the Assembly. Removed from office, he returned to England and served in Parliament until his retirement in 1780. He wrote *The Administration of the Colonies,* an argument for improved colonial policy.

William Prendergast. Leader of a tenant uprising, for which he was sentenced to death; he was later pardoned by the king.

Israel Putnam (1718–1790). After fighting in several campaigns in the French and Indian War he returned to his Connecticut farm. He was active as a Son of Liberty from the time of the Stamp Act and according to the legend left his plow and set off for the battlefield upon hearing news of Lexington in April 1775. He was appointed a major general in the Continental Army, but was not cut out for the conduct of an army or strategy. In 1779 a paralytic stroke forced his retirement.

Walter Quackenbos. A Dutch baker in New York, he collaborated with Isaac Sears in the street violence against British soldiers leading to the "Battle of Golden Hill" in January 1770.

Paul Revere (1735–1818). Boston silversmith and engraver who became a leader of the Sons of Liberty and probably took part in the Boston Tea Party. He was an important political organizer and a member of the committee of correspondence, and as official courier for the Massachusetts Provincial Assembly he alerted the countryside on the night of April 18, 1775, that Gage's troops were headed for Concord to seize supplies. After the war he returned to his business and from his copper and brass foundry supplied materials for the USS *Constitution* and plates for the boilers of Robert Fulton's steamboats.

Charles Lennox, Duke of Richmond (1735–1806). A distinguished military figure who was also active in government from the 1760s. A liberal, he opposed the ministries of Bute, Grenville, and North, and the war, voting consistently against measures that would harm the colonies.

James Rivington (1724–1802). He emigrated to America in 1760 and opened bookstores in Philadelphia, New York, and Boston. In 1773 he began publishing the *New York Gazetteer,* which was attacked for its loyalist tendencies, and in 1775 Isaac Sears destroyed his printing plant. He went to London in 1776 and returned the following year as the king's printer. From then until 1783 he published a loyalist paper, and he remained in the city after the war. Convincing evidence exists that he was a spy for the patriots from 1778 on. But his business fared poorly and he was in debtors' prison from 1797 to 1801.

Charles Watson-Wentworth, Marquis of Rockingham (1730–1782). English Whig statesman whose 1765–1766 coalition government attempted conciliation with the colonies and oversaw repeal of the Stamp Act against opposition from Grenville and George III. In 1778 he proposed immediate recognition of American independence.

Philip Schuyler (1733–1804). A cousin of the DeLanceys, the patrician Schuyler, owner of an immense estate near Albany, parted ways with them politically and embraced the patriot cause. Although he suffered from poor health, he fought in the French and Indian War and was one of Washington's major generals. After the war he developed canal navigation on the Mohawk River. His daughter Elizabeth married Alexander Hamilton.

John Morin Scott (1730?–1784). A founder of the New York Sons of Liberty, Scott was a member of "the triumvirate" with William Livingston and William Smith, Jr. They opposed the DeLancey interests, including the founding of King's College as an Anglican institution and the establishment of an American episcopate. He was a brigadier general in the war and fought on Long Island. He was also secretary of state of New York (1778–1784) and a member of the Continental Congress.

Samuel Seabury (1729–1796). This ardent advocate of an American episcopate defended the Anglican domination of King's College. He feared that independence would cause an attack on Anglican churches, and his inflammatory loyalist pamphlets signed "A. W. Farmer" (for A Westchester Farmer) provoked spirited replies by the young Alexander Hamilton. He served as chaplain during the British occupation of New York, and after the war traveled to Scotland to receive his consecration as first bishop of the Episcopal Church in America.

Isaac Sears (1730–1786). Like Alexander McDougall, Sears was a privateer in the French and Indian War. He lost his ship, however, and went into the West Indies trade, subsequently becoming a merchant. Greatly feared by the conservatives, he seemed to have a mob at his beck and call, and during the Stamp Act crisis and at other times he led popular riots in New York. His chosen role was to organize and direct rough tactics. When news of Lexington reached the city, for example, he seized arms from the Custom House and effectively took charge of the city. He went back to privateering during the war, operating out of Boston. After the Revolution he died on a voyage to China.

Thomas Secker (1693–1768). The son of a dissenting minister, he converted to the Church of England as a young man and rose to become archbishop of Canterbury in 1758 and a favorite of George III. He strongly supported the idea of an American episcopate.

William Petty, second Earl of Shelburne (1737–1805). An ally of Chatham, he opposed Townshend's revenue policy for America and subsequent coercive measures, but voted in favor of the Boston Port Act. He hoped for conciliation until 1782, when he accepted America's independence and helped negotiate the peace. He resigned from Parliament after being accused of yielding to American pressure and failing to protect loyalists' interests.

William Smith (1697–1769). English-born, he became a prominent New York lawyer and trained others, including his son William, Jr., John Morin Scott, and William Livingston—"the triumvirate." He frequently served as counsel in cases where he tried to restrict the governor's prerogative, and he served as a counsel for John Peter Zenger who was tried for seditious libel. An associate justice of the New York Supreme Court, he helped establish the Presbyterian College of New Jersey (later Princeton) and opposed Anglican domination of King's College in New York.

William Smith, Jr. (1728–1795). A Yale graduate, like his father, and trained in the law by his father, he went into partnership with William Livingston, whose sister Janet he married. He wrote a history of the province of New York, published in 1757, and kept a remarkable diary, or memoirs, of the years 1763–1778. He was an adviser to several governors (though not to the lieutenant governor, Cadwallader Colden, whom he despised) and was a member of the Council. He refused in 1778 to take the oath of allegiance to the revolutionary state, and when New York was evacuated by the British he went to England and then became chief justice of Canada.

Charles Townshend (1725–1767). A witty member of Rockingham's and Chatham's ministries, he became chancellor of the Exchequer in the latter, and when Chatham was incapacitated by mental and physical illness, Townshend effectively took charge. He suspended activities of the New York Assembly and pushed through measures taxing paper, glass, and tea in the colonies.

Barlow Trecothick (c. 1719–1775). A Boston merchant before settling in London in the 1750s, he was deeply involved in trade with the colonies. In 1765 he worked with Rockingham to influence public opinion against the Stamp Act. He was agent for the colony of New Hampshire starting in 1766, and served as alderman, sheriff, and mayor of London. As a member of Parliament his was a conciliatory voice.

Horace Walpole, fourth earl of Orford (1717–1797). Third son of Sir Robert Walpole, he was a prolific writer of letters and memoirs, which provide a vivid picture of Georgian England. He never entered politics and did not take his seat in the House of Lords, but opposed North's ministry and the war with the colonies. The architecture of his Strawberry Hill mansion and his popular novel *The Castle of Otranto* did much to inspire the Gothic revival.

Robert Walpole, first Earl of Orford (1676–1745). Generally regarded as the first "prime minister" of England, though the term was often used to disparage his near-tyrannical control over Parliament. During the reigns of George I and George II he increased the ascendancy of the cabinet and made the House of Commons, rather than the House of Lords, the nexus of power. He applied his financial skills to stabilize the country's economy and favored the landed gentry by reducing their taxes, while encouraging commerce. His hands-off policy toward the American colonies was known as "salutary neglect."

George Washington (1732–1799). A Virginia planter, surveyor, and militia colonel, he rose to prominence during the French and Indian War. As a member of the province's House of Burgesses, he opposed British legislation affecting the colonies. He was a delegate to the First and Second Continental Congresses, which chose him as commander in chief of the Continental Army. After the war he advocated a strong national union and was president of the Constitutional Convention in 1787. Two years later he was elected the nation's first president, and he served two terms before retiring to his estate, Mount Vernon.

John Watts (1715–1789). Born in New York City, he was allied by marriage to the DeLanceys and was a member of the Assembly and the Council. A wealthy merchant, landowner, and philanthropist, he helped found the city's first library and hospital. Accompanied by another Council member, Roger Morris, he sailed from New York on May 11, 1775—twenty-two days after the fighting at Lexington and Concord. He never returned, but lived in London until his death in 1789. All of his property in New York State—which included parcels in New York City, plus numerous tracts in Westchester and Dutchess counties and elsewhere in the state—was confiscated because of his "adherence to the State's enemies."

John Watts, Jr. (1749–1836). Last royal recorder of New York City, he sat in the New York Assembly, was a member of Congress 1793–1796, and from 1802 to 1808 was a judge in Westchester County. He and his brother Robert repurchased their father's land on Manhattan Island from the Commissioners of Forfeiture in 1789. The 131-acre Rose Hill Farm on the East River between 22nd and 30th streets and west to Broadway went to John, Jr. Robert obtained the lot on what is now Pearl Street, between Whitehall and Broad, where his father's three-story mansion once stood.

John Wilkes (1725–1797). A member of the Hell-fire Club, which met in an abandoned abbey to indulge in parodies of Roman Catholic ritual. His attack on George III for falsehood in No. 45 of his paper, the *North Briton,* led to his prosecution for libel and expulsion from the House of Commons. He was reelected, expelled again, reelected, and expelled, and became the idol of the mob, shouting "Wilkes and Liberty!" He was a popular hero of American patriots. As lord mayor of London and (finally) a member of Parliament, he championed colonial rights.

Isaac Wilkins (1741–1830). The son of a wealthy Jamaican planter, he prepared for the ministry but did not take holy orders. After settling in Westchester County, he was elected a member of the New York Assembly, where he exerted considerable influence. He opposed sending delegates to the Continental Congress and delivered an eloquent speech defending his position. In 1775, Wilkins left New York for England, but he returned to Long Island, where he sat out the war. His Westchester estate was not listed in the Act of Attainder and he sold it at a considerable loss. For a time he lived in Nova Scotia and elsewhere in Canada; he became a minister, and in 1799 returned to Westchester to serve the parish there for thirty-one years.

Marinus Willett (1740–1830). An alumnus of King's College, a well-to-do merchant and property owner, he served in the French and Indian War with Oliver DeLancey's New York regiment and was an avid Son of Liberty. Most of his military experience during the war was in the Mohawk Valley. He was mayor of New York, 1807–1811.

Patience Wright (1725–1786). Daughter of a Quaker farmer on Long Island, she started modeling clay and dough figurines as a child. She went to Philadelphia, where she married Joseph Wright, a wealthy cooper, and after her husband's death worked with her sister making portraits in wax. Eventually she went to London and created "bustos" of many notable individuals, including the king and queen, Benjamin Franklin, and the Earl of Chatham. Her being such a gossip gave rise to unsubstantiated suspicions that she was a spy.

BIBLIOGRAPHY

1. PRIMARY SOURCES

ADAMS, JOHN. *Diary and Autobiography of John Adams.* Ed. L. H. Butterfield. Cambridge: Harvard University Press, 1961. Vol. 2.

———. *The Works of John Adams.* Ed. Charles Francis Adams. 10 vols. Boston: Little, Brown, 1856.

American Loyalists. Transcript of the Manuscript Books and Papers of the Commissioners of Enquiry into the Losses and Services of the American Loyalists Held under Acts of Parliament of 23, 25, 26, 28, and 29 of George III preserved amongst the Audit Office Records in the Public Record Office of England. Examinations in London and New York. 1783–1790. 60 vols. New York Public Library.

ASPINWALL PAPERS. *Collections of the Massachusetts Historical Society.* Vol. IX and X. Fourth Series. Boston: 1871.

BANGS, EDWARD, ed. *Journal of Lieutenant Isaac Bangs, April 1 to July 29, 1776.* Cambridge, Mass.: Wilson, 1890.

BOUCHER, JONATHAN. *Reminiscences of an American Loyalist, 1738–1789.* Ed. Jonathan Bouchier. Boston: Houghton Mifflin, 1925.

COLDEN, CADWALLADER. *The Colden Letter Books, 1760–1775.* New-York Historical Society Collections, I–II, 1876–1877.

———. *The Letters and Papers of Cadwallader Colden, 1711–1775.* New-York Historical Society Collections, I–VII, 1917–1923.

———. *Additional Papers, 1715–1748, 1749–1775.* New-York Historical Society Collections, 1934, 1935.

FORCE, PETER, ed. *American Archives: Fourth Series, Containing a Documentary History of the English Colonies in North America from the King's Message to Parliament of March 7, 1774, to the Declaration of Independence by the United States.* 6 vols. M. St. Clair Clarke and Peter Force, Washington, D.C., 1837–1846.

GEORGE III. *The Correspondence of King George the Third from 1760 to December 1783.* Ed. Sir John Fortescue. 6 vols. London: Macmillan, 1927–28.

HONYMAN, ROBERT. *Colonial Panorama, 1775: Dr. Robert Honyman's Journal for March and April.* Ed. Philip Padelford. San Marino, Calif.: Huntington Library, 1939.

JAY, JOHN. *John Jay: The Making of a Revolutionary, Unpublished Papers, 1745–1780.* Ed. Richard B. Morris. New York: Harper & Row, 1975.

O'CALLAGHAN, E. B., ed. *The Documentary History of the State of New York.* 4 vols. Albany, N.Y.: Weed, Parsons, 1849. CD, Fine Books Company, Abilene, Texas.

Papers of the Lloyd Family of the Manor of Queens Village, Lloyd's Neck, Long Island, New York, 1654–1826. 2 vols. Ed. Dorothy C. Barck. New York: New-York Historical Society, 1927.

SCULL, G. D. ed. *Journals* of Colonel James Montresor, 1757–1759, and Captain John Montresor, 1757–1778. New-York Historical Society *Collections,* 1881.

B. F. Stevens: Facsimiles of Manuscripts in European Archives Relating to America, 1773–1783. Vol. 24, No. 2045. Ambrose Serle to Earl of Dartmouth, Nov. 8, 1776. AMS Press Film Service.

SULLIVAN, JAMES, ed. *Minutes of the Albany Committee of Correspondence, 1775–1778.* Vol. 1. Albany, N.Y.: University of the State of New York, 1923.

WALPOLE, HORACE. *The Letters of Horace Walpole.* 9 vols. Ed. Peter Cunningham. Edinburgh: John Grant, 1906.

WATTS, JOHN. *Letter Book of John Watts, Merchant and Councillor of New York.* Jan. 1, 1762–Dec. 22, 1765. Ed. Dorothy C. Barck. New-York Historical Society Collections, LXI, 1928.

The Library of Congress

Peter Atkinson: "Memo Book of my journey as one of the Commissioners on Treaty with the Six Nations of Indians, 1754." Papers of Peter Force: Series 8, Manuscript Collections.

The Pierpont Morgan Library, New York, N.Y.

Gilder Lehrman Collection

The following works are from the Gilder Lehrman Collection on deposit in the Pierpont Morgan Library, New York, N.Y.

Act for importing salt from Europe into New York, 1730 GLC 3562.02

John Adams to Catharine Macaulay, Aug. 9, 1770 GLC 1784.01; Apr. 19, 1773 GLC 1785.01; Jun. 28, 1773 GLC 1786; Dec. 11, 1773 GLC 1787; Dec. 28, 1774 GLC 1788

John Adams to Richard Henry Lee, Nov. 15, 1775 GLC 3864

John Adams to Joseph Palmer, Oct. 3, 1775 GLC 1725

Resolution signed by John Adams, Silas Deane, and George Wythe, Oct. 24, 1775 GLC 505.01

James Bowdoin, Samuel Pemberton, and Joseph Warren to Catharine Macaulay, Mar. 23, 1770 GLC 1789.02

Broadside signed Brutus, to "Free and Loyal Inhabitants of the City and Colony of New-York", May 16, 1770 GLC 2552

John Butler to Joshua Mauger, Oct. 28, 1775 GLC 3902.64

Thomas Clark to William Winslow, July [?] 1745 GLC 1450.614.02

Samuel Cleaveland to John Beague, Dec. 9, 1774 GLC 1450.047

John Dickinson to Catharine Macaulay, Oct. 31, 1770 GLC 1790.01; Dec. 17, 1770 GLC 1790.02

Benjamin Franklin to his brother John, Mar. 16, 1755 GLC 5267

Benjamin Franklin to John Hunter, Dec. 3, 1755 GLC 1656

Benjamin Franklin to William Smith, May 3, 1753 GLC 1722

"The examination of Doctor Benjamin Franklin before an August Assembly, relating to the Repeal of the Stamp Act" [London 1766] GLC 1719

Thomas Gage to Gov. Hopkins of R.I., March 26, 1764 GLC 1450.257

Thomas Gage to Sir William Johnson, June 22, 1766 GLC 3238

Capt. A. Harrington to Maj. Genl. Seth Williamson, Nov. 20, 1765 GLC 278

Richard Henry Lee to Catharine Macaulay, Mar. 30, 1770 GLC 1792

Resolution signed by Peter Van B. Livingston, May 29, 1775 GLC 418

Philip Livingston to Jillis Fonda, Apr. 16, 1772 GLC 184.28

Advertisement signed by Philip Livingston, James Duane, John Alsop, John Jay, and Isaac Low, July 5, 1774 GLC 2440

William Livingston to Catharine Macaulay, Sept. 21, 1769 GLC 1793

William Livingston to Major Samuel Hayes, Jul. 10, 1770 GLC 1150

Advertisement signed by Isaac Low, July 9, 1770 GLC 2554

Receipt from Thomas and Richard Penn, July 28, 1769 GLC 2548

Richard Peters to Sir William Johnson [?], Feb. 12, 1761 GLC 766

Timothy Pickering, Jr., to his father, Feb. 23, 1778 GLC 2325

Peter Porter to Elijah Leonard, July 3, 1755 GLC 1450.298

John Read to Capt. Christopher Whipple, Dec. 29, 1774 GLC 1450.432

Mercy Otis Warren to Catharine Macaulay, Dec. 29, 1774 GLC 1800.01; Aug. 24, 1775 GLC 1800.02

Brooks Watson to Joshua Mauger, Oct. 18, 1763 GLC 3902.01; Oct. 25, 1763 GLC 3902.02; Dec. 19, 1765 GLC 3902.04; Oct. 15, 1774 GLC 3902.17

Henry Wendell to his uncle, Apr. 12, 1755 GLC 1450.259

Proclamation by Benning Wentworth, Feb. 28, 1757 GLC 1450.545

Advertisement signed "By Order of a Number of the Inhabitants," July 7, 1770 GLC 2553

Proclamation "To the Inhabitants of the City and Colony of New-York," printed by John Holt, c. 1774 GLC 2439

Museum of the City of New York

Peter R. Livingston to Dear Sir, Jan. 19, 1769 [Ms. collection, cab. 3, box 155]

New-York Historical Society, New York, N.Y.
Misc. Mss. Alsop, John

George Bancroft Papers: R. R. Livingston Papers

Goldsbrow Banyar Papers

Beekman Family Papers
James Beekman, in BV Beekman, Letterbook B
Bancker, Christopher ledger, 1718–1755; Evert Bancker, Jr. ledger, 1765–1774. BV
    Bancker
Samuel Deall account book. BV Deall

Debating Club minutes. In Misc. Mss. Van Schaack, Peter

Oliver DeLancey Papers
William DeWitt daybook. BV DeWitt, William

James Duane Papers
Andrew Elliot Correspondence, 1747–1777. BV Elliot, Andrew

William Edgar Papers

Ellison Family Papers
Thomas Gage to Sir William Johnson, May 11, 1767, May 20, 1770. Misc. Mss. Gage,
    Thomas
Thomas Gage Orderly Books. BV Orderly Books

Emmet Collection
Sir Henry Moore to Gov. Bernard, Feb. 23, 1767
James Duane to [?], Feb. 17, 1767

Hardwicke Collection

Richard Harison Papers
Alexander Colden to George Harison, Dec. 18, 1755; Jan. 24, May 21, Jun 22, Jun. 30,
    Aug. 12, 1756; Mar 4, 1757

John Lamb Papers
Joseph Allicocke to John Lamb, Nov. 21, 1765
Deposition of John Abeel and James Abeel, Mar. 19, 1766
William Bradford to Messrs. Lamb, Sears, Willey, and Mott, Feb. 15, 1766
Major Durkee to Capt. Isaac Sears, Feb. 10, 1766
Nicholas Ray to New York Sons of Liberty, Jul. 28, 1766
Albany Committee of Correspondence to New York Committee, May 24, 1766
New Hampshire Sons of Liberty to Sons of Liberty in Connecticut and New York,
    1766

New York Sons of Liberty to Philadelphia Sons of Liberty, May 11, 1770
Resolves of Oyster Bay Sons of Liberty, Feb. 22, 1766
Philadelphia Sons of Liberty to New York Sons of Liberty, Feb. 1766
Letter from Providence to New York Sons of Liberty, Feb. 17, 1766
Doctor Thomas Young, Boston, to John Lamb, May 13, 1774

Livingston Family Papers

Robert R. Livingston Papers
Misc. Mss. Lydius, John H.

Alexander McDougall Papers

Myers Collection

Joseph Reed Papers
BV Rhinelander
Philip Rhinelander Letterbook and Orderbook 1774–1784
Frederick Rhinelander to Messrs Smith, Son & Russel. Nov. 7, 1776
Frederick Rhinelander to Messrs Rawlinsons & Chorley, Dec. 28, 1776
Misc. Mss. Van Schaack, Peter
Peter Van Schaack to New York Committee [?] Jan. 25, 1777

Robert Watts Papers
BV Stevens, Phinehas
Nicolaes Bleecker invoice to Storke & Gainsborough, Nov. 15, 1734
Henry Bostwick to [?], Dec. 10, 1764
James DeLancey to Cadwallader Colden, Nov. 4, 1757
James DeLancey to Colonels of Ulster and Dutchess Counties
James DeLancey to Jacob Glen and John V. Rensselaer, Sep. 1, 1754
James DeLancey to Maj. Gen. Johnson, August [?] 1755
Jacob Glen invoice to Storke & Gainsborough, Sep. 10. 1736
Lord Hillsborough to Sir William Johnson, Dec. 4, 1771; Jul. 1, 1772
List of Indian attacks, 1746–1759

2. SECONDARY SOURCES CONTAINING PRIMARY MATERIALS

BARBER, JOHN W., and HENRY HOWE. *Historical Collections of the State of New York.* New York: Tuttle, 1842.
BENSON, ADOLPH, ed. *Peter Kalm's Travels in North America: The English Version of 1770.* New York: Dover, 1987.
CRARY, CATHERINE S. *The Price of Loyalty: Tory Writings from the Revolutionary Era.* New York: McGraw-Hill, 1973.

DUFFY, JOHN J., ed., with Ralph H. Orth, Kevin Graffagnino, and Michael A. Bellesiles. *Ethan Allen and His Kin.* Correspondence, 1772–1819. 2 vols. Hanover, N.H.: University Press of New England, 1998.

EVANS, CHARLES, ed. *American Bibliography: A Chronological Dictionary of All Books, Pamphlets, and Periodical Publications Printed in the United States of America . . . 1630 . . . to . . . 1820.* 12 vols. Chicago, 1903–1934.

FORD, PAUL LEICESTER. *The Journals of Hugh Gaine, Printer.* Vol. 1. New York: Dodd, Mead, 1911.

FRANKLIN, BENJAMIN. *The Papers of Benjamin Franklin.* 34 vols. Ed. Leonard W. Labaree. New Haven, Conn.: Yale University Press, 1959–1998.

GAGE, THOMAS. *The Correspondence of General Thomas Gage with the Secretaries of State, and with the War Office and the Treasury, 1763–1775.* 2 vols. Ed. Clarence Edwin Carter. Hamden, Conn.: Archon, 1969.

[GRANT, MRS. ANNE]. *Memoirs of an American Lady, with Sketches of Manners and Scenery as They Existed Previous to the Revolution.* 2 vols. London: A. K. Newman, 1817.

KERKKONEN, MARTTI. *Peter Kalm's North American Journey: Its Ideological Background and Results.* Helsinki, Finland: Finnish Historical Society, 1959.

KLEIN, MILTON M., ed. *The Independent Reflector, or Weekly Essays on Sundry Important Subjects, More particularly adapted to the Province of New York.* By William Livingston and Others. Cambridge, Mass.: Belknap Press of Harvard University Press, 1963.

M'ROBERT, PATRICK. *A Tour Through Part of the North Provinces of America.* Edinburgh, 1776. Offprint from the *Pennsylvania Magazine of History and Biography,* April 1935, by the Historical Society of Pennsylvania.

SEABURY, SAMUEL. *Letters of a Westchester Farmer, 1774–1775.* Ed. Clarence H. Vance. New York: Da Capo Press, 1970.

SMITH, WILLIAM. *Historical Memoirs of William Smith.* 3 vols. Ed. William H. W. Sabine. New York: Colburn & Tegg, 1956.

STOKES, I. N. PHELPS. *The Iconography of Manhattan Island, 1498–1909.* 6 vols. New York: The Lawbook Exchange, Ltd., 1998.

WILLARD, M. W., ed. *Letters on the American Revolution, 1774–76.*

3. GENERAL WORKS

ABBOTT, CARL. "The Neighborhoods of New York, 1760–1775." *New York History* 55 (1974): 35–54.

ALBERTS, ROBERT C. *The Most Extraordinary Adventures of Major Robert Stobo.* Boston: Houghton Mifflin, 1965.

ALDEN, JOHN RICHARD. *General Gage in America.* Baton Rouge: Louisiana State University Press, 1948.

———. *A History of the American Revolution.* New York: Knopf, 1969.

AMMERMAN, DAVID. *In the Common Cause: American Response to the Coercive Acts of 1774.* New York: Norton, 1974.

ANDERSON, FRED. *Crucible of War: The Seven Years' War and the Fate of Empire in British North America, 1754–1766.* New York: Knopf, 2000.

APPLEBY, JOYCE. "The Social Origins of American Revolutionary Ideology." *Journal of American History* 64 (4) (March 1978).

BAILYN, BERNARD. *Faces of Revolution: Personalities and Themes in the Struggle for American Independence.* New York: Knopf, 1990.

BARROW, THOMAS C. "Background to the Grenville Program, 1757–1763." *William and Mary Quarterly,* 3rd Ser., vol. 22, no. 1 (January 1965).

BASKERVILLE, CHARLES A. "The Foundation Geology of New York City." *Geological Society of America Reviews in Engineering Geology* 5 (1982).

BECKER, CARL LOTUS. *The History of Political Parties in the Province of New York, 1760–1776.* Madison: University of Wisconsin Press, 1968.

BELOFF, MAX, ed. *The Debate on the American Revolution, 1761–1783.* Dobbs Ferry, N.Y.: Sheridan, 1989.

BLIVEN, BRUCE, JR. *Battle for Manhattan.* New York: Holt, 1956.

———. *Under the Guns: New York, 1775–1776.* New York: Harper & Row, 1972.

BONOMI, PATRICIA U. *A Factious People: Politics and Society in Colonial New York.* New York: Columbia University Press, 1971.

———. "Political Patterns in Colonial New York City: The General Assembly Election of 1768." *Political Science Quarterly* 81 (1966).

BRANDT, CLARE. *An American Aristocracy: the Livingstons.* Poughkeepsie, N.Y.: privately published, 1990.

BRIDENBAUGH. CARL. *Mitre and Sceptre: Transatlantic Faiths, Ideas, Personalities, and Politics, 1689–1775.* New York: Oxford, 1967.

BROWNING, REED. "The Duke of Newcastle and the Financing of the Seven Years' War." *Journal of Economic History* 31 (1971).

BULLION, JOHN L. *A Great and Necessary Measure: George Grenville and the Genesis of the Stamp Act, 1763–1765.* Columbia: University of Missouri Press, 1982.

BURROWS, EDWIN G., and MIKE WALLACE. *Gotham: A History of New York City to 1898.* New York: Oxford, 1999.

CALHOON, ROBERT M. "William Smith Jr.'s Alternative to the American Revolution." *William and Mary Quarterly,* 3rd ser., vol. 22, no. 1 (January 1965).

CARMER, CARL. *The Hudson.* New York: Farrar & Rinehart, 1939.

CARVER, JONATHAN. *Travels Through the Interior Parts of North America in the Years 1766, 1767, and 1768.* London: Dilly, 1781.

CHAMPAGNE, ROGER J. *Alexander McDougall and the American Revolution in New York.* Schenectady, N.Y.: Union College Press, 1975.

———. "The Sons of Liberty and the Aristocracy in New York Politics, 1765–1790." Ph.D. thesis, University of Wisconsin, 1960.

CHASTELLUX, MARQUIS DE. *Travels in North America in the Years 1780, 1781, and 1782.* Trans. by Howard C. Rice, Jr. Chapel Hill: University of North Carolina Press, 1963.

CHRISTEN, ROBERT J. *King Sears: Politician and Patriot in a Decade of Revolution.* New York: Arno Press, 1982.

COLLEY, LINDA. *Britons.* New Haven, Conn.: Yale University Press, 1992.

CONGER, MARY DE PEYSTER RUTGERS MCCREA. *New York's Making: Seen through the Eyes of My Ancestors.* London: Methuen, 1938.

COOK, DON. *The Long Fuse: How England Lost the American Colonies, 1760–1785.* New York: Atlantic Monthly Press, 1995.

COUNTRYMAN, EDWARD. *A People in Revolution: The American Revolution and Political Society in New York, 1760–1790.* New York: Norton, 1989.

CUMMING, WILLIAM P. *British Maps of Colonial America.* Chicago: University of Chicago Press, 1974.

CURREY, CECIL B. *Road to Revolution: Benjamin Franklin in England, 1765–1775.* Garden City, N.Y.: Anchor, 1968.

DAVIDSON, MARSHALL B. *The Horizon History of the World in 1776.* New York: American Heritage, 1975.

DAVIDSON, PHILIP. *Propaganda and the American Revolution, 1763–1783.* Chapel Hill: University of North Carolina Press, 1941.

DAVIS, DAVID BRION, and STEVEN MINTZ. *The Boisterous Sea of Liberty: A Documentary History of America from Discovery through the Civil War.* New York: Oxford, 1998.

DAWSON, HENRY B. *The Sons of Liberty in New York.* New York: Arno Press, 1969.

———. *New York City during the American Revolution.* New York: Mercantile Library Association, 1861.

DECKER, MALCOLM. *Brink of Revolution: New York in Crisis, 1765–1776.* New York: Argosy Antiquarian, 1964.

DE LANCEY, EDWARD F. "Memoir of the Hon. James DeLancey, Lieut. Gov. of the Province of New York." *Documentary History of the State of New York.* Vol. 4.

DEMOS, JOHN. *The Unredeemed Captive.* New York: Knopf, 1994.

DILLON, DOROTHY RITA. *The New York Triumvirate: A Study of the Legal and Political Careers of William Livingston, John Morin Scott, William Smith, Jr.* New York: Columbia University Press, 1949.

DRAPER, THEODORE. *A Struggle for Power: The American Revolution.* New York: Vintage, 1997.

EINSTEIN, LEWIS. *Divided Loyalties: Americans in England During the War of Independence.* London: Cobden-Sanderson, 1933.

ELLIS, JOSEPH J. *Founding Brothers: The Revolutionary Generation.* New York: Knopf, 2000.

FARRAGHER, JOHN MACK. *Daniel Boone: The Life and Legend of an American Pioneer.* New York: Holt, 1992.

FISCHER, DAVID HACKETT. *Paul Revere's Ride.* New York: Oxford, 1994.

FLEXNER, JAMES THOMAS. *Mohawk Baronet: Sir William Johnson of New York.* New York: Harper, 1959.

———. *George Washington: The Forge of Experience (1732–1775).* Boston: Little, Brown, 1965.

———. *George Washington in the American Revolution (1775–1783).* Boston: Little, Brown, 1968.

————. *States Dyckman, American Loyalist.* Boston: Little, Brown, 1980.

FLICK, ALEXANDER C., ed. *The American Revolution in New York.* Albany: University of the State of New York, 1926.

FREEMAN, DOUGLAS SOUTHALL. *George Washington.* 6 vols. New York: Scribner's, 1948–1954.

FRIEDMAN, BERNARD. "The Shaping of the Radical Consciousness in Provincial New York." *Journal of American History* 56 (4) (March 1970).

GIPSON, LAWRENCE HENRY. *The British Empire Before the American Revolution.* 15 vols. New York: Knopf, 1936–1970.

————. *The Coming of the Revolution, 1763–1775.* New York: Harper, 1954.

GRAFFAGNINO, J. KEVIN. *Ethan and Ira Allen: Collected Works.* 3 vols. Benson, Vt.: Chalidze Publications, 1992.

GREENE, EVARTS B., and RICHARD B. MORRIS. *A Guide to the Principal Sources for Early American History (1600–1800) in the City of New York.* New York: Columbia University Press, 1929.

GREENE, EVARTS B., and VIRGINIA D. HARRINGTON. *American Population Before the Census of 1790.* New York: Genealogical Publishing Co., 1993.

GREGORY, JAMES, compiler. *Narratives of the Revolution in New York.* New York: New-York Historical Society, 1975.

HAMILTON, EDWARD P. *The French and Indian Wars.* Garden City, N.Y.: Doubleday, 1962.

HARRINGTON, VIRGINIA D. *The New York Merchant on the Eve of the Revolution.* Gloucester, Mass.: Peter Smith, 1964.

HINDLE, BROOKE. "A Colonial Governor's Family: The Coldens of Coldengham." *New-York Historical Society Quarterly* 15 (3) (July 1961).

HINKHOUSE, FRED JUNKIN. *The Preliminaries of the American Revolution as Seen in the English Press.* New York: Octagon Press, 1969.

HOBHOUSE, HENRY. *Seeds of Change: Five Plants That Changed Mankind.* New York: Harper & Row, 1985.

HOERMANN, ALFRED R. "A Savant in the Wilderness: Cadwallader Colden of New York." *New-York Historical Society Quarterly* 62 (1978).

HOMBERGER, ERIC. *The Historical Atlas of New York City.* New York: Holt, 1994.

JAMES, LAWRENCE. *The Rise and Fall of the British Empire.* London: Abacus, 1998.

JONES, ALICE HANSON. *Wealth of a Nation to Be: The American Colonies on the Eve of the Revolution.* New York: Columbia University Press, 1980.

JONES, THOMAS. *History of New York During the Revolutionary War.* 2 vols. Ed. Edward Floyd DeLancey. New York: New-York Historical Society, 1879.

KALLICH, MARTIN, and ANDREW MACLEISH, eds. *The American Revolution through British Eyes.* Evanston, Ill.: Row, Peterson, 1962.

KALLINEN, MAIJA. "Pehr Kalm (1716–79)—Explorer, professor of economics." Unpublished paper.

KAMMEN, MICHAEL G. *A Rope of Sand: The Colonial Agents, British Politics, and the American Revolution.* Ithaca, N.Y.: Cornell University Press, 1968.

KETCHUM, RICHARD M., ed. *The American Heritage Book of the Revolution.* New York: American Heritage, 1958.

———. "England's Vietnam." *American Heritage,* June 1971.

———. *Saratoga: Turning Point of America's Revolutionary War.* New York: Holt, 1997.

KEYS, ALICE MAPELSDEN. *Cadwallader Colden: A Representative Eighteenth Century Official.* New York: AMS Press, 1967.

KIERSCH, GEORGE A. "Environmental/Engineering Geology of Alluvial Settings." *Engineering Geology* 45 (1996): 325–46.

KNOLLENBERG, BERNHARD. *Origin of the American Revolution: 1759–1766.* New York: Macmillan, 1960.

KOUWENHOVEN, JOHN A. *The Columbia Historical Portrait of New York.* New York: Columbia University Press, 1953.

LEAKE, ISAAC Q. *Memoir of the Life and Times of General John Lamb.* Albany, N.Y.: Joel Munsell, 1857.

LLOYD, ALAN. *The King Who Lost America: A Portrait of the Life and Times of George III.* Garden City, N.Y.: Doubleday, 1971.

LONG, J. C. *Mr. Pitt and America's Birthright: A Biography of William Pitt the Earl of Chatham, 1708–1778.* New York: Stokes, 1940.

LONG, J. H., ed. *Atlas of Historical County Boundaries.* New York: 1993

MACALPINE, IDA, and RICHARD HUNTER. *George III and the Mad-Business.* New York: Pantheon, 1969.

MACDOUGALL, WILLIAM L. *American Revolutionary: A Biography of General Alexander McDougall.* Westport, Conn.: Greenwood Press, 1977.

MCCARDELL, LEE. *Ill-Starred General: Braddock of the Coldstream Guards.* Pittsburgh, Pa.: University of Pittsburgh Press, 1958.

MCFARLAND, PHILIP. *The Brave Bostonians: Hutchinson, Quincy, Franklin, and the Coming of the American Revolution.* Boulder, Colo.: Westview Press, 1998.

MCKEE, SAMUEL. *Labor in Colonial New York, 1664–1776.* New York: Columbia University Press, 1935.

MAIER, PAULINE. "John Wilkes and American Disillusionment with Britain." *William and Mary Quarterly,* 3rd ser., vol. 20 (July 1963).

———. "Popular Uprisings and Civil Authority in Eighteenth-Century America." *William and Mary Quarterly,* 3rd ser., vol. 27 (1970).

———. *The Old Revolutionaries: Political Lives in the Age of Samuel Adams.* New York: Knopf, 1980.

———. *From Resistance to Revolution: Colonial Radicals and the Development of American Opposition to Britain, 1765–1776.* New York: Norton, 1991.

MAIN, JACKSON TURNER. *The Social Structure of Revolutionary America.* Princeton, N.J.: Princeton University Press, 1965.

MILLER, JOHN C. *Origins of the American Revolution.* Boston: Little, Brown, 1943.

———. *Sam Adams, Pioneer in Propaganda.* Boston: Little, Brown, 1936.

MOORE, FRANK. *Diary of the American Revolution.* 2 vols. New York: Charles Scribner, 1860.

MORGAN, EDMUND S., and HELEN M. MORGAN. *The Stamp Act Crisis: Prologue to Revolution.* Chapel Hill: University of North Carolina Press, 1953.

MORRIS, RICHARD B. "James DeLancey: Portrait in Loyalism." Ed. Philip Ranlet. *New York History,* April 1999.

MORRIS, RICHARD B., et al. *The Development of a Revolutionary Mentality.* Washington: Library of Congress, 1972.

NEWBOLD, ROBERT C. *The Albany Congress and Plan of Union of 1754.* New York: Vantage, 1955.

NICOLSON, COLIN. "Governor Francis Bernard, the Massachusetts Friends of Government, and the Advent of the Revolution." *Proceedings of the Massachusetts Historical Society* 103 (1991).

O'CALLAGHAN, E. B., ed. *Documents Relative to the Colonial History of the State of New York.* 15 vols. Albany, 1853–1857.

PARES, RICHARD. *Merchants and Planters.* Cambridge, England: Cambridge University Press, 1960.

[PENHALLOW, SAMUEL]. *Penhallow's Indian Wars.* Ed. Edward Wheelock. Reprint of the 1726 edition. Boston, 1924.

PHILLIPS, KEVIN. *The Cousins' Wars: Religion, Politics, and the Triumph of Anglo-America.* New York: Basic Books, 1999.

PLUMB, J. H. *England in the Eighteenth Century.* Baltimore, Md.: Penguin, 1966.
———. *The First Four Georges.* New York: Wiley, 1967.

RANLET, PHILIP. *The New York Loyalists.* Knoxville: University of Tennessee Press, 1986.
———, ed. "Richard B. Morris's James DeLancey: Portrait in Loyalism." *New York History,* April 1999.

RANTOUL, ROBERT S. "The Cruise of the 'Quero': How We Carried the News to the King." *Historical Collections of the Essex Institute* 36 (1) (January 1900).

RITCHESON, CHARLES R. *British Politics and the American Revolution.* Norman: University of Oklahoma Press, 1954.

ROSEBROCK, ELLEN F. *Farewell to Old England: New York in Revolution.* New York: South Street Seaport Museum, 1976.

SABINE, W. H. W. *Suppressed History of General Nathaniel Woodhull.* New York: Colburn & Tegg, 1954.

SCHUTZ, JOHN A. *Thomas Pownall, British Defender of American Liberty.* Glendale, Calif.: Arthur H. Clark, 1951.

SELLERS, CHARLES COLEMAN. *Patience Wright: American Artist and Spy in George III's London.* Middletown, Conn.: Wesleyan University Press, 1976.

SELLERS, CHARLES G., JR. "Private Profits and British Colonial Policy." *William and Mary Quarterly,* 3rd ser., vol. 8 (1951).

SELLERS, LEILA. *Charleston Business on the Eve of the American Revolution.* Chapel Hill: University of North Carolina Press, 1934.

SHY, JOHN. *Toward Lexington: The Role of the British Army in the Coming of the American Revolution.* Princeton, N.J.: Princeton University Press, 1965.

SINGLETON, ESTHER. *Social New York under the Georges, 1714–1776.* New York: Appleton, 1902.

SMITH, WILLIAM, JR. *The History of the Province of New York.* Ed. Michael Kammen. 2 vols. Cambridge, Mass.: Harvard University Press, 1972.

SOSIN, JACK M. *Agents and Merchants: British Colonial Policy and the Origins of the American Revolution, 1763–1775.* Lincoln: University of Nebraska Press, 1965.

STEELE, IAN K. *Betrayals: Fort William Henry and the "Massacre."* New York: Oxford, 1990.

STEINER, BRUCE E. *Samuel Seabury, 1729–1796: A Study in the High Church Tradition.* Oberlin: Ohio University Press, 1971.

SWEET, WILLIAM WARREN. "The Role of the Anglicans in the American Revolution." *Huntington Library Quarterly* 2 (1947–1948).

TIEDEMANN, JOSEPH S. *Reluctant Revolutionaries: New York City and the Road to Independence, 1763–1776.* Ithaca, N.Y.: Cornell University Press, 1997.

TOURTELLOT, ARTHUR BERNON. *William Diamond's Drum: The Beginning of the War of the American Revolution.* New York: Doubleday, 1959.

VAIL, R.W.G. "The Loyalist Declaration of Dependence of November 28, 1776."

VALENTINE, ALAN. *Lord North.* Norman: University of Oklahoma Press, 1967.

VAN DOREN, CARL. *Benjamin Franklin.* New York: Viking, 1938.

WARFEL, HARRY R., RALPH H. GABRIEL, and STANLEY T. WILLIAMS. *The American Mind: Selections from the Literature of the United States.* New York: American Book Co., 1937.

WERTENBAKER, THOMAS JEFFERSON. *Father Knickerbocker Rebels: New York City During the Revolution.* New York: Scribner's, 1948.

WESLAGER, C. A. *The Stamp Act Congress: With an Exact Copy of the Complete Journal.* Newark: University of Delaware Press, 1976.

WESTBROOK, NICHOLAS. "Like Roaring Lions Breaking from Their Chains; The Highland Regiment at Ticonderoga." *The Bulletin of Fort Ticonderoga* 16 (1) (1998).

WILCOX, RUTH TURNER. *The Mode in Furs.* New York: Scribner's, 1951.

WRIGHT, ESMOND. *Franklin of Philadelphia.* Cambridge, Mass.: Belknap Press, 1997.

————, ed. *Benjamin Franklin: His Life as He Wrote It.* Cambridge, Mass.: Harvard University Press, 1996.

4. REFERENCE SOURCES

BOATNER, MARK MAYO III. *Encyclopedia of the American Revolution.* New York: David McKay, 1966.

MORRIS, RICHARD B. *Encyclopedia of American History.* New York: Harper & Row, 1961.

SABINE, LORENZO. *The American Loyalists, or Biographical Sketches of Adherents to the British Crown in the War of the Revolution.* Boston: Charles C. Little and James Brown, 1847.

SOURCE NOTES

Like my earlier books on the American Revolution, this book is based as far as possible on contemporary evidence—on the written testimony of eyewitnesses who were on the scene in those deeply troubling, challenging years. Anyone who is truly interested in history finds a way, sooner or later, to get into the shoes of the people of that other day, to try to see things as they saw them, to understand the problems that confronted them. Once you have done so you appreciate that we cannot judge the people of another time in the light of what we know today, or how our society chooses to assess right and wrong. Judge, if you will, but on their terms and from the perspective of their times.

Although it sometimes seems miraculous that so much of our past has been preserved in the form of letters, journals, diaries, and newspapers, it is sadly true that what we have is a mere fraction of what once existed. In deciding to concentrate on New York City, I was aware of the wealth of firsthand accounts accessible in a number of truly great repositories—the New-York Historical Society, the New York Public Library, the Morgan Library, the Museum of the City of New York, Columbia University, and others. In fact, the riches were almost too much; I have had to omit many illuminating or entertaining documents simply because they repeated what was available from another source. And yet, paradoxically, there is never really enough.

Take three of the important protagonists in this book: James DeLancey, Sr., Alexander McDougall, and Isaac Sears. Of the three, only McDougall left behind a substantial quantity of letters, and most of those in the prewar period deal with a relatively brief portion of his activities—mainly his trial and involvement with the Sons of Liberty. From the paucity of the evidence, I concluded that neither DeLancey nor Sears was much of a writer. Where others talked or wrote, Sears took action, and it is hard to avoid the feeling that those documents from his hand that survive were written grudgingly and quickly, because he had no time to waste. DeLancey's case is somewhat different. He was, of course, in a position of considerable authority through much of his working life, and his involvement in affairs was often recorded in the form of notes taken by a secretary. But he was also, and primarily, a politician, and a politician's bargains are best kept from prying eyes, as DeLancey knew.

The following notes indicate the principal sources of quotations or assertions for the guidance of the general reader interested in learning more or knowing what books I found most helpful. I have not provided citations for the many sources consulted for background information—only those whose contents deal specifically with the events described here. Neither have I cited sources where the text makes clear that it is, for example, a newspaper of a specific date. Works cited are usually identified as briefly as possible, and their presence there is the best indication that they were valuable—in some cases invaluable—to me.

A word about abbreviations. The so-called Aspinwall Papers, published by the Massachusetts Historical Society, are listed here as MHS IX and X. N-YHS is New-York Historical Society. NYPL is New York Public Library.

Prologue
Alice DeLancey Izard's March 23, 1776, letter to her mother, Mrs. Peter DeLancey, is in the Museum of the City of New York, DeLancey Family Reminiscences, 1850, #49.48.68.

1. A Most Splendid Town
For a description of New York City in the eighteenth century an indispensable source is Isaac Newton Phelps Stokes's six-volume *The Iconography of Manhattan Island, 1498–1909*. It has been enormously useful throughout the writing of this book, for in addition to the extraordinary collection of maps and views of the city within its pages, it has what amounts to a day-by-day account of events, drawn largely from local newspapers and letters for the entire period of my study. The quotations in the opening paragraph are from Carl Carmer's *The Hudson* 61–62 and Stokes 1:114.

Another superb source is John Kouwenhoven's *The Columbia Historical Portrait of New York,* in which the story is told entirely through contemporary illustrations and maps, with Mr. Kouwenhoven's incisive captions. The first chapter of Esther Singleton's charming *Social New York under the Georges, 1714–1776* has a number of quotations from visitors to the city, and her book is extremely useful in terms of the habits and lifestyles of the more affluent inhabitants. For population figures, Abbott and Singleton are helpful. Stokes 4:716, Jan. 1761, gives a figure for that date of 2,737 houses; I used the rounded-off figure of 2,000 houses in Greene and Harrington 101fn.

From Singleton 4–5 come the city's dimensions and the quotation on what advantages they gave tradespeople.

My information on Franklin's activity as postmaster general is from Carl Van Doren's splendid one-volume biography, 211–13.

Bruce Bliven's excellent *Under the Guns: New York: 1775–1776* describes the semiannual arrivals of English merchant ships, 43.

The comments of Anne Watts and Anne Moore on the social scene are contained in some delightful gossipy letters from the two young ladies to Anne DeLancey, from the DeLancey Family Reminiscences at the Museum of the City of New York.

Singleton 265 mentions the arrival of the governor with "gouff clubs."

Harrington 21–33 provides a well-rounded picture of the merchant prince's milieu and includes the acid comment from John Adams.

Descriptions of the city at this time are in Stokes 1:165, 184, and 200; Bliven *Guns* 179–80; Ketchum *Saratoga* 4; and Singleton 24.

Information on beaver and the fur trade comes from the *New-York Gazette* of Feb. 3, 1766, and Wilcox 78–80 and 103.

Mrs. Grant, who lived with the Schuyler family for years, provides a delightful inside look at Albany and what life was like on an immense estate in the upper Hudson Valley.

Dawson's incomparable *New York City during the American Revolution* is by far the best source of information on lower Manhattan, its streets, public buildings, churches, and other landmarks, the people who lived there, and the merchants who traded and counted their money there.

The issue of the *New-York Mercury* cited was Feb. 25, 1765. The number of churches was determined from Ratzer's 1767 map of Manhattan, a superb piece of work which gives us an exact scheme of the city more than two and a third centuries ago.

Descriptions of the merchants' homes are in Wertenbaker 13, Dawson *New York City* 13–15, Harrington 25fn, and Stokes 4:710.

In two of his chapters, "Income and Property" and "Standards and Styles of Living," Main offers interesting comparisons of the cost of living for lower and upper classes that give a good picture of life in colonial times.

Flexner *Dyckman* 11 describes the terrain and roads at the upper end of Manhattan. Burrows and Wallace 105 mentions the tidy toll arrangement Frederick Philipse had across Spuyten Duyvill Creek. My description of the west side of Manhattan Island draws on Wertenbaker 15–16 and Dawson *New York City* 15–17 and 28–29.

Thomas Jones's house on Mount Pitt is described in his *History of New York* lix–lxi. The value of DeLancey's estate as estimated by Watts appears in a letter from Richard Peters to Monckton on Aug. 21, 1760, and in another on Sept. 11. They are in MHS IX 304 and 319.

Abbott 50 gives the grim picture of New York's slums, and Burrows and Wallace 182 discusses press-gangs and the reaction to them. Robberies and "whippings at the cart's tail" are mentioned in Stokes 4:711 and the free school is cited on 4:714. Singleton 4 notes conditions in the Out Ward.

The smallpox outbreak in Boston is mentioned in a letter from Elizabeth Lloyd Fitch to her father on Long Island and appears in Lloyd Family Papers II, 591.

Abbott 49–50 discusses the state of King's College at this time and Stokes 4:711 and 714 takes note of the funds voted for a pesthouse and a new jail. Burrows and Wallace 172 has the figures on population for New York, Boston, and Philadelphia.

The Scottish visitor—in the years 1774 and 1775—was Patrick M'Robert, and his letters are among the very best in travel literature, based on acute observation. He speaks only casually of the growing difficulties between colonies and mother country; his interest is in the basics of life—farming, industry, trade, the value of the many kinds of coins passed from hand to hand in the various provinces; the roads existing in North America, running from New York to Charleston, to Canada, and to Boston, from Long Island to New York on the Post Road, and from Louisbourg to the mouth of the Mississippi River, with mileages between each town along the route. In Nova Scotia he found the best grazing land he had seen in North America; on the island of St. John's he visited the governor's experimental vegetable garden and assessed the local horses, cattle ("a very good kind, and neat"), and sheep. And his final note before leaving for home has to do with the "unhappy contest" which means that "many fine industrious families, lately in affluence, now do not know where to turn to avoid the dreadful stroke of a desolating war."

2. Salutary Neglect

The late J. H. Plumb's trenchant studies of England during this period are well written, filled with insights into the principal characters, and extremely useful for the background they provide. "The Age of Walpole" in *England in the Eighteenth Century* is of particular interest.

Theodore Draper's excellent *A Struggle for Power* 27–32 has a valuable analysis of British trade policies.

For Kalm, see Benson's *Peter Kalm's Travels in North America.* In the early stages of researching this book I spent many happy hours reading Kalm's account of his travels through the colonies from 1748 to 1751, during which he visited a good many of America's men of science, saw some of the important cities as well as the countryside of the land, and witnessed at first hand the frightening warfare on the frontier. His comments on the natural world are of special interest, for he was exploring at the behest of Sweden the plants that might be commercially useful to that country.

J. C. Long 39 and 96, Plumb's *The First Four Georges* 86–90, and Lloyd 37 have helpful assessments of Pitt and George II during the Seven Years' War.

To appreciate the scope and extraordinary amount of information in Lewis Evans's 1755 map takes hours of careful study and makes one realize how difficult it must have been for the cartographer to assemble so many facts and such an accurate portrayal of the colonies at that early date. Evans had help, to be sure, but it was he who did the fieldwork on this remarkable project.

Lawrence Gipson's monumental study of the British Empire prior to the Revolution—especially 5:304–51—was helpful on the background of the French and Indian War that became the Seven Years' War in Europe. Other sources on Washington's involvement were Edward Hamilton's *The French and Indian Wars* 147–48; Flexner's *Mohawk Baronet* 106; and McCardell's fine study of the Braddock expedition. Colden's observations to Governor Clinton are in his Papers IV 298.

3. Year of Wonders

Gipson 5:323–25 mentions the fruitless discussions between the English and French commissaries about the fighting on the colonial frontier.

Lee McCardell's book is an excellent source of information on the ill-starred Braddock expedition—one that involved so many men who were to go on to considerable fame, among them Benjamin Franklin, George Washington, Thomas Gage, Horatio Gates, Daniel Morgan, Daniel Boone, Christopher Gist, George Croghan, Charles Lee, and Pontiac.

Hamilton 147–59 is another source on the Braddock campaign, as are Alberts 148 for the Stobo episode and Flexner's *Washington: Forge of Experience* 119–31.

Johnson's fight with Dieskau and the "Bloody Morning Scout" are covered in Steele 44–56 and Hamilton 212. The latter also includes on pp. 180–83 a discussion of events at Fort Oswego.

J. C. Long 270 describes Cumberland's disaster at Hastenbeck, and Decker 23 has the quotation from Pitt announcing that he can save the country.

The most recent account of Abercromby's campaign is the excellent article by Nicholas Westbrook in *The Bulletin of Fort Ticonderoga* 16(1) (1998). Carefully researched and well written, using a wealth of previously unpublished documents, it reveals the errors in many eighteenth- and nineteenth-century histories and sheds new light on the participants and events.

Pitt's plans for North America and events there are described in Hamilton 214–59 and J. C. Long 266–313.

The 1759 letter from Samuel Denny to his nephew in Suffolk came to me through the kindness of Sydney N. Stokes, Jr. It is from his family's papers.

The fall of Quebec is described in Hamilton 277–90 and J. C. Long 312–15.

Walpole's comments are in his *Letters* 3:250, 259.

A summary of what Britain achieved in the Seven Years' War appears in Fred Anderson's superb *Crucible of War* 453–56. This is by all odds the best book I have read on the French and Indian Wars of the eighteenth century; it makes the very important point that these conflicts on the fringe of the colonies were at the root of the American Revolution.

Linda Colley describes the portrait of George II by Robert Edge Pine, with a reproduction of the painting, in her *Britons* 204–5. Her excellent assessment of George III's reign appears on pp. 204–36. Much of this, of course, has to do with the post-Revolution period.

In Ketchum, *The American Heritage Book of the Revolution,* the chapter "The World Beyond America," by J. H. Plumb, is an excellent depiction of Britain and the continent at this period.

4. Join or Die

According to Anderson 410, the British force present at the surrender of Montreal was some 10,000 regulars, 6,500 provincials, and 700 Iroquois.

Events in various sections of the colonies in 1760 are described in letters in MHS IX 303–65 *passim.* The letter from Richard Peters to Monckton is on pp. 299–301.

The best description of DeLancey's final hours appears in William Smith's *History of the Province of New York* 2:244. Colden alludes to DeLancey's death in MHS IX 1–2, and the lieutenant governor's complaint about his temper is in Colden Papers IV 125.

A fine appraisal of James DeLancey, Sr., and his political career may be found in Tiedemann 32–34, an excellent book covering this period in New York history.

Patricia Bonomi's splendid study, *A Factious People,* discusses the structure of New York's government on pages 158–59.

Smith's *History* 2:132–35, has the account of Osborn's arrival, his depression, and subsequent suicide. One of the joys of researching a project such as this one is of making the acquaintance of a man like William Smith, Jr. His *History of the Province of New York,* mentioned above, took the story to 1762. In 1916 the New York Public Library purchased Smith's papers, observing that they "constitute a remarkable collection of primary evidence on the administrative and political history of New York in its most stirring period—1763–83." William H. W. Sabine assembled these thousands of pages of handwritten documents chronologically, and typed them, following Smith's spelling, punctuation, and capitalization exactly. The result, as Sabine wrote in his Foreword, is a verbatim copy of the "Memoirs of a man who was a member of the Legislative council of the Province of New York from 1767 to the departure of the British in 1783, of a man who recorded many of the most secret transactions of those years which saw the Revolution preparing and of those during which it struggled to victory." Smith was "a Whig who adhered to the Crown," who was "mildly outlawed by his own party, and coldly received by the Tories . . . [and] held firmly to the principle of a united Empire. He foresaw that America would one day be the greatest of all."

A detailed account of the Albany Congress is in Newbold. Van Doren 221–27 discusses Franklin and the congress, making clear how far ahead of his fellow countrymen Franklin was on the subject of unity and how his ideas were to influence the Constitution. The Plan of Union is printed in the Colden Papers IV 452–57.

Peter Livingston's comments on the feud between his family and the DeLanceys is in his letter to an unknown recipient, Jan. 19, 1769, at the Museum of the City of New York.

Clare Brandt's fascinating study of the Livingston family and Patricia Bonomi's *A Factious People* 69–75 describe the holdings of some of the great landowners in the Hudson Valley and how they came by their property.

Thomas Jones's history of New York is written from the viewpoint of an embittered Tory, so his judgments have to be weighed carefully. On the other hand, few observers were closer to the scene or as knowledgeable about what was happening in the city. On the opposite side of the fence politically were the members of "the triumvirate," whose *Independent Reflector* was immersed in the fight over King's College. That paper (see Klein 34–35) is the source of the value of land donated to the college by Trinity Church. Stokes 4:832, 1773, has details about the site and the view from the college. The triumvirate and their *Reflector* are discussed in Sabine's introduction to Smith's *Memoirs* 1:1–2

Observations on Smith, Scott, and Livingston are in Thomas Jones 1:xi, 1, 3, and 5, Klein 17, and Seabury 9fn.

Livingston's attitude is documented in Klein 24, and some of the material on the three men and *The Independent Reflector* is from the splendid introduction by Milton M. Klein to the book of that name.

5. George—Be a King

Hoermann's article is useful on Colden and his background. Another source is the only biography of Colden, written by Alice Keys. The quotation from Watts is from MHS X 590.

Colden's Letter Books I 48–49 and 55 contain a flurry of letters to various dignitaries advising them of the death of George II, the accession of a new king, and the problem of the warrants for the Great Seal. The proclamation of the accession of George III is in Colden's Papers VI 6–7.

The doggerel warning against the Stuarts is in Bridenbaugh 207.

For material on George III I have drawn on Plumb's *First Four Georges* 92–95; Knollenberg's excellent summary 18–23 entitled "George II Becomes King"; Cook 7–11; Lloyd 40–44, 46, 50, and 135–136; and Colley 206–7.

The excerpt from the king's first speech to Parliament is in Bullion 15–16. The phrase from Pitt is in Draper 4, where the pamphlet war is discussed, 3–11.

The quotation about the value of a French Canada is from Edmund Burke, writing anonymously.

For Franklin's views on the subject of Canada, Van Doren 288–89 and Draper 11–14 are instructive. The excerpt from the *London Magazine* is in Wright's *Franklin of Philadelphia* 156.

John Adams's letter to Mr. Calkoen is quoted from Charles Francis Adams, ed., *The Works of John Adams* 7:266.

Samuel Johnson's endorsement of a French Canada is in his *Taxation No Tyranny* 84, published in London in 1775. The writer complaining about American motives of private interests is quoted in Draper 23.

My section on taxation owes much to Reed Browning's useful analysis of the Treasury under Newcastle's guidance, esp. 375fn.

Material on Pitt's final days in office in 1760 may be found in J. C. Long 372–88 and Cook 29–32. The figures on the workings of patronage on membership in Parliament and votes controlled by various wealthy landowners are also from Cook 26–29.

Burke's remark about how traditional liberties could be preserved in the face of a strong presiding power is from Colley 102.

6. Gentle Shepherd

The Comte de Vergennes's prediction of American independence is from Stokes 1:302.

John Watts's letter is in his *Letter Book* 137–38.

Cook 52 and 55 records George III's comments on Grenville. Ritcheson 8–9 has a good discussion of Grenville's ministry. Colley 197 mentions the prime minister's unwillingness to pay for real estate around Buckingham House.

The American newspaper quoted on customs officials was the *Virginia Gazette* of May 27, 1773. Miller *Origins* 81 *et seq.* is most informative on smuggling and other evasions of the customs and Britain's efforts to remedy them. Tiedemann 59–60 also discusses efforts at reform.

The quotation from Walpole comes from Draper 97–98.

Lloyd 411 has the origin of the Gentle Shepherd nickname for Grenville.

The exchange between Amherst and Johnson is in Flexner's *Mohawk Baronet* 239–41.

Watts's comments are in a Sept. 3, 1763, letter to Monckton, MHS X 490.

Richard Peters's letter to Johnson is in Davis and Mintz 136–37.

The contretemps over Amherst's demands for troops is in Weyman's *New-York Gazette* of Nov. 21, 1763; also see Watts to Monckton, MHS X 505.

Watts's Papers from June 7, 1763, to Sept. 22, 1764, are filled with horror stories from the frontier.

The Proclamation of 1763 is described and quoted in part in Davis and Mintz 144–46.

Draper 198–99 quotes Washington's views on the proclamation.

Knollenberg 104–5 and 138–49 *passim* explains the Sugar Act.

I am much indebted to the remarkable book by Henry Hobhouse and especially for his chapter on the addictive food sugar and its impact on the slave trade and the tax on the colonies. The "five plants that changed mankind" are quinine, sugar, tea, cotton, and the potato—a fascinating book.

Leila Sellers's book on Charleston business is informative on the slave trade, esp. 124–25.

Gipson's *The Coming of the Revolution* 60–68 deals with smuggling, as does Draper 203–4.

Richard Pares 38 is my source for the story of George III and Pitt.

Weslager 28–31 has a section on the shortage of currency.

Stokes 6:169, the John Watts Estate; Watts *Letter Book* x–xiii. Watts is a classic example of how common intermarriage was between the better families of New York. He was himself kin to the Van Rensselaers and Van Cortlandts and married Ann DeLancey, a daughter of Stephen and Ann Van Cortlandt DeLancey and granddaughter of Stephen and Gertrude Schuyler Van Cortlandt. Her sister married Sir Peter Warren (Sir William Johnson's uncle). Her oldest brother was James DeLancey. Another brother married Elizabeth Colden, Cadwallader's daughter. John and Ann Watts had ten children, of whom seven survived and had issue.

Watts's remarks about his children are in his Papers 109–10, and his comments on the Sugar Act are on pp. 212 and 218.

Weyman's *New-York Gazette,* Sept. 17, 1764, quotes the Assembly.

Dawson 57–60 and 64 prints the memorial to the House of Commons.

James Otis's comments are in Morgan 34.

Valentine 116 quotes No. 45 of *The North Briton.*

Gibbon's seemingly unlikely praise for Wilkes appears in Lloyd 147.

Much material on Wilkes may be found in Valentine 115–22, Plumb's *First Four Georges* 119–23, Ritcheson 32–33, and Knollenberg 31–41. The Hogarth caricature is reproduced in Ketchum, *The American Heritage Book of the Revolution* 19.

7. A Stamp Tax

James Otis's treatise on colonial rights is quoted in Weslager 50.

The lively exchange between the New Yorker and the Londoner appeared in the *New-York Gazette* on Jan. 28, 1765, and Feb. 10, 1766.

Samuel Adams is quoted in Draper 219, the Assembly on p. 220.

Smith's complaint appears in his *Memoirs* 1:27.

Letters from Robert R. Livingston are in the George Bancroft Papers: to Robert Livingston in June 1764; to Henry Beekman on July 13, 1764.

Whately's letter to Temple appears in Ritcheson 24fn.

The Colden Papers VI 338–39, has Halifax's request; Colden's letter to the attorney general is in the Letter Books I 405.

Watts's woes appear in his *Letter Book* 163.

Baron and Smith made a fascinating study of killing frosts in New England during the period 1697–1947 and discovered how hard hit the area was by droughts and early or late killing frosts, especially in the years 1760–1764, making it extremely difficult for farmers to make a decent living. As the British discovered, it was no time to plague farmers with new taxes. The figures I have used come mainly from pp. 14–19.

Information on McCulloh and his notion about a stamp tax appears in Charles G. Sellers's article, 548–49.

Bullion 75 notes Jenkinson's involvement with McCulloh and Cruwys. It discusses preliminaries to the Stamp Act 64–77, as does Ritcheson 20–21.

Grenville's soothing words to members of Parliament appear in Morgan 76, and the *New-York Gazette* of Oct. 1, 1764, has the Londoner's jibe at the rich colonials. The latter was echoing Grenville's own remarks in the House of Commons, noted in Bullion 153–59. Kammen's *A Rope of Sand* 3–15 discusses the colonial agents.

The bitter exchange between Townshend and Barré is in Morgan 67–68.

The diagnosis of George III's illness then and two centuries later is discussed at length in Macalpine and Hunter, and his symptoms in 1765 are described on p. 180.

The physical description of the stamps and the selection of distributors in the colonies appears in Weslager 70–73; and Bullion discusses Grenville's ouster, 191. Ritcheson 35–36 has more on this.

James Otis's telling comment is in Bullion 202.

Information on Patrick Henry is in Freeman's *Washington* 3:105–6 and 592–95; the Frenchman's account appears in "Journal of a French Traveler in the Colonies, 1765," *American Historical Review* 21 (1920–1921).

The aftermath of Henry's speech and the Virginia Resolves is discussed fully in Morgan 90–103. Professor Morgan also has an interesting summary on p. 293 of how Henry's speech—while not as violent as men remembered it—was the first breakthrough in the monopoly Speaker Robinson and the elder statesmen had on the House of Burgesses.

8. Slavery Fenced Us In

The information on General Gage is drawn largely from Alden's *Gage* 12–68 *passim*; and in Billias's *George Washington's Opponents* 3–9.

The *New-York Gazette or, the Weekly Post-Boy* of Apr. 15, 1765, carried news of the Stamp Act's terms; the issue of Nov. 7, 1765 included the letter pronouncing that "Slavery . . . fenced us in. . . ."

Robert R. Livingston's depiction of the "general disgust" is in a letter to Monckton, MHS X 559. Maier, in her fine, aptly titled book *From Resistance to Revolution,* quotes Mayhew, 32 and 52. The remarks from Watts appear in MHS X 568 and 572, and Smith's remarks, in a letter to Monckton, are in the same volume, p. 571.

The excerpts from Montresor's diary are dated July 13, 20, and 21 and Sept. 11 and 12.

Members of Boston's Loyal Nine are identified (via John Adams) in Maier 307.

The mob's assault on Oliver's house is described in Morgan 121–25.

The plight of the stamp men McEvers, Hood, and Ingersoll is depicted in the Colden's Papers VI 56–57 and 77–78; and Morgan 152–55.

Robert R. Livingston's comment on the demise of the stamp distributors is in a letter to Monckton, MHS X 559.

The Boston mob's destruction of Hutchinson's home is in Morgan 126–27, and the likely motives in Maier 58.

Weslager quotes from the Massachusetts circular letter 60–61, describes the arrival of the South Carolina delegation 92–93, and gives Colden's reaction 116.

Watts's several letters to Monckton about Colden's behavior are in MHS X 537 and 547–48. Smith's comments are in MHS X 553.

Colden's woes are described in Weslager 118–19, and his discussion of the delegates and their arrival in New York is on pp. 67–99 *passim.*

9. Petitions and a Dagger

Much of the material for this chapter is drawn from C. A. Weslager's *The Stamp Act Congress,* a full account of that signal event. It includes a copy of the journal of the congress, which Mr. Weslager tracked down in a search that proved worthy of a detective novel. After the congress adjourned, an original and twelve replicas of the journal were made. The author found that only two of the replicas and a transcript of a third survived, and of these, only the one taken back to Connecticut by that colony's delegates was complete and accurate.

Two other first-rate studies of the subject are John L. Bullion's *A Great and Necessary Measure* and Edmund S. and Helen M. Morgan's *The Stamp Act Crisis.*

The question of a chairman and the delegates' activities after the close of each session are in Weslager 122–23. The quotation from Judge Livingston is from Brandt 97. Gage's comments on the proceedings are in his Papers I 69–70, Oct. 12, 1765. Reaction in London is noted in Weslager 120–21.

Colden's hasty return to town and his reaction are in his Letter Books II 33–34. The "Negro plot" is described in Barber and Howe, 295–96.

The exchange between Gage and Colden is in Shy 210; Montresor's subsequent report to Colden is summarized in the latter's Papers VII 46 and 73–74 and Colden's Letter Books II 30, 34.

Gage's troop movements are covered in Alden 116–17 and in Gage *Correspondence* I:77.

Colden's preparations and maneuvering during this period can be seen in his Letter Books II 29–30, 32–33, and 33–37.

The Assembly's threat appeared in the *New-York Gazette* of May 24, 1764. Dillon's study of the triumvirate, 88, notes the appointment of a committee of correspondence.

Pauline Maier's chapter "The Making of an American Revolution," in her *From Resistance to Revolution,* is especially good, particularly 227–48. Also, her earlier remarks on the origins of the term "Sons of Liberty" are instructive.

John Watts's reaction to Scott's anonymous essay is in his *Letter Book* 357–58.

Livingston's comment on Colden is in MHS X 560. Colden's remark about the "virulent papers" is in Dawson's *Sons of Liberty* 71. Dillon 88–89 has the denial that Americans desired independence.

Morgan 107–13 is especially good on the different voices and personalities that moved the Stamp Act Congress toward a decision—a line that fell far short of independence but one that clearly indicated where Parliament should stop and go no further.

As noted above, Weslager reproduces the complete journal of the congress. Also, pp. 142–157 cover the discussions in the meetings, and 238–49 deal with the aftermath. P. 251fn, has the quotation from Otis.

Colden's instructions to Captain Kennedy are in Letter Books II 47, and Montresor 336 describes the enraged New Yorkers at the Battery. (See below, in Notes for Chapter 12, information on Montresor's *Journal.*)

The manner in which the stamps were packed is noted in Dawson *Sons of Liberty* 79 and fn. Colden's Papers VII 63, 79, 48, and 50 deal with efforts to unload the *Edward* and with Colden's lack of instructions.

"The last day of Liberty" is mentioned by Livingston: MHS X 560.

Colden's Letter Books II 52, 80, 64, and 66 have his son David's request to the stamp commissioners in London, and the old gentleman's dilemma over enforcing the Stamp Act.

Holt's *New-York Gazette* describes the situation in the city and harbor.

Judge Livingston's Nov. 8, 1765, letter to Monckton , describing the events on the night of November 1, is in MHS X 559–67.

That same letter, and Montresor's *Journal* 336, have details on how the fateful night ended.

10. The City in Perfect Anarchy

The warning about a threat to Major James and Colden's appeal for help are in Colden's Papers VII 85–86 and Letter Books II 53.

Dawson in *Sons of Liberty* has a long footnote on p. 83 offering evidence that Major James indeed threatened to cram the stamps down the throats of the Sons of Liberty.

The description of events on the night of November 1, 1765, is in Judge Livingston's November 8 letter to Monckton, in MHS X 559–67.

Gage's letter to Conway is in his *Correspondence* 1:71. Evidence of Gage's state of mind may be judged from his letters to Conway from Dec. 4, 1765, to Jan. 16, 1766.

Colden's dismay and anger are voiced in Letter Books II 55.

Carther's account of the riot is in Dawson's *New York City during the American Revolution* 42–29. From the same source, 48, comes a description of the trashing of Vauxhall, and Montresor's *Journal* 337 has more.

The best accounts of the Stamp Act rioting are, as noted earlier, Judge Livingston's Nov. 8, 1765, letter to Monckton, MHS X 559–67; Montresor 336–37; and Smith's letter of Nov. 8 to Monckton in his *Historical Memoirs* 1:30–32.

The threat to Colden and his requests for help and advice from the Council and then from Kennedy appear in his Papers VII 84–85, 64–65, and 86. The oystershell message is noted in VII 88, and Montresor's report on the fort's defenses in VII 87–88.

Montresor 338 has the story of "stragglers" from Connecticut and Colden's flight to the *Coventry.*

Allicocke's letter to Lamb is from Lamb Papers, Reel 2, N-YHS.

Colden's Papers VII 67 and 68 note the pressure on him to deliver the stamps, and his determination that the Corporation should handle them.

Gage's warning to Colden are in Montresor 352 and Colden's Papers VII 70.

Watts's disgust with Colden is evident in his letters to Monckton, MHS X 580 and 590, written on Oct. 12, 1765, and Feb. 22, 1766.

Livingston's letter to his cousin is quoted in Bonomi, *A Factious People* 234. His letter to Monckton, describing nonimportation, is in MHS X 565–67.

Smith's concern over civil war is clear from his *Historical Memoirs* 1:30.

11. Madness and Folly

John Watts told Monckton of his misgivings regarding Governor Moore: MHS X 575–76.

Burrows and Wallace 200, Tiedemann 78, and Gage *Correspondence* 1:73 all mention Moore's decision to let New Yorkers suffer the consequences of their own acts.

Colden's Letter Books II 66 and Papers VII 88 mention the warning from Benevolus and Colden's decision to avoid Moore.

Captain Harrington's opinion on dismantling the fort's defenses is from the Pierpont Morgan Library's Gilder Lehrman Collection 00278, Harrington to Williamson, Nov. 20, 1765.

Good material on Isaac Sears exists. Pauline Maier has a splendid chapter on him in *The Old Revolutionaries,* and he is the subject of a good dissertation by Robert Jay Christen, *King Sears: Politician and Patriot in a Decade of Revolution.*

Thomas Jones's apt description of Sears is in his *History* 1:340–41.

For a description of Lamb, I have drawn on Leake's biography, esp. 5–16.

Gage's comments appear in his *Correspondence* 1:78–81. Shy 215 notes the general's shift of troops closer to New York.

Worsening economic conditions are depicted in Harrington 323.

Watts's gloomy forecast is in his Papers 396.

Montresor was no admirer of Governor Moore; his comments are on p. 346 of his *Journal*.

Peter DeLancey's arrival is noted by Watts (*Letter Book* 403).

Hood's escape and capture are chronicled in Gaines's *Mercury*, Dec. 2 and 9, 1765.

Watts's lowering confidence in the government at "Home" is evident in such letters as those to Monckton (Watts *Letter Book* 400–401, 404) and Franks (398, 406).

The Adams diary is quoted in Anderson 683–84, and 686.

The annoyance of king and ministry over Colden's behavior during the Stamp Act riots is in Colden Papers VII 96–98 and in Keys 330–31. Kennedy's punishment is in Colden's Letter Books II 103–7, while reassurance to the likes of Major James appears in Colden Papers VII 98–101.

12. An Act to Repeal an Act

A gloomy letter from Watts to General Monckton is in MHS X 587.

Pauline Maier deals with popular uprisings in her article "Popular Uprisings and Civil Authority," and I have drawn on material from pp. 24–27 and 27fn.

Montresor 349 has his impression of Gage's attitude. In 1778, when Captain John Montresor embarked for England with his wife and family, he devoted many days at sea to writing about his service in America. It was a remarkable story, to say the least. As he observed, he had gone from ensign to chief engineer for the king between 1755 and 1776. He had served under fourteen commanders in chief, among them Braddock, Abercromby, Amherst, Gage, Haldimand, Howe, Clinton, Wolfe, Monckton, and James Murray, whom he described as "a madman." One of those brave, unsung heroes of the British Empire, Montresor had endured unbelievable hardship and fought ("altho' an Engineer," as he says) in numerous engagements against the French and Indians and, later, the Americans. He was responsible for building and rebuilding many a fort, blowing up works, and laying the guns for sieges. A sampling of his notes covers a scout he led from Quebec to Topsham, Maine, between Jan. 26 and Feb. 20, 1760, when he and his men suffered terribly from cold, hunger, and exhaustion. On Feb. 9 they ate the last of their food and were reduced to "eat their leather breeches and raw woodpeckers." Toward the end they ate their bullet pouches and belts, having already devoured the netting and strings from their snowshoes. A later scout—in June and July, fortunately—produced a journal that fell into the hands of Benedict Arnold, to whom it suggested the route he followed in 1775 on his expedition to join Schuyler at Quebec.

The John Lamb Papers at the New-York Historical Society are filled with communications to and from Sons of Liberty in many of the colonies, indicating the extraordinary level of activity of those in New York.

Tiedemann's discussion of the alliance of Sears with the DeLanceys is useful, and Smith's portrayal of the alliance is in his *Historical Memoirs* 1:95.

Oliver DeLancey's understandable nervousness about the family papers is revealed in his letter of Jan. 10, 1766, in the Oliver DeLancey Papers.

Montresor's *Journal* 349–50 has information on Pintard and Williams.

Watts's comments on Colden are in MHS X 586–87.

Montresor's *Journal* 350–57 is my source for much of the material in this chapter.

Leake describes the episode involving Lieutenant Hallam, and the John Lamb Papers contain Bogert's deposition of Mar. 20, 1766.

Dartmouth's remarks about unemployment in England appear in Ritcheson 42fn. The Rockingham dinner parties and the efforts of London merchants to break the impasse are described in Sosin 74–77.

George III's surprising concession on repeal is in Fortescue 1:269.

Jackson's letter to Governor Fitch and many of the actions leading to repeal are discussed in Morgan 266–80. Sosin 79–80 is helpful also. The *Briton's* comment on Franklin was published in the *New-York Gazette* of May 5, 1766

As for details concerning Franklin's remarkable appearance before the House and his testimony, this appears in Van Doren 340–52.

The *New-York Gazette* of May 21 and 26, and June 30, 1766, carried news of repeal and its celebration in London. Montresor's acid comments are from his *Journal* 368.

The appearance of the Liberty Pole is noted in Stokes 4:765, May 21, 1766; and in Countryman 63–64.

Philadelphia's wild enthusiasm for Franklin's achievement and his own uneasiness about the future are in Van Doren 353–55.

The admonitions of the London merchants appeared in the *New-York Gazette,* June 30, 1766.

Leake 35–36 tells of the Liberty Boys' revelry.

13. An Unsupportable Burden

The Gage *Correspondence* 1:xi discusses the magnitude of his assignment in the colonies.

Conway's letters to Gage on Oct. 24, Dec. 15, and Dec. 1765 urge the general to do what he can to reduce tensions and "insure the future Tranquillity & Prosperity of the Colonies." Gage 2:27–32.

Shy 110, 305–8, and 332 has useful information about conditions in the British army at the time.

Gage 1:91–92 and Tiedemann 108–9 describe the contagious "spirit of Riot" and the growing animosity between redcoats and citizens. Gage 1:49 has his letter to Halifax on desertions.

Tiedemann 90–91 speaks of problems raised by the Quartering Act, and Shy 210 explains Gage's dilemma.

Gage's frustrations in trying to get action out of the Assembly are evident in 1:77 in his letter of Dec. 21, 1765, to Conway. His letter to Governor Wright of Georgia is in Alden 125.

Moore's trying time with civil authorities is in Stokes 4:760, Jan 13, 16, 1766.

Feuding between the Moores and the Gages is in Tiedemann 112–13.

The theater riot is reported in *New-York Gazette,* May 8, 1766, and Montresor *Journal* 364. Countryman's discussion of this, 55–56, is especially good.

Stokes 4:739, Jan. 15, 1764, has the story of the initial fight between soldiers and civilians.

Montresor *Journal* 372–73 describes the understandable anger of the troops held aboard ship. The *New-York Gazette,* Aug. 14, 1766, provides details on the felling of the Liberty Pole. Subsequent events are noted in Leake 32–33, Montresor 382–83, Champagne's thesis 121–22, and Stokes 4:769.

Gage's letters from Boston are in Gage 1:204 and 223.

Many had begun to wish Canada were French again; Watts's thoughts are in MHS X 591–92.

Decker 88 mentions the flow of new money.

Shelburne's orders on quartering are in Gage 2:44–45.

The Assembly's astounding refusal to quarter troops is in Champagne's thesis 129–32.

Franklin's remark on petitioning was in the *London Chronicle* of Apr. 9, 1767, quoted in Christen 109, which also has the Watts comment.

Draper 295–98 has a good description of Townshend and the ill-considered Chatham administration; Long 462–63 has Burke's remarks.

Burke's criticism of Townshend appears in Draper 303, which also has, on p. 302, an excerpt from Franklin's letter to Galloway.

The New York tradesman is quoted in Stokes 4:779, Dec. 14, 1767.

Maier *From Resistance to Revolution* 113fn has a succinct assessment of why the Townshend Act was such a threat to colonial assemblies.

14. A Tax on Tea

Brandt 92–94 has an evocative description of the Judge and his wife. Their town house is mentioned in Dawson *New York City* 15.

Christen 120 quotes Sears on the iniquitous lawyers.

Phillips, in the preface and on p. 4, deals with religious disputes.

Seabury's letter about the SPG is quoted in Ranlet 185.

The quotation from Secker appears in Knollenberg 77.

Apthorp's arrival in Boston and his mansion are mentioned in Bridenbaugh 212 and 215–17. The same book is the source of quotations here from John Adams (237), Henry Cruger (256), William Gordon (244–45), and Jonathan Mayhew (202–3).

Lewis Morris's bill to exempt Protestants from taxes to support a church to which they did not belong is in Stokes 4:793, Apr. 6, 1769.

Auchmuty's letter comes from Seabury 3–4.

Stokes 4:778, Aug. 26, 1767, notes the Presbyterians' petition.

The continuing worries over an Anglican bishop and the election of 1768 are discussed in Tiedemann 125–28. Bonomi *A Factious People* 239 takes up the terrible "Contagion of Politiks" and deals with the election, 239–46.

Franklin's letter to a friend, describing the chaos in London, is in Van Doren 381.

Tiedemann 99–100 has a good explanation of Smith's plan of government. Schutz 15–40 *passim* describes what Pownall had in mind. The praise for Pownall by John Adams comes from Cook 141.

Miller *Origins of the American Revolution* 278 has Lord North's thoughts on reconciliation.

15. Incentive to Rebellion

Miller *Origins* 258–61 discusses the Massachusetts circular letter and its reception in London.

Hillsborough's threat appeared in the *New-York Journal*, Oct. 20, 1768.

The appearance of the *Letters* is noted in Stokes 4:779.

Quotations from Dickinson's *Letters* are taken from Warfel *et al.* Cook 125–27 has a good summary of Dickinson and the impact of his writing.

Mr. G. Taylor's account of his visit to New York is summarized in Stokes 4:787–88. In that same volume (766) appears a notice of the equestrian statue of Pitt, and (782) mention of money passed by the Assembly to pay for that and the king's statue. Praise and criticism for the theater is also in Stokes 4:779–81. Maunsell's complaints are in Stokes 4:775.

Smith's remarks appear in MHS X 600, and in his *Historical Memoirs* 1:44.

Miss McVickar's appraisal of Sir Henry Moore appears in Carmer 100.

Chatham's reaction to the petition Moore sent is in Christen 107. The response of Sears and his friends to Hillsborough's instructions is in the same volume, 127–28, and the sense of the resolves on 132.

Moore's words in dissolving the Assembly on Jan. 2, 1769, are reported in Stokes 4:790.

Colden, writing to Hillsborough on Sept. 13 and Oct. 4, 1769, is quoted in the Letter Books II 187–89.

Tiedemann 141–42 does a good job of summarizing the complicated negotiations between Colden and the Assembly. Colden explains his position to Hillsborough in the Letter Books II 194.

Judge Livingston's gloomy forecast is in Brandt 101.

The bizarre method of secretly posting handbills by having a man carry a small boy on his back in a box is set forth in Moore 1:55.

The full text of the handbill appears in Smith *Historical Memoirs* 1:426–30.

16. The Wilkes of America

A vivid description of opening day of Parliament on Jan. 9, 1770, appeared in the London *Gazetteer and New Daily Advertiser* on the 10th and 11th of the month, supplemented by a report in the London *Gazette,* No. 11007 of Jan. 6–9, 1770.

Chatham's speech is reported in detail in J. C. Long 482–86, and Cook 145–146 also reports this signal event. Chatham's final unhappy words on the affair appear in the *Gazetteer and New Daily Advertiser* for Jan. 15, 1770.

Walpole's characterization of North is quoted in Cook 148.

Sears's warning to the Livingstons is quoted in *New-York Journal,* May 10, 1770.

Champagne *Alexander McDougall and the American Revolution* 18–21 discusses McDougall's ideology and ideals.

MacDougall 15 quotes Livingston's estimation of McDougall, and pp. 3–16 tell of his career; more on the career is in Champagne *Alexander McDougall* 5–10.

McDougall's encounter with the chief justice and his letter from jail are reported in the *New-York Journal,* Feb. 15, 1770.

Thomas Jones's comment on Sears and the jurors is in his *History* 1:28–29.

McDougall's conviction and release on bail are described in Champagne *Alexander McDougall* 31–34 and Dillon 113–14. The McDougall saga is chronicled in Thomas Jones 1:23–33, Tiedemann 150ff, Smith 1:73–76, Dillon 107–8, and Champagne *Alexander McDougall* 27–40.

The indictment of McDougall is in N-YHS McDougall Papers, Apr. 27, 1770. His defiance of the Assembly is reported in *New-York Gazette,* Dec. 24, 1770; MacDougall 37; and Champagne *Alexander McDougall* 42–43.

The letter from Benjamin Franklin to McDougall, dated Mar. 18, 1770, is in the Hawkes Collection.

17. Battle of Golden Hill

Colden's letter to Hillsborough is quoted in Christen 181.

The letter from "A.B." appeared in *New-York Journal,* Jan. 18, 1770.

Unless otherwise noted, McDougall's trial and events before and during the Golden Hill battle are from the Supplement to the *New-York Journal* dated Mar. 10, 1770. The New Yorker's letter to a London friend is in Dawson *Sons of Liberty in New York* 117–18fn.

Gage's remarks on the event are in his *Correspondence* 1:248.

Colden's Letter Books II 210–11, contain his accusations.

The antics concerning the Liberty Pole are described in Stokes 4:804–5, for Jan. 30 and Feb. 2, 3, and 6; also Champagne *Alexander McDougall* 26.

Stokes 4:801 notes the dispute between Colden and the new governor.

The comments of Rivington and Duane are from Christen 193.

New-York Journal, Apr. 3, 5, and 19, 1770, has the "Watchman"–"Americanus" argument. Christen 197–201 offers more details.

A letter from Evert Bancker to David Ogden, Jan. 7, 1765, is in N-YHS Bv. New Netherland Vol. Fol. 73.

Rivington's caustic letter to Hays, June 11, 1770, is from the NYPL, Myers Collection #2178.

The London tradesman's letter is in *New-York Journal,* May 10, 1770.

The quotations from George Washington and George Mason appear in Freeman 3:251, 275, and 275fn 50.

The letter reputedly from Franklin is in Gipson *Coming of the Revolution* 193.

Cook 149 has the king's comment on the tea duty. The remark about preserving Parliament's honor is in *New-York Journal,* May 3, 1770.

The Boston Massacre is described in Gage 1:248–51 and was reported in Parker's *New-York Gazette,* Mar. 19, 1770.

Fischer 23 describes Revere's prints.

18. Coercive Measures

These Adams-Macaulay letters in the Gilder Lehrman Collection are dated Aug. 9, 1770, and Dec. 28, 1774.

John Watts's thoughts on the relationship between Britain and America are set forth in a Feb. 16, 1769, letter to Monckton in the Chambers Papers at the New York Public Library.

Marshall Davidson's *World* 62–68 and Ritcheson 68, 79–82, and 155 are informative on Chatham and the East India Company. Tiedemann 175 discusses the company's financial dilemma. Hobhouse 95–137 has an extremely perceptive account of tea and the role of the British East India Company.

Tiedemann 176 notes the arrival of the *Lord Dunmore* and British plans.

The appearance of "Alarm No. 1" is in Christen 278–79.

The whale, the earthquake, and Tryon's letter to Dartmouth are in Stokes 4:841, Oct. 25, 27, and Nov. 3, 1773.

Christen 282–83 mentions the activities of Sears, McDougall, and the "Mohawks."

John Adams's Dec. 11, 1773, letter to Catharine Macaulay is in the Gilder Lehrman Collection.

Samuel Adams's decision to strike a blow is in Miller's *Adams* 285–88.

Smith's *Historical Memoirs* 1:157–62 has his thoughts on the Sons and their deliberations, the reaction of the governor and Council, and the meeting. All Smith items listed hereafter are from *Historical Memoirs.*

The quotation from Hutchinson and propaganda by the Sons are in Philip Davidson 50–51, 58–62.

Smith 1:163 describes Revere's arrival: "The History Place" Web site has an "eyewitness account" of the Boston Tea Party by George Hewes.

Revere's accomplishments are detailed by Fischer 301–2.

Comments on the Tea Party appear in Miller's *Adams* 294–95.

Tryon's correspondence with Dartmouth is in Colden's Papers VII 199–200, where the governor's illness is also noted.

Reference to Sears's nom de plume of Tom Bowline is in Christen 294.

Tiedemann 175–83 has an excellent summary of New Yorkers' response to the Boston Tea Party; Smith 1:163–66 and 173 has more, including Smith's draft of the letter for incoming ships. Tryon's letter to Dartmouth is in Stokes 4:844, Jan. 3, 1774.

Smith 1:166–67 describes the fire in the governor's house.

The letter from New York Sons to those in Boston is in Christen 296.

A report on the voyage of the *Nancy* is in Stokes 4:845, Jan. 6, 1774, and Tryon's departure is mentioned on page 849.

Judge Livingston's letter to Mrs. Tryon is in his Papers at the N-YHS, Apr. 1774. Smith's remarks are in Smith 1:182.

The Chambers incident may be found in Gaine's *New-York Gazette; and the Weekly Mercury* of Apr. 25, 1774; Leake 82–84; Christen 302–3; Smith 1:185; and Stokes 4:849–51.

Morris's comment on the "mobility" is in Philip Davidson 78.

The king's message to Parliament appears in Colden's Papers VII 215.

Alden's *History* has Hutchinson's argument for the supreme authority of Parliament and the Massachusetts House's rebuttal.

John Adams to Macaulay, June 28, 1773, is in the Gilder Lehrman Collection.

Wedderburn's attack on Franklin was reported in the *New-York Journal* of Apr. 14, 1774, and is described by Cook 181–86. Wright's *Life* 209 has Franklin's comment to Cushing; Sosin 160–61 notes the rejection of the charges against Hutchinson. See also Sosin 151–61; Van Doren 444–78.

Burke's advice to the New York Assembly is noted by Sosin 191 and the same source, 170, cites Franklin's agreement with the ministry's decision to close Boston's port.

The king's remark about the Stamp Act repeal is in Sosin 171. Van Doren 369 has Franklin's description of Versailles.

Burke's remarks on the coercive measures are in Colden's Papers VII 232.

19. An Act of Tyranny

Lord North's observation about who was in charge is in Draper 417. Knollenberg 246 lays out the effects of the Coercive Acts.

The report New Yorkers read was in a Supplement to the *New-York Journal* dated June 16, 1774.

Dartmouth's decision to use force is in Draper 418–19.

The reaction to the Quebec Act is in Knollenberg 247; Ritcheson 158–67; and *New-York Journal*, Aug. 25, 1774.

Ritcheson 167–68 and Long 501–3 have Chatham's remarks.

The curious story of Patience Wright and her activities in London is told in Charles Coleman Sellers.

News of the Boston Port Bill and the reaction in New York is in N-YHS: Alexander McDougall, Political Memorandums relative to the Conduct of the Citizens on the Boston Port Bill (hereafter McDougall Memoranda); Champagne *Alexander McDougall* 53 and endnote; Smith 1:186, May 18, 1774; and *New-York Journal,* May 19, 1774.

The Liberty Boys' decision to lobby for a congress and to aid Bostonians is in McDougall Memoranda, May 12 and 14, 1774; Champagne thesis 318; Stokes 4:982; and McDougall's Addenda for May 15, 1774, has a good discussion of the first call for a congress. Christen 314–17 notes the decision to dispatch the messenger to Boston.

Smith's regrets over the ministerial policy and his entreaties to McDougall are in Smith 1:186–87.

McDougall Memoranda *passim,* Colden's Papers II 341–67 *passim,* Jones 1:41fn, and Smith 1:186, 188 all have examples of the prevalent name-calling.

Isaac Low's appeal for an end to party bickering is in Force IV 1:294.

The makeup of the committee is in McDougall Memoranda, May 16, 1774, and Champagne thesis 344, n. 17.

Colden's Papers II 339–43 have his letters to Dartmouth and Tryon.

Thurman's hopes for a lasting union are in Stokes 4:854.

Smith's role as peacemaker are in Smith 1:187.

McDougall Memoranda, May 22, 1774, notes the arrival of Revere and his departure two days later with the committee's letter and McDougall's message. Christen 327–28 and 337–40 narrates the activities of McDougall and Sears.

20. The Mob Begin to Think

Smith 1:188–89 describes the actions of the Committee of Fifty-one, Smith's comparison of New York's fervor with that of South Carolina, and his thoughts on buying land.

Rivington's *New York Gazetteer* has the story of the meeting breaking up.

Thomas Jones 1:35 contains Jones's comments on personalities.

Colden's letters to Dartmouth and Tryon are in the Letter Books II 346–49.

Gouverneur Morris to Mr. Penn, May 20, 1774, is quoted in Champagne thesis 323.

The letters in *New-York Journal* are in Aug. 25 and Oct. 13, 1774, issues.

Colden to Tryon is in Letter Books II 351; Champagne thesis 350–51 reveals the lack of interest in outlying counties.

Gage 1:360–61 downplayed the Boston situation in writing Dartmouth.

Population statistics come from Greene and Harrington 91.

John Adams's commentary on New York and the people he met are set forth in his *Diary,* Aug. 20–27, 1774. Tiedemann 198–99 also has some of Adams's observations.

The conservatives' view of what Congress should do is noted in Champagne thesis 355.

The *New-York Gazette; and the Weekly Mercury,* Aug. 15, 1774, has the story of Duane's son; the *Gazette* of Sept. 5 carried the story of the delegates' departure from the city.

21. Blows Must Decide

Gage's mission that alarmed Boston is in Alden 213–14 and in Gage's Sept. 2, 1774, letter to Dartmouth, *Correspondence* 1:369–72.

Adams's *Works* 9:347 has his letter.

Gage's comment on Worcester is in *Correspondence* 1:36 and his remarks on the Suffolk Resolves in 1:374. Draper 421 and 471–72 has more on this.

The general's concerns about desertions and security, with his appeals for reinforcement and the cold reception in London, are in his Sept. 12 and 25, 1774, letters to Dartmouth (*Correspondence* 1:375) and Ritcheson 170.

Barrington's comment on American courage is in Lloyd 217. The appalling logistical difficulties are mentioned in Ketchum "England's Vietnam" 10–11. Ritcheson 172–75 has an excellent discussion of Barrington's and the king's attitudes, the navy's weakness and the reasons for it, and North's persistent economy measures.

Valentine 332–38, Bonomi 281fn, and Burrows and Wallace 215 deal with the franchise in England and the colonies and with the evils of patronage in Parliament.

John Jay's comments are in Jay 135–36.

Debate on Galloway's plan and the views of such men as Lee, Henry, Low, Jay, and Duane are in Stokes 4:865–66, Draper 429–32, and Ranlet 46.

Jay's "Address" is covered in Jay, 137–38.

Duane is described in Burrows and Wallace 221–22, and the new committee is mentioned in *New-York Journal,* Nov. 29, 1774.

The views of opposing segments of society in New York are covered most effectively in Countryman 103–12, which also describes where the loyalties of different counties lay.

22. Affairs Grow Serious

The views of Smith are in Stokes 4:866, Sept. 7, 1774; those of Thurman in Stokes 4:854, May 18, and 866, Sept. 14, 1774. The several news items concerning activity in the city are from Stokes 4:845 and 851.

The newspaper stories concerning "Lewis XIV" and "Lewis XV" and the death of Adam Garley are from the *New-York Gazette; and the Weekly Mercury,* Aug. 15, 1774.

Most helpful on the subject of Samuel Seabury is Seabury *Letters of a Westchester Farmer, 1774–1775,* edited by Clarence H. Vance. I have chosen excerpts from pp. 7–9, 13–15, 23–25, 33, 35, 44–64 *passim,* 52–53, and 59–60.

James Beekman's letter about the state of business is in the N-YHS: Beekman Family Papers, Dec. 11, 1774.

The return visit of the Massachusetts delegates, the change of heart of New York's representatives, and the revised makeup of the new committee are discussed in Adams *Diary* 102, Smith 1:203, and Christen 353–54.

The *James* and *Beulah* episodes may be found in Christen 358–61, Tiedemann 205–6, and Jay 143–44.

The broadside attacking Elliot is "To the PUBLIC" in Evans, #13666; it is quoted in the *New-York Gazette; and the Weekly Mercury,* Jan. 9, 1775. The response to Elliot's reply is #13658 in Evans, "To the inhabitants of New York."

McDougall's message to Cooper in Boston is in Tiedemann 204; N-YHS McDougall Papers, Feb. 9, 1775.

Smith 1:209–10 has more on Watson and his ship, as does Christen 358–59.

23. The Sword Is Drawn

Duane's letter to Kempe is in N-YHS Duane Papers, quoted in Tiedemann 211.

Rumors about who was to receive what are in Force IV 2:508–9. Smith 1:213 cites North's putative bribes in New York.

Force IV 2:255–56 has Dr. Joseph Warren's letter to Arthur Lee, reporting the movements of Lord Percy's brigade outside Boston.

Dartmouth's letter to Colden is in the latter's Papers VII 261–62.

Force IV 2:282, 313, has a sampling of attitudes in outlying towns.

Colden's messages to Dartmouth on the actions of the Continental Association and the convening of a provincial congress are in the Letter Books II 382–84, 388–91, and 395.

Thomas Jones 1:38 has Jones's caustic remarks about his favorite whipping boys. Their meeting was described in *New-York Journal,* Mar. 9, 1775. Isaac Low's decision to resign is in Stokes 4:878.

The incident involving Ralph Thurman, Sears, and Willett is described in Force IV 2:282 and 344–50; Christen 370–71; and Smith 1:219–20.

The tenant rising at Livingston Manor is the subject of Lynd's article in Gregory's *Narratives of the Revolution in New York,* esp. 170–75.

Dartmouth's controversial letter condemning the Continental Congress is in Smith 1:213.

Colden's Papers VII 296, has Dartmouth's letter of May 23, 1775, to Tryon. Colden's instructions to desist from making further grants in the disputed territory is in the Papers VII 124–25. More on this is in Countryman 81 and Smith 1:185. J. H. Long 55–57 shows the boundaries of Cumberland County.

Colden's complaint to Dartmouth is in Letter Books II 396–98, 400.

Force IV 2:315 has the point of view of those on the east side of the Green Mountains.

Rumblings of trouble are reported in Force IV 2:318–19; and *The Gentleman's Magazine* 45 (Sept. 1775) 445; and the tale of prisoners taken by Taunton minutemen is in Force IV 2:340.

New-York Journal, Feb. 23, 1775, reported the Wethersfield story.

Letters from abroad were quoted in *New-York Mercury,* Apr. 24, 1775; and Force IV 2:344–45.

Dartmouth's crucial letter to Gage is in Gage *Correspondence* 2:179–83.

Franklin's reported involvement in a last-minute conciliation appears in Currey 377–80.

Alden 233–50 has a good account of the secret orders the general received from Dartmouth and the action Gage took.

Dartmouth's April 15, 1775, letter to Gage is in Gage 2:191–92.

24. You Must Now Declare

Fischer's definitive book on Paul Revere's ride is the source of much of my discussion of the event—particularly pp. 129–49, 178–95, and 248–49. Force IV 2:363–66 is filled with the reports that were circulating, bringing news of the fighting at Lexington and Concord. These include Palmer's messages, and the one from Williams. Champagne *Alexander McDougall* 82 states that "Israel Bissell reached New York around two o'clock Sunday afternoon, April 23. . . ." Fischer (map, 272) cites New York's receipt of news as "Apr. 23, 4PM." Thomas Jones 1:39 says it was "Sunday morning, the 23rd." See also "The Lexington Broadside" in Stokes 4:pl. 42A, opp. page 832, for this and subsequent reports received in New York. It is not really clear whether or not Bissell brought the message to New York; it *is* clear that he took it as far as Connecticut.

Sears's actions on hearing the news are recorded in Christen 380–81.

Smith 1:221 has his statement about the Council's powerlessness.

The ominous letter from Wethersfield appears in Force IV 2:362–63. Colden's Letter Books II 424 contains his June 7 report to Dartmouth.

How the news spread from one town to another may be traced by following its progress in Force IV 2:363–69.

The capture of Ticonderoga—Colden's version—is in O'Callaghan 4:14, 919.

Gage's report to Barrington of the fighting is in Gage 2:673–74, and to Dartmouth on the same date in 1:396–97. Dartmouth's replies on June 1 and July 1 are in Gage 2:198–200.

The extraordinary story of the *Quero,* the enterprising Captain Derby, and how he took the news to England is in Rantoul's article.

The exchanges of letters between Colden, Major Hamilton, and Captain Montagu are in the Colden's Papers VII 293 and 297–300.

Willett's exploit is in Dawson's *New York City during the American Revolution,* 299–300.

Colden's messages to Hamilton and Hicks are in Letter Books II 426–28.

N-YHS John Alsop Papers, May 12, 17, and 24, June 5, 14, and 24, 1775, have provided the communications between Alsop and Christopher Smith. The same source, May 23 and 27, 1775, has his letters from Peter Keteltas.

James Beekman to Messrs. Pomeroy is in N-YHS BV Beekman, Letterbook B.

Judge Livingston's Apr. 27 and May 3, 1775, letters to his wife, Margaret, are in NYPL Livingston-Bancroft transcriptions. His letter to his son and the letter from Duane are quoted in Brandt 111.

Brandt 114–15 recounts the tragedies inflicted on Margaret Livingston.

25. The Proposition Is Peace

The Earl of Chatham is quoted in Lloyd 220. Excerpts from Burke's speech are in Cook 218.

Van Doren 482, 488, 513, 519, 522–23, and 529 accounts for Franklin's activities after leaving London, and has Jefferson's observation. The letter from the Philadelphian, quoting Franklin, is in Stokes 4:885, May 8, 1775.

Currey 344–49 mentions Franklin's contacts with businessmen and ship captains.

Britain's slowness to take action is noted in Ritcheson 198–99, and Chatham's criticism is in Lloyd 220.

North's Conciliatory Proposition is discussed in Ritcheson 186–88 and Maier 245–46.

The scene in New York City is described in Bliven *Guns* 93 and 301–2. Smith 1:222 and 224 has Smith's thoughts on the situation.

Colden's communications to Dartmouth and North are in the Letter Books II 404–6.

The unloading of Watts's ships is in Stokes 4:882.

The Apr. 29, 1775, broadside from White is in Evans.

A threatening letter to DeLancey and his friends was in Bradford's *Pennsylvania Journal,* Apr. 26, 1775, Evans #14028. Watts's letter to his son-in-law is from N-YHS Robert R. Livingston Papers, film reel 1, John Watts to Sir John Johnson, Sept. 2, 1775. His later claim is in John Watts Memorial to the Commissioners, Mar. 22, 1784, American Loyalists, Transcript of the Manuscript Books and Papers of the Commissioners of Enquiry into the Losses . . . (hereinafter Loyalist Transcripts), vol. 46, 432–33, 438.

The source of the footnote concerning the harassment of Sir John Johnson is Jones 1:76–77.

James DeLancey's activities before his departure and the notice of his flight are in Ranlet's article in *New York History,* 196–97 and 201–2.

Samuel Seabury's trials are in Seabury 30–35.

Cooper's narrow escape is recounted in Thomas Jones 1:59–60, and the effects on the college are in Stokes 4:886, May 24, 1775.

The letter about Auchmuty is from Willard *Letters on the American Revolution* 183 and is also noted in Seabury 33 fn. 117.

Colden's letter to Dartmouth about Wilkins is in the Letter Books II 406. The broadside urging Wilkins's capture is Evans #14509, May 4, 1775.

Rivington's *Gazetteer,* May 11, 1775, printed Wilkins's farewell letter.

Andrew Elliot's amusing account of the Connecticut boys is in N-YHS, Andrew Elliot Correspondence, 1747–1777.

Pettit's uncomfortable position among New Jersey Tories comes from N-YHS Joseph Reed Papers, Charles Pettit to Reed, Aug. 10, 1775.

Smith 2:xxix–xxv mentions the Livingston family's split. The Morris family is discussed in Lorenzo 704.

26. Full Exertion of Great Force

The arrival of the New England delegates is chronicled in Rivington's *Gazetteer* of May 11, 1775; and Stokes 4:983, May 7.

General Washington's appearance on the scene is in Flexner *George Washington in the American Revolution* 24, and Stokes 4:894, June 25, 1775, describes the festive reception.

The awkward coincidental arrival of Washington and Tryon is described in Jones 1:55–57 and Smith 1:228c and d. See also Freeman 3:462–68, Flexner *George Washington in the American Revolution* 23–26, and Bliven *Guns* 2–12.

Washington's gracious and welcome reply is in Freeman 3:470, where, the author states, the text is "Garbled in *N.Y. Gazette and Weekly Mercury,* July 3, 1775." In the same volume, pp. 469–71, Washington's cavalcade beds down for the night and heads for Watertown. See also Flexner *George Washington in the American Revolution* 26–28 and Bliven *Guns* 9–13.

Jones 1:58 has the story of Schuyler's faux pas.

Advertisements noted here were in *New-York Journal* of Mar. 9, 1775.

References to New York's preparations for war are scattered through the pages of Stokes 4:888–99, May 25–Aug. 8, 1775. The incident of the *Asia* bombarding the city is in Stokes 4:900, Aug. 23–24, 1775, and Bliven *Guns* 35–38. Pastor Shewkirk's diary is quoted in Stokes 4:901, Aug. 28.

Rivington's running feud with Sears is in Stokes 4:876, 877, 880, 885, 886, 888, 889, and 891.

John Jay's embarrassment is in Jay 188.

For Sears's raid on Rivington's shop, see Bliven *Guns* 59, 62–69, 71.

Tryon's tribulations are discussed in N-YHS: NYC Misc. Mss. Box 11, #6. Whitehead Hicks to William Tryon, Oct. 14, 18; Isaac Low to Hicks, Oct. 17; William Tryon to Hicks, Oct. 14, 19, 1775. Bliven *Guns* 47–48.

Tryon's candid report to Dartmouth is quoted in Ranlet *New York Loyalists* 61.

George III's speech was published in *The Gentleman's Magazine* 46 (May 1776): 218, quoted in Kallich and MacLeish.

The question "Pray, what is a Tory?" with its answer was printed in *New-York Journal,* Feb. 9, 1775.

John Harris Cruger wrote on July 13, 1775, to James Duane about his friendship to America's liberties (in N-YHS: James Duane Papers). Jones 1:108–9 tells of Cruger's unhappy experience, and that of Augustus Van Cortlandt and the plight of other loyalists 110–11.

Jones 1:185–87 also has the tragic story of the DeLancey women.

Epilogue

Boatner 797 supplies Lee's comment on New York.

Ranlet *New York Loyalists,* appendix 2, deals with this extremely difficult and interesting question.

Einstein 193 reports Justice Oliver's remark.

Crary 437–40 recites Ann Watts Kennedy's feelings of injustice.

The quotation from Samuel Curwen is in Einstein 215.

The Act of Attainder is printed in Jones 2:510–23. Jones, of course, was one of the victims.

The unnamed New York loyalist is quoted in Crary 360, and the same source, 225 n. 4, repeats Gouverneur Morris's bloodthirsty remark.

Peter Van Schaack's story appears in Jay 80–81 and 331–32; also in Einstein 263–66.

ACKNOWLEDGMENTS

Carl Brandt suggested the idea of a book about how the Revolution came to one town, and my first task was to find the right town—a small community, I decided, that could serve as a microcosm of many such towns in colonial America.

Peter Drummey, Librarian at the Massachusetts Historical Society, was immensely helpful as always, and set me on the trail of a number of possibilities. George Billias encouraged me to concentrate on Marblehead, and Karen MacInnis of that town's historical society was a valuable source of information about its resources. Peter Seamans put me in touch with a number of people in Salem, including Will LaMoy and Jane Ward of the Peabody Essex Museum, who were generous with their time and suggestions. In Marshfield, Janet Peterson and Cynthia Krusell were most informative. In Cambridge I spent many hours perusing card files and talking with the knowledgeable Warren Little in the Cambridge Historical Society.

Reluctantly I concluded that none of those towns possessed the abundance of primary sources I needed, and I decided that New York City and the communities upriver to Albany were my destination. (So much for a small community—but of course New York City was, in the second half of the eighteenth century, a small town.) My inclination to pursue my project there was confirmed in a conversation with Pauline Maier, the author of a number of authoritative books and articles related to the subject.

It was clear that most of the material I needed was in four or five institutions in the city, but it was equally clear that I could afford neither the time nor money to spend the next year or two in New York doing research. Hoping to locate a well-qualified graduate student who could undertake some of this work, I spoke with Patricia Bonomi, formerly of NYU, and her successor there, Karen Ordahl Kupperman, and with Mark Carnes and Herb Sloan of Columbia. Thanks to their efforts I found Matthew Abramovitz, who assisted me until he could take no more time from his dissertation; James Delbourgo, who eventually ran into the same problem; and Laura Kopp, who worked with me until the research was finished. Like the other two, she is highly capable, meticulous, with real initiative, and enabled me to complete the writing in far less time than would otherwise have been possible. Richard Snow of *American Heritage* and Thomas Fleming were kind enough to suggest other candidates to me.

John Morton Blum wrote a dazzler of a letter for me when I was in need of one. Charles Bulterman did his best to help me understand the Dutch. Osborne Day introduced me to the papers of his ancestor, John Watts, who plays a significant role in the book and bequeathed a fine sense of humor to his descendant. John and Wini Hawkes gave me a book about *his* ancestor, Alexander McDougall, and made available copies of certain McDougall papers (thanks also to Alana Johnson). The Reverend John Mitchell lent me a seventeenth-century Anglican prayer book. Sydney Stokes, Jr., shared with me a letter from his family's papers. Mark Madison and Nancy Oltedal came to my rescue on computer problems from time to time, and my grandson Derek Murrow was a calm, reassuring adviser when the computer turned inscrutable and my panic level peaked.

For assistance in obtaining illustrations and permissions I am indebted to Laurie Platt Winfrey and Carousel Research.

A number of historical societies and libraries were essential to my inquiries, and I have included in the following list the names of individuals who went out of their way to be helpful. Thanks to a generous fellowship from the Gilder Lehrman Institute of American History, I began my research at the Pierpont Morgan Library, which houses the extraordinary Gilder Lehrman Collection, and there I was aided immeasurably by Leslie Fields, the assistant curator. I appreciate the continuing interest in my project by Lesley Herrmann of the Gilder Lehrman Institute. The remarkable collections at the New-York Historical Society were of paramount interest and importance to me, and I am most grateful for the assistance of Betsy Gotbaum, former president; Margaret Heilbrun, Director of the Library; and Melissa Haley, Phillip Lauer, and Alyssa Shirley. Throughout this project I took frequent advantage of the facilities at the New York Public Library, whose immense collections are in many respects unsurpassed. Others who provided guidance and assistance are James DeLancey Harris; William Young of the American Antiquarian Society in Worcester, Mass.; Gail Bumgardner and others at the Dorset (Vt.) Public Library; John W. Tyler, Editor of Publications at the Colonial Society of Massachusetts in Groton, Mass.; Gail Rice and the staff at the Mark Skinner Library in Manchester, Vt.; William Fowler, Peter Drummey, Virginia Smith, and Brenda Lawson at the Massachusetts Historical Society, Boston; Robert Parks, Curator of Literary and Historical Manuscripts at the Pierpont Morgan Library in New York City, and Inge Dupont, Head of Reader Services there; the staff at the Museum of the City of New York, especially Elizabeth Ellis and Eileen Kennedy Morales; Robert Fickies of the New York State Geological Survey in Albany, N.Y.; Mervi Aho of Porin Kaupunki, Satakunnan Museo, Hallituskatu, Finland, and Maija Kallinen of the Finnish Historical Society in Helsinki for information concerning Pehr Kalm; in Washington, D.C., Katherine Grayson Wilkins and Elizabeth Harrison Hadley; the staff of Special Collections at the University of Vermont; and the staff at the Williams College Library in Williamstown, Mass.; and the staff at the Northshire Book Store in Manchester, Vt.

The copy editor Edward Johnson has done an excellent job, saving me from a number of goofs. At Henry Holt, Katy Hope and Judy Sisco have been extremely helpful.

Writing a book is totally involving for long periods of time, which in our case, since we have a farm, means that numerous chores have to be handled by others. For their assistance I am deeply indebted to Robert Matteson, Daniel O'Leary, and Virginia Pearson.

For their unflagging support, enthusiasm, and encouragement, I would like to thank a number of people, beginning with my family—my wife, Barbara Bray Ketchum, our daughter, Liza Ketchum, and her husband, John Straus, our son, Thomas Bray Ketchum, and his wife, Pauline, our grandsons, Derek and Ethan Murrow. Others whose support is greatly appreciated are Kate Canning; Harvey Carter; John O. Chesley, Jr.; Austin Chinn; Castle Freeman; John Hand; J. Robert Maguire; David McCullough; Thomas O'Brien; Janet Whitehouse; Donald Wickman; and Corinna Wildman.

Extra thanks go to Carl Brandt, whose idea this was in the first place. My editor John Macrae, who has a broad knowledge of history, has given me many perceptive suggestions, and happily we have seen eye-to-eye on just about everything.

Once again my wife, Barbara Bray Ketchum, has accompanied me on another long project, and I have benefited from her incisive comments, her advice, and an enthusiasm that has brightened many a dark moment.

INDEX

ABOUT THE AUTHOR

RICHARD KETCHUM is the author of thirteen books, including the Revolutionary War classics *Decisive Day, Winter Soldiers,* and *Saratoga.* He was the cofounder and editor of *Blair & Ketchum's Country Journal.* He and his wife live on a sheep farm in Vermont.